The Law of Nations and Britain's Quest for Naval Security

Scott Andrew Keefer

The Law of Nations and Britain's Quest for Naval Security

International Law and Arms Control, 1898–1914

palgrave
macmillan

Scott Andrew Keefer
Bournemouth University
Poole, United Kingdom

ISBN 978-3-319-39644-6   ISBN 978-3-319-39645-3   (eBook)
DOI 10.1007/978-3-319-39645-3

Library of Congress Control Number: 2016953885

Cover image © Chronicle / Alamy Stock Photo
Cover design by Henry Petrides

Printed on acid-free paper

This Palgrave Macmillan imprint is published by Springer Nature
The registered company is Springer International Publishing AG
 The registered company address is: Gewerbestrasse 11, 6330 Cham, Switzerland

To Katie

ACKNOWLEDGEMENTS

There are a number of individuals and institutions I owe a debt of grati-
tude for supporting me in the preparation of this book. The project grew
out of a Fulbright Fellowship undertaken while I was practicing as international lawyer, leading me away from Washington, DC to Heidelberg,
Germany, and I am forever indebted to the Council for International
Exchange of Scholars and the Fulbright Program for providing this path in
life. Funding from the German–American Fulbright Commission allowed
me to investigate comparative attitudes toward international law and security in the modern world. I began researching contemporary international
law, investigating what led states to employ multilateral institutions such
as international law in managing security, gradually shifting to an historical
angle, evaluating the arms control initiatives of a century earlier.

I would like to thank Reiner Rohr, Ines Horbert, and Catharina
Hänsch at the Berlin office of the Fulbright Commission for their support
through the project. While on the Fulbright Fellowship, I worked as a
guest researcher at the Max Planck Institute for Comparative Public Law
and International Law in Heidelberg, enjoying access to many obscure
sources of law, and would like to thank and Rüdiger Wolfrum for welcom-
ing me to the Institute, and also thank Peter Macalister-Smith for bringing
the library alive and providing new avenues of research.

I am indebted to the staff at the National Archives in Kew, the British
Library, the Bodleian Library, and the Cambridge University Library for
support while researching the project and assistance in locating documents. In addition, I would like to thank Robin Harcourt Williams, the
Archivist at Hatfield House for his advice in accessing Lord Salisbury's

manuscripts. I am also grateful for the support and friendship of Rosemary Wiseman of Richmond, my hostess during numerous trips to the archives at Kew.

The book incorporates materials from two previously published articles in *The International History Review* and *War in History*, and I wish to acknowledge these journals, and thank Hew Strachan and the anonymous reviewers of these periodicals for their insightful comments. Additionally, I would like to thank Isabel Hull of Cornell University, for taking the time to review part of my text and for providing outstanding insights. Thanks also are due to MacGregor Knox for comments and advice on a draft chapter. I wish also to thank Commissioning Editor at Palgrave Macmillan, Emily Russell, and Angharad Bishop for their editorial assistance.

The book started as a doctoral thesis under David Stevenson at the London School of Economics and Political Science, and I would like to thank him for not only his tireless support throughout this project, but also his close reading of manuscripts, and endless knowledge of topic. Thanks also to Joe Maiolo and John Keiger, my doctoral committee members, for their comments and encouragement. It should go without saying, but is worth mentioning that while my I have benefitted immeasurably from the assistance of numerous people, any mistakes or omissions are solely my responsibility.

Finally, the work would not have been possible without the constant encouragement of my wife Katie Terkanian, who has travelled from Washington to Germany and beyond in support of my project, and to whom the book is dedicated.

CONTENTS

LIST OF TABLES

CHAPTER 1

Introduction

The historian's art consists in conveying how those in the past perceived their present and imagined their future. The history of arms control before 1914 reveals more about what statesmen expected from the future than how that future unfolded. To the British Foreign Office, the limitation of naval armaments was a realistic possibility, and a way of removing a significant contention with an increasingly erratic and aggressive Germany. To understand how these statesmen perceived their world, the historian must seek a fuller comprehension of the strategic situation, and the tools at the disposal of policy-makers. While the diplomacy of the pre-war era has been exhaustively studied, as have many of the tools of policy-making, such as naval strategy and war planning, one crucial element remains neglected – international law.

Without this foundational knowledge of law, our understanding of treaties – from arbitration and arms agreements to alliances, guarantees of state neutrality, and rules of war – reflexively reverts to commonplace misunderstandings about how law functioned. In turn, if historians fail to grasp how statesmen expected law to work, then arguments built around key treaties lose critical theoretical foundations. Mistaken impressions about international law arise honestly, as often international lawyers, comfortable working within their discipline, assume an understanding of core legal concepts and omit them in their discussions. But the absence of discussion of these core concepts has left historians to speculate about the nature of law. When candidly expressed, historians' misconceptions significantly undermine the validity of their claims.

© The Editor(s) (if applicable) and The Author(s) 2016
S.A. Keefer, *The Law of Nations and Britain's Quest for Naval Security*, DOI 10.1007/978-3-319-39645-3_1

More often, historians equate the international legal system with its domestic counterpart by focusing on legislative, judicial, and executive institutions. Thus, when analyzing a treaty, historical accounts often seek evidence of a world court or international police powers for enforcement, and assume that no treaty could function as law in their absence. In discussing disarmament at the First Hague Peace Conference, Arthur Marder judged "[t]here was no possible means of guaranteeing that such a self-denying ordinance would be observed, except perhaps through an army of international inspectors, and this would lead to friction."[1] Similarly, a leading historian of arms limitation, Merze Tate, wrote "[i]n the European society of the nineteenth century, without an international executive to enforce engagements on recalcitrant states, disarmament was impossible."[2] In reality, statesmen were perfectly comfortable working without such a safety net.

What the layman seeks in courts and cops, the international lawyer metes out in prose and cons. Beneath the florid language of treaties lay assumptions of political costs and power relationships. By going to the trouble of formalizing an agreement in a treaty, vested with symbolic significance and an aura of permanence, statesmen increased the political costs of violations, making breaches less likely. Yet violations remained possible and good lawyers anticipated them. While law could not eliminate the possibility of violations, it could make behavior more predictable.

Additionally, law could enshrine national interests. Under sweeping statements of universal humanitarian sentiment, more often than not lurked cold calculations of national interest. Well-crafted treaties betrayed little of these calculations, appearing more as moral platitudes than diplomatic bargains. Within all treaties lay estimations of power, questions of who could enforce what obligations under which set of circumstances; and legal instruments provided a veneer of legitimacy to these machinations. Law is a struggle for power, and states engaged in treaty-making to legitimize their national interests. "[*T*]*he majestic equality of the laws ... forbid rich and poor alike to sleep under the bridges, to beg in the streets, and to steal their bread.*"[3] Law functioned as an element of foreign policy-making,

[1] Arthur J Marder, *The Anatomy of British Sea Power: A History of British Naval Policy in the Pre-Dreadnought Era, 1880–1905*, 3rd Edition 1972 ed. (London: Frank Cass, 1940), 342.

[2] Merze Tate, *The Disarmament Illusion: The Movement for a Limitation of Armaments to 1907*, 2nd edn. 1971 ed. (New York: Russell and Russell, 1942), 347.

[3] Anatole France, *The Red Lily* (New York: Boni & Liveright, 1917), 75.

employing recognized diplomatic practices for resolving disputes and pursuing national interests. International law, as understood and practiced by statesmen in the nineteenth century, functioned without powerful legal institutions.

This book aims to correct some of these misassumptions about international law and its role in foreign policy decision-making. In doing so, it argues that law was employed by statesmen in order to advance national goals, and, when utilized pragmatically, recognizing its limitations, law could contribute to national security. The Foreign Office acted rationally by acknowledging that law alone could never guarantee security, but in the words of one statesman, could serve as "an obstacle, though not a barrier."

Arms limitation presents a unique case study, highlighting an effective role for law in strengthening national security. Unlike prior studies of arms limitation, the focus here is squarely upon rational state interest, rather than popular pacifist movements or other non-state actors. As the emphasis will be on British interests in arms limitation, the primary emphasis will be on naval rather than land armaments. Several scholars in the recent past have studied the European land arms races, including David Stevenson and David Herrman. Stevenson's work, *Armaments and the Coming of War: Europe 1904–1914*, provided limited coverage of international legal issues relating to arms control and discussed the 1907 Hague Conference, but retained a focus on the continental land armaments race.[4] Herrman also exclusively covered the land arms race and did not concentrate on arms control.[5] Jonathan Grant's *Rulers, Guns, and Money: The Global Arms Trade in the Age of Imperialism* should also be mentioned. Grant shifted away from the core European great power competition to the Balkan, South American, and Russo-Japanese arms races, tracing the manner in which imperialism and technology diffusion contributed to these races.[6] However, Grant did not detail the use of international law in these cases, with only occasional references to treaties such as the one resolving the Argentine-Chilean arms race in 1902.[7]

[4] David Stevenson, *Armaments and the Coming of War: Europe 1904–1914* (Oxford: Oxford University Press, 1996), 105–11, 417.

[5] David G. Herrmann, *The Arming of Europe and the Making of the First World War* (Princeton, NJ: Princeton University Press, 1996).

[6] Jonathan A. Grant, *Rulers, Guns, and Money: The Global Arms Trade in the Age of Imperialism* (Cambridge: Harvard University Press, 2007), 6.

[7] *Id.*, 133–34.

The intention is not to revisit the contentious historiography of British naval policy prior to 1914, but to discuss the role of international law in the formation of national security policies through the evaluation of naval arms control. Assumptions regarding the necessity of international enforcement mechanisms prevalent in older studies, such as those of Marder and Tate, need to be questioned. A reassessment can assist the historian in making sense of British foreign policy decision-making, taking the advocacy of arms control out of a simplified view of arms limitation treaty-making as either utopian or Machiavellian, by demonstrating practical means in which law could contribute to security. Even if Anglo-German arms control efforts ultimately faltered as a result of the incompatible goals of each side or German intransigence, the negotiations provide evidence of British expectations about the future.

An appreciation of legal strategies helps make sense of arms limitation goals as well as turn of the century attitudes towards future conflict. For instance, if international law could be most effectively enforced by neutral great powers, then treaties regulating wartime use of weaponry had to be built around an assumption that powerful neutrals would remain on the sidelines. In contrast, arms control treaties functioned in peacetime rather than in war, allowing a wider range of enforcement mechanisms, such as attaché visits. In turn, verification through such mechanisms was a strategy better suited to naval arms control than to the limitation of land armaments, and was one best matched to a state like Britain which possessed a significant advantage in capital ship numbers.

One central challenge faced by the Foreign Office at the time of the Hague Peace Conferences lay in the shift from limited naval rivalry of a few powers to a general multilateral competition. In the hundred years between 1815 and 1914, the number of powers with significant navies ebbed and flowed, with Spain and the Ottoman Empire rebuilding fleets at several points and then declining, and new major naval powers entering competition towards the end of the century (Tables 1.1, 1.2, 1.3 and 1.4). At the time of the Hague Conferences, the number of great power competitors rose significantly, while the shift to the Dreadnought added to uncertainty as the new battleship became accepted as a the standard even among smaller powers. Many smaller states lacking the capacity and finances to maintain large fleets purchased dreadnoughts, adding to the risk that the tightening naval balance could be rapidly tipped by the sale of these expensive warships, leading Winston Churchill to decry the threat of "loose

Table 1.1 Ships of the line 1820–1860

	Britain	France	Russia	Ottoman	US	Spain	Netherlands	Sweden	Denmark	Portugal	Naples	Brazil	Austria
1820	112	48	43	17	7	14	7	12	3	9	1	0	2
1830	82	33	47	8	7	3	5	8	4	4	1	2	0
1840	77	23	46	19	7	2	5	8	6	1	2	1	0
1850	3/70	1/25	0/47	0/12	0/7	0/1	0/5	0/8	0/5	0/2	0/2	0/1	0
1855	31/50	17/26	4/39[a]	0/12	0/7	0/2	0/5	1/6	0/4	0/1	0/2	0	0
1860	62/25	35/8	9/9	4/3	0/7	0/2	0/2	2/7	1/3	0/1	1/1	0	1/0

This table is divided into steam/sail ships of the line from 1850 onwards.

[a]Russian figures for 1855 represent 1853 totals

Table 1.2 Ironclad and pre-dreadnought capital ships

Table	Britain	France	Russia	US	Italy	Germany	Austria-Hungary	Japan	Other
1860	0	1/0/0	0	0	0	0	0/0/0	0	0
1865	10/4/1	11/0/0	2/0/12	0/1/42	2/6/2	0/2/0	0/5/0	0/1/0	7/7/6
1870	23/10/5	17/8/4	2/1/20	0/0/43	2/9/1	3/2/0	2/5/0	0/1/1	10/16/34
1875	23/12/9	16/9/6	2/2/21	0/0/16	4/9/1	5/3/0	6/2/0	0/1/1	9/20/46
1880	18/24/13	13/18/8	1/6/22	0/0/16	5/7/1	8/2/0	6/5/0	0/4/1	4/26/48
1885	11/28/14	9/20/11	1/7/22	0/0/14	6/8/1	8/5/0	5/5/0	0/4/1	3/27/41
1890	19/25/14	15/13/9	4/8/10	0	6/5/0	6/6/1	2/8/0	0/3/1	4/20/40
1892	19/27/9	14/14/8	3/12/2	0/0/1	7/4/0	4/6/2	2/7/0	0/3/1	3/21/40
1894	24/25/7	13/13/11	4/13/5	0/0/2	8/3/0	7/6/6	2/7/0	0/3/0	3/17/30
1896	25/24/11	14/12/11	6/13/4	3/2/6	9/3/0	6/7/8	1/8/0	1/3/1	1/13/20
1898	28/24/9	17/13/10	7/12/4	4/1/6	8/4/0	6/9/8	1/7/3	3/3/1	1/12/22
1900	32/24/7	20/11/10	10/11/3	7/1/6	7/3/0	6/7/8	1/5/3	4/4/1	1/10/27
1902	38/22/4	18/12/10	14/9/3	10/1/8	6/6/0	12/5/8	1/4/3	6/4/1	1/9/30
1904	40/30/3	16/10/7	18/10/3	12/1/10	5/8/0	16/4/8	0/6/3	4/1/0	1/7/32
1906	43/22/3	16/11/6	5/6/0	18/1/11	5/8/0	20/3/8	0/6/3	6/1/0	0/6/34
1908	41/19/0	17/11/5	5/4/0	25/1/10	8/8/0	21/4/8	0/8/3	6/1/0	0/6/35
1910	36/16/0	17/8/5	8/5/0	24/2/10	6/7/0	20/3/8	1/8/3	7/0/0	0/8/35
1912	32/17/0	17/12/2	8/4/0	21/4/10	6/5/0	20/2/8	3/8/3	7/1/0	0/7/32
1914	28/13/0	14/9/2	7/5/0	19/4/10	6/5/0	18/4/8	3/6/3	7/1/0	2/7/32

This table is divided into first-class ironclads/(second-class and cruising ironclads)/coastal-defense vessels. The table is adapted from John F. Beeler's *British Naval Policy in the Gladstone-Disraeli Era, 1866–1880* (Stanford: Stanford University Press, 1997) at 198, with the addition of Japan and other powers, and with first-class battleships reduced to second class after 15 years, and all vessels removed from the list after 25 years

Table 1.3 Heavy cruisers

	GB	Fr	R	US	It	G	AH	J	Other
1894	0/10	3/1		1/0			1/0		4/0
1896	0/11	5/1	1/0	2/0			1/0		8/0
1898	0/15	6/1	2/0	2/0	1/0	0	1/0		9/0
1900	0/18	6/3	3/0	2/0	2/0	1/0	2/0	5/0	10/0
1902	7/20	8/4	3/0	2/0	4/0	2/0	2/0	6/0	10/0
1904	20/21	17/4	4/0	2/0	4/0	4/0	2/0	8/0	10/0
1906	29/21	19/4	2/0	11/0	5/0	6/0	3/0	8/0	10/0
1908	34/21	20/4	4/0	15/0	5/0	8/0	3/0	10/0	10/0
1910	35/21	21/3	4/0	15/0	8/0	9/0	3/0	11/0	10/0
1912	35/21	23/3	6/0	15/0	9/0	9/0	3/0	12/0	11/0
1914	35/21	23/3	6/0	15/0	9/0	9/0	3/0	12/0	11/0

This table is divided into armored cruisers/protected cruisers over 7000 tons completed since 1890

Table 1.4 Dreadnought battleships and battlecruisers

	Britain	France	Russia	Germany	Austria Hungary	Italy	US	Japan	Argentina	Brazil	Chile	Spain	Greece	Turkey	Netherlands
1906	1														
1908	1/2														
1910	7/3			4			4								
1912	15/7			9/3	1		8	2		2	2				
1914	22/10	4	4	14/5	3	3	10	2/2	1	2	2		1	3	
1916	32/10	12	7/4	20/7	5	6	14	4/4	2	3	3		3	2	1

This table is divided into battleships/battlecruisers. 1916 list includes ships in existence in 1914, along with ships under construction or projected to begin construction in 1914. Data for the tables was compiled from John F. Beeler, *British Naval Policy in the Gladstone-Disraeli Era, 1866–1880*, (Stanford: Stanford University Press, 1997); George Modelski &William R. Thompson, *Seapower in Global Politics, 1494–1993* (London: Macmillan, 1988); Jan Glete, *Navies and Nations: Warships, Navies and State Building in Europe and America, 1500–1860*, Vol. II; Robert Gardiner, ed., *Conway's All the World's Fighting Ships, 1860–1905*; Robert Gardiner, ed., *Conway's All the World's Fighting Ships, 1906–1921*

dreadnoughts" on British security.[8] Around 1909–1910, the Foreign Office responded to the possibility of a Latin American naval arms agreement with horror, as it might suddenly release a number of dreadnoughts onto the international market and from there into the German Navy.

British statesmen found no perfect solution to the problem of multilateral negotiations prior to 1914. The Foreign Office drew upon its experience with regional bilateral agreements in trying to address the arms competition. After the Hague Conferences, bilateral Anglo-German negotiations continued against a background of increased naval construction by all the powers. The smaller powers could be brought into line through great power control of export markets and finances, a method which assisted in resolving the Argentine-Chilean arms race in 1902. Additionally, the Foreign Office contemplated novel legal strategies, such as the creation of global norms through declarations, as a means of reducing the destabilizing influence of small power purchases of warships. The Foreign Office still needed to develop other strategies to manage the core competition among the great powers, developing concepts such as escape clauses within bilateral treaties for third party construction, regular renegotiation of annual building holidays, multilateral exchanges of information, and most importantly, the further elaboration of attaché visit procedures. Experience negotiating with Germany also confirmed that binding legal commitments would provide greater security than informal or non-binding gentlemen's agreements. While no answer to the multilateral arms race resulted, the challenge forced statesmen to shift multilateral negotiations away from unrealistic formulas of disarmament as well as away from unwieldy fora such as the Hague Conferences, and towards real workable terms. The application of arms limitation strategies demonstrated how a great power could harness international law to furthering national interests.

International law and arms control efforts assume only a subsidiary role in most diplomatic and naval histories of the 1899–1914 era. The main accounts usually mention the attempts to limit armaments at The Hague in 1899 and 1907, noting the utopian and impractical nature of the schemes. No author writing on the Anglo-German naval arms race has treated the efforts in depth. In earlier histories, this may be in part due to a lack of source material, while later historians have tended to relegate international legal negotiations to specialist works devoted to the topic of

<hr/>

[8] Churchill to Grey, Oct. 24, 1913, Gooch and Temperley, eds., *British Documents*, Vol. IX, 721.

legal history. The result is a gap in the literature: Legal histories offer little coverage of arms control, and histories of the arms race provide limited space to discussions of international law.

General accounts of the Anglo-German naval arms race by E. L. Woodward and Arthur Marder mentioned the Hague Conferences, but provided little discussion of international law.[9] Woodward stressed the inadvertent nature of Anglo-German conflict, providing a fatalistic account of efforts to halt the race.[10] In discussing the Hague Conference, he made no mention of the course of negotiations on arms control, finding the initiative doomed from the outset, and of little importance to his central account of Anglo-German naval rivalry.[11]

Arthur Marder published several volumes on British naval policy, including *The Anatomy of British Sea Power*, which covered events between 1880 and 1905, and the five-volume successor work on British policy from 1905 through 1919, *From the Dreadnought to Scapa Flow*.[12] While the second series detailed the Anglo-German arms race in Volume I, *The Road to War, 1904–1914*, its predecessor provided greater information on the nature of naval armaments in the late nineteenth and early twentieth centuries, explaining more fully the arms race phenomenon. Marder mentioned international law, discussing the effectiveness of law in times of war and the lack of enforcement mechanisms, but his account was limited by a lack of understanding of law. Like many, his conception of international law focused on the creation of utopian institutions while ignoring practical forms of legal regulation. While he discussed the Hague Conferences, Marder placed the efforts at legally managing the arms race in the context of an inexorable slide toward war, chronicling them alongside other futile initiatives.

General histories of international law have devoted little space to arms limitation. However, such works often develop larger themes and explore trends evolving over centuries, making it difficult to focus upon discrete topics. Wilhelm Grewe and Arthur Nussbaum provided standard accounts, tracing the history of international law back to the Middle Ages in Grewe's *Epochs of International Law*, and back to antiquity in Nussbaum's *History*

---

[9] E. L. Woodward, *Great Britain and the German Navy*, 2nd edn (London: Frank Cass and Co., 1964).

[10] *Id.*, 5.

[11] *Id.*, 134.

[12] Marder, *The Anatomy of British Sea Power*; Arthur J. Marder, *From the Dreadnought to Scapa Flow*, 3rd edn (London: Oxford University Press, 1972), Vol. 1, 1904–14: The Road to War.

of International Law.[13] Both works were targeted towards international
lawyers, and assumed a familiarity with key concepts of law while providing evidence of trends and chronology. For these authors, the Hague
Peace Conferences provided evidence of shifts within international law,
with the creation of international institutions and the formalization of a
regular global forum for discussing legal issues.

The Hague Peace Conferences have received the greatest coverage of
any international legal topic of the era, due to their ambitious scale and
agenda, as well as the hopes they engendered. The conferences included
nearly all recognized nations of the world, making them a de facto world
congress. Delegations at the conferences were drawn from the highest
circles of military and diplomatic affairs, with numerous international
lawyers in attendance. These delegates prepared the first generation of
histories of the conferences, some autobiographical in nature, others reci-
tations of the conference proceedings, interspersed with commentary. The
works of Joseph Choate, Andrew D. White, Karl von Stengel, Frederick
W. Holls, and James Brown Scott fall into this category.[14] Even Captain
Alfred Thayer Mahan published an account of his experiences with disarmament at The Hague, giving a military perspective on the value of law in
wartime.[15] James Brown Scott and A. Pearce Higgins provided more thorough accounts, producing massive books on the negotiations, with Scott
translating multiple volumes of the conference *travaux* into English.[16]

[13] Wilhelm G. Grewe, *The Epochs of International Law*, trans. Michael Byers (Berlin: Walter
de Gruyter, 2000); Arthur Nussbaum, *A Concise History of the Law of Nations* (New York:
Macmillan Co., 1947).

[14] Joseph Choate, *The Two Hague Conferences* (Princeton, NJ: Princeton University Press,
1969), Frederick W. Holls, *The Peace Conference at the Hague and Its Bearing on International
Law and Policy* (London: Macmillan and Co., 1900), James Brown Scott, *The Hague Peace
Conferences of 1899 and 1907: A Series of Lectures Delivered before the Johns Hopkins University
in the Year 1908*, 2 vols. (Baltimore, MD: Johns Hopkins Press, 1909), Karl von Stengel,
Weltstaat Und Friedensproblem (Berlin: Verlag Reichl, 1909). Andrew Dickson White, *The First
Hague Conference* (Boston: World Peace Foundation, 1912). The accounts of Holls and Choate
also tended toward self-congratulation, exaggerating their roles in crafting compromises.

[15] Alfred Thayer Mahan, *Armaments and Arbitration: Or, The Place of Force in the
International Relations of States* (New York: Harper and Brothers, 1912).

[16] Scott, *The Hague Peace Conferences of 1899 and 1907*; James Brown Scott, ed., *The
Proceedings of the Hague Peace Conferences: Translation of the Original Texts. Conference of
1899* (New York: Oxford University Press, 1920); A. Pearce Higgins, *The Hague Peace
Conferences and Other International Conferences Concerning the Laws and Usages of War:
Texts of Conventions with Commentaries* (Cambridge: Cambridge University Press, 1909).

While most of the works by international lawyers expressed cautious optimism about the pre-war development of law, a distinct minority utterly opposed arms limitation. Besides Mahan, German delegate Karl von Stengel wrote two scathing accounts of the dangers of disarming in the midst of potential enemies.[17] However, the support of German international lawyers for the Hague project even surpassed that of their Anglo-American colleagues, with Walter Schücking and Hans Wehberg expressing unreserved confidence in law.[18] Schücking championed the cause of "progressive codification of international law" through regular conferences like those at The Hague, while Wehberg prepared the most extensive account of arms limitation prior to 1914.[19] While these works reflected a range of opinion, they generally failed to reflect state interest in international law.

Subsequent scholars provided critical evaluations of the arms limitation movement before 1914, drawing on greater access to official records. But as international lawyers moved on to newer subjects, the topic was increasingly left to historians, with the inevitable result that much of the legal insights in the record have not been fully exploited. Merze Tate wrote one of the first overall accounts of the pre-war arms limitation movement, in her 1942 work, *The Disarmament Illusion*.[20] Utilizing published diplomatic records, she assessed the state role in the disarmament movement while also addressing the contributions of lawyers, public opinion, and pacifists. Tate's book, appearing during the Second World War, reflected contemporary pessimism about arms limitation. While Tate discussed academic legal writing on disarmament, her work displayed no real familiarity with state practice of international law. As with other works, her view of

---

[17] Stengel, *Weltstaat Und Friedensproblem*, 134–37. See also Karl von Stengel, *Der Ewige Friede* (Munich: Carl Haushalter, 1899).
[18] Walther Schücking, *The International Union of the Hague Conferences*, trans. Charles G. Fenwick (Oxford: Clarendon Press, 1918); Hans Wehberg, *Die Internationale Beschränkung Der Rüstungen* (Stuttgart: Deutsche Verlags-Anstalt, 1919). Works by non-lawyer Alfred H. Fried, a noted peace activist, should also be included in the discussion of the conferences. Alfred H. Fried, *Die Zweite Haager Konferenz: Ihre Arbeiten, Ihre Ergebnisse, Und Ihre Bedeutung* (Leipzig: B. Elischer Nachfolger, 1908).
[19] Wehberg, *Die Internationale Beschränkung Der Rüstungen*; Hans Wehberg, *The Limitation of Armaments: A Collection of the Projects Proposed for the Solution of the Problem, Preceded by an Historical Introduction*, trans. Edwin H. Zeydel (Washington: Carnegie Endowment for International Peace, 1921).
[20] Tate, *The Disarmament Illusion*.

international law remained heavily influenced by grandiose projects for powerful institutions associated with disarmament, obscuring the more mundane diplomatic practices which made law workable.[21]

Calvin Davis wrote the definitive accounts of America's role in the Hague Conferences, *The United States and the First Hague Peace Conference*, and *The United States and the Second Hague Peace Conference*.[22] Sketching a broad overall account of the conferences, including the pre-conference diplomacy, the personalities at The Hague, and on the social aspects of the gatherings, he provided thorough coverage of all the topics under discussion. Jost Dülffer provided greater detail of European diplomacy surrounding the conferences in his *Regeln gegen den Krieg? Die Haager Friedenskonferenzen von 1899 und 1907 in der internationalen Politik*.[23] For both authors, the armaments issues were only a small part of the overall agenda at The Hague, and received limited coverage, Davis dedicating only 14 pages of his 1899 study, and a meager five pages in his 1907 conference work to armaments.[24] Moreover, particularly with Davis's work, arms limitation efforts at The Hague were interpreted as only preliminary steps in the evolution of an embryonic subject of international law and longer term efforts to halt the arms race, rather than attempts to harness existing legal practices to armaments issues.[25] More recent works have provided a richer analysis of the available material, including essays by Andre T. Sidorowicz and Keith Neilson, in *Arms Limitation and Disarmament: Restraints on War, 1899–1939*. Sidorowicz and Neilson traced efforts at arms control at The Hague in 1907, connecting British arms control efforts to Liberal campaign promises of budgetary reductions and to practices of maritime warfare, respectively.[26]

[21] *Id.*, 347.

[22] Calvin DeArmond Davis, *The United States and the First Hague Peace Conference* (Ithaca, New York: Cornell University Press, 1962); Calvin DeArmond Davis, *The United States and the Second Hague Peace Conference: American Diplomacy and International Organization 1899–1914* (Durham, North Carolina: Duke University Press, 1975).

[23] Jost Dülffer, *Regeln Gegen Den Krieg? Die Haager Friedenskonferenzen Von 1899 Und 1907 in Der Internationalen Politik* (Berlin: Ullstein, 1981).

[24] Davis, *The United States and the First Hague Peace Conference*, 110–24; Davis, *The United States and the Second Hague Peace Conference*, 215–19.

[25] Davis, *The United States and the Second Hague Peace Conference*, vii–viii.

[26] Andre T. Sidorowicz, *The British Government, the Hague Peace Conference of 1907, and the Armaments Question*, in B. J. C. McKercher, ed., *Arms Limitation and Disarmament: Restraints on War 1899–1939* (Westport, Conn: Praeger, 1992), 16; Keith Neilson, "The British Empire Floats on the British Navy": British Naval Policy, Belligerent Rights, and Disarmament, 1902–1909, in *Id.*, 21.

A brief mention should be made at this point to the newer naval historiography of Jon Sumida and Nicholas Lambert.[27] Sumida and Lambert have challenged much of the traditional Marder account of British naval policy of the era. They have cumulatively provided an interpretation which downgrades the Admiralty perception of a German threat relative to the threat posed by long-term Franco-Russian competitors, while also diminishing the importance of battleships in Admiralty planning.[28] If the Admiralty was unconcerned with a conventional battleship threat posed by Germany in the early 1900s, then it could be argued that efforts at naval arms control might have been of lesser importance to the British government. This historiography will be discussed in greater depth in Chap. 5, but as a preliminary observation, regardless of the threat the Admiralty expected to encounter in a future war, the battleship continued to have a peacetime function in diplomacy. This peacetime function was one which the Foreign Office grasped, even if its leadership was unaware of changing naval policy being debated at the Admiralty. Moreover, if one challenger could have been contained through treaty law, resources would have been freed to meet other threats, a rationale for arms limitation regardless of which nation was perceived as presenting the biggest threat.

A thorough study of the role of international law in arms limitation will illustrate how statesmen intended law to function. The perspective of the predominant sea power on naval arms control will provide further insight into how law was expected to enhance national security in a vital strategic area. Rather than viewing law as a hindrance to sea power, the Foreign Office conceived of law as a means to reinforce strategic advantages. This stands in stark contrast to the attitudes of Germany, the preponderant land power, towards arms limitation. Finally, this study offers insights into effective strategies a dominant great power may take in managing the rise of competitors, and how law can contribute to security and stability in such a period of transition.

---

[27] Jon Tetsura Sumida, *In Defence of Naval Supremacy: Finance, Technology and British Naval Policy, 1889–1914* (London: Routledge, 1989); Nicholas A. Lambert, *Sir John Fisher's Naval Revolution* (Columbia, SC: University of South Carolina Press, 1999).

[28] The theories have developed, in turn, a contentious historiographical debate. See, for example, Matthew S. Seligmann, "The Renaissance of Pre-First World War Naval History," *Journal of Strategic Studies* 36, no. 3 (2013): 454–479; Nicholas A. Lambert, "On Standards: A Reply to Christopher Bell," *War in History* 19, no. 2 (2012): 217–240; Christopher M. Bell, "Sir John Fisher's Naval Revolution Reconsidered: Winston Churchill at the Admiralty, 1911–14," *War in History* 18, no. 3 (2011): 333–356.

Discussions on armaments shifted away from grandiose schemes for disarmament to arms control, a regulation of arms competition which left sovereign states with the capacity for self-defense. Disarmament could only succeed through a radical cession of power to an international government capable of enforcing obligations, an unrealistic goal which served only to discredit more feasible plans for arms control. Between the calling of the First Hague Peace Conference in 1898 and the outbreak of war in 1914, arms control overtook disarmament as the conceptual framework. British legal policy also shifted in the period, towards greater engagement with the international community through treaty negotiation, demonstrated in differing attitudes towards arms limits in 1899 and 1907. Moreover, as Britain became more engaged in arms negotiations, it infused discussions with pragmatic proposals drawn from a century of experience in limited bilateral arms treaties. However, as naval arms competition became increasingly multilateral in the 1890s, strains emerged in the application of bilateral models to a progressively more complex strategic environment. The employment of international law by British statesmen provides evidence for how they perceived this changing environment, exposing their assumptions about the international community, about their views of future conflict, and management of security. This work details the British role in the evolution of naval arms control from 1787 to 1914, with an emphasis on negotiations from 1898 to 1914. Beginning with an assessment of arms control precedents in the first chapter and an explanation of how statesmen expected law to contribute to security in the second, later chapters build upon this foundation while reevaluating the Hague Peace Conferences of 1899 and 1907, as well as subsequent Anglo-German negotiations. What will emerge throughout is the employment of law as an element of a larger national security policy. Like all elements of national security, law was incapable of independently ensuring safety, yet played a pivotal role in an integrated strategy.

CHAPTER 2

Arms Control Antecedents in the Nineteenth Century

Armaments Competition and National Interest in the Nineteenth Century

The disarmament movement seemingly broke out onto the international scene with the Hague Conferences of 1899 and 1907, but in reality it had a rich history of antecedents. While calls for general disarmament yielded no results throughout the century, limited legal agreements assisted statesmen in managing specific issues. Grounded in security planning, nineteenth-century international law provided a framework for developing legal norms relating to security concerns.

In the nineteenth century, the terminology of arms limitation remained rudimentary. General disarmament referred to both advocacy of complete disarmament, as pacifists sought, and broad arms limitation among the great powers. In the modern era, this distinction is more precise. Disarmament signifies the entire elimination of all defenses or an entire class of weapon, while the modern term arms control involves the regulation of weaponry in order to manage competition. In the modern sense, disarmament is utopian, requiring a fundamental alteration in the nature of international relations. In contrast, arms control assumes conflict will remain among states, and seeks to channel competition into less volatile and destabilizing weapons acquisitions. However, early nineteenth-century authors used "disarmament" to cover both concepts, sometimes distinguishing between "general and total disarmament" and "peace footing," with the former term corresponding to disarmament and the latter conforming to ideas of arms control. The

© The Editor(s) (if applicable) and The Author(s) 2016   15
S.A. Keefer, *The Law of Nations and Britain's Quest for Naval Security*, DOI 10.1007/978-3-319-39645-3_2

lack of precision in terminology often lent itself to muddled debating, and influenced international attempts at regulating war and peace.

The role of pacifists in arms limitation has been broadly explored, yet the often-unexamined government initiatives played a larger role. While Richard Cobden and the Manchester School influenced British economic policy, pacifist arguments held little sway over official policy.[1] Motivations were often complex,[2] and genuine humanitarian concerns played a role, but the common theme in calls for limitation was a desire to maintain the national interest. For this same reason most efforts towards a *general* limitation failed. Often if one monarch saw an advantage in disarmament, his peers often had a counter-interest in maintaining arms levels. Never did all the great powers simultaneously hold an interest in limitation, ending many of these initiatives. Thus, in 1816, Czar Alexander I's calls for a limitation gained little traction. Prince Metternich quickly noticed that Russia posed the greatest potential threat to peace as its large army had not demobilized from Napoleonic War levels.[3] When French King Louis Philippe called for a general arms limitation in 1832, Metternich noted that the French were more concerned with the economically destabilizing effects of armaments expenditures and potential army involvement in anti-monarchical palace intrigue than with any common European arms problem.[4] Napoleon III made several calls for a general arms limitation between 1859 and 1870, also motivated by a mixture of altruism and realism. One ascribed desire was to curry favor with agrarian elements in France by limiting military service.[5] Influenced by a desire to preserve a French voice in the momen-

[1] David Nicholls, "Richard Cobden and the International Peace Congress Movement, 1848–1853," *Journal of British Studies* 30, no. 4 (1991): 367–69; Alexander Tyrrell, "Making the Millennium: The Mid-Nineteenth Century Peace Movement," *Historical Journal* 21, no. 1 (1978): 75 et. seq.; Tate, *The Disarmament Illusion*, 161–63.

[2] Dan L. Morrill, "Nicholas II and the Call for the First Hague Conference," *Journal of Modern History* 46, no. 2 (1974): 313.

[3] Tate, *The Disarmament Illusion*, 8–9.

[4] Metternich to Apponyi, Oct. 28, 1831, *in* Klemens von Metternich, *Memoirs of Prince Metternich*, ed. Prince Richard Metternich, trans. Gerard W. Smith, Vol. V, 1830–1835 (London: Richard Bentley & Son, 1882), 111–12. Moreover, Metternich perceived the proposed disarmament as asymmetrical, as the French peacetime establishment excluded the *Garde Nationale* while other states included the *Landwehr* as an integral party of the army, thus proportionate reduction of forces would leave France with a larger potential military force. He despaired of any treaty setting fixed numbers. "It would be vexatious, because it would demand a reciprocal control; it would be useless, because such a control is impossible." Metternich to Apponyi, June 3, 1831, *in* Metternich, *Memoirs of Prince Metternich*, 113–14.

[5] Lyons to Clarendon, Jan. 30, 1870, *in* Lord Newton, *Lord Lyons: A Record of British Diplomacy*, Vol. Volume I (London: Edward Arnold, 1913), 248.

tous changes taking place in Germany, Napoleon III coaxed Britain into attempting to mediate an arms limit with Prussia in 1868–1870. Prussia naturally refused to limit its military while remaining the smallest of the great powers hemmed in by large military nations.[6]

Statesmen feared the fiscal expense of armaments more than the danger of war resulting from an arms race. The concept of an arms race, including an understanding of the spiral dynamic that often accompanied arms competition, was well understood. However, skyrocketing armaments costs appeared to be a greater threat to national stability, reviving lingering fears of revolution after 1815. Military expenditures rose dramatically during the century, especially with the unprecedented leaps in technology, but state capacity to pay climbed along with the costs. Armies grew dramatically as the ability to supply a force in the field improved.[7] The French Revolutionary nation in arms, and the 1860s Prussian experience with mass conscription, provided models for contemporary armies. Where eighteenth-century armies tended to be small, highly trained peacetime forces, the nineteenth century witnessed a shift towards large conscript forces. Prior to the nineteenth century, technological evolution was incremental and slow, but by mid-century it yielded to revolutionary changes, particularly in naval affairs.[8]

Perceptions, tied to the fear that the public might stage a tax revolt, proved more important than actual costs.[9] Prince Metternich noted:

[6] Bismarck to Bernstorff, Feb. 9, 1870, *in Id.*, 263.

[7] Michael Howard, *War in European History* (Oxford: Oxford University Press, 1976), 99–100.

[8] *Id.*, 101–02; William H. McNeill, *The Pursuit of Power: Technology, Armed Force, and Society since A.D. 1000* (Chicago: University of Chicago Press, 1982), 232, 72.

[9] In the nineteenth century, states also perceived the need for a standing army as a defense against domestic social unrest. In some cases, this concern actually served as a limit on the growth of the military. German authorities believed a smaller, professional army, drawn from the rural provinces, possessed greater loyalty and resistance to revolutionary ideals than recruits from the growing urban centers. Arming the urban masses would only increase the danger of revolution. *See* Holger H. Herwig, "Strategic Uncertainties of a Nation-State: Prussia-Germany, 1871–1918," in *The Making of Strategy: Rulers, States and War*, ed. Williamson Murray (1996), 242, 48. Industrialization of war raised risks that armies composed of social discontents would be more likely to revolt, while simultaneously increasing the tax burden on the populace. The threat of revolution was a significant factor to a generation of leaders who had not seen a general European war since 1815, yet had lived through repeated revolutions. Excessive armaments posed a question of European survival, thus, "[i]l leur est indispensable de sortir, et à tout prix, de cette situation, s'ils ne veulent avec le temps devenir les victimes des *barbares de l'intérieur* ..." [Italics in original.] Count Kamarowski, "Quelques Réflexions Sur Les Armements Croissants De L'europe," *Revue de Droit International et de Législation Comparée* 19 (1887): 481–82.

[a] very large army presents a considerable danger even when maintained for preserving domestic order of a State, because it exhausts resources which are indispensable for a wise administration of the people. This danger is particularly great at the present time (1816), when armies themselves are imbued with revolutionary ideas and given up to aspirations which cannot be realized without overturning the existing order of public affairs.[10]

Similarly, at the 1831 Paris conference the delegates of France, Great Britain, Austria, Russia, and Prussia recognized "the purpose of strengthening the general peace and relieving the peoples of the burden of extraordinary armaments which have been imposed upon them ..."[11] However, German Colonel Gross von Schwarzhoff spoke for many at The Hague in 1899 when he noted "as far as Germany is concerned, I am able completely to reassure her friends and to relieve all well-meant anxiety. The German people is not crushed under the weight of charges and taxes."[12]

Richard Cobden exploited these concerns where pacifists had failed, by appealing to rational self-interest. His influential theory of interdependence advocated gradually eliminating the need for offensive weapons, and utilizing cheaper means of defense. As a corollary to Cobden's theories, interdependence required a denser network of international connections. International law supplied the means of framing that network, and treaties were increasingly used to regulate a myriad of issues incapable of unilateral resolution. Telegraphy, weights and measures, postal, and patent and trademark regulation, all came under international treaty regulation. The Anglo-French commercial treaty of 1860 provided the centerpiece of Cobden's program of improving relations and ending a succession of naval panics.

International law proved an instrument facilitating a denser network of relationships in the nineteenth century. The trend was pronounced from mid-century onwards, with the movement for the "progressive codification of international law"[13] providing the goal of integration

---

[10] Prince Metternich, Memorandum, in *Documents Relating to the Program of the First Hague Peace Conference: Laid before the Conference by the Netherland Government*, (Oxford: Clarendon Press, 1921), 5.

[11] As quoted in Wehberg, *Limitation of Armaments*, 9.

[12] Scott, *The Hague Peace Conferences of 1899 and 1907*, Vol. 1, 657.

[13] Progressive codification was the goal of standardizing legal obligations, by taking the complex tangle of international custom and creating a unified code, thereby reducing conflict as rules of international conduct would be clearly set and understood. Hannis Taylor, *A Treatise on International Public Law* (Chicago: Callaghan and Co., 1901), v, 93–95.

through legal relationships. Beyond the occasional initiatives for broad, general limitations of armaments, and beyond the petitions framed by the sporadic gatherings of the peace movements, lay a more concrete role for international law in managing competition in weaponry. Statesmen had a rich legal and practical base from which they could craft practical agreements for limited purposes.

Great Britain played a central role in the development of arms control in the era. As the largest naval power, the dominant trading nation for much of the century, and the possessor of extensive overseas interests, Britain had a disproportionate influence on the development of international law. The Foreign Office utilized its predominant position to shape international law to British requirements. A number of arms initiatives were stifled by British opposition, due to the larger political questions involved or the perceived impact upon British naval strategy. A study of these arms initiatives provides a broader sense of how international law meshed with strategic planning, and how statesmen perceived law.

THE ANGLO-FRENCH NAVAL DECLARATIONS OF 1787

International projects for limiting arms competitions date back into antiquity, but while many were rooted in utopian schemes for peace, statesmen also placed practical and limited regulations into agreements. The Treaty of Utrecht included a ban on French fortifications at Dunkirk, to provide greater security for its Channel neighbor, Great Britain.[14] One of the earliest agreements negotiated specifically for the purpose of limiting armaments dates to 1787. These treaties between Great Britain and France regulated naval armaments during a crisis between the two states, providing an opportunity for tensions to subside while reducing mutual fears of attack by the other party.

The immediate crisis arose from an uprising in the Netherlands. France had forged an alliance with the Netherlands in 1785, following a rupture in the long-term Anglo-Dutch relationship that occurred during the War of American Independence. To the British, this new alliance presented the

---

[14] Treaty of Peace and Friendship between France and Great Britain, signed at Utrecht, Apr. 11, 1713, Clive Parry, ed., *Consolidated Treaty Series* (Dobbs Ferry, New York: Oceana Publications, 1969), Vol. 27, 482, Art IX. In 1766, Austria proposed a three-quarter reduction of standing armies to Prussia, although the offer met no success. Tate, *The Disarmament Illusion*, 7.

specter of a great power controlling the Scheldt estuary harbors on the English Channel. When the Netherlands was convulsed by revolution in the winter of 1786–1787, Great Britain and Prussia sided with the ruling House of Orange, against the French-supported Patriots. In July 1787, a Prussian expeditionary corps was formed to oust the Dutch Patriots.[15] In response, the French formed an army at Givet, with many in the French government urging intervention on behalf of their Dutch ally.

Alongside the immediate tensions relating to the Dutch revolution, lay Anglo-French competition in the East and West Indies. The Dutch alliance offered the opportunity for attacks on British–Indian trade from bases in the Cape Colony and Ceylon, and coincided with a reinvigorated French trading presence in the region.[16] In the summer of 1787, tensions over the Dutch revolution fueled rumors of naval and military expeditions being organized by France and Britain against each other. These rumors variously held that their neighbor was planning an expedition to the Indies in anticipation of war. The British also feared French intervention in the Netherlands.[17] The combination of tensions over the Netherlands and the Indies made both France and Great Britain nervous and highly sensitive to movements of troops and ships. In order to resolve the immediate crisis in Europe, the two powers needed greater confidence that neither would launch a pre-emptive strike on the other.

It was in these circumstances that envoy to France, William Eden, entered into naval disarmament negotiations with the French Foreign Minister, the Comte de Montmorin. Both sides sought an agreement that would reduce the risk of attack, by clarifying intentions about naval movements and by limiting the number of commissioned ships. One peculiar feature of the negotiations was that rather than focusing solely upon the

---

[15] J. H. Rose et al., "The Missions of William Grenville to the Hague and Versailles in 1787," *English Historical Review* 24, no. 94 (1909): 280–81.

[16] Munro Price, "The Dutch Affair and the Fall of the Ancien Regime, 1784–1787," *Historical Journal* 38, no. 4 (1995): 877. Many, although by no means all, prominent French leaders preferred better relations with Great Britain, including the King and the new Foreign Minister Montmorin, but the Dutch alliance kept alive a strategic option if war did occur. Moreover, French activity in India could have taken a provocative course in reasserting French influence in the region. *See* G C Bolton and B E Kennedy, "William Eden and the Treaty of Mauritius, 1786–7," *Historical Journal* 16, no. 4 (1973): 681–85.

[17] Eden to Marquess of Carmarthen, June 18, 1787, *in* Eden, FO 27/25 (May–Sep. 1787), at 64; Eden to Carmarthen, Aug. 2, 1787, *Id.*, at 178; Whitehall to Eden, Aug. 10, 1787, *Id.*, at 226.

number of warships built or under construction, concern centered upon the relative state of preparedness. In this era, navies generally possessed a number of warships in mothballs, in varying states of readiness, which required a significant amount of time to mobilize. British calculations focused upon French forces that could be made ready to go to sea in a short period of time, and arms control discussions emphasized preparedness, and means of verifying levels of warlike-preparations.

Eden's instructions required him to determine the number and size of ships "actually fit for immediate Service, the Number and Size of those now building, and their different Degrees of Preparation, as well as the State of the naval Magazines of Stores and Provisions."[18] Montmorin, in replying to this request for information in August, not only detailed the size of the fleet, but also listed those ships that were in good repair, those without masts and rigging, those that were unmanned, and those that were being sheathed in copper in preparation for sea service.[19] After a series of requests for clarification brought by both Britain and France, Eden offered to regularize the exchange of information in a declaration.[20] Montmorin initially replied with an offer to disarm the French squadron when the British reciprocated, and later suggested both states limit mobilized naval forces to six warships, for the duration of the present crisis.[21]

Eden and Montmorin finalized these negotiations in a joint declaration. The British government expressed an interest in making the arrangement permanent, but both parties recognized the need to expressly limit its application to the "present circumstances" and consider the effects a permanent treaty would have on other naval stations.[22] Naval forces were

---

[18] Whitehall to Eden, June 29, 1787, *in* FO 27/25 at 132.

[19] Eden to Carmarthen, Aug. 9, 1787, *in* FO 27/25, at 187. The lack of information was endemic. The British heard rumors of a large supply of salted provisions shipping out of London bound for the French Fleet at Brest, and could only confirm the shipment from their own capital by asking the French. Whitehall to Eden, Aug. 10, 1787, *in* FO 27/25, at 225. Montmorin agreed that if such a report was true, the British could halt the shipment. Eden to Carmarthen, Aug. 16, 1787, *in* FO 27/25, at 265–266.

[20] Eden to Carmarthen, Aug. 4, 1787, *in* FO 27/25, at 186.

[21] *Id.*; Eden to Carmarthen, Aug. 16, 1787, *in* FO 27/25, at 265. France had initially mobilized six ships-of-the-line in response to a British squadron organized in the summer. Eden to Carmarthen, Aug. 4, 1787, *id.* at 187.

[22] Whitehall to Eden, Aug. 24, 1787, *id.* at 294. "[D]ans la position actuelle des affaires." Reciprocal Declaration between France and Great Britain, signed at Versailles, Aug. 30, 1787, *in* Parry, ed., *Consolidated Treaty Series*, Vol. 50, 211.

numerically limited to *"l'établissement de paix,"* active commissioned warships were limited to six ships-of-the-line, and each party had to give notice prior to altering its naval preparations.[23]

In September, the situation deteriorated, following Prussian military intervention in the Netherlands, threatened French invasion, and subsequent British preparations. Throughout October, war appeared likely, until France backed down with some embarrassment. The French lacked funds to initiate a major war in both the East Indies and the Netherlands, yet were prepared to fight if pressed. Montmorin expressed himself as "horrified beyond measure" with having to "keep pace with [British] armaments";[24] thus arms limitation appealed to France for financial reasons. Great Britain, for its part, feared that France was using the lengthy period of negotiations to prepare its fleet for war, and sought to reaffirm the mutual commitment to restrict naval forces.[25]

The parties negotiated a further disarmament treaty, reaffirming their commitment to resolve the crisis peacefully. Given the precarious nature of French finances on the eve of the Revolution, Great Britain achieved nearly all its goals. France sought to remove Prussian armed forces from the Netherlands as part of the agreement, but Prussia refused, and the British disavowed any ability to bind their ally – signaling an Anglo-Prussian victory in the entire Dutch affair.

The October agreement related solely to naval armaments. Differences in levels of actual peacetime preparations made a meaningful comparison of French and British forces difficult. Great Britain maintained a number of "guard ships" in semi-active status, while France had fewer ships in service, but at a higher state of readiness. Montmorin expressed a desire to emulate the British system of guard ships, drawing objections from the Foreign Office, which viewed such measures as a de facto increase.[26] The ultimate use of the term *"le pied de l'établissement de la paix"* was

[23] *Id.* The "Peace Establishment" referred specifically to normal mobilized forces, later set at active forces as of January 1, 1787.

[24] Eden to Carmarthen, Oct. 17, 1787, *in* Eden & Grenville, FO 27/26 (Sep.–Dec. 1787), at 223.

[25] Whitehall to Eden, Oct. 14, 1787, *id.* at 208. Moreover, the British sought to signal to Spain that the Dutch affair was unlikely to lead to war, in order to coax the latter state to reduce its naval preparations. As in 1912, Mediterranean calculations influenced British negotiations, making bilateral arms control more challenging.

[26] Whitehall to Eden, Oct. 24, 1787, *id.* at 247–248.

intended by Britain to reject such a possibility, with both parties agreeing to revert to their naval status as of the beginning of 1787. Foreign Office instructions requested Eden to gain assurance that France had not intended to intervene in the Netherlands, nor would it seek to do so in the future, a suggestion that Eden wisely sidestepped as both offensive to French national honor and unlikely to provide any real security in a legal agreement.[27] Verification might have provided a more effective measure, and both sides contemplated exchanging naval officers to confirm the state of preparedness at major ports. However, Eden noted that it would still be easy to disguise many preparations, and verification provisions might only fuel suspicions and ill-will. Hence the topic was quietly shelved.[28]

The final agreement differed from the August declaration in consisting of a declaration and counter-declaration exchanged by each party simultaneously, with a third joint declaration between them. The use of separate notes was common in contemporary negotiations, allowing each party to explain its views more fully in its own preamble, while retaining nearly identical wording of the binding provisions. British wording in the first declaration was expressly conditional (*"seraient discontinués"*) and only on receiving French assurances did the British agree that armaments *"seront discontinués."*[29] The attention to wording and an explicit Foreign Office insistence on the simultaneous exchange of notes reflected a concern with how each party might be held to the agreement.[30] Both states deemed the agreement to be binding, even though termed only a "Ministerial Declaration."[31]

---

[27] "I beg leave to submit that it is easier to give such a suggestion than to [execute] it: – and if it were practicable, which I apprehend it is not, it does not appear that it would be of any utility. – I conceive that no Court ever was required by another to make such a promise; and also, that if made, it would afford a most slender security." Eden to Carmarthen, Oct. 11, 1787, *id.* at 187.

[28] Eden to Carmarthen, Nov. 1, 1787, *id.* at 258.

[29] Reciprocal Declarations between France and Great Britain, signed at Versailles, Oct. 27, 1787, *in* Parry, ed., *Consolidated Treaty Series*, Vol. 50, 245.

[30] Whitehall to Eden, Oct. 15, 1787, *in* FO 27/26, at 211.

[31] The Foreign Office stressed that the "engagement should be positive" and consistently discussed it as a legally binding document, right down to consideration of the documents that would need to be laid before Parliament on its conclusion. *Id.* at 213. Moreover, despite the somewhat conditional language in the declarations, both parties repeatedly indicated to the other that they regarded the obligations as binding. *Id.* at 215.

The Anglo-French Declarations of 1787 provided a precedent for later arms control agreements. In contrast to later discussions, negotiations focused on the state of preparations rather than on numbers of warships, presaging Churchill's goal of reducing Anglo-German mobilized naval forces in May 1914. The intervening wars through 1815 and a failure to build upon this model meant that arms control law did not directly progress from the 1787 agreements. However, the agreement was not forgotten.[32] These early discussions showed that the nature of the arms race was understood at the beginning of the nineteenth century. The process of competitive armaments was seen to contribute directly to "*les jalousies nationales et des défenses inutiles.*"[33] International agreements could relieve the situation by providing an exchange of information as well as verification of defense arrangements. Finally, statesmen affirmed as a principle of international law that national defenses, when they menaced their neighbors, were a legitimate topic of regulation.

RUSH-BAGOT AGREEMENT OF 1817

Another early agreement, also involving naval armaments and Great Britain, played a larger role in the long-term development of arms control law. The Rush-Bagot Agreement of 1817 regulated British and American naval forces on the Great Lakes, and still remains in force, making it the world's the longest-lasting arms control agreement, although it has been modified by diplomatic notes in the twentieth century. In its long tenure, this agreement has reflected the challenges of regulating naval forces and predicting technological evolution. More centrally, the continued existence of this treaty, despite numerous initiatives to terminate it, highlights the enduring value of law in shaping policy. In spite of violations and challenges to its continued effectiveness, the existence of a treaty increased the political costs of shifting national policy enough to help prevent any radical change of course.

The treaty was part of the post-war settlement following the War of 1812. The conflict featured savage warfare, the burning of Washington in retaliation for the American sacking of York, atrocities against civilians, and

[32] For instance, a book on the 1817 Rush-Bagot Agreement published shortly before the 1899 Hague Peace Conference referenced it. James Morton Callahan, *The Neutrality of the American Lakes and Anglo-American Relations* (Baltimore: Johns Hopkins Press, 1898), 19–20.

[33] Eden to Carmarthen, Aug. 16, 1787, *in* FO 27/25, at 265.

a state of almost fratricidal warfare in the Great Lakes region.[34] Relations remained embittered following the 1814 Peace of Ghent, with the United States protesting that British warships still fired upon their merchants in the Great Lakes.[35] The possibility of renewed conflict remained real. Both sides had built up large naval forces on the Great Lakes during the war, the British maintaining 28 warships, including one 74-gun and one 60-gun ship of the line, comparable to heavy warships on the oceans.[36] The Great Lakes, as enclosed seas lacking navigable access to the ocean, offered a unique regulatory advantage. In 1815, a treaty limiting warships on the Great Lakes could not be violated by one party bringing in ships from the high seas, where Great Britain enjoyed an overwhelming naval superiority.

Following the War of 1812, both sides sought to increase their naval armaments upon the lakes, and the Americans, fearing the expense of an arms race and concerned that British actions on the lakes might spark a renewed conflict, sought an agreement. The United States planned a fleet of nine ships-of-the-line and a dozen heavy frigates at sea. On the lakes, both powers had three-deck ships-of-the-line under construction, including the 130-gun USS *Chippewa*, which had it been finished, would have been one of the most powerful ships in the world.[37] The concept of an arms race was clearly expressed in American correspondence, which recognized the need for an international solution.[38] In addition to the

[34] Ernest Crosby, "A Precedent for Disarmament: A Suggestion to the Peace Conference," *North American Review* 183, no. 6 (1906): 776.
[35] Adams to Castlereagh, Mar. 21, 1816, *in* Message from the President of the United States, in Response to Senate Resolution of April 11, 1892, Relative to the Agreement between the United States and Great Britain Concerning the Naval Forces to Be Maintained on the Great Lakes, Dec. 7, 1892, S. Exec. Doc. No. 9, at 4 (1892) [*hereinafter* Presidential Message].
[36] Bagot to Monroe, Nov. 4, 1816, *in id.* at 9. Exact figures for the United States are unclear, although one authority lists them as 25 vessels. Henry Sherman Boutell, "Is the Rush–Bagot Convention Immortal?" *North American Review* 173, no. 3 (1901): 335.
[37] Kenneth Bourne, *Britain and the Balance of Power in North America, 1815–1908* (London: Longmans, Green & Co., 1967), 9, 12.
[38] "The increase of naval armaments on one side upon the lakes, during peace, will necessitate the like increase on the other, and besides causing an aggravation of useless expense to both parties must operate as a continual stimulus of suspicion and of ill will upon the inhabitants and local authorities of the borders against those of their neighbors." Peace should be "cemented ... by reliance upon good faith far better adapted to the maintenance of national harmony than the jealous and exasperating defiance of complete armor." Adams to Castlereagh, Mar. 21, 1816, *in* Presidential Message, *supra* note 35.

naval construction rivalry, the Americans accused the British of boarding American vessels on the lakes, reminiscent of actions that had led the United States to war in 1812. Castlereagh initially opposed a limit, noting that the defense of Canada depended on forces being available at the start of a conflict, as the United States could out-build the Canadians after war had erupted.[39] Moreover, the British recognized control of the Great Lakes as key to the outcome of any future conflict.[40] Echoing contemporary legal doctrine, a British delegate at the Ghent Conference, Henry Goulburn, noted that the United States had no grounds to complain of British armaments if they were proportionate to growth of population and did not "exceed the necessity of the case."[41]

The American proposals arrived at an awkward time in London. Following a quarter-century of high naval budgets during the French Revolutionary and Napoleonic wars, the Admiralty faced significant spending cuts in 1816.[42] As a result, the specter of renewed American conflict was exploited to maintain funding in annual estimates debates, leading American Ambassador John Quincy Adams to despair of the arms control project. However, soon after the estimates had been passed, Castlereagh revived the American proposition to limit warships, leaving Adams scrambling to belatedly frame a formal proposal.[43] Negotiations shifted to Washington in the summer of 1816, being conducted between American Secretary of State James Monroe, and Charles Bagot, the British Minister in Washington. Trans-oceanic communications repeatedly hamstrung negotiations. Bagot, like Adams, was initially unprepared to begin negotiations before instructions arrived, and then only able to undertake talks *ad referendum*, or subject to ratification in London. Ultimately, the trans-Atlantic delays in finalizing the agreement led American negotiators

---

[39] Adams to Monroe, Feb. 8, 1816, *in* Presidential Message, *supra* note 35. Adams noted that this had been apparent during the peace negotiations at Ghent in 1814, at which point Great Britain proposed that one party control the whole territory of the Great Lakes, including the shores, thus obviating the need for naval armaments. *Id.*

[40] Frank A. Updyke, *The Diplomacy of the War of 1812* (Baltimore: Johns Hopkins Press, 1915), 458–60.

[41] *Id.*, 460–61.

[42] C. J. Bartlett, *Great Britain and Sea Power, 1815–1853* (Oxford: Clarendon Press, 1963), 15–17.

[43] Castlereagh to Bagot, Apr. 23, 1816, *in* Castlereagh to Bagot, Drafts FO 5/113, (1816) at 16.

to suspect treachery. A clear informal agreement was only worked out in November 1816, and a formal treaty followed in April 1817. As British debates over naval estimates demonstrated broad support for naval superiority at all costs, the American negotiators offered flexible terms. American goals included both a reduction in naval forces as well as restrictions on activities on the lakes, to reduce the risk of collision. While preferring a reduction in forces, Adams initially offered a status quo limit which would have kept the large forces in place.[44] After talks were renewed in Washington, Madison suggested only one warship per party be allowed on all the lakes, increasing the offer to four ships when Bagot demurred.[45] Any British inferiority in local construction facilities could be overcome by framing and maintaining keels ready for launching in an emergency.[46] Uncompleted ships could be launched if this was necessary for their preservation. However, once negotiations had moved beyond status quo and had centered on actual reductions, Monroe demanded legal parity in any agreement, either temporary or permanent, recognizing that it would be politically unpalatable to accept any less during an election year.[47]

Once negotiations began, both sides showed more flexibility in making major cuts, and discussions focused more on the form and status of the final agreement. Both non-binding informal agreements and a formal legally binding treaty were employed in the negotiations. The parties initially reached an informal "gentlemen's agreement" in April 1816, pending further negotiations, but they did not set out the terms in writing, leading each side to form a different impression of what had been

---

[44] Adams to Monroe, Feb. 8, 1816, *in* Presidential Message, *supra* note 35. The latter condition alarmed Bagot, who read this as a limit on the use of ships on the lakes. Bagot to Castlereagh, Aug. 12, 1816, *in* Bagot to Castlereagh, FO 5/115, at 1.

[45] *Id.*

[46] Bagot to Castlereagh, May 3, 1816, *in* Bagot to Castlereagh, FO 5/114, Part 2, at 48. Moreover, Monroe held that the status quo would preserve an extant British superiority on Lake Ontario, which was critical for the defense of Canada, while the US would have superiority on Lakes Erie and Huron, allowing rapid movement of troops for defense against Native American tribes living along the lakes. Monroe to Adams, May 21, 1816, *in* Presidential Message, *supra* note 35.

[47] *See* Bagot to Castlereagh, Aug. 12, 1816, *in* FO 5/115. Like the British stance *vis-à-vis* the United States in 1920s arms negotiations, Bagot recognized that once accorded legal parity, the United States would be unlikely to build up its authorized levels. *See* Gregory C. Kennedy, "The 1930 London Naval Conference and Anglo-American Maritime Strength, 1927–1930," in *Arms Limitation and Disarmament*, 149, 154.

decided.[48] In his instructions to Bagot, Castlereagh preferred a non-binding agreement to remove the immediate problem, but would have accepted a binding treaty if the Americans insisted.[49] The Americans did insist, placing Bagot in a bind over the summer of 1816. He repeatedly promised to "give effect to any general understanding" to temporarily limit armaments while sending a formal proposal back to London. But he cagily refused to term even this informal agreement as provisional.[50] After sending formal proposals back to London in August, the parties agreed to an informal status quo arrangement, finalized in November 1816 with the exchange of lists of ships in service.[51] The *pourparlers* followed a standard pattern in arms negotiations prior to 1914. Negotiations shifted from informal to formal agreements, with exchanges of information on naval forces forming essential parts of the final bargain. As with the 1787 Anglo-French Declarations, this negotiating process was not seen as innovative or a noteworthy departure from practice.

The challenge of fixing a strategic balance and then preventing violations also followed predictable patterns. Castlereagh and Bagot each independently expressed concerns about the disparity in construction capabilities on the Great Lakes, and Monroe and Adams separately anticipated and acknowledged these concerns. The Americans also feared British duplicity – Monroe suspecting the lengthy negotiations were drawn out to allow Britain to concentrate naval artillery on the lakes.[52] The British Admiralty had already thought of ways to circumvent the strategic balance without drawing suspicion. In July 1816, the Admiralty discussed the possibility of building heavily timbered ships comparable to the *Princess Charlotte*,

[48] Adams wrote home that beyond troop transports, "the British Government did not wish to have any ships in commission or in active service," while Castlereagh informed Bagot that "they would keep in Commission the smallest number of vessels that was compatible with the ordinary routine of a Peace Establishment." Adams to Monroe, Apr. 15, 1816, *in* Presidential Message, *supra* note 35; Castlereagh to Bagot, Apr. 23, 1816, *in* FO 5/113, at 16.

[49] *Id.*

[50] Bagot to Monroe, Aug. 6, 1816; Bagot to Castlereagh, Aug. 12, 1816; Bagot to Monroe, Aug. 13, 1816, all *in* FO 5/115, at 1 *et. seq.*

[51] Bagot to Monroe, Nov. 4, 1816 & Monroe to Bagot, Nov. 7, 1816, both *in* Presidential Message, *supra* note 35.

[52] Monroe to Adams, Nov. 14, 1816, *in* Presidential Message, *supra* note 35. Tensions remained so high that the Americans feared the British had undertaken the lengthy negotiations merely to "amuse us" while preparing for renewed hostilities, as they had failed to give their lead diplomat any authority to bind his country. *Id.*

"observing that whilst peace continues it may be proper as on Ontario to call them Corvettes, but strong enough in Timber to have another Deck build over on appearance of war."[53] The Admiralty sent instructions to Canada to prepare to build similar ships on Lake Erie, with the clear intention of misleading the Americans.[54] The vague informal agreement of April 1816, at least under the British interpretation, did not forbid such naval preparations, highlighting the risks of unclear, non-binding agreements.

Seeking greater stability and clarity, the Americans pressed for a formal treaty. Adams suggested a basic formula in August 1816 which ultimately became the Rush-Bagot Agreement. The parties agreed to a numerical limit on warships allowed on the Great Lakes, with provision for one vessel on Lake Ontario, two on the upper lakes, and one on Lake Champlain.[55] The agreement was also the first to feature both size limitations and armament regulation, as vessels were restricted to 100 tons, and to one 18 pound cannon.[56] All other extant vessels were to be "dismantled" and no further construction would be allowed.[57] The interpretation of dismantling allowed warships then under construction in the Great Lakes to be maintained in an unfinished condition for future use, which both parties did for many years, by building sheds over the incomplete hulls.[58] At Adams's insistence, the Rush-Bagot Agreement also contained an express provision for terminating the agreement, requiring either party to give six

---

[53] Admiralty to Byam Martin, July 6, 1816, *in* Admiralty Special Minutes, ADM 3/262, (1816–1824).

[54] *See* Bourne, *Britain and the Balance of Power in North America*, at 16–17. I agree with Bourne's conclusion that the subterfuge was made in the absence of any real obligation to the United States, and was most likely the result of a lack of inter-departmental communications between the Admiralty and Foreign Office.

[55] Exchange of Notes between Great Britain and the United States Relative to Naval Forces on the American Lakes, signed at Washington, Apr. 28, 29, 1817, *in* Parry, ed., *Consolidated Treaty Series*, Vol. 67, 154. [*hereinafter* Rush-Bagot Agreement]. Lakes Ontario and Champlain were separated from the upper lakes, making three distinct sub-regions.

[56] *Id.* An 18-pounder cannon refers to the nominal weight of a cannonball fired from this cannon. In the early nineteenth century, the heaviest warships carried naval artillery nearly twice the size, up to 32 pounders. R Ernest Dupuy and Trevor N Dupuy, *The Encyclopedia of Military History: From 3500 B.C. To the Present*, 2nd edition (New York: Harper and Row, 1986), 666–67. Both these methods of limiting naval weaponry became central to twentieth century treaties, most notably the Washington Convention of 1922.

[57] 1817 Rush-Bagot Agreement.

[58] C. P. Stacey, "The Myth of the Unguarded Frontier 1815–1871," *American Historical Review* 56, no. 1 (1950): 12.

months' notice.[59] Finally, the parties restricted actions that their navies could undertake on the lakes, which would "in no respect interfere with the proper duties of the armed Vessels of the other Party."[60]

The agreement, initialed a year after negotiations began, took the form of a pair of notes exchanged by Bagot and Richard Rush, the Acting American Secretary of State. The use of diplomatic notes, which had also been employed in the Anglo-French declarations, and the absence of further acts of ratification in either Washington or London, almost immediately led to confusion as to the status of the agreement within international law. Neither statesman had initially been given authority to conclude a binding treaty; only "a provisional arrangement" had been desired, in order to alleviate an immediate problem without necessarily creating a long-term relationship.[61] The statesmen sought a way of reducing the inordinate number of warships in enclosed seas, as they were unable to redeploy them to other stations. A diplomatic exchange of notes provided an ideal method for resolving this temporary dispute, but left questions as to whether a long-term arrangement had been anticipated. A year after the notes were signed, now-President Monroe suffered doubts about whether or not the agreement had been ratified as a binding treaty, and submitted it to the Senate for its advice and consent.[62] The United States did not formally resolve the question of whether or not the agreement was binding until after the Civil War, although throughout the century the Americans acted in the belief that they were bound.[63] This ambiguity over the exchange of notes has also subsequently confused his-

---

[59] 1817 Rush-Bagot Agreement.

[60] *Id.*

[61] Monroe to Bagot, Aug. 12, 1816, *in* Presidential Message, *supra* note 35.

[62] Presidential Message, *supra* note 35, at 12. The agreement was technically an executive agreement under presidential powers, although the domestic form did not affect its international legal status. John Bassett Moore, *A Digest of International Law* (Washington: Government Printing Office, 1906), Vol. I, 692–93.

[63] As late as 1892 the State Department had to explain that the exchange of notes remained binding. While the American government possessed no evidence that Great Britain had ratified the agreement, which suggested that it might have been considered non-binding by the British, the Secretary of State provided numerous other examples of exchanges of notes creating binding obligations. Presidential Message, *supra* note 35, at 13–15. Secretary of State Seward referred to the agreement as "informal" when discussing it in 1864, although he acknowledged that the ratification by the Senate was consistent with a treaty. *Id.* at 27–28. In 1892, Secretary of State Foster noted that it was more of a "reciprocal regulation of a matter within the administrative competence of each." *Id.* at 33.

torians about whether the agreement was legally binding.[64] Ultimately, notification requirements stipulating the only manner in which the agreement "shall cease to be binding" indicated an intention to create a binding agreement.[65]

After an agreement had been reached, warships laid up in ordinary were allowed to fall into disrepair. The United States still maintained the dismantled ships-of-the-line *Chippewa* and the *New Orleans* in readiness for future launching, the latter remaining on the navy list into the 1880s. Moreover, the United States continued to build naval facilities at Sackett's Harbor, the second most expensive American naval base after Boston.[66] Both sides continued to make naval preparations allowed by the treaty, but expenses gradually decreased. More significantly, the British came to appreciate the agreement as the balance of power shifted. Recognizing the rising costs of defending Canada, an agreement which reduced these costs was welcomed by the British, to the extent that violations of the treaty were increasingly tolerated.

Over the course of the nineteenth century, both parties violated the agreement, arguing self-defense, but the relationship anchored by the treaty remained important enough to overlook occasional breaches and remained in force. The British were the first to violate the agreement, when responding to a rebellion in Canada in 1838. A group of rebels, self-styled "Canadian Patriots," seized an island in the Niagara River and used it as a base to attack and burn a British ship and to plot further attacks.[67] As the forces authorized under the treaty were insufficient to quell the uprising, the British notified the American government that they would temporarily need to build a naval force.[68] The American government

---

[64] *See, for example,* Alvin C. Gluek, "The Invisible Revision of the Rush-Bagot Agreement, 1898–1914," *Canadian Historical Review* 60, no. 4, (Dec. 1979): 466, 467–468.

[65] 1817 Rush-Bagot Agreement.

[66] Bourne, *Britain and the Balance of Power in North America*, at 31–32.

[67] Presidential Message, *supra* note 35, at 15–16.

[68] Fox to Forsyth, Nov. 25, 1838, *in* Presidential Message, *supra* note 35. This same set of circumstances also led Britain to enter American territory and burn an American vessel called the *Caroline* before it could transport supplies to the rebels. The resulting outcry and diplomatic exchange led to the formation of the *Caroline* Dictum, setting out the international legal standard for preemptive self-defense. "[W]hile it is admitted that exceptions growing out of the great law of self-defense do exist, those exceptions should be confined to cases in which the 'necessity of that self-defense is instant, overwhelming, and leaving no means, and no moment for deliberation.'" Moore, *A Digest of International Law*, Vol. 2, 412.

attempted to confirm if the agreement remained operative, and when the British failed to respond, insisted on "rigid compliance with the terms of the convention."[69] In addition, President Van Buren commissioned military forces under Major General Winfield Scott to verify British compliance. However, the realities of the frontier terrain prevented effective verification, as Scott had only five officers to spare for a task involving hundreds of miles of coastline. Not only did the Americans have to rely upon rumors in their final report, but one of the officers, a General Brady, confessed that prior to his assignment he had never heard of the Rush-Bagot Agreement, and that "during the border troubles he frequently had a piece of ordnance on board the steamboat in the employ of the United States," unwittingly violating the agreement.[70]

Unable to independently confirm British forces in the region, and armed with rumors of 500-ton British steamers plying the lakes, the American Navy built the *Michigan*, its first iron-hulled warship. Weighing 498 tons and carrying six guns, the ship clearly exceeded the treaty limitations, consuming more than the total tonnage allowed for the squadron.[71] Both sides questioned whether the agreement applied to steamers. Colonial Secretary Lord Stanley suggested that Britain contract with private companies to provide steamers capable of conversion in wartime.[72] The episode showed the challenges of regulating rapidly evolving naval technology. The agreement made more sense in 1817, as warship design had not evolved significantly over the prior 150 years.[73] By the mid-nineteenth century, when

[69]Webster to Fox, Nov. 29, 1841, *in* Presidential Message, *supra* note 35. The United States also noted repeatedly that British ships were pierced to carry more than one gun, highlighting a problem with the armament limitation in the treaty. Mason to Calhoun, Sep. 4, 1844, *in* Presidential Message, *supra* note 35. Like the question of gun elevation which arose after the 1922 Washington Treaty, not every potential issue could be foreseen and incorporated into an agreement.

[70]H.R. Exec. Doc. No. 26–246, July 1, 1840 Message from the President of the United States, Naval Forces on the Lakes, at 2 (1840).

[71]"No effective steamer for any purpose, it is believed, would be built on a tonnage of 100 tons." Mason to Calhoun, Sep. 4, 1844, *in* Presidential Message, *supra* note 35. Conway's lists the armament as one 18pdr. Robert Gardiner, ed., *Conway's All the World's Fighting Ships, 1860–1905* (London: Conway Maritime Press Ltd., 1979), 118.

[72]"It is fair to say that it is a question whether the Convention extended to Steamers: still the construction of Vessels of such size, and the supply of shot and shells for them in time of profound peace can hardly be considered consistent with the spirit of the agreement." Stanley to Peel, Sep. 5, 1844, *in* Paul Knaplund, "Documents: The Armaments on the Great Lakes, 1844," *American Historical Review*, 40, no. 3 (Apr. 1935): 473, 474.

[73]McNeill, *The Pursuit of Power*, 225.

steam power was supplanting sail, when exploding shells replaced solid shot, and when iron was mounted on the sides of warships in response, technological change became the norm. From that time forward, the challenge of adequately regulating unforeseeable technological changes in a legal agreement provided ample opportunities for circumventing a treaty's intention. The ship served on the Great Lakes into the 1920s without being replaced – its paddlewheels churning the freshwater into the age of submarines and aircraft.

During the Civil War, the Americans also violated the agreement, on the basis of self-defense, following a Confederate plot to seize an American warship, raid prisoner of war camps on the lakes, and spread havoc.[74] More significantly, the American Civil War altered Anglo-American relations. As the relative power shifted to the United States, Americans increasingly raised objections to the treaty, while the British sought to retain it in order to bolster their own position. The United States officially gave notice to withdraw from the treaty in 1864, but rescinded the notice before the end of the mandatory six-month period.[75]

BLACK SEA NEUTRALIZATION OF 1856

The third major arms control agreement of the era again involved naval armaments, with Great Britain as its promoter. The Black Sea Treaty of 1856, part of the settlement of the Crimean War, banned both Russia and Turkey from maintaining warships in the Black Sea beyond six small steam vessels of 800 tons weight and four smaller craft under 200 tons.[76] The agreement regulated numbers of warships and their size, like the Rush-Bagot Agreement of 1817, although the treaty did not limit their armament. Notably, the victorious allies imposed the treaty upon an unwilling

---

[74] Macdonell to MacDonald, Sep. 20, 1864, enclosure in Monck to Cardwell, Sep. 26, 1864, Correspondence with Canada upon the use of Armed Vessels upon the American Lakes, and on Piratical Attempts there, and the Best Means of Prevention, Dec. 6, 1864, *in* Armed Ships on Great Lakes, FO 5/2598 (1892–1905).

[75] Presidential Message, *supra* note 35, at 26–27. This course of action raised complex constitutional questions, and as late as 1892, questions still remained as to whether the treaty still existed. *Id.* at 32–34.

[76] Convention between Russia and Turkey, limiting their Naval Force in the Black Sea, Art. II, *in* Michael Hurst, ed., *Key Treaties for the Great Powers 1814–1914* (Newton Abbot: David & Charles, 1972), Vol. 1, 331. [*hereinafter* Black Sea Neutralization Treaty].

Russia.[77] As a result, the long-term stability of this arms control regime rested upon a slender support.[78] However, the agreement did succeed in temporarily stabilizing the region, the immediate goals of the British negotiators.

The settlement of the Crimean War, at the Paris Peace Conference, also included a Tripartite Guarantee Treaty protecting Turkey, a treaty neutralizing the Åland Islands in the Baltic, and a treaty demilitarizing the Turkish Straits, in addition to the general Peace of Paris.[79] Britain and France had fought the Crimean War to contain Russian expansion, in particular the naval threat posed to Constantinople by the Russian Black Sea fleet.[80] The war began with a stunning Russian victory over the Ottoman fleet at Sinope, in which new Russian shell-firing cannons decimated the wooden walls of their Turkish enemy.[81] British policy throughout the ensuing conflict focused on countering the challenge of Russian naval expansion. The main land campaign in the Crimea revolved around the siege of the primary Russian naval base in the region, Sevastopol, and resulted in the complete destruction of the Black Sea Fleet.

As part of the peace negotiations, the British insisted upon Russian naval disarmament in the Black Sea, this becoming one of the points in the Austrian ultimatum delivered to Russia.[82] By eliminating the risk of a

---

[77] The agreement had precedents in Russian experience. Russia had imposed similar naval limitations on vanquished foes in the past, forcing Persia to accept demilitarization of the Caspian Sea in the 1828 Peace Treaty signed at Turkmanchai. Russia also had been obliged to accept demilitarization of the Black Sea in 1739. "[L]a Russie ne pourra ni sur la mer de Zabache, ni sur la mer Noire, construire & avoir de flotte & d'autres navires." Definitive Treaty of Peace between the Emperor and Turkey, signed at Belgrade, Sep. 18, 1739, Art. III, *in* Parry, ed., *Consolidated Treaty Series* Vol. 35, 431.

[78] On the fate of the agreement, see next chapter.

[79] Additionally, the parties ratified the Declaration of Paris, regulating maritime warfare, discussed *infra*. On the Declaration of Paris, *see* Jan Martin Lemnitzer, *Power, Law and the End of Privateering* (Houndmills, Basingstoke: Palgrave Macmillan, 2014). This work will refer to the agreements collectively as the Peace of Paris, unless specifically referring to one of the agreements.

[80] David Wetzel, *The Crimean War: A Diplomatic History* (Boulder: Columbia University Press, 1985), 114–15.

[81] Dupuy and Dupuy, *The Encyclopedia of Military History*, 825. Marder, *The Anatomy of British Sea Power*, 4.

[82] Winfried Baumgart, *The Peace of Paris 1856: Studies in War, Diplomacy, and Peacemaking*, trans. Ann Pottinger Saab (Santa Barbara: ABC Clio, 1981), 114.

naval landing, the Turkish defenders could focus on the two land routes from Russia. Of these, the western route through the Principalities of Moldavia and Wallachia had been neutralized by the Peace of Paris, and the victorious allies acquired a stake in protecting the territory as it moved towards independence in the 1860s. The eastern route traversed remote mountainous territory far from the center of Ottoman power, preventing a rapid attack from destabilizing Turkey. In these circumstances, Russia could not hope to rapidly overthrow the Ottoman Empire by a *coup de main* on Constantinople, and Turkey would be given time to strengthen its institutions and revitalize its position.[83] While Russia lacked a naval force on the Black Sea, the Turks could maintain a fleet beyond the Straits in the Sea of Marmara, and could also call upon allied assistance if attacked.[84] Thus the Black Sea neutralization played a key part in the scheme to restore the regional balance.

Prior to the Paris Peace Conference, Russia had accepted a general limitation on its Black Sea naval forces in principle, leaving delegates at the gathering to resolve the details. Russia and Turkey would be limited to maintaining light vessels in the Black Sea, while other powers would generally be banned from sending warships through the Bosphorus, neutralizing the sea.[85] Moreover, Russia agreed not to rebuild naval arsenals on the Black Sea. However, the parties had not exactly defined either the extent of the Black Sea or what "light vessels" included. As to the first issue, Russia claimed an exemption for its main surviving naval works at Nicolaev, thirty miles from the coast on the Bug River, arguing that if this riverside establishment was banned, there would be no natural limit to how far inland the treaty would operate.[86] Moreover, Russia considered

---

[83] See generally E. Hammond, Memorandum – Russia and Turkey and the Treaties of 1856, Nov. 1, 1870, FO 881/1816 (1870).

[84] As with the 1817 Rush-Bagot Agreement and 1922 Washington Treaty balance between France and Italy, parity did not imply strategic equality.

[85] The Straits traditionally had been regulated by the Ottoman Empire as an internal matter, and after 1841 the Convention of London closed them as a matter of international law. Convention Respecting the Straits of the Dardanelles and of the Bosphorus, signed in London, July 13, 1841, *in* Hurst, ed., *Key Treaties*, Vol. I, 259. A specific exception was allowed, granting each state the right to maintain two small vessels at the mouth of the Danube as part of the new legal regime opening the river to navigation.

[86] Clarendon to Palmerston, Mar. 5, 1856, *in* Paris Conference, Archives, Lord Clarendon to Lord Palmerston, Drafts, FO 27/1168 (Feb. 17–Mar. 12, 1856) at 157.

the Sea of Azov to be inland waters beyond the scope of the ultimatum.[87] The Foreign Office sought advice from the Law Officers, who advised that, technically, the Russians were correct. The Sea of Azov, like ports up the Bug River, was not part of the Black Sea. However, Palmerston seized upon their broader argument that the goal of neutralizing the Black Sea required regulation of all adjacent regions. If Russia could easily bypass the agreement by stationing a fleet in the Sea of Azov, a treaty could not achieve its broader goal of neutralizing the Black Sea.[88] Ultimately, Russian delegate Orlov pledged not to use Nicolaev as a naval base, beyond supporting the minor naval force allotted to Russia under the treaty, and the British let the matter rest.

Technical questions relating to warship regulations proved more complex, although Russia generally acceded to British demands. The British negotiators demonstrated a sophisticated understanding of verification challenges. Policies were developed in coordination with Admiralty experts, and framed around feasible restrictions. The British sought to reduce naval armaments on the Black Sea to the minimum level necessary for police duties. Russia continually pushed back, seeking as powerful a force as possible allowable under the Austrian ultimatum. Initially, Russia claimed that the limitation to light vessels would allow the construction of frigates, the smallest vessels capable of standing in the line of battle. Armed with a single deck of forty to fifty guns, a frigate was far smaller than the three decker ships-of-the-line. As a modern frigate could equal the fighting capability of an older ship of the line, the Foreign Office refused to accept this claim, fearing it would vitiate the entire agreement if Russia maintained such a squadron.[89] Russia then sought to build corvettes under the agreement. Another memo went out from the Foreign Office explaining this type of warship to Foreign Secretary Earl of Clarendon, and noting that these also were far too big and powerful and did not "answer the Description of light vessels for the service of the Courts and for the Prevention of Piracy mentioned in the Austrian ultimatum."[90]

---

[87] Clarendon to Palmerston, Mar. 9, 1856, *id.* at 172–173. However, Russian delegate Orlov did admit that the waters of the Sea of Azov were too shallow to operate large warships, and as a result Russia had no building establishments there. *Id.*

[88] Palmerston to Clarendon, Feb. 22, 1856, *in* Lord Clarendon Paris Conference Drafts, FO 27/1163 (Feb.–Apr. 1856), at 9–11.

[89] Palmerston to Clarendon, Mar. 2, 1856, *in* FO 27/1163 at 46–47.

[90] Palmerston to Clarendon, Mar. 3, 1856, *id.* at 56. A corvette was defined as a vessel carrying twenty to thirty guns. *Id.*

Even when the interpretation of "light vessel" had been narrowed down to a vessel under 50 meters in length, Russia sought other means of circumventing the limit. Orlov requested a number of "hulks," to house harbor guards.[91] Traditionally, navies utilized older warships of the line as hulks, often removing rigging and making the ships stationary. While Clarendon and French Admiral Hamelin thought the key issue would be ascertaining that the vessel was truly stationary and immobile, the Foreign Office vetoed the idea, fearing the ships could be re-converted into ships-of-the-line, and would undermine the stability intended by the treaty.[92]

Finally, after the tentative number of light vessels had been set at six, the Russians sought to augment this force with a number of military transports for moving troops when policing coastal areas. Initially, the Foreign Office opposed this demand, fearing that Russia would build large ships that could be converted into frigates or ships-of-the-line,[93] allowing Russia to maintain warship-building arsenals under the cover of transport construction.[94] When Orlov and the French delegation agreed to an additional four small vessels for Russia, Clarendon accepted it, reasoning that nothing could prevent Russia from building transports under "a Commercial disguise." Britain would "run less risk by giving a formal sanction to 800 tons more for small armed vessels than to 2000 or 3000 more tons for transports."[95]

Underlying much of these negotiations were concerns regarding verification. An international agreement was of little value if it could be easily circumvented, and would not increase confidence in Turkey or the West if it was perceived to be faulty. Clarendon's instructions vigorously sought to prevent future loopholes, as well as attempting to avoid unrealistic expectations as to what verification could accomplish. The instructions repeatedly referred to length, weight, and number of guns as the standards to be set on light vessels. The British sought limits of 400 tons and four guns, on 50 meters length. Ultimately, Admiralty advice held that weight was a more important characteristic than either length or number of guns, which could be altered when needed.[96] The final agreement allowed both

[91] Clarendon to Palmerston, Mar. 11, 1856, *in* FO 27/1168, at 215–216.

[92] Palmerston to Clarendon, Mar. 11, 1856, *in* FO 27/1163, at 82–83.

[93] Palmerston to Clarendon, Mar. 13, 1856, *in* FO 27/1163, at 89–90.

[94] Palmerston to Clarendon, Mar. 14, 1856, *in* FO 27/1163, at 93–94.

[95] Clarendon to Palmerston, Mar. 18, 1856, *in* Paris Conference, Archives, Lord Clarendon to Lord Palmerston, Drafts, FO 27/1169 (Mar. 13–Apr. 20, 1856), at 23–24.

[96] Palmerston to Clarendon, Mar. 24, 1856, *in* FO 27/1163, at 138. It would be impossible to regulate unarmed transports, as these might carry guns for signal purposes or on the pretext of relocating artillery. Clarendon to Palmerston, Mar. 18, 1856, *in* FO 27/1169, at 23.

Russia and Turkey to maintain six vessels of up to 800 tons and 50 meters waterline length, and four light vessels of up to 200 tons.[97] No mention was made of allowable armament in the final text. Length could be easily determined, and weight derived from a ship's size. These two components could be easily verified, and in turn would limit the power of any engine. Moreover, Palmerston insisted on the presence of British consuls in Russian ports to verify compliance.[98]

The agreement was contained in a separate bilateral treaty between Turkey and Russia. However, the Treaty of Paris incorporated the regulations of the Black Sea Treaty, preventing either Turkey or Russia from altering its disposition without the consent of all the parties to the peace treaty.[99] The Treaty of Paris also forbade the maintenance of any "Military-Maritime Arsenal," thereby hobbling the ability of Russia to rebuild a navy.[100] An additional agreement prohibited Russia from maintaining military or naval establishments or building fortifications in the Åland Islands in the Baltic.[101] Great Britain, despite pressure from some quarters did not push for a harsher disarmament in the Baltic. A Russian Baltic Fleet was deemed necessary for the defense of the capital. Additionally, the fleet had not been used aggressively, and more importantly, it remained intact at its fortified base.

In 1856, negotiations indicated the importance the Foreign Office placed upon easily verifiable arms control terms. Clarendon repeatedly rejected Russian counter-offers in order to craft an agreement that could be verified through consular officials. The painstaking deliberations provided a model for future arms control. The following chapter will detail the subsequent history of the Black Sea Treaty, as its termination posed central questions of international law, but the significance of the agreement in 1856 lay in this emphasis on verifiable obligations.

---

[97] Black Sea Neutralization Treaty, Art. II.

[98] Andrew Lambert, *The Crimean War: British Grand Strategy, 1853–56* (Manchester: Manchester University Press, 1990), 333. Clarendon to Cowley, Nov. 29, 1855, Clarendon Papers, C. 257, ff.21–23.

[99] Treaty of Paris, signed Mar. 30, 1856, Art. XIV, *in* Hurst, ed., *Key Treaties*, Vol. I, 321.

[100] Significantly, this provision was inserted directly into the Treaty of Paris rather than merely appearing in the Black Sea Treaty. Treaty of Paris, Art. XIII.

[101] Convention Respecting the Aland Islands, signed at Paris, Apr. 27, 1856, Art. I, *in* Hurst, ed., *Key Treaties*, Vol. I, 333.

St. Petersburg Declaration of 1868 – "Explosive Missals"

The final major arms control agreement of the century differed from the other three by banning a specific weapon type for ostensibly humanitarian purposes.[102] The St. Petersburg Declaration of 1868 banned exploding bullets from use among its signatory parties, preventing the new ammunition from gaining general acceptance. Like the Hague Peace Conference called by the Czar Nicholas II in 1898, Russian initiative led to the 1868 gathering. The summit followed the precedent set by the Geneva Conference of 1868, an important early gathering held to codify rules respecting the Red Cross in wartime. The resulting declaration was significant in creating a precedent for humanitarian arms control later developed at The Hague in 1899. Additionally, the 1868 debates at St. Petersburg highlighted differing opinions regarding technology and war.

The exploding bullet was designed to attack artillery caissons, allowing a sniper to hit and detonate enemy ammunition supplies on the battlefield. Following the 1863 introduction of the weapon by Russia, several European nations developed exploding bullets in the early 1860s, including Prussia, Austria, Switzerland, and Bavaria.[103] These bullets, fired by ordinary rifles, generally featured a hollow shell containing a fulminating substance designed to explode upon hitting a target. The earlier version built by Russia was designed to detonate only upon hitting a hard substance, such as a wooden artillery case, but later versions could explode upon striking a soft surface, such as a human being or horse.[104]

Although designed for use against inanimate targets, the Russian government feared that this ammunition might end up being used against soldiers or horses.[105] Initial Russian regulations only supplied ten of the

---

[102] The following section summarizes arguments made in Scott Keefer, "'Explosive Missals': International Law, Technology, and Security in Nineteenth-Century Disarmament Conferences," *War in History* 21, no. 4 (2014): 445.

[103] Mémoire sur la Suppression de l'Emploi des Balles Explosives en Temps de Guerre, 2, *enclosed in* St. George to Pakington, Nov. 15, 1868, *in* Use of Explosive Projectiles in Time of War, FO 83/316 (1868–1869).

[104] *Id.* at 3.

[105] Contemporary international law forbade the infliction of superfluous wounds. It was generally held that a soldier would be put out of combat merely by being struck by a bullet, thus making the additional chemical burns and wounds caused by explosions unnecessary. *Id.* at 3; Henry Wheaton, *Elements of International Law, with a Sketch of the History of the Science* (Philadelphia: Carey, Lea & Blanchard, 1836), 249–50.

special bullets per soldier and regulated their use, but concerns remained that in the heat of an engagement, a soldier would use them against the enemy. The czar called for an international regulation of the ammunition in May 1868, and after negotiation on the scope of prohibition in a second circular, the Russian government issued a third circular in July, calling for a conference at St. Petersburg.[106]

Initially, the Russian government had hoped that after canvassing foreign powers about their general opinion in their first circular, their draft protocol in the second circular would be met with acclamation. However, Prussia sought a broader prohibition on all weapons causing excessive harm, requiring collective discussion to resolve the matter.[107] While Prussian Minister President Bismarck may have broadened the scope unrealistically in an attempt to kill off the proposal, diplomats now had to respond to a formal call for a more general humanitarian ban. Unable to resolve the matter by correspondence, the Russian government thus organized a conference to be held at St. Petersburg.[108] The level of attendance at the ensuing conference promoted progressive codification of international law as Spain was the only major European country not to attend.[109] As in 1899, Russian invitation policy excluded Latin America; as in 1856, the United States refused to participate.[110]

Between the issuance of three circulars and the conference held in October, debate focused on the breadth of the regulation. Prussia sought a broader law-making conference, such as the one that formulated the Declaration of Paris in 1856. In part, Prussia feared that a vaguely worded declaration against exploding bullets would also forbid exploding artillery shells.[111] While Prussia sought a more general rule of international law, Great Britain resisted, fearing that such a regulation could halt technologi-

---

[106] Mémoire, *supra* note 103, at 4–10.

[107] Buchanan to Stanley, 14 July 1868; Communication Prussienne, 10 July 1868, *both in* FO 83/316.

[108] Mémoire sur la Suppression de l'Emploi des Balles Explosives en Temps de Guerre, 4–10 *supra* note 103.

[109] Protocole No. 1, Commission Militaire Internationale, Oct. 28, 1868, at 1, [for purposes of simplicity, Western dates will be utilized in this work except where specifically mentioned], *in* FO 83/316 (1868).

[110] Other states were allowed to adhere to the declaration, Brazil ratifying it in 1869. Buchanan to Clarendon, Oct. 28, 1869, *in* FO 83/316.

[111] Buchanan to Stanley, July 14, 1868; Communication Prussienne, July 10, 1868, *both in* FO 83/316.

cal development of weaponry. While the British were not concerned specifically with exploding bullets, as a capital-intensive state they depended disproportionately on technical advances for defense and would not easily abandon their advantage.

[W]hile the numerical force of the British army was less than that of any Great Power, the mechanical resources, the inventive talent and the wealth of England were probably not exceeded, if indeed they were equalled [*sic*], by those of any other country: and it followed therefore that any understanding which tended to limit the application of mechanical or chemical arts to war would operate, so far as it was effective, to reduce rather than to augment the military force of this country as compared with that of other nations.[112]

Likewise, Sweden expressed reservations at the conference, noting that with the recent invention of the mitrailleuse, "*qu'on ne peut pas préjuger les progrès de la science.*" The Swedish delegation unsuccessfully advocated that a margin be built into regulations "suffisante à l'esprit d'invention."[113] The final text banned exploding munitions lighter than 400 grams, thereby maintaining the legality of artillery shells.[114] The Prussian goal of a prohibition on excessive injury while allowing legitimate weapons was enshrined in the Preamble to the Declaration.[115] While this conference was held before the last great wave of imperialism, the British clearly had in mind the question of utilizing technological superiority in defending the empire, with the Sepoy Rebellion of 1857 serving as a recent reminder of the risks faced by a small occupying force in hostile territory.

Initially, the British refused to attend the conference, but ultimately participated and signed the resulting declaration.[116] Their decision to

---

[112] Buchanan to Stanley, July 25, 1868, *in* FO 83/316.

[113] Protocole No. 2, Commission Militaire Internationale, Nov. 1, 1868, at 2, *in* FO 83/316.

[114] "Declaration of St. Petersburg, of 1868 to the Effect of Prohibiting the Use of Certain Projectiles in Wartime, Nov. 29, (Dec. 11) 1868," *American Journal of International Law* 1, no. 2 Supplement (1907): 95.[*hereinafter* Declaration of St. Petersburg].

[115] *Id*. Preambles generally did not contain binding obligations, and were used to restate general principles and motivations behind agreements, which could be used in interpreting the duties contained in a treaty.

[116] Russia also would have accepted Britain's initial plan of adhering to the new rule by means of a separate document, rather than through the jointly ratified text, seeking universal adherence to the rule while accommodating British reluctance. Buchanan to Stanley, June 30, 1868, *in* FO 83/316. This procedure was also followed at the Hague Peace Conference after British reticence to sign further arms restrictions.

attend was influenced in no small part by the decision to make the legal obligations contained in the Declaration reciprocal.[117] Only parties to the Declaration could claim the protection of its provisions, thus Europeans could utilize the weapons against non-parties, including Asian and African peoples. Thus, a new legal norm intended for humanitarian purposes was effectively limited to the sphere of European international law, without regard to the mass of humanity outside its protection.

If diplomats truly believed that the injuries caused by exploding bullets were excessive and unnecessary for military purposes, there would have been no reason to attach a reciprocity clause. Notably, the other major contemporary humanitarian treaty, the 1864 Geneva Convention, lacked any explicit requirement of reciprocity.[118] Possibly the parties acknowledged that the munitions were too barbaric for use amongst themselves yet perceived advantages in using them against non-European enemies lacking sophisticated technology. Thus, the munitions were barbaric but were perceived as necessary. The British and Russian delegations sought a reciprocity clause for this reason. As the majority of mankind remained unprotected by the agreement, its underlying purpose could not reasonably be construed as humanitarian. The Declaration must be seen rather as an attempt to check the rapid development of weaponry in an avenue that appeared to be a likely next step.

The negotiations highlighted the difficulties in regulating rapidly evolving military technology. Statesmen in numerous countries expressed fears that regulations could be framed too broadly, either preventing the adoption of new technology or resulting in recrimination by belligerents as to the exact nature of the ban. When negotiating the text, the parties argued about whether Congreve rockets, mitrailleuses, or even standard explosive artillery shells would be banned by the new rule.[119] The British govern-

---

[117] The British delegate was only authorized to sign after confirming that the Declaration would not apply to Central Asia, and would be based on reciprocity. *See* Transcription of Telegram from Buchanan to Stanley, Nov. 10, 1868, *in* FO 83/316; War Office to Stanley, Nov. 11, 1868, *id.*; Stanley to Buchanan, Nov. 13, 1868, *id.*

[118] 1864 Geneva Convention for the Amelioration of the Condition of the Sick and Wounded of Armies in the Field, 22 Aug. 1864, *in American Journal of International Law* 1, no. 2 (Supplement Apr. 1907), pp. 90–92.

[119] *See* for example Protocole No. 1, Commission Militaire Internationale, *supra* note 109, at 4–5.

ment struggled to keep up to date on the technology being regulated. Even the terminology proved too complicated, their correspondence perpetuating an unintended pun (or Freudian slip) by repeatedly referring to regulations of "explosive missals."[120]

Underlying these questions were tensions between national power and humanity. Arguments raged as to how war could best be made more humane. Noting that the vast majority of casualties came from illnesses spread in camp, some argued that the more humane course would be to adopt weapons that made war as short as possible.[121] Modern weapons were also seen as serving a deterrent function, as the horror of their use prevented states from going to war.[122] A country could not abandon unique national advantages, including advanced technology, for abstract principles of humanity. Without its technological advantages, the small British army would be no match for a continental foe, and would be insufficient to maintain a vast overseas empire. In framing the Declaration of St. Petersburg, the British delegate sought to preserve national advantage.

CUSTOMARY LIMITS ON ARMAMENTS

Besides arms limitation agreements, international law regulated armaments through many other obligations. A preoccupation with stability and security underlay international law in the nineteenth century. Arms control agreements and many other areas of legal regulation reflected the underlying premises. A number of treaties negotiated in the century developed principles of arms control, although few of these agreements focused specifically upon armaments. More often, treaties covering a broad range of topics contained arms control provisions in a few articles. Mostly, these treaties included the dismantling of fortresses; occasionally they regulated

---

[120] War Office to Foreign Office, Nov. 20, 1868, *in* FO 83/316; Foreign Office to War Office, Nov. 23, 1868, *id.* The British government also failed to effectively coordinate with the Admiralty, informing them of the negotiations only after they had been completed, despite the application of the rule to war at sea. Admiralty to Foreign Office, Dec. 18, 1868, *id.*

[121] "Foreign Intelligence," Dec. 8, 1868, *The (London) Times*, at 8 D. Additionally, the article noted that grenades remained legal, despite causing similar wounds. *Id.*

[122] "Editorial," Dec. 9, 1868, *The (London) Times*, at 8 E.

naval forces and armies.[123] The term disarmament also applied to the demobilization of forces at the end of a crisis, sometimes imposed upon a vanquished state.[124]

In addition to treaty provisions regulating armaments, international custom also created limits. Statesmen justified these limits as necessary for maintaining the balance of power or for preventing humanitarian abuses. States possessed the right to self-defense, which included the right to amass armaments and enter into alliances.[125] At the same time, neighboring states had a right to live in security, which could be violated by a neighbor's disproportionate arms increase. While states theoretically possessed full liberty to arm themselves, "some modification of [the right] appears to flow from the equal and corresponding rights of other nations, or at least to be required for the sake of the general welfare and peace of the world."[126] A state could also voluntarily bind itself not to increase armaments.[127] These legal rights and duties did not automatically translate into national policy, but could be the basis of arguments made to the international community when taking actions to limit foreign threats.

[123] Among the first group, the Second Treaty of Paris 1815 dismantled fortifications at Hämingue, an 1864 convention dismantled fortresses on Corfu, the 1867 Treaty of London dismantled the fortress of Luxembourg as part of neutralization of the state, and the 1878 Treaty of Berlin dismantled Bulgarian fortresses on the Danube River. *See generally*, Wehberg, *Limitation of Armaments*, at 11, fn. 1. Among the other early agreements regulating naval forces, the Russo-Turkish Treaty of 1739, the Russo-Persian Treaty of 1828, and the Franco-Tripolitan Treaty of 1830 should be mentioned. *See* Jost Delbrück, ed., *Friedensdokumente Aus Fünf Jahrhunderten: Abrüstung, Kriegsverhütung, Rüstungskontrolle* (Strasbourg: N.P. Engel, 1984), Vol. 2, 437. Among the more interesting land disarmament agreements of the period was the Preliminary Bolivian-Peruvian Peace Treaty of 1831, which limited total land forces in each country, and included one of the earliest clauses for verification. Preliminary Treaty of Peace between Bolivia and Peru, signed at Tiquina, Aug. 25, 1831, Parry, ed., *Consolidated Treaty Series*, Vol. 82, 150; *see also* Preliminary Convention of Peace and Commerce between Bolivia – and Peru, signed at Lima, Apr. 19, 1840, Parry, ed., *Consolidated Treaty Series*, Vol. 90, 104.

[124] The Treaty of Tilsit of 1807 is a prominent example.

[125] John Westlake, *Chapters on the Principles of International Law* (Cambridge: Cambridge University Press, 1894), 114, 21, Sir Robert Phillimore, *Commentaries Upon International Law*, 3rd ed. (London: Butterworths, 1879), Vol. I, 312–13. Customary law was compiled in textbooks, and was viewed as authoritative by the Foreign Office, as discussed in the following chapter.

[126] Phillimore, *Commentaries Upon International Law*, Vol. I, 312–313; Wheaton, *Elements of International Law*, 82–83.

[127] H. W. Halleck, *Elements of International Law and Laws of War* (Philadelphia: J. B. Lippincott & Co., 1866), 57–59; Wheaton, *Elements of International Law*, 82.

States had a duty to explain extraordinary armaments increases, and possessed a corresponding right of self-defense in the face of such increases by neighbors.[128] "Armaments suddenly increased to an extraordinary amount are calculated to alarm other nations, whose liberty they appear, more or less, according to the circumstances of the case, to menace. It has been usual, therefore, to require and receive amicable explanations of such warlike preparations; the answer will, of course, much depend upon the tone and spirit of the requisition."[129] State practice followed theory. In 1793, Foreign Secretary William Grenville sought explanations from France for its sudden increase in naval armaments, basing the right to this information upon international law.[130] Similarly, Palmerston warned Russia that its naval build-up in 1833 was causing misunderstandings, and sent a similar note to France in 1840.[131] Again in 1855, Clarendon explained to the Russian government, "if it was true that Russia might keep up the force she pleased within her own limits, it was also true that other Powers had a right to require explanations, and upon their not being satisfactory to declare war."[132]

By the 1800s, legal theory recognized the community-wide nature of armaments competition.[133] Anglo-American theorists went so far as to justify preemptive strikes to redress the balance of power,[134] validating the earlier British strike on the Danish fleet at Copenhagen in 1807. Law provided a continuum of responses to strategic threats from neighboring states, legitimizing actions ranging from arms treaties to preemptive strikes. The balance of power underlay these principles of international

---

[128] Phillimore, *Commentaries Upon International Law*, Vol. I, at 312–13; Westlake, *Chapters on the Principles of International Law*, 114. But see Westlake at 121 suggesting a state has a right to increase its armaments "in a fair proportion to its population and wealth and to the interests which it has to defend." Yet even this definition linked armaments to legitimate purposes, indicating that a state did not possess an unfettered right to amass armaments.

[129] Phillimore, *Commentaries Upon International Law*, Vol. I, 313.

[130] *Id.*

[131] Bartlett, *Great Britain and Sea Power 1815–1853*, 94, 137.

[132] Clarendon to Russell, Mar. 26, 1855, Clarendon Papers, C. 267, at 76.

[133] Phillimore commented on the aggressive nature of states seeking territorial expansion, contributing to "the great evil of enormous standing armies, perpetual menaces to the liberties of mankind ..." Phillimore, *Commentaries Upon International Law*, Vol. I, 584.

[134] *Id.*, Vol. I, 313–14; Wheaton, *Elements of International Law*, 203.

law.[135] A central goal of international law was to maintain the state system. International law used this premise to justify intervention in the affairs of neighboring states, and to put down revolution.[136] In assessing threats to the international balance, population and economic growth rates did not warrant international action, but the decision of a state to increase its armaments could be a justification for a military response.[137]

Besides enshrining principles relating to the peacetime balance of power, international law regulated permissible wartime conduct. States could also enter into treaty obligations that remained in force during war-time, such as the St. Petersburg Declaration of 1868. Custom also pro-vided regulations, such as the banning of poisons.[138] International legal requirements obliging military forces to be under the control and regular military discipline of the state limited the employment of levées en masse and colonial troops. Although international law did not ban their employ-ment, it did regulate their use.[139]

International law proscribed the use of weapons deemed inhumane, although often initial moral disapproval faded as weapons gained accep-tance.[140] Law could evolve around a community-wide approbation of a new technology, as occurred with exploding bullets. However, initial moral outrage often did not coalesce in a clear community-wide rule,

---

[135] Phillimore, *Commentaries Upon International Law*, Vol. I, 589; See Chap. 3.

[136] *Id.*, Vol. I, at 574. However, legal scholars took care in circumscribing this right of intervention to cases of extreme necessity, noting that claims of maintaining the balance of power were regularly abused. Thomas Joseph Lawrence, *A Handbook of Public International Law* (Cambridge: Deighton, Bell & Co., 1885), 31–33.

[137] *But see* Phillimore, *Commentaries Upon International Law*, Vol. I, at 614, fn. (a), quot-ing Lord Bacon as saying that increased trade could threaten the balance of power and justify action.

[138] Henry Sumner Maine, *International Law, a Series of Lectures Delivered before the University of Cambridge, 1887* (New York: Henry Holt & Co., 1888), 134–35. The use of artillery firing glass and metal fragments was also banned, as was the employment of blood-hounds and wild animals. Taylor, *A Treatise on International Public Law*, 478.

[139] Lawrence, *A Handbook of Public International Law*, 84–85. Phillimore also held that the use of savages and cannibals was "universally reprobated." Sir Robert Phillimore, *Commentaries Upon International Law* (Philadelphia: T. & J.W. Johnson & Co., 1857), Vol. III, at 144. International law also banned the use of privateers after 1856, through the Declaration of Paris.

[140] Muskets, bayonets, and rifled firearms were all deemed immoral initially, without a gen-eral rule against their use evolving. Maine, *International Law*, 139–40; Taylor, *A Treatise on International Public Law*, 481.

leaving statesmen to argue whether a particular weapon was legitimate. From the mid-nineteenth century onwards, a dizzying revolution in military technology, particularly naval technology, raised numerous questions of law. Torpedoes, naval mines, and rams could all rapidly sink an enemy warship, leading to doubts as to the legitimacy of their employment.[141] Confusion in terminology as well as technology often marked discussions of weapons, with the rule of 1868 regulating "explosive missals" linked to the archaic use of red-hot shot at sea.[142] This particular debate was largely irrelevant as technology was moving beyond wooden ships which could be burned by this shot towards ironclads which could not, as well as away from smoothbore muzzleloaders to rifled breechloaders incapable of handling such ammunition.

The principle underlying these regulations was that the means of injuring an enemy in warfare were not unlimited, and that a state could inflict no more harm than was necessary to render an enemy combatant *hors de combat*. Warfare was seen not as a situation of total license to wreak harm, but as a vindication of rights, through a trial by combat.[143] As a corollary, states could inflict only the harm necessary to bring the enemy to terms.[144] International law limited the scope of warfare, in part to make war more humane, and in part to assist in the resumption of relations after a brief, sharp conflict. Incorporated within international law were nineteenth-century conceptions of limited war.

INTERNATIONAL LAW AND SECURITY IN THE NINETEENTH CENTURY

In addition to armaments regulations, international law affected peace and security in numerous other ways. Both alliances and neutralization treaties attempted to increase predictability in interstate relations. Diplomats codified the system of alliances in legally binding agreements, in the belief

---

[141] Maine, *International Law*, 141.
[142] William Edward Hall, *A Treatise on International Law*, 3rd edn (London: Henry Frowde, 1890), 530–31; George B. Davis, *Outlines of International Law: With and Account of Its Origin and Sources of Its Historical Development* (New York: Harper and Brothers, 1887), 224–25.
[143] Maine, *International Law*, 132–33; Phillimore, *Commentaries Upon International Law*, Vol. III, 59.
[144] Phillimore, *Commentaries Upon International Law*, Vol. III, 99–100.

that law increased their effectiveness. Neutralization treaties attempted to limit the geographical range of warfare, removing key territories such as Belgium, Luxembourg, Switzerland, the Greek Ionian Islands, and the Suez Canal from direct military competition.[145] Often the great powers accompanied these treaties with military guarantees, vesting these states with a stake in the success of the treaty regime.

Arbitration agreements attempted to reduce the recourse to war by providing a peaceful means of settling disputes. Interest in arbitration grew dramatically over the century, culminating in major advances at the Hague Peace Conferences of 1899 and 1907. The *Alabama* claims arbitrated between Britain and the United States in 1871 also provided a key example of the new system. In this instance, the United States complained of the damages caused to American maritime trade by a Confederate commerce raider outfitted by a British shipyard. Both states agreed to resolve the matter amicably, Gladstone's government motivated partly by a desire to promote arbitration. Undoubtedly, the government also sought to delegitimize commerce raiding, a form of warfare uniquely suited to undermine British maritime trade. Ultimately, states rarely arbitrated claims, and most arbitration agreements contained exceptions for "vital interests" or national honor.[146] Direct negotiation remained the preferred method for peaceful dispute settlement, limiting the influence of arbitration.

*   *   *

The crystallization of the rules of war provided another key example of the role international law played in security. Nineteenth-century diplomats attempted to codify the customary international law of war, taking the confused tangle of regulations and moral proscriptions and creating a concise statement of law. The Brussels Conference of 1874 was held to achieve this aim, but reflected the divisions among states, and the manner

---

[145] Similarly, the Black Sea Neutralization Treaty was often referred to as a neutralization agreement, claiming to neutralize the region. This claim remained contentious in international law, as generally treaties only bound ratifying parties, non-parties having no formal obligation to obey. In this case, the United States refused to abide by a treaty it did not negotiate, sending Admiral Farragut to the Straits with the large frigate *Franklin* in 1868. E. Hertslet, Memorandum Respecting the Passage of Foreign Ships of War through the Straits of the Dardanelles and Bosphorus, Nov. 18, 1870, FO 881/1825 (1870) at 10.

[146] Grewe, *The Epochs of International Law*, 522–23.

in which law could enshrine national interest. Germany and Russia, large land powers, sought to define rules of war which would grant an occupying power greater leeway in stamping out resistance, in response to experiences during the recent Franco-Prussian War.[147] The smaller states vigorously opposed this initiative, attempting to preserve legal protections for irregular combatants rising up in the defense of their country.[148] France, still embittered by its recent experience at the hands of Prussia, also opposed regulations that would condemn *franc-tireurs*.[149] Fundamentally, the conference was held too soon after the 1870–1871 war for a dispassionate discussion of the rules of war. Great Britain opposed the inclusion of naval warfare within the terms of discussion, and ultimately doomed the declaration by refusing to ratify it.[150]

The Brussels Conference indicated the manner in which international law could be shaped to advance national interests. This was a struggle over law, with states arrayed in opposing camps, on polarizing topics of conquest and survival. The intensity of negotiations indicated that the laws of war mattered. Smaller countries, which relied heavily upon hastily mobilized forces, could neither afford to sacrifice a significant part of their defenses, nor accept the alternative expenses of peacetime conscription. Britain rallied the smaller states in opposition to what it termed a "Code

[147] Horsford to Derby, Aug. 16, 1874, *in* Conference at Brussels on the Rules of Military Warfare Correspondence with Major-General Sir A. Horsford, FO 412/18 (July–Sep. 1874). The Prussians experienced great difficulty after winning the initial campaign of this war, as they were forced to maintain long supply lines while besieging Paris. All the while, French citizens were spontaneously rising in defense of their homeland. Germany sought a new rule that would broadly define the front line, thus allowing large and relatively unoccupied areas to be deemed under effective occupation. This would allow any guerrilla actions taken against occupying soldiers to be treated as criminal behavior, such as murder, rather than as a legitimate act of war, in turn justifying harsher punishment.

[148] *Id.* The Belgian delegate, Baron Lambermont, declared "that if citizens were to be sacrificed for having attempted to defend their country at the risk of their lives, they need not find inscribed on the post at the foot of which they were to be shot, the Article of a Treaty signed by their own Government which had in advance condemned them to death." Horsford to Derby, Aug. 21, 1874, *id.* This discussion raised the question of an arms race, as states faced a choice between mass conscription in peacetime or a spontaneous popular rising in wartime. *See* Buchanan to Derby, June 17, 1874, *in* Conference at Brussels on the Rules of Military Warfare Correspondence, Part I, FO 412/15 (Apr.–July 1874).

[149] Lyons to Derby, July 22, 1874, *in* Conference at Brussels on the Rules of Military Warfare Correspondence, Part II, FO 412/16 (June–July 1874).

[150] Derby to Her Majesty's Representatives in Countries Invited to Take Part in the Brussels Conference, July 4, 1874, *in* FO 412/15; Maine, *International Law*, 128–29.

of Conquest."[151] The Russian sponsors of the project just as adamantly needled those "who are naturally addicted to the defensive" for their unwillingness to accept limits.[152]

At the conference, the regulation of armaments arose indirectly. The Swedish delegation proposed an extension of the 1868 Declaration to cover soft lead bullets, which, unlike hard lead bullets, had a tendency to expand when hitting flesh.[153] The resulting Declaration forbade the use of "arms, projectiles, or substances which may cause unnecessary suffering" and affirmed the general principle that the "laws of war do not allow to belligerents an unlimited power as to the choice of means of injuring the enemy."[154] Although the Declaration never entered force, it influenced the future codification of international law at The Hague in 1899, and found its way into numerous military manuals issued by European states.[155]

The Brussels gathering failed largely because of British influence. Derby's Foreign Office initially opposed the conference out of fear that regulations could limit its ability to utilize sea power, and ultimately because the rules weighed heavily against smaller countries, as well as countries like Britain which lacked a large army manned by universal conscription. This episode illustrated not only how contemporary diplomats viewed the importance of international law, but also the extraordinary ability of the British government to shape the law to fit its strategic needs. As the dominant sea power, and possessing only a small peacetime army, the British sought

---

[151] Lumley to Derby, July 7, 1874, *in* FO 412/16.

[152] Ribeiro to Cobbold, Feb. 17, 1875, *enclosure in* Cobbold to Derby, Feb. 27, 1875, *in* Brussels Conference Volume V, Rules of War and Miscellaneous, FO 83/485 (Sep. 28, 1874–Aug. 31, 1875).

[153] As most of the continental powers utilized soft lead bullets, the Prussian delegate claimed that the expense of changing to hard lead bullets made the proposal problematic. Horsford to Derby, July 31, 1874, No. 7, *in* 412/18.

[154] "Project of an International Declaration Concerning the Laws and Customs of War, Adopted by the Conference of Brussels, Aug. 27, 1874," *American Journal of International Law* 1, no. 2 Supplement (1907). Arts. XII & XIII (e).

[155] The most famous example of such a manual was the earlier Lieber's Code, issued by the United States Army during the American Civil War, which had influenced the Brussels Declaration. Francis Lieber, *Instructions for the Government of Armies of the United States in the Field* (New York: D. Van Nostrand, 1863). These codes were not binding within international law, but formed a clear expression of customary international law and were recognized for this reason. *See* Maine, *International Law*, 129–30.

specific rules that favored the type of warfare they assumed they would confront in the future.

* * *

The larger question remained the value of law as an instrument of policy. A state could never be sure that a treaty-partner would uphold its obligations. International law presented both opportunities and risks, as highlighted in debates over the 1856 Declaration of Paris. As many statesmen noted, no international police force existed to enforce obligations. States had to defend their own rights, by generating international support for their position, and ultimately by force of their own arms. Additionally, the existence of a treaty could lull a public into a false sense of security, and could be exploited by politicians to cut defenses. The British government recognized this risk, weighed the benefits and disadvantages of agreements, and still believed that law could contribute to security.[156]

In spite of uncertainties in international law, statesmen often utilized treaties when planning national defenses and in defusing disputes. Great Britain proved no exception to this rule, and was pivotal in shaping arms control law in the nineteenth century. British statesmen made conscious decisions to utilize or avoid law based on an assessment of national interests. This implicitly presumed that law had some effect on these interests. This in turn raises the question of what influence statesmen expected international law to have upon national security.

CONCLUSION

Statesmen had a wealth of precedents in both arms limitation agreements and in general international law. Law was utilized in numerous ways in shaping the security environment, both in peacetime and during war. This foundation provided negotiators at the turn of the century with a framework when considering the possibility of limiting armaments by treaty. The issues raised at The Hague in 1899 and 1907, and later during Anglo-German naval discussions, had their precursors in these earlier negotia-

---

[156] Admiralty to Foreign Office, June 28, 1907, *in* Further Correspondence respecting the Second Peace Conference at the Hague, FO 412/86, (Jan. 1906–June 1907).

tions. While international law could play a role in defense policy, statesmen were acutely conscious of its limits at the same time. Diplomats crafted agreements in the nineteenth century while recognizing the limits of law, and attempted to get the most that could be realistically hoped from treaty agreements. Treaty provisions had to reflect the absence of international institutions capable of verifying restrictions, as well as a limited public attention span that might not long maintain the will to enforce obligations. At the same time, while working within these confines, law was able to make a contribution to defense policy.

Britain's role in this development reflected an assessment of self-interest as a global power. Armament agreements were used to reduce the immediate risk of conflict, and to defuse limited regional tensions, as in the Great Lakes and the Black Sea. Support for arms limitation was not dogmatic, and British opposition to restrictions on new technology or on rules for naval warfare reflected the concerns of a naval power seeking to maintain a world empire with a small army. Britain showed a willingness to engage the world and to shape law in a manner to reinforce British interests. Yet in order to fully grasp what Britain hoped to achieve through international law, it is necessary to understand how international law was perceived, which the following chapter will address.

CHAPTER 3

International Law in the Nineteenth Century

An International Police Force

"There's th' internaytional coort, ye say, but I say where ar-re th' polis? A coort's all r-right enough, but no coort's anny good unless it is backed up be a continted constabulary, its counthry's pride, as th' pote says. Th' Czar of Rooshya didn't go far enough. Wan good copper with a hickory club is worth all th' judges between Amsterdam an' Rotterdam … But I suppose it wud be just th' same thing as it is now in rale life."

"How's that?" asked Mr. Hennessy.

"All th' biggest crooks wud get on th' polis force," said Mr. Dooley.[1]

Mr. Dooley, the fictitious barman/philosopher, often struck closer to home in his soliloquies on turn of the century affairs than was immediately apparent. In 1906, Mr. Dooley was discussing with his patron Hennessy the prospects for a world court. When newspaperman Finley Peter Dunne put these words in the mouth of Mr. Dooley, he encapsulated both the conventional view of international law as well as its real significance. Legal systems are commonly assessed in terms of their legal institutions, the executive capacity being salient in determining the effectiveness of law. International and domestic law can be clearly distinguished by the utter absence of any international enforcement capacity in the latter system.

[1] Finley Peter Dunne, *Dissertations by Mr. Dooley* (New York: Harper & Bros., 1906), 161.

© The Editor(s) (if applicable) and The Author(s) 2016   53
S.A. Keefer, *The Law of Nations and Britain's Quest for Naval Security*, DOI 10.1007/978-3-319-39645-3_3

However, Dunne hinted at the real significance of international law. The great powers would likely dominate any international police force, just as they employed the international legal system to further their individual national interests. At its core, the international legal system reflected the power and interests of the states engaged in it.

While historians have addressed numerous aspects of foreign policy decision-making, one crucial element remains neglected – international law. The result is an underdeveloped interdisciplinary dialogue between historians and international lawyers. The lack of understanding of how statesmen expected international law to function hampers an accurate assessment of treaties, conferences, and other efforts at incorporating law into national policy. This chapter provides insight into the workings of international law between 1815 and 1914, employing British examples of diplomatic and international legal practices to illustrate what law meant to contemporaries. By advocating or avoiding legal engagements, the opinions of the British Foreign Office are noteworthy, as Britain, the predominant naval power of the era, took a central role in numerous negotiations.[2]

THE DECLARATION OF LONDON, 1871

In October 1870, as Europe was preoccupied with the Franco-Prussian War, Russian Foreign Minister Prince Gorchakov announced that because of violations of the 1856 Peace of Paris, Russia would no longer be bound by the Black Sea Treaty. The unilateral Russian pronouncement challenged the integrity of the international legal system, and threatened to add an eastern war to the ongoing western conflict. The episode that followed provided a rare glimpse into contemporary attitudes towards international law generally, and to issues of arms control specifically.

Russia immediately turned to overthrowing the Black Sea Treaty after 1856, viewing the imposed disarmament much as Germany would perceive the Versailles Treaty after 1919. The treaty limited Russia and Turkey to six warships of up to 800 tons each and four light vessels of up to 200 tons on the Black Sea, further prohibiting the maintenance of naval arsenals. Russia gained French diplomatic support for a revision in 1859, in return for Russian military assistance against the Austrian Empire. However,

---

[2] This chapter expands upon themes discussed in Scott Keefer, "'An Obstacle, though not a Barrier': The Role of International Law in Security Planning during the Pax Britannica," *International History Review* 35, no. 5 (2013): 1.

Napoleon III only offered vague support at a future conference, ending the initiative. The resulting Franco-Russian treaty contained a nonspecific obligation, "the High Contracting Parties will agree to the modification of existing treaties..."[3]

During the Austro-Prussian War in 1866, Russia prepared a circular ending the treaty, but the rapid conclusion of the war preempted Russian plans.[4] Four years later, the Franco-Prussian War presented a more opportune moment. The war incapacitated one of the key guarantors of the Peace of Paris, France, at a time when Austria-Hungary appeared preoccupied with domestic affairs. Gorchakov brandished the same circular he had prepared in 1866, announcing the unilateral repudiation of the Black Sea Treaty.[5]

The Russian Circular of October 1870 claimed violation of the neutralized sea by whole squadrons of warships, undermining Russian security in the region, and noted "the advent of ironclads constituted a change in circumstances unforeseen in 1856."[6] Foreign Secretary Lord Granville disputed the Russian factual claims, but focused on the challenge to the international legal system posed by the unilateral abrogation of a treaty:

Yet it is quite evident that the effect of such doctrine, and of any proceeding which, with or without avowal, is founded upon it, is to bring the entire authority and efficacy of Treaties under the discretionary control of each one of the Powers who have signed them; the result of which would be the entire destruction of Treaties in their essence. For whereas their object is to bind Powers to one another, and for this purpose each one of the parties

---

[3] As quoted in B. H. Sumner, "The Secret Franco-Russian Treaty of 3 March 1859," *English Historical Review* 48, no. 189 (1933): 78. It is also noteworthy that the obligations in this article were undertaken by the *state*, while most of the remaining articles established a duty on behalf of the two emperors. Early nineteenth-century legal doctrine distinguished between personal obligations which ended with the rule of the monarch, and those undertaken by the state, which would survive. Grewe, *The Epochs of International Law*, 514. The use of both styles of obligation indicated an intention that these provisions would remain in existence for a long time, but without promise of immediate fulfilment.

[4] Baumgart, *Peace of Paris 1856*, 192–93.

[5] W. E. Mosse, *The Rise and Fall of the Crimean System 1855–1871: The Story of a Peace Settlement* (London: Macmillan & Co., 1963), 161–62.

[6] Oct. 19/31 1870 Gortschakow's Telegram Ending the Neutralization of the Black Sea, *in* Wilhelm G. Grewe, ed., *Fontes Historiae Iuris Gentium: Sources Relating to the History of the Law of Nations*, 3 vols., Vol. 3 (Berlin: Walter de Gruyter, 1992), 473. However, as the earliest ironclads had been tested by French forces in the Crimea, their development was not entirely unforeseen.

surrenders a portion of its free agency, by the doctrine and proceeding now in question, one of the parties in its separate and individual capacity brings back the entire subject into its own control, and remains bound only to itself.[7]

The unilateral Russian action threatened to undermine the doctrine of *pacta sunt servanda*, the concept that nations must honor their treaty obligations. This implicit principle of good faith underlay all treaties, forming a cornerstone of the legal system. On the other hand, *rebus sic stantibus*, or the doctrine of changed circumstances, allowed abrogation of agreements when conditions had materially altered in an unforeseeable manner. This latter doctrine stood in an uneasy relationship with nineteenth century international law, challenging the orderly revision of treaties.[8]

The resulting crisis threatened war, pitting Great Britain, Austria-Hungary, Italy, and Turkey against Russia.[9] Prussia could not afford to alienate Russia during the Franco-Prussian War, and was expected to side with Russia, expanding a western conflict into an eastern one. Granville feared crystallizing the division of Europe into two camps, and sought a diplomatic solution. At Bismarck's suggestion, the powers met at London to defuse the situation in January 1871. The London Conference side-stepped the Russian Circular, reaffirmed the principle that treaties could only be altered by mutual consent of all the parties in the Declaration of London, then jointly confirmed the end of the Black Sea neutralization.

In the wake of the conference, Parliament assembled to discuss the embarrassing episode, revealing contrasting expectations for the international legal system. Many observers believed the conference had only papered over a Russian breach of international law, leading to two critiques. The first critique decried the weakness of the international legal system, as no international body existed which could enforce a treaty.[10]

---

[7] Granville to Buchanan, Nov. 10, 1870, *in* Correspondence respecting the Treaty of March 30, 1856, FO 881/1901 (Nov. 1870–Feb. 1871).

[8] *See* David J. Bederman, "The 1871 London Declaration, Rebus Sic Stantibus and a Primitivist View of the Law of Nations," *American Journal of International Law* 82, no. 1 (1988): 8.

[9] Bloomfield to Granville, Nov. 24, 1870, *in* FO 881/1901; Paget to Granville, Nov. 19, 1870, *in* FO 881/1901.

[10] Sir Charles Dilke, *Hansard* 3rd ser., CCV, 901, 915, Mar. 30, 1871; Somerset Beaumont, *id.* at 917.

Radical liberals, and even Gladstone, sought international tribunals with ability to enforce judgments. The second view decried national failure to uphold a treaty obligation. Liberals like Sir Charles Dilke called for robust national enforcement, by war if necessary, while Conservatives sought to scale down national obligations, summed up by Lord Salisbury: "if they will not adapt their promises to their powers, or their powers to their promises, I foresee a time of terrible humiliation to this country which may shake our institutions to their centres."[11] Two contrasting views of the international legal system emerged, one focusing upon powerful international institutions and the other upon national enforcement.

Diplomatic historians decried the result as a "fiction" and a "sop to the British public in exchange for abandonment of the Black Sea clauses."[12] In contrast, international lawyers have had less difficulty with the episode, recognizing the need to modify treaties and viewing the era overall as one of "contractual fidelity."[13] This view was best expressed by Philip Muntz in the House of Commons in 1871. Muntz acknowledged that the government never intended the agreement to be permanent. On the contrary, "if they looked into the history of such treaties, they would find that like piecrust, they were made to be broken, and always had been broken when opportunities presented themselves."[14]

Palmerston, like most British negotiators, did not expect these provisions, crafted through wartime compromises, to last more than ten years.[15] The treaty had to accomplish its goals within that timeframe. Turkey gained breathing space to undertake internal reforms, while halting Russian ability to project force in the region for a more extensive period. In fact, the treaty lasted 15 years. During this period, Russian maritime industries received no contracts, skilled workmen sought other employment, and new workers received no training. At this point, the Russian naval industries had withered away and had to be cultivated from scratch. Russia could not begin the process of regenerating the maritime industries

---

[11] Marquess of Salisbury, *Hansard* 3rd ser., CCIV, 1367, Mar. 6, 1871. Radical Liberals also followed this logic, but advocated a more isolationist policy, avoiding any treaty obligations.

[12] Baumgart, *Peace of Paris 1856*, 194; Mosse, *Rise and Fall of the Crimean System*, 182.

[13] Grewe, *The Epochs of International Law*, 514–15. Nussbaum, *A Concise History of the Law of Nations*, 198–99; Bederman, "1871 London Declaration," 39–40.

[14] Muntz, *Hansard* 3rd ser., CCV, 927, Mar. 30, 1871.

[15] Lord Granville, *Hansard* 3rd ser., CCIV, 246–247, Feb. 14, 1871.

until after 1871. Russia required another decade to fully recover and begin the lengthy process of building major warships.[16]

Six years after ending the treaty, Russia could not even build small craft in the Black Sea, and sought British-built torpedo boats for its Black Sea fleet, specifying that these vessels needed to be capable of railroad shipment.[17] The first coastal ironclads had to be built in the Baltic, shipped in sections by train, and reassembled in the Black Sea. Russia did not complete its first sea-going battleship in the Black Sea until 1889, and did not possess an ironclad squadron until 1894.[18] With these developments, Britain's anxieties about its position in the Mediterranean reemerged, but benefitted from an extended period with a diminished naval threat from one quarter.[19] Had Russia utilized its fledgling maritime industries in the Black Sea to begin reconstruction of its fleet in 1856, it might have directly resumed its position. The maritime industries left to wither took more than a decade to recover.

Russia consistently sought to overturn the *diktat* over the 14 years following 1856. But the treaty created obstacles to Russian policy-making, too great even for an autocracy to overcome. Law had a major effect in preventing a great land power from unshackling itself from an extraordinarily unpopular treaty. Russia abrogated the agreement only when Europe was preoccupied with the Franco-Prussian War. Russia's reluctance to rebuild its fleet did not arise solely from the threat of great power intervention, as great power interests shifted in the years following the 1856 peace. Of the three powers enforcing the obligations on Russia, two of them, Austria and France, were at war with one another by 1859 and were willing to sacrifice the agreement in order to gain Russian support. The existence of the agreement in itself created an obstacle in altering policy. Once an agreement had been ratified, diplomacy tended towards inertia – states consciously had to decide to alter course, accepting the repercussions of removing the treaty. Hence, diplomats needed to uphold the fiction that

[16] Roger Parkinson, *The Late Victorian Navy: The Pre-Dreadnought Era and the Origins of the First World War* (Chippenham, United Kingdom: Boydell Press, 2008), 51. On the complexity of maritime industries and industrial dependency on government orders, *see* Marder, *The Anatomy of British Sea Power*, 37–42.
[17] Grant, *Rulers, Guns, and Money*, 93.
[18] Gardiner, *Conway's All the World's Fighting Ships, 1860–1905*, 177, 78.
[19] The relative Russian naval ascendancy in the region was due as much to Turkish disinterest in maintaining its fleet after 1876 as to Russian efforts to bolster its fleet. Grant, *Rulers, Guns, and Money*, 80–81.

treaties could only be altered by consent, as credence in the fiction created a real obstacle to state action.

The Black Sea Treaty was a British success. It was nearly forty years before Russia posed a naval challenge in the Black Sea, for the first 15 years directly because of the treaty restrictions, and for the following twenty-odd years because of the lack of maritime industries resulting from the treaty. While Britain and Russia continued to spar throughout Central Asia and the Far East, the treaty prevented a direct Russian maritime challenge until the 1890s, and then only in conjunction with France. While the Black Sea Treaty was unilaterally breached by Russia in 1870, with some diplomatic discomfort to the British government, Russian Black Sea maritime development had been hampered for most of the remaining years of the nineteenth century.

A simplistic assessment of international law might view this agreement as an abject failure. But the fate of the agreement was less important than its influence, and this treaty substantially furthered British interests. A more sophisticated understanding of international law, as held by Palmerston when creating this treaty, would see the long-term security benefit it conferred. The ultimate value of any agreement, and of international law more generally, lies in shaping behavior into paths that allow states to predict and plan their policy.

In 1870, the continued validity of the international legal system was at stake. Following two decades of upheaval, the post-Napoleonic Vienna settlement, based on an orderly change of treaties, had been forcibly dismantled. International law remained as it had always been, a thin social system capable of channeling behavior, but incapable of controlling it. The 1871 Treaty of London was a fiction in as much as all law is a fiction; that is, its strength depended upon the context in which it was invoked. Nonetheless, both this affirmation of *pacta sunt servanda* and the Black Sea Treaty played an important role in shaping conduct and setting expectations. The painstaking negotiations involved in codifying this rule at the London Conference evidenced the significance underlying these words. Law was more than diplomatic formality.

This extraordinary episode raises questions regarding the meaning of international law in the nineteenth century. Historians and lawyers have reached different conclusions about the Black Sea crisis, reflecting a lack of common appreciation of legal concepts. Ideas such as the binding nature of treaties, enforcement of legal obligations, and even sovereign equality of states have both a commonplace and a technical meaning. In order to properly assess foreign policy in the era, the historian must fully comprehend how these concepts were understood by nineteenth-century diplomats, and more broadly, the nature of international law as practiced by states.

THE CONTEXT OF INTERNATIONAL LAW

Such is the unity of all history that any one who endeavours to tell a piece of it must feel that his first sentence tears a seamless web.[20]

International law has always offered more than its critics have admitted and less than its champions have hoped. As an institution of interstate relations, law has influenced state conduct, without ever fully constraining independent action. While international law has not fully fettered sovereignty, it has changed the cost structure of individual diplomatic choices, channeled activities in both war and peace into commonly accepted paths, and arguably has helped shape national interests. The role played by international law needs to be understood in order to evaluate the manner in which statesmen have sought to incorporate it into security planning.

Law was most effective when it coincided with national interest and with power. In the 1871 parliamentary debates after the London Conference, statesmen advocated two solutions to the perceived failings of law, calling either for stronger international institutions or more robust national enforcement – making obligations match British means, to paraphrase Salisbury. Britain chose to craft treaties that matched national enforcement capabilities, undertaking obligations that could be upheld, signaling a pragmatic stance rather than a utopian view of law.

The focus will be on international law as it was practiced in the nineteenth century. State practice largely revolved around treaties and custom, interpreted by states and enforced through self-help. Law served as a universal grammar for resolving disputes, by providing an understood system for raising claims, and functioned entirely through existing diplomatic practices. Non-lawyers often harbor misconceptions about international law, portraying it as a set of utopian schemes of world government, or as vague principles of morality lacking effective sanction. While many lawyers and diplomats hoped that international law would evolve into a

---

[20] F. W. Maitland, "A Prologue to a History of English Law," *Law Quarterly Review* 14, no. 53 (1898): 13.

more powerful system, and called for the creation of powerful international institutions,[21] day-to-day diplomacy functioned in their absence. International law reflected power relations as much as it included moral aspirations.

This is not to suggest that statesmen always had a firm grasp of the law when wielding it. Nor should it be assumed all administrations followed the same approach. A drive for international organization played a more prominent role in some administrations, such as Gladstone's, than in others, such as Salisbury's. However, even the latter statesman exploited international law in advancing national goals and could eloquently express the same hopes for the legal system.[22] Statesmen of both parties worked within the existing system, utilizing law as a tool of diplomacy in meeting national interests.

Earlier works have highlighted different aspects of international law, focusing on either law as a system of communal values or law as a practical tool of national policy. Martti Koskenniemi emphasized the aspirational goals of international law, stressing what law could become through interdependence and common values.[23] Other authors, such as Gerry Simpson, have focused on the role of law in furthering national interest. Simpson reflected on the role of power in shaping law, noting a tension between legitimacy and functionality in the nineteenth century. In this latter view, the great powers sought to make the legal system more functional by acknowledging a special role for powerful states, yet repeatedly had to

---

[21] See Schücking, *The International Union of the Hague Conferences* on the goal of world federation; John Austin, *The Province of Jurisprudence Determined* (London: John Murray, 1832) on the lack of effective sanction in international law. Martti Koskenniemi described the reformist element in nineteenth-century international law, epitomized by the early history of the Institute of International Law. See Martti Koskenniemi, *The Gentle Civilizer of Nations: The Rise and Fall of International Law 1870–1960* (Cambridge: Cambridge University Press, 2001), 91. This branch of legal scholarship was driven by a goal of reforming international society, and its accounts of international law focused upon what law might become rather than what statesmen perceived it to actually be. Often critical of older generations of legal scholarship, with their descriptive accounts of extant legal relationships, primarily expressed through treaties negotiated out of expediency rather than universal principles, the reformers sought an international legal system based firmly upon concepts of interdependence.

[22] "[T]his federation of Europe is the embryo of the only possible structure of Europe which can save civilization from the desolating effects of a disastrous war." Lord Salisbury's Speech on the Lord Mayor's Day, *in* "The Guildhall Banquet," *The Times*, Nov. 10, 1897, at 6.

[23] Koskenniemi, *The Gentle Civilizer of Nations*.

return to the principle of sovereign equality of states in order to legitimize great power actions.[24]

The state provides an ideal point to begin an investigation of international law, as the core elements of law can most easily be explained through an appreciation of national interest. Moreover, the focus is historically warranted, given the marked positivism and voluntarism of nineteenth-century international law, which accorded states greater liberty in accepting or rejecting legal obligations than in other eras. As Stephen Neff noted, this was the era of Clausewitz, in which war was seen as an extension of politics, and in which statesmen wielded international law, like war, for narrowly conceived conceptions of national interest rather than out of community obligations.[25]

The practice of international law involved the advocacy of legal rights as specified in treaties and custom, through a range of legitimate state enforcement actions. Despite paltry legal institutions, law as a policymaker's tool served key functions. The importance attached to legal obligations made violations more costly, reducing the likelihood of breaches. By reducing the chances of unacceptable conduct, law could increase predictability in international affairs, assisting states in long-term planning.

International law was not static. Law evolved over the course of the century to legitimize a broader great power role in maintaining the balance of power. It also changed with the movement for progressive codification in the last third of the century, and through the creation of broader treaty networks regulating a growing myriad of topics. But the utilization of law in meeting state goals remained a constant.

While statesmen often sought powerful international institutions to make relations more orderly, it remained another question if such institutions would merely mirror the power structure in the world at large, or whether it could truly make great power behavior more law-like. Ultimately, statesmen lacked the luxury of waiting for such utopias, yet could cope manageably within the existing system. The failure of arms control prior to 1914 cannot be attributed to a lack of developed legal institutions. Law provided a comprehensive structure for ordering state behavior, and by and large statesmen knew it.

[24] Gerry Simpson, *Great Powers and Outlaw States. Unequal Sovereigns in the International Legal Order*, (Cambridge: Cambridge University Press, 2004), 91 *et. seq.*

[25] Stephen C. Neff, *War and the Law of Nations. A General History* (Cambridge: Cambridge University Press, 2005), 162.

Scholars and Official Law

International law must be understood within the context of the nineteenth-century legal system. International legal theory varied from country to country, but core principles remained universally accepted. International law was embodied in standard forms, largely through treaties and custom. To make sense of the unwritten custom, states accorded great weight to compilations by leading scholars, many of whom were governmental advisors writing from experience. These treaties and customs, and what statesmen expected from them, must be explored. It also needs to be determined if *legal* obligations added anything to international agreements, and whether statesmen perceived international law as an actual legal system.

International law evolved as a distinct category of legal education in the nineteenth century. Prior to mid-century, legal studies had often been undertaken on an ad hoc basis, as more of an apprenticeship than a modern course of study. Within universities, the era witnessed a shift from teaching international law within philosophy faculties to law faculties. Older chairs in the Law of Nature and of Nations in philosophy departments were replaced by chairs in International Law in law departments.[26] The process was gradual, with the first British chairs in international law being occupied at Oxford in 1859, and Cambridge in 1866. Germany, despite its rich tradition of legal education, did not follow suit until after 1900.[27] Russia also joined late, having only one major scholarly work translated into Russian prior to 1880.[28]

International law possessed no single standard regarding how states should incorporate international legal obligations into domestic law. Each state determined how international law fitted within its domestic legal structure in a manner reflecting its unique historical experiences. However, there were broad cross-border trends within international law, and leading scholars influenced the development of theory beyond their home states. The system of international law in the nineteenth century was largely a European phenomenon, although the addition of states in the Americas led to the gradual broadening of the legal community. The evolution of terminology from "European public law" to "general international law" reflected this change, as did the shift from "Christian states" as mentioned

---

[26] Nussbaum, *A Concise History of the Law of Nations*, 237.
[27] Koskenniemi, *The Gentle Civilizer of Nations*, 33, 209.
[28] Nussbaum, *A Concise History of the Law of Nations*, 231–32.

in treaties in the early part of the century to "civilized states" in the second half. The 1856 Treaty of Paris constituted a milestone by incorporating the non-Christian Ottoman Empire into the legal community.

Within this system of international law, continental and Anglo-American schools existed, mirroring their domestic civil and common law systems respectively. At the turn of the century, government-sanctioned German legal theorists placed international law below domestic law, stressing the limits of international law, and allowing national sovereignty to trump treaty obligations.[29] The United States held its constitution as the supreme law of the land, above Acts of Congress and treaties.[30] British statesmen occasionally argued that their unwritten constitution prevented them from accepting binding alliance obligations, as ratified agreements would illegally bind future governments, although this rationale was only utilized sporadically and did not prevent Great Britain from contracting numerous treaty obligations, all of which bound future governments.[31] Moreover even when raised, this argument was associated with treaties of alliance, rather than the myriad range of treaties into which Great Britain willingly entered. British governments did not question whether treaties were binding as a matter of British law, only whether certain types of treaties, such as alliances, could be made, and whether these agreements had to be placed before Parliament for ratification.[32]

While each state determined how legal obligations would interact with domestic law, this fact did not alter obligations on the international level.

---

[29] See generally Koskenniemi, The Gentle Civilizer of Nations, 210–11. Most legal theories implicitly acknowledged this reservation, see, e.g., Moore, A Digest of International Law, Vol. V, 221. However, few theorists emphasized this reservation over the general rule. Isabel Hull has further explored differences in German international legal theory as practiced in wartime, demonstrating how exceptions trumped law. Isabel Hull, Absolute Destruction: Military Culture and the Practices of War in Imperial Germany (Ithaca: Cornell University Press, 2005); A Scrap of Paper: Breaking and Making International Law during the Great War (Ithaca: Cornell University Press, 2014).

[30] US Const. Art. 6. Moreover, in the nineteenth century, the United States government argued that its constitution prevented it from contracting binding alliances, as treaties were ratified solely by the Senate, but Article I of the Constitution placed the power to declare war in the hands of both houses of Congress. See Christopher H. D. Howard, Britain and the Casus Belli, 1822–1902: A Study of Britain's International Position from Canning to Salisbury (London: Athlone Press, 1974), 128.

[31] See generally id., especially 126 et. seq.

[32] On the binding nature of treaties as a source of national law, see Samuel B. Crandall, Treaties, Their Making and Enforcement (New York: Columbia University Press, 1904), 151 et seq., especially 59–60.

Treaties still remained binding within international law.[33] Even if a state held a ratified treaty to be incompatible with domestic law, its treaty partners could still assert the obligation and seek some form of compensation for violations. As constitutional differences caused variations in treaty ratification procedures, domestic law influenced the creation of legally binding obligations. Early in the century, for example, absolute monarchies had greater authority to enter into treaties, so ratification could be implied at the time of signature. More democratic states reserved this authority for legislative bodies, which could significantly delay, or even jeopardize, the ratification process.[34] Nations were put on notice of notoriously fickle systems, and recognized that a state was not bound until the agreement had been ratified in accordance with domestic law.

National interpretations in turn found their way into scholarly writing on international law. As customary law remained a largely unwritten source of binding obligations, governments relied upon compilations of custom by leading scholars. The diplomatic world furnished countless international law scholars, many of whom continued to advise their governments on contemporary legal questions while writing and whose works reflected their diplomatic experience. The major scholarly works were considered by states to be a significant supplementary source of international law.[35]

International Law is *not* a body of rules which lawyers have evolved out of their own inner consciousness: it is *not* a system carefully thought out by University Professors, Bookworms, or other theorists in the quiet and seclusion of their studies. It is a living body of practical rules and principles which have gradually come into being by the custom of nations and international agreements. To the formation of these rules Statesmen, Diplomatists, Admirals, Generals, Judges and publicists have all contributed.[36]

Foreign Office memoranda made liberal use of quotes from legal scholars, particularly in matters of custom, as reflecting the extant state practice. Foreign Office files on bombardment, laws of war, and other topics were

---

[33] "*Pacta sunt servanda* is the pervading maxim of International, as it was of Roman jurisprudence." Sir Robert Phillimore, *Commentaries Upon International Law* (Philadelphia: T. & J.W. Johnson Law Booksellers, 1855), Vol. II, 56.

[34] Wheaton, *Elements of International Law*, 187.

[35] Phillimore, *Commentaries Upon International Law*, Vol. I, 62.

[36] A. Pearce Higgins, *The Binding Force of International Law* (Cambridge: Cambridge University Press, 1910), 3.

littered with passages from scholarly texts.[37] The Foreign Office sought out international legal advice from a range of sources, retaining private attorneys, and employing officials such as the Lord Chancellor, the Queen's Advocate, and the Law Officers, calling upon the latter daily for advice.[38] These attorneys represented the government in different capacities, and with respect to different subjects. For instance, the Queen's Advocate represented the monarch in ecclesiastical and admiralty matters. The Foreign Office would present correspondence to its attorneys and allow them to frame the legal issue and response.[39] Law Officers' reports covered a wide variety of legal issues, from private claims for property in foreign lands to extradition requests. Additionally, the Foreign Office sought advice on the repercussions of prospective treaties on British law, and the Law Officers advised on the revision and ratification of treaties.[40] The Foreign Office librarians, particularly the long-serving Edward Hertslet, provided another avenue of advice. As the third-generation Hertslet serving as Foreign Office librarian, he entered government service in 1840 at the age of 16, remaining until 1896.[41] While untrained as a lawyer, his long experience gave him an encyclopedic knowledge of diplomatic affairs, and the Foreign Office often called upon him to provide memoranda summarizing current legal obligations.[42]

Leading figures in British legal circles, such as Travers Twiss and Robert Phillimore, served as consultants for the Foreign Office: Phillimore and Twiss had similar careers, both becoming noted figures in ecclesiastical and international law, and both writing on maritime and defense issues from the 1840s onwards. While Phillimore served in Parliament and held

[37] In preparing for an international conference to be held on bombardment, the Foreign Office sought to explain the current state of the law on the topic. The Foreign Office organized a file with numerous excerpts from scholarly works, indicating the influence of these experts on official opinion. Papers respecting the Bombardment of Unfortified Towns, Requisitions, etc., FO 83/1652 (1834–1898).

[38] Clive Parry, 'The Legal Advisers of the Crown' *in* Clive Parry, (ed.), *A British Digest of International Law, Part VII Organs of States* (London: Stevens & Sons, 1965), 242 *et. seq.*

[39] *Id.*

[40] *See, for example*, Foreign Office to the Law Officers of the Crown, Sep. 18, 1899, *in* Reports by the Law Officers of the Crown, FO 881/7356 (1899) advising on legal ramifications of the 1899 Hague Conventions.

[41] "Sir Edward Hertslet Obituary," Aug. 5, 1902, *The (London) Times*, 5.

[42] For instance, Herstlet was called on to provide advice regarding the existence of any treaty limiting the number of British ironclads stationed in the Mediterranean, holding there was no obligation. Edward Herstlet, Memorandum Respecting the Number of British and Foreign Ships of War in the Mediterranean, FO 881/5716, (January 28, 1889).

judicial posts, Twiss taught at King's College London and Oxford. Both served as a Queen's Advocate and Admiralty Advocate General, positions where they were called on to provide advice to the Foreign Office on international law.[43] In turn, their writings reflected prevailing Foreign Office attitudes. Indeed, Phillimore has been criticized for taking a parochial view, limiting his influence beyond Anglo-American schools of thought.[44] However, for this same reason, Phillimore's works are particularly useful for understanding official British perceptions.

Throughout the era, agents responsible for shaping international law on behalf of their nations contributed to legal scholarship. Naval figures like Vice-Admiral Charles H. Stockton, military officers like J. B. Porter, Major George B. Davis, General H. W. Halleck, and politicians including Elihu Root and Senator Cushman Davis all contributed to international legal theory.[45] Even noteworthy figures such as Alfred Thayer Mahan and General Helmuth von Moltke participated in legal debates, if only to argue against further extension of regulations over their fields of endeavor – contributions that should not be overlooked.[46] Many military officers received training in international law, and in the execution of their duties they were often required to determine the legality of different courses of action. The leaders' statements indicated likely wartime conduct, which in turn indicated the actual extent of the law. Declarations of military law, such as Lieber's Code, proved influential in the subsequent development of the law of war.[47] Additionally, state papers and diplomatic correspondence served as a source of international law, indicating actual state practice.[48]

[43] See Howard, *Britain and the Casus Belli*, 94–95; Parry, "The Legal Advisers of the Crown," 251.

[44] Nussbaum, *A Concise History of the Law of Nations*, 235–36. Unlike his near-contemporary Wheaton, Phillimore was never translated.

[45] Charles H. Stockton, *Outlines of International Law* (New York: Charles Scribner's Sons, 1914); Davis, *Outlines of International Law*; Halleck, *Elements of International Law*; J. B. Porter, *International Law, Having Particular Reference to the Laws of War on Land* (Fort Leavenworth, Kansas: Press of the Army Service Schools, 1914); Elihu Root, "The Sanction of International Law," *American Journal of International Law* 2, no. 3 (1908); Cushman K. Davis, *A Treatise on International Law Including American Diplomacy* (St. Paul, Minnesota: Keefe-Davidson Law Book Co., 1901).

[46] Mahan, *Armaments and Arbitration*; Helmuth von Moltke and Johann Kaspar Bluntschli, "Les Lois De La Guerre Sur Terre," *Revue de droit international et de législation comparée* 13 (1881).

[47] Lieber, *Instructions for the Government of Armies of the United States in the Field*.

[48] Phillimore, *Commentaries Upon International Law*, Vol. I, 68.

The topics addressed by experts and practitioners centered on state-to-state relations, or public international law, differentiating the topic from law governing relationships between individuals of separate states, or private international law. Nineteenth-century legal texts were generally divided into major sections on peacetime law and the law of war. Often, texts began with an account of the fundamental principles of international law, founded on either natural or positive law. Subsequent sections covered the extent of national jurisdiction, practices of diplomatic etiquette such as ambassadorial immunity, and the various types of legal relations established between states. These texts usually covered the settlement of international disputes in a spectrum, starting with negotiation and mediation, then moving to sanctions and war.

SOURCES OF LAW AND NON-BINDING AGREEMENTS

Public international law, a term that came into use in the nineteenth century,[49] included treaties, customs, and judicial opinions among its sources. Judicial opinions often summarized state practice, and were influential in areas such as naval prize law, in which national courts adjudicated the legality of seizing merchant vessels in war, relying upon international precedent. Custom referred to unwritten practices accepted as binding by states, or *opinio juris*, as evidenced by state action.[50]

Custom is probably the hardest concept for non-lawyers to grasp, given the unwritten nature of this source of law. Practices regularly engaged in by states could gradually take on a binding nature.[51] As no authoritative government work listed binding custom, diplomats and lawyers working for the government often prepared textbooks summarizing these obligations. Despite the absence of official compilations, states deemed custom to be as binding as treaty law. Prior to the codification movement in the late nineteenth century, the most authoritative compilations of customs were those contained in these scholarly works, which the Foreign Office widely utilized. In this respect, the distinction between scholarly international law

---

[49] The term had been coined by Jeremy Bentham in the late eighteenth century, and well into the nineteenth century other terms such as "the public law of nations" remained in currency.

[50] Phillimore, *Commentaries Upon International Law*, Vol. I, 39–41.

[51] "Custom is the older and the original source of International Law in particular as well as of law in general." Lassa Oppenheim, *International Law: A Treatise*, 2nd ed. (London: Longmans, Green and Co., 1912), Vol. I, 22.

and state practice was more apparent than real. Scholarly works provided a significant source of information on the bulk of unwritten international law, by perpetuating customs reflected in prior state practice. When considering the dense web of international custom reported in legal texts, it should also be kept in mind that law only provided a set of rights and obligations, but did not dictate the manner in which states should raise these issues or uphold them. Ultimately, the decision to raise a legal claim was a policy decision to be made by the state. Law merely provided the generally recognized rationale for framing these claims.

Treaties formed a key part of the international legal system, binding the parties who contracted them.[52] The role of treaties as a source of *general* international law, obligating non-parties as well as parties, was increasingly advocated during the nineteenth century, but usually their effect was considered to be limited to the signatories.[53] A certain amount of confusion exists regarding the status of treaties as *sources of international law*.[54] The use of the term "source of international law" in the nineteenth century was reserved for sources of *general* obligation binding *all* states, while current usage tends to define any legal obligation, whether specific to a single state or general to the whole community, as a "source of law."[55] A modern international lawyer studying nineteenth-century texts can easily make the mistake that since treaties were not usually listed as "sources of international law" in older works they were not considered legally binding, but the evidence indicates otherwise. Legal treatises uniformly described treaties as binding within international law, and state practice confirmed this expectation. International legal scholars often analogized these obligations to domestic contract law. Treaties were agreements willingly entered into

---

[52] G. F. Von Martens, *A Compendium of the Law of Nations*, trans. William Cobbett (London: Corbett & Morgan, 1802), 47–48; Wheaton, *Elements of International Law*, 49–50, 188; Phillimore, *Commentaries Upon International Law*, Vol. I, 38; "[t]he most useful and practical part of the Law of Nations is, no doubt, instituted or positive law, founded on usage, consent, and agreement;" Maine, *International Law*, 32; Hall, *A Treatise on International Law*, 323; Westlake, *Chapters on the Principles of International Law*, 78, 83; Thomas Joseph Lawrence, *The Principles of International Law*, 4th ed. (Boston: Heath and Co., 1910), 101 et. seq., 326–27. This was not merely a matter of scholarly theory but of state practice, as seen with the Declaration of London.

[53] Lawrence, *The Principles of International Law*, 101 et. seq.

[54] E.g. Clive Parry, "Foreign Policy and International Law," in *Foreign Policy under Sir Edward Grey*, ed. F. H. Hinsley (Cambridge: Cambridge University Press, 1977), 91.

[55] The classic statement on sources of international law is Article 38 of the Statute of the International Court of Justice.

by the parties, containing obligations that could be avoided only on narrowly drawn grounds, and which entailed a right to remedies if a breach occurred.[56]

International law utilized treaties to manage some of the core questions of international relations. Treaties considered binding within international law included many of the alliances of the era, such as the Triple Alliance and the Franco-Russian Alliance.[57] The treaty system enshrined the balance of power within the international legal order, specifically referencing its maintenance as a goal.[58] Treaties also specified spheres of influence[59] and set national boundaries,[60] often codifying expectations in order to preserve peace or to restore international stability. Treaties also specified rules of conduct in wartime to limit the repercussions when efforts to keep the peace failed.[61]

* * *

This leaves the question of whether legally binding obligations contributed anything to the impact of an agreement. Law was not the only means of communicating state interests. Statesmen could employ many other means to convey their vital national interests and signal their intentions,

---

[56] Hall, *A Treatise on International Law*, 323 et. seq.

[57] Additionally, the Anglo-French and Anglo-Russian ententes were enshrined in binding legal documents. But while these created legal obligations, they contained no binding duties to intervene militarily, and only regulated colonial and policy disputes. The broader policies enshrined in ententes remained outside of any legal obligation.

[58] Phillimore, *Commentaries Upon International Law*, Vol. I, 576–77; Treaty of Constantinople, Mar. 12, 1854, Preamble "[T]heir said Majesties being fully persuaded that the existence of the Ottoman Empire in its present Limits is essential to the maintenance of the Balance of Power among the States of Europe ..."; Treaty of Stockholm, Nov. 21, 1855, Preamble "[The parties] being anxious to avert any complication which might disturb the existing Balance of Power in Europe ..." *both in* Hurst, ed., *Key Treaties*, Vol. I, 299, 315. Many legal texts recognized the balance of power as a precondition for international law. *See* Alfred Vagts and Detlev Vagts, "The Balance of Power in International Law: A History of an Idea," *American Journal of International Law* 73, no. 4 (1979).

[59] *For example*, Declaration Between the United Kingdom and France respecting Egypt and Morocco, Apr. 8, 1904; Hurst, ed., *Key Treaties*, Vol. II, 760.

[60] The Treaty of Berlin provided a key example.

[61] "Declaration of Paris, Apr. 16, 1856," *American Journal of International Law* 1, no. 2 Supplement (1907); Geneva Convention for the Amelioration of the Condition of the Sick and Wounded of Armies in the Field, Aug. 22, 1864; Declaration of St. Petersburg; the Hague Conventions of 1899 and 1907.

including parliamentary speeches, state papers, diplomatic negotiations, military maneuvers, and fleet visits. Even royal visits abroad could indicate changes in policy, leading diplomats to carefully balance travel itineraries in order to prevent international panics. Statesmen utilized legal instruments for specific reasons, when predictability outweighed flexibility in decision-making. By framing policy in a binding agreement, an additional message could be expressed.

The use of non-binding instruments provides evidence that legally binding obligations were intended to have an additional effect. Otherwise, all agreements could simply have been termed binding. Not all international agreements were binding as a matter of law. States could enter into gentlemen's agreements, understandings, *modi vivendi*, non-binding exchanges of notes, and other forms that would currently be termed soft-law agreements. Diplomats drafted these documents specifically to avoid legal obligation, often to clarify informal arrangements while leaving greater liberty of action. Non-binding instruments had the advantage of simplicity and often circumvented complex ratification procedures. Additionally, the use of these non-binding documents as an alternative to binding treaties conveyed a specific message, indicating that a different level of obligation was intended.

Salisbury's first 1887 Mediterranean Agreement with Austria-Hungary and Italy provides a classic example of a non-binding agreement. This agreement concerned a coordinated response by the parties to any changes in the territorial status quo within the Mediterranean, Aegean, and Black Seas. Salisbury pledged only that "[i]t will be the *earnest desire* of H.M.'s Government to give their best co-operation … in maintaining these cardinal principles of policy" while recognizing that "[t]he character of that co-operation must be decided by them, when the occasion for it arises, according to the circumstances of the case."[62] The elder statesman consciously chose this type of instrument, with no firmer obligation than an "earnest desire" and no duties other than cooperation, a vague term to be defined solely by Britain.[63] Britain sought to coordinate policy with

---

[62] Emphasis added. British Note to the Italian Government in Regard to a Mediterranean Agreement, Feb. 12, 1887, Hurst, ed., *Key Treaties*, Vol. 2, 635.

[63] Compare this language to that of the Triple Alliance of 1882: Article II stated in case Italy was attacked by France, "the two other Contracting Parties *shall be bound* to lend help and assistance *with all their forces* to the Party attacked." First Treaty of Triple Alliance between Austria-Hungary, Germany and Italy, May 20, 1882. Similarly, the initial draft of 1892

Italy and Austria-Hungary, without becoming obliged to enter a war on behalf of these Triple Alliance partners. By avoiding a binding assurance to the two Mediterranean states, Salisbury reduced the likelihood that Italy and Austria-Hungary would act aggressively in the expectation that Britain would back them up.[64] Britain could frame policy based upon present circumstances, in this case during a Franco-Italian war scare, signaling to France an intention to support Italy, without becoming locked into a long-term obligation to the Triple Alliance.

Despite Salisbury's occasional claims to the contrary, his actions indicated that he considered treaties binding. On certain occasions he set British policy through binding treaties, while on other occasions nonbinding documents were used. Had he truly believed treaties conveyed no legal weight, there would have been no reason to avoid their use. Nonbinding agreements would have allowed him to negotiate without parliamentary review, but his administration was clearly not concerned about avoiding legislative scrutiny. He had no qualms about hiding a binding treaty made with Portugal from Parliament in 1899.

British avoidance of firm treaty commitments to the Triple Alliance in the 1880s and 1890s reflected a conscious weighing of advantage between freedom of action and obtaining firm commitments from the other parties. Similarly, the Anglo-French and Anglo-Russian ententes, while legally binding treaties, contained no provisions relating to mutual security arrangements. The caution shown by various diplomats, including Lord Salisbury and Sir Edward Grey, in denying that Britain had undertaken *legal* obligations, indicated a belief that treaty obligations bound the state in a manner that non-binding agreements did not. States sought on the one hand to record these alliances in legally binding documents;

Franco-Russian Military Convention provided strong obligations: At Article 1 "If France is attacked by Germany, or by Italy supported by Germany, Russia *shall employ all her available forces to attack Germany*" creating an outright obligation not only to fight but to actually attack Germany, the article going on to state that in the case of attack on Russia, France "*shall employ all her available forces* to fight Germany." Draft of Military Convention between France and Russia, 1892. Emphasis added. *Both in* Hurst, ed., *Key Treaties*, Vol. II, at 611, 668.

[64] Earlier in the century, Clarendon had preferred to keep the exact nature of British obligations vague, in order to prevent guaranteed states like Portugal and Belgium from flaunting unconditional British support at their enemies. *See* Howard, *Britain and the Casus Belli*, 96. These concerns also influenced British alliance negotiations with Japan, although ultimately Britain accepted formal treaty obligations. *See* Draft Dispatch from Lansdowne to MacDonald, Dec. 24, 1901, CAB 37/59/142 (1901) at 2.

Great Britain, by contrast, often sought to avoid writing them down. This indicates that the character of being legally binding had some independent value within agreements.

*   *   *

International law did not then, nor does it now, possess a firm means of enforcement. A common misconception among non-lawyers is that international law encompasses only obligations under the jurisdiction of a world court or other international institutions capable of adjudicating disputes and enforcing settlements. The reality is that international law was, and remains, very much a system of self-help.

In the nineteenth century, legal scholar John Austin reassessed international law in light of the lack of enforcement authority. According to Austin and his followers, the law "properly so-called" required an authority to compel its enforcement, and the absence of this authority in the international sphere relegated international law to "positive morality" at best.[65] Austin influenced Anglo-American circles of scholars more than continental ones, where another school of positivists emerged after 1815. While Anglo-American scholars increasingly had to address this critique, Austin's theory did not predominate among them, and was not held as an official view by the British government.[66]

The response to Austin rested on perceptions of law.[67] Law can be viewed either in terms of institutions or in terms of its function within society. The *institutions* of legal systems include a legislature, judiciary, and executive. While a rudimentary legislature can be discerned in the

---

[65] Austin, *The Province of Jurisprudence Determined*, 138, 46–48, 208.

[66] Grewe, *The Epochs of International Law*, 509–10. While foreign ministers like Salisbury commented on the lack of binding nature of treaties, the Foreign Office never subscribed to this view and continued to treat treaties as legally binding. Moreover, Salisbury's conduct indicated that his own views were more complex than he admitted in political speeches. *See generally* Howard, *Britain and the Casus Belli*. and specifically, 126 et. seq.

[67] "The capability of being enforced by compulsory means is not the only or the most essential characteristic of Law. That characteristic lies much more in this – that it is the rule and order governing all human communities in all spheres and dimensions of private and public life, and also of the social relations of Peoples and States with one another, which is also International Law. Compulsion only issues from the community as such. This is the order which ought to be upholden – the life regulated by law is the common life of States." Kaltenborn, *as translated in* Phillimore, *Commentaries Upon International Law*, Vol. I, 77. Lawrence, *The Principles of International Law*, 3, 9–11; Halleck, *Elements of International Law*, 54.

development of treaty networks and customary law, a judiciary capable of defining legal obligations rarely existed, and an independent executive with police powers was entirely absent. An institutional view of law, such as Austin's, would find that international law is not truly law. On the other hand, if one focuses upon the *function* of law, then international law can be viewed as truly law, albeit weaker than domestic law. The function of law within society lay in establishing predictability in behavior.[68] Law accomplished this function by setting expectations for mutual conduct, and through fear of repercussions. Law only needed a sufficiently effective sanction to deter most proscribed conduct, even if it was unable to enforce all obligations.[69] Rather than deterring every violation, law only had to influence enough behavior to set expectations and allow individuals to plan.[70] When viewing law as a function within society, recognized and sanctioned by the state, then international law is law.[71]

Contemporary lawyers recognized this distinction, noted the weakness of domestic law, and focused upon the functions of law. After assessing legal institutions such as police forces one author noted:

> ... they are not essential to the conception of law, any more than ermine and sealing wax, and any attempt to exaggerate their importance can only result in exhibiting them in the light of cumbrous and clumsy excrescences on the essential characteristics of what law is.[72]

[68] "Municipal law itself is constantly and systematically violated by the average citizen ... We do not ask of law that it should absolutely suppress all action which is opposed to its dictates; its function is performed when it imposes a definite and powerful check upon any such action; more we cannot require of it." Thomas Baty, "The Basis of International Law," *Macmillan's Magazine* 78, no. 466 (1898): 280.

[69] Lawrence, *The Principles of International Law*, 3.

[70] For instance, domestic law has not eliminated bank robberies, only made them rare enough that the public has confidence placing its money within banks. A vast proportion of law is regularly disobeyed, including speed limits on the highways, but the rules are enforced sufficiently to keep the highways relatively safe. Law enforcement is always relative and contextual, dependent upon numerous factors, varying upon neighborhood, time of day, and even weather, as witnessed by the prevalence of crime in many cities during the dog days of summer.

[71] As a normative question, each state determines for itself the nature of its domestic legal obligations. The question of whether international law was truly law can be simply answered by recourse to national legal texts. In the nineteenth century, Great Britain held international law to be legally binding. *See* Edward Wavell Ridges, *Constitutional Law of England* (London: Stevens & Sons, 1905), 424–26.

[72] Baty, "The Basis of International Law," 279.

The British Foreign Office utilized this sophisticated understanding of law when negotiating agreements in the nineteenth century, ever cognizant of the limitations of law but sharply aware of how law could promote British interests.

THE FUNCTION OF INTERNATIONAL LAW: "AN OBSTACLE THOUGH NOT A BARRIER"

Statesmen utilized legally binding agreements for a number of reasons: to increase predictability in international relations; to communicate vital interests to other parties; and to create and strengthen mutual interests. The question of enforcing a binding engagement when one party was recalcitrant arose only secondarily. While the threat of sanctions lay at the root of international legal obligations, law functioned more by altering the cost structure of decision-making by communicating acceptable avenues of conduct. As a violation of law justified retaliation and could lead to international isolation, statesmen used greater care both when entering into legal obligations and when attempting to exit from them. Politicians recognized that the existence of a treaty, while unlikely to entirely elimi-nate proscribed conduct, could inhibit a state from taking actions deemed illegal by raising the political costs of such actions. This circumscribed range of options constituted the binding effect of international law.

Law's Function in Increasing Predictability

Politicians warily approached the legal obligations which treaties engen-dered. Many leaders publicly expressed a cavalier attitude towards treaty obligations, the most famous example being Bethmann Hollweg "scrap of paper" comment regarding the 1839 Belgian guarantee. The truth was subtler. Even autocratic governments like Wilhelmine Germany approached new obligations cautiously, the Germans refusing to accept broad obliga-tions at the Hague Conferences. Had Germany attached no weight to these agreements, then it could have avoided the onus of scuttling various nego-tiations in 1899 and 1907 by simply signing and then promptly ignoring the resultant treaties.[73] Treaty obligations ratified by domestic procedures

---

[73] The Kaiser impatiently claimed this as his policy. "To prevent *him* [the Russian Czar] from making a fool of himself before all Europe, *I* have agreed to this nonsense. But in practice I will continue as before to trust only in God and my sharp sword! And will shit on all the

carried political weight both at home and abroad, raising the political costs of casually breaching obligations. In a famous example, British Foreign Secretary Lord Stanley attempted to water down Britain's obligations under the new 1867 treaty guaranteeing Luxembourg by claiming that the "collective guarantee" was inherently ineffectual.[74] When he posed this interpretation in Parliament he drew immediate rebuke from Lord Russell as well as diplomatic protests from Bismarck, and hastily disavowed the statement.[75]

Although international law was breached, agreements given the imprimatur of law could not easily be abandoned without entailing political consequences.[76] Throughout the era, British statesmen recognized this effect of law and utilized binding agreements for this reason. For instance, in the mid-1880s the British government sought to protect its extensive submarine telegraphic cable network by treaty. Reversing its earlier position, the government hoped to delegitimize cable cutting in wartime, preserving Britain's strategic advantage in its global telegraphic network by institutionalizing a rule favorable to Britain's specific position. Yet the government recognized that a treaty could offer only imperfect advantages, a member of the Colonial Defence Committee noting that they were:

> well aware that no Treaty obligations will suffice to secure absolute immunity for cables in time of war. They consider, however, that if a sentiment against this mode of injuring an enemy, sufficient even to cause a certain measure of reluctance to adopt it, can be promoted, there would be a direct gain for the Empire.[77]

resolutions!" Norman Rich, *Friedrich Von Holstein: Politics and Diplomacy in the Era of Bismarck and Wilhelm II* (Cambridge: Cambridge University Press, 1965), 607. However, the record of German treaty ratification indicated that agreements were cautiously entered into.

[74] He claimed that "collective guarantees" made by all the great powers, such as the 1867 agreement, could only be brought into effect if *all* powers agreed to participate in the defense of the guaranteed state, an unlikely situation as these same nations were the only parties likely to invade the guaranteed state. If one of them invaded Luxembourg, there would be no collective defense of the hapless state. Howard, *Britain and the Casus Belli*, 79. A collective guarantee required intervention only when other guarantors intervened, but an invasion of the guaranteed state by one of these parties would not excuse the others of this duty. Oppenheim, *International Law: A Treatise*, 601–02.

[75] Howard, *Britain and the Casus Belli*, 79–80.

[76] The political cost of breaching legal obligations also depended on the nature of the breach, and the array of states capable of sanctioning the conduct. See the following section on this point.

[77] Memorandum of the Colonial Defence Committee, Jul. 19, 1886, *quoted in* Committee of Imperial Defence, The Hague Conference: Notes on Subjects which might be raised by Great Britain or by other Powers, at 5, CAB 38/10/76 (Oct. 26, 1905).

Again when discussing rules of war prior to the Second Hague Conference, the Committee of Imperial Defence (CID) held:

> All international agreements are liable to be set aside by a belligerent who considers he could secure definite advantage by violating them, and believes himself powerful enough to ignore neutral protests; or by a neutral who strongly favours a belligerent, and who is prepared to disregard the interests of other neutrals. At the same time, the existence of international agreements must create some measure of reluctance to appear publicly in the part of a violator, and must tend to develop a community of sentiment in regard to the methods of conducting operations of war.[78]

When discussing the possibility of a mediation clause in the 1856 peace agreement, Clarendon noted that while causes for war might still exist, "[n]evertheless I thought a general declaration in favour of the principle of mediation would be a fitting corollary to the treaty and oppose an obstacle though it might not prove a barrier to the renewal of war."[79] By creating an obstacle to proscribed conduct and setting an expectation regarding future behavior, law could increase predictability in international affairs, even if it could not create a total barrier against violations.

The process of treaty ratification can in turn shape state interest. States accept legal obligations in the international sphere in order to communicate a firm intention of guiding their policy with reference to agreed terms. Policy can be expressed in many forms, but law added another layer of obligation, solidifying commitments. To breach an agreement, after taking extraordinary pains to reach a common policy, and after convincing a domestic audience of the wisdom of undertaking treaty obligations, involved higher domestic political costs. Coalitions were formed to ensure ratification of a treaty, and proponents of the engagement placed their political credibility on the line to gain domestic allies.[80]

Law's Function in Communicating Vital Interests

Some historians have decried the limited utility of law, holding that if national interest dictates a particular course of action, a state will follow

---

[78] The Hague Conference, at 9, CAB 38/10/76.

[79] Clarendon to Palmerston, Apr. 15, 1856, *in* FO 27/1169.

[80] For an excellent exposition of this process, *see* Abram Chayes, "An Inquiry into the Working of Arms Control Agreements," *Harvard Law Review* 85, no. 5 (1972).

these interests regardless of the existence of a treaty.[81] This view echoes statements made at the time. "If the interests exist, you will have the support of those whose interests are similar to your own, with or without alliances; if the interests have changed, you will not secure them by alliances which have no longer any binding force."[82] As an example of this interpretation, Great Britain did not need a treaty guaranteeing Belgium: If it was in the British interest to defend Belgium, Britain would do so, and if it was not in Britain's interest, no treaty obligations could secure British intervention. But this narrow view ignores the value of law in both communicating vital interests to third parties, and strengthening and channeling national interests.

Treaty obligations communicated vital interests to other parties. The British participation in the Belgian guarantees signaled a long-standing interest in preventing any great power from gaining control of the Scheldt estuary and harbors near British territory across the English Channel. Moreover, the guarantee could be and was used to rally public support for British intervention when Belgium was invaded. Indeed, Clarendon recommended binding obligations to spare future British governments from the temptation to neglect national interests.[83]

The existence of a treaty could reduce the likelihood that force would be necessary to defend national interests. In 1906, the government contemplated a guarantee of Spanish territory opposite Gibraltar in return for a Spanish promise never to cede the territory to another power. While expressing dislike of guarantees, the Admiralty noted "it seems very doubtful whether we should ever be called upon to fulfil this obligation to Spain by force of arms, if we frankly announced our attitude (and gave a 'hands off' notice to the world thereby.)"[84]

The guarantee of Sweden in 1855 similarly was intended to signal British commitment to Scandinavian independence. British Prime Minister Palmerston noted that Britain had fought the Crimean War to counter Russian aggression in Turkey, and that as Britain had a similar interest in halting Russian expansion into the north, "if we can do so by Inkshed instead of by Bloodshed surely it is wise to take the opportunity to do so." He further explained:

[81] Howard, *Britain and the Casus Belli*, 172.

[82] Sir William Harcourt, *Hansard*, 4th ser., LVIII, 1420, June 10, 1898.

[83] Clarendon to Palmerston, Apr. 12, 1856, Clarendon Papers, C. 135, ff. 540–541.

[84] Charles Ottley, Memorandum, Dec. 14, 1906, *in* Admiralty – Grey Correspondence: Admiralty 1905–1913, FO 800/87, (1905–1913), 88–89.

First of all the Knowledge of such a Treaty would be a powerful check upon Russia and would prevent her from pressing Sweden .... In the next Place Sweden if left free to act as she liked might have Inducements held out to her which might make her willing to consent to what Russia wants ... the Swedish Government if unshackled might think the Bargain a good one for Sweden, but it would be a very bad one for us; and yet if there was no Treaty we should have no Right to object.[85]

Palmerston also acknowledged a third justification for legally binding agreements here by remarking on the creation of mutual interests. In the absence of an agreement, Swedish policy might have evolved in an opposite direction into the Russian orbit, but a decision to enter into a treaty made such a reversal more difficult politically.

Law's Function in Strengthening Mutual Interests

Law could strengthen mutual interests, thus the existence of a treaty might prevent a state from drifting into an antagonistic position. Great Britain entered into an alliance with Japan in 1902, partly in order to preempt a Russo-Japanese arrangement.[86] After Japan's victory over Russia in 1905, it became more important to Great Britain to keep Japan on friendly terms, and thus the treaty was repeatedly renewed.[87] International law channeled Japanese policy into a parallel course with British interests. Both Japan and Great Britain were compelled to make public decisions about the future course of their foreign relations when entering into the alliance, which closed other doors. Had statesmen believed that national interest operated purely independently of international law, there would have been no point in attempting to keep Japan on friendly terms through a treaty. Moreover, British diplomats were not alone in their use of alliances. Bismarck's com-

[85] Palmerston to Clarendon, Sep. 25, 1855, Clarendon Papers, C. 50, ff.98–99. See Howard, *Britain and the Casus Belli*, 57.

[86] Ian H. Nish, *The Anglo-Japanese Alliance: The Diplomacy of Two Island Empires 1894–1907* (London: Athlone Press, 1966), 167, 94–95, 230. Nish noted that while Great Britain and Japan had interests in common, "it was necessary to codify their common interests in the diplomatic language of a treaty ...", 239–240. Marder, *The Anatomy of British Sea Power*, 427–28.

[87] Marder, *Dreadnought*, Vol. I, 238. Although outside the timeframe of this present study, in 1921, the British attempted to gain American adherence to the Anglo-Japanese alliance, recognizing explicitly the value of the treaty in keeping Japanese policy aligned with that of the West. One correspondent described it as placing a bad elephant "between two good elephants to behave." Memorandum by Fletcher of a Conversation with Willert, May 31,

plex system attempted to prevent Germany's neighbors from sliding into antagonistic positions.[88] While the Prussian statesman may have shown disdain for the concept of international law, Bismarck still utilized it in securing Germany's future.

* * *

International legal agreements, at the very least, could serve to warn third parties of a state of relations, thus deterring conflict. Agreements could also channel the expectations of the parties, by specifying what behavior was acceptable. Additionally, agreements could create national interests, by creating factions with a government tied to passage of the treaty, and by creating awareness among the public of certain concerns. Law played a role by creating an obligation that was expected to be binding. Statesmen feared entering into binding agreements without serious consideration of the consequences; thus if an agreement was concluded, it was after serious reflection and some measure of acceptance of the obligations by at least some factions within the state. While law could perform a limited function by increasing international stability, enforcement remained a significant means of ensuring that stability.

ENFORCEMENT OF LEGAL OBLIGATIONS AND EXPECTATIONS OF WAR

Even if the British Foreign Office held international law to be as binding as other forms of domestic law, the means of enforcing it remained weak and uneven. States enforced international law through a spectrum of measures ranging from peaceful negotiation to open war. With no international court capable of determining rights and duties, the legal system

---

1921, Dep. of State 741.9411/96, *as quoted in* Thomas H. Buckley, *The United States and the Washington Conference, 1921–1922* (Knoxville, Tennessee: University of Tennessee Press, 1970), 30. Prior to the Washington Conference of 1921, the British stressed the goal of maintaining the alliance "as we cannot afford to risk the open hostility of Japan." Victor Wellesley, General Survey of Political Situation in Pacific and Far East with Reference to the Forthcoming Washington Conference, Oct. 20, 1921, *in* Washington Conference Memoranda, FO 412/118 (1921) at 3.

[88] W. N. Medlicott, *Bismarck, Gladstone, and the Concert of Europe* (London: Athlone Press, 1956), 41–44. In 1880 Russia sought an alliance with Germany to circumvent that nation's hostility, rather than to affirm common interests. *Id.*, 41.

remained largely one of self-help, although public opinion and self-interest also motivated third parties to uphold the law. As previously mentioned, no international court existed that was capable of determining rights and duties. More importantly, even if adjudication was possible, increasingly in the form of arbitration, no international police force existed that was capable of enforcing a decision. However, compliance with international law more often came about from subtle influences, and this compliance was sufficient for statesmen to set expectations of future behavior.

Legal compliance usually did not require legal enforcement, and the threat of compulsion generally arose secondarily as a motivation. Even Bismarck, no champion of morality in international affairs, recognized the value of law:

> [T]he plain and searching words of a treaty are not without influence on diplo-
> macy when it is concerned with precipitating or averting a war; nor are even
> treacherous and violent governments usually inclined to an open breach of
> faith, so long as the *force majeure* of imperative interests does not intervene.[89]

Compliance usually arose from habit and the realization that self-interest required cooperation.[90] The interests of states "meet and cross each other at so many points that there is generally, before long, some point at which the offender is made to feel the loss of sympathy which his conduct has

---

[89] Otto von Bismarck, *Otto Von Bismarck, The Man and the Statesman*, trans. A. J. Butler (New York: Harper & Brothers, 1899), Vol. II, 270–71. The crux of Austin's theory was that without the threat of compulsion and the authority to administer it, law "properly so-called" did not exist. But "the largest number of rules which men obey are obeyed unconsciously from a mere habit of mind. Men do sometimes obey rules for fear of the punishment which will be inflicted if they are violated, but, compared with the mass of men in each community, this class is but small ..." Maine, *International Law*, 50.

[90] "There must be a coercive force somewhere, because mankind obeys that law, nations obey it. In the first place there is the force of opinion. In the next place, there is the force of pacific retaliation, of restrained intercourse, of international boycotting and outlawry, of unfriendly legislation. And then, finally, there is the supreme arbiter and coercive force of war." Davis, *A Treatise on International Law*, 26, see 26–28; "In reality the source of its strength are three: (i) a regard – which in a moral community often flickers but seldom entirely dies – for national reputation as affected by international public opinion; (ii) an unwillingness to incur the risk of war for any but a paramount national interest; (iii) the reali-sation by each nation that the convenience of settled rules is cheaply purchased, in the major-ity of cases, by the habit of individual compliance." Frederick Erwin Smith, *International Law*, 2nd edn (London: Dent and Co., 1903), 16; *See also* Maine, *International Law* (1888) 50; Halleck, *Elements of International Law*, 54.

occasioned."[91] A state contemplating a breach of one of the many treaty obligations could expect a response.

A state injured by a breach of a legal obligation could calibrate its response depending upon the circumstances. A minor infraction by an ally might draw only a diplomatic protest, whereas a similar breach by an unfriendly nation might justify the abrogation of a treaty relationship. Moreover, international law did not dictate the manner of response. A state could choose to nullify a treaty that had been breached or abrogate a separate agreement. Direct negotiation was the primary method for resolving disputes. If negotiation failed, states could also undertake retorsion, which involved treating subjects of the offending nation in a similar manner to that complained of, reprisals, by seeking compensation in other areas, or embargo.[92]

*   *   *

Ultimately, war remained as an option to enforce claims of legal right. Prior to the Kellogg–Briand Pact of 1928, war remained a legitimate means of upholding legal rights, although states had to exhaust all peaceful means first.[93] Legal scholars of the era likened war to trial, albeit a medieval sort of trial by combat.[94] Phillimore compared war to criminal law, as a necessary result of the depraved nature of society,[95] although he also made a finer distinction, noting that international law held no truly criminal sanctions. Unlike criminal law, where sanctions could be levied against individuals, the law of war held that an aggrieved state only had the right to take actions necessary for compensation, but had no further right to punish. Generally, international law held that conceptions of limited warfare prevailed, as states had no authority to take action beyond that necessary to vindicate rights.[96] This limitation upon the rights within war could also

---

[91] Westlake, *Chapters on the Principles of International Law*, 7.

[92] Travers Twiss, *The Law of Nations Considered as Independent Political Communities*, Vol. I On the Right and Duties of Nations in Time of Peace (Oxford: Oxford University Press, 1861), 18, 20–21; Phillimore, *Commentaries Upon International Law*, Vol. III, 59–67.

[93] Phillimore, *Commentaries upon International Law*, (1857) Vol. III, 60.

[94] Travers Twiss, *The Law of Nations Considered as Independent Political Communities*, Vol. II On the Rights and Duties of Nations in Time of War (Oxford: Oxford University Press, 1863), vii.

[95] Phillimore, *Commentaries Upon International Law*, Vol. III, 99.

[96] *Id.*, Vol. III, 100; Twiss, *Law of Nations*, Vol. I, vii; Wheaton, *Elements of International Law*, 249–53.

be seen in the intricate relations existing between neutrals and belligerents described in most legal texts of the period. A state of law continued to exist between belligerents, and between belligerents and neutrals.

This conception of war had two implications. The first implication was that limited war justified wartime regulations. It had long been recognized that treaty relations could continue between belligerents in time of war, if the states specified this within the treaty.[97] In effect, states could limit their rights by treaty, just as they could limit other rights in peacetime. Moreover, concepts of humanity had traditionally been recognized in warfare – for instance, prohibitions on the use of poisons dated back to antiquity.[98] These prohibitions were never absolute, and coexisted in an uneasy tension with the dictates of national survival, held to be the primary obligation of the state.[99] But implicitly it was recognized that states could limit their freedom in areas central to the exercise of sovereignty.[100] This evolution underlay the nineteenth-century development of the law of war, including much of arms control law.

Second, the concept of limited war spoke volumes about nineteenth-century perceptions about the future of war, and of the nature of international relations. International law was predicated on expectations of limited war, as neutrals were vital to wartime enforcement. International law possessed different means of enforcement in peacetime and in wartime. In peacetime, a state could respond to a breach of a legal obligation in many ways, by voiding treaty obligations even in unrelated areas. Generally, a state had fewer options to prevent a breach of law in wartime, other than the threat of retaliation. When discussing the failure of the Brussels Conference to discuss the limitation of reprisals, it was noted:

At the same time her Majesty's Government cannot conceal from themselves that, in passing over these Articles in silence, the Delegates really evaded one of the principal difficulties inherent in any scheme for the preparation of Rules of War to be observed by belligerents, namely the question how those rules are to be enforced. Rules of international law in which the interests of

---

[97] Wheaton, *Elements of International Law*, 191; Lawrence, *A Handbook of Public International Law*, 66–67; Von Martens, *A Compendium of the Law of Nations*, 56–57.

[98] Phillimore, *Commentaries Upon International Law*, Vol. III, 143. Even if these rules were not always observed, their breach gave rise to rights, including retaliation.

[99] Wheaton, *Elements of International Law*, 81.

[100] *Id.*, 82.

neutrals and belligerents are concerned can be enforced in the last resort by recourse to war. In the case, however, of countries already engaged in hostilities, there will be no means, except by reprisals, for either Belligerent to enforce upon the other the observance of any set Rules.[101]

The other means of enforcement in wartime was through neutral pressure.[102] Third parties often had vested interests in upholding legal rights as neutrals, for instance with the right to conduct maritime trade with belligerents. Belligerents like Great Britain sought to use a preponderance of naval power to halt the maritime trade of an opponent. When overzealousness in halting trade led to stretching the laws of blockade and maritime capture, neutrals who lost their shipping on the high seas protested. The willingness of the United States to go to war with Great Britain in 1812 over perceived violations of maritime rights exemplified the possibility of enforcement by a neutral, as did its declaration of war on Germany in 1917.

The expectation of neutral enforcement of international law betrayed a belief that a general Europe-wide war was unlikely. As many of its principles could only be enforced by neutral third parties, the volumes written on this avenue of enforcement indicated a belief that future conflict would leave numerous powerful states as neutrals – states which would be capable of upholding the law. This assumption reflected the model of European conflict between 1815 and 1914, in which no more than two or three great powers were directly involved in warfare at any point.

Even before 1815, the French Revolutionary and Napoleonic wars provided the "Great War" by which statesmen measured total warfare, and throughout the course of these wars, there were always neutral great powers capable and willing to intervene. Unlike the total warfare of the twentieth-century world wars, in which powers generally fought to the bitter end on one side or the other, during the era 1792–1815, all five great powers only simultaneously engaged in war once, and then only briefly between the collapse of the summer armistice in 1813 and the April 1814 abdication of Napoleon – eight months out of the 23-year period. After the rise of Napoleon, most of the wars, with the notable exception of the Spanish conflict, involved rapid campaigns and capitulations, followed by a reshuffling of the diplomatic deck. With the exception of Anglo-French hostility, all the other powers – Prussia, Austria, Russia, Spain if it

---

[101] Foreign Office to Loftus, Jan. 20, 1875, *in* FO 83/485.
[102] Westlake, *Chapters on the Principles of International Law*, 232–33.

is included as a power – either switched sides or were willing to do so, and even English commitment to the anti-French crusade was doubted by the continental powers.[103] The diplomatic situation remained fluid to the very end, with the possibility of a breakup of the coalition during the Congress of Vienna. To the nineteenth-century diplomat, total war still involved rapid campaigns and multiple opportunities to switch sides, leaving at all times at least one neutral great power capable of entering the conflict. International law of the era provided rationales as well as pretexts for such interventions, seen not only in maintaining the legitimacy of ruling dynasties, but in the League of Armed Neutrality and American protests against British maritime practices in 1812.

This belief in the future of war was partially justifiable. Statesmen could reasonably anticipate America would uphold its interpretations of maritime law as well as adhere to its policy of non-engagement in European affairs, thus serving as a neutral great power in future wars. With regard to maritime war, Britain could realistically expect the legal system to function. It was partly with regard to such a contingency that the Foreign Office sought clear rules of maritime warfare at the London Conference in 1908–1909, reasoning '[i]t would tend to draw a ring fence round the belligerents, and eliminate the risk of a simultaneous contest with a second Power.'[104] But with regard to the laws of war on land, there was no comparable reliably neutral great power with an automatic interest in upholding the rules. The principles upon which lawyers and statesmen spent significant energy were not workable in a general war on the model of the later world wars.

---

[103] Prussia began the period as part of the anti-revolutionary coalition, returned to benevolent neutrality towards France until 1805, fought against France briefly in 1806–1807 before becoming a quasi-satellite providing troops guarding the flank of the French invasion of Russia, then switching sides again in early 1813. Russia remained neutral much of the first decade, entering the coalition against France before Napoleon's seizure of power, then following the peace of Tilsit in 1807 schemed with France in plans to divide Europe before ending up as enemies again in 1812. Spain started in the first coalition against France, soon switching sides until invaded by the French. Austria never sided openly with France, but as late as 1813, sought to maintain Napoleonic France as a counter-weight to Russia, reluctantly entering the war when peace negotiations failed.

[104] The Declaration of London from the Point of View of its effects on Neutral Shipping and Commerce, Feb. 1, 1911, *in* CAB 37/105/6 (1911) at 6. But see Christopher Martin, suggesting that the Admiralty feared intervention by smaller Mediterranean neutral states rather than great powers. Christopher Martin, 'The Declaration of London: A Matter of Operational Capability', *Historical Research* lxxxii, no. 218 (2009): 742–744. Either way, the rules had been crafted to prevent neutral intervention.

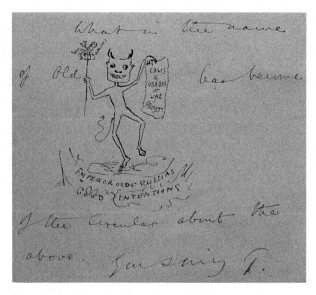

Foreign office sketch of Brussels conference of 1874 (Courtesy of National Archives)

Foreign Office take on the 1874 Brussels Conference project to codify the rules of war: In a hand-drawn sketch incorporated in Foreign Office correspondence, Old Scratch dances on the Emperor of Russia's good intentions while skewering the presiding Russian diplomat at the gathering, Baron Jomini, on a pitchfork and waving the Brussels Declaration. Jan. 27, 1875, in Brussels Conference on the Rules of War, FO 83/485 (1874–1875).

In turn, contemporary opinions of neutral enforcement betrayed an assumption of a shared rationality in interstate politics. Neutral states were expected to offset hegemonic ambitions by great powers. When discussing advances in the laws of war at the 1899 Hague Peace Conference, the *London Times* noted:

A powerful State involved in a life-and-death struggle would be under a strong temptation, if it discovered that it were [*sic*] being hampered by these changes [in the rules of war], to denounce and disregard them ... [H]ow long would a Napoleon have consented to be bound by them after it had become plain that they were costly to him and saved his foes from being utterly crushed? Happily, there is not much likelihood that the world will soon be visited again by another Napoleon. There are so many States of the first order in these days that the power of neutral opinion is very formidable, and it is for the interest generally of neutrals that the horrors, and even the inconveniences, of war should be limited and mitigated.[105]

This assumption that a future Napoleon would bow to the threat of international action would be sorely tested in the twentieth century. Yet in spite of its uncertainty, statesmen at least partially predicated the rules of war on this expectation that shared interests would keep the legal system functional.

When discussing obligations of neutrals states in warfare prior to the 1907 Hague Peace Conference, the CID reasoned:

> The weaker Powers will frequently be unable to do more than protest against violations of their neutrality, unless backed by the strong neutrals. Uniformity of neutrality rules, therefore, appears to be in the interests of all neutrals. The greater the divergence, the greater will be the probability of violations of neutrality at the expense of weak Powers by a belligerent. *A combination of powerful neutrals would be able to exercise a controlling influence over the actions of belligerents.* Failing such a combination, uniformity of neutrality rules – between Great Britain and the United States especially – would be to our advantage if both Powers were neutral. Similarly, our interests as belligerents would best be served if we could count upon the observance by an enemy of definite rules.[106]

The CID hedged its bets, seeking to foster common interests with the United States in case powerful neutrals failed to uphold the legal system. But this remained the contingency plan, and the optimal goal remained the common enforcement of standardized rules by the great powers.

International law evolved in anticipation of short wars, with higher frequency of conflict. As seen from the 1874 Brussels Conference negotiations, statesmen consciously shaped humanitarian rules of war with an intention of limiting lingering hostility after war ended, by reducing the displacement and atrocities attendant on military conflict. Statesmen expected that wars would be brief and sharp, and the goal of the international community would be to heal the wounds as quickly as possible, preventing the development of long-term hatred among adversaries.[107]

---

[105] "Untitled," Aug. 1, 1899, *The (London) Times*, 9.

[106] Emphasis added. The Hague Conference, at 9, CAB 38/10/76.

[107] Phillimore argued that states had to obey rules in war in order to allow peace negotiations. Phillimore, *Commentaries Upon International Law*, Vol. III, 146.

States also had to design law in a manner that reflected the diverse situations they might find themselves in during a war. Great Britain had to carefully frame maritime policy around its role as the world's largest shipping nation requiring protection as a neutral, while not hampering its ability to effectively utilize its sea power as a belligerent.[108] The legal system crafted by diplomats had to reflect assumptions about the scale of war likely to be encountered. If the place of war in the legal system remained a blind spot, the possibility of general war constituted a low-frequency, but high-cost problem. In this sense, the inconsistency appears more glaring to students of twentieth-century world affairs than to nineteenth-century diplomats. Statesmen designed the legal system to avoid war and minimize its effects, and effectively employed treaties as part of overall national security strategies for much of the era between 1815 and 1914.

LEGAL ENFORCEMENT AND INTERNATIONAL ORDER

Nineteenth-century conceptions of international law were intrinsically bound up with perceptions of international order. After 1815, the central preoccupation of the state system was in preventing a further revolution on the model of France in 1789. Lawyers and statesmen devised broad theories justifying great power intervention in the internal affairs of other states to prevent revolution from occurring, by arguing that revolution inherently posed an international threat.[109] More generally, after 1815, the international legal order broadly acknowledged a special role to be played by the great powers, the Concert of Europe, in preserving European peace and order.[110] By the second half of the century, many argued that the European Concert was evolving into an institution of law enforcement. Gerry

[108] Edmund Slade made this point during the London Conference in an internal memo while discussing the laws of contraband: "Also, we must not forget that we are not always belligerent. During the last century we have more often been neutral than belligerent, and during the century before more often belligerent than neutral." Edmund Slade, Memorandum of Dec. 14, 1908, at 3, *in* London Conference on International Maritime Law, ADM 116/1079, Part 2 (1908–1909).

[109] Phillimore justified intervention upon the balance of power. Phillimore, *Commentaries Upon International Law*, Vol. I. 574, 76–77. The doctrine of intervention remained problematic in international law, and subject to abuse. Thus, it did not receive full acceptance by all authorities. See Lawrence, *A Handbook of Public International Law*, 31–33.

[110] Twiss, *Law of Nations*, Vol. II, 16; Thomas Joseph Lawrence, *Essays on Some Disputed Questions in Modern International Law*, 2nd ed. (Cambridge: Deighton, Bell & Co., 1885), 209.

Simpson explored the cyclical shift between equality and great power hegemony within international law more extensively, noting that the early nineteenth century witnessed a high point for great power hegemony.[111] The notion of a special status for the great powers grated with the long-standing conception of equality among states in international law, but state practice appeared to confirm this evolution.[112] As T. J. Lawrence put it in 1885:

> The foregoing examples [from 1815 to 1882] by no means exhaust the subject; but they are sufficient to shew [sic] that the Great Powers have by modern usage a position of preeminence in European affairs, which is so marked, and has such important legal results, that the old doctrine of the absolute equality before International Law of all sovereign states is no longer applicable. It is not merely that the stronger states have influence proportionate to their strength; but that custom has given them what can hardly be distinguished from a legal right to settle certain questions as they please, the smaller states being obliged to acquiesce in their decisions.[113]

The great powers used the occasional meetings of the Concert of Europe to resolve standing questions threatening the general peace.[114] The Concert met in various forms prior to 1878, not as a formally organized body, but ad hoc. Despite the lack of formality to the system, the geopolitical weight behind its great power members, and the role they assigned to the Concert in resolving questions, lent authority to it as an institution. While few statesmen would openly admit this growing authority, as it would offend long-standing notions of equality of states, treaty practice tended to confirm it.[115] Some international lawyers believed that the Concert of Europe increasingly possessed both legislative and judicial powers, and was capable of enforcing its decisions on small states.[116] Without judging the morality of this evolution, it was hoped that a system of the great powers could eventually evolve into a true international institution.[117] These assessments

---

[111] Simpson, *Great Powers and Outlaw States*, 115.

[112] Lawrence, *A Handbook of Public International Law*, 51–52.

[113] Lawrence, *Essays*, 226–27. See also Westlake, *Chapters on the Principles of International Law*, 92, 98 recognizing the existence of the European Concert while not conceding legal inequality.

[114] *See* Grewe, *The Epochs of International Law*, 429 et. seq.

[115] *See,* for example, Foreign Secretary Viscount Castlereagh's views on the role of great powers in Simpson, *Great Powers and Outlaw States*, 99.

[116] Lawrence, *Essays*, 228, 30.

[117] Westlake, *Chapters on the Principles of International Law*, 100–01; Lawrence, *Essays*, 232–33.

were not based on a sanguine view of the great powers' motivations, but merely a realistic appraisal of their role in international society. Moreover, the Security Council of the United Nations has since evolved to fulfill a similar function within international law. The great powers possessed the capability to enforce the law in disputes involving smaller states, even if they lacked the full capacity to uphold the law in controversies with other great powers. At its heart was the understanding that law had to reflect existing power structures. This is not to say law merely abdicated its place to politics, as law could also slow the drift of states into proscribed behavior. It is merely to say that while law could have an effect, it could best do so when it harnessed existing forces in the international environment. Similarly, the balance of power, while sometimes referred to as a political institution, was generally seen as integral to the system of international law.[118]

However, the European Concert, the balance of power, and international law generally, proved an uncertain source of order. Lawrence hoped that the system of alliances could eventually serve a legal function and ensure peace, but his view was not universally accepted.[119] Phillimore noted that a "league of protection" would better uphold the law on behalf of small states, and that the policy of law founded upon a single principle of international law, namely order, at the expense of other principles, would be fatal to the peace.[120] Large states were far more likely to get away with breaching their obligations than small states, an observation confirmed by the CID comments on the violations of neutral rights in the previous section.[121] This consequence flowed naturally from the self-help aspect of enforcement. "What is the sanction of international law? It is self-help in its most licentious form: for international law professes itself unable to regulate the occasions on which resort may be made to war, the litigation of states."[122] While international law may be considered true

---

[118] Phillimore, *Commentaries Upon International Law*, Vol. I, 589. Wheaton held the view that the balance of power was political and lay outside the law, although states that truly disturbed the European equilibrium generally did so overtly, furnishing substantive grounds to justify war. Wheaton, *Elements of International Law*, 82–83. *See generally*, Vagts and Vagts, "Balance of Power in International Law."

[119] Westlake, *Chapters on the Principles of International Law*, 265–66. Koskenniemi suggests that the *Institut de droit international* also rejected Henry Maine as a member because of his defense of alliances. Koskenniemi, *The Gentle Civilizer of Nations*, 75.

[120] Phillimore, *Commentaries Upon International Law*, Vol. I, 588–89.

[121] The Hague Conference, at 9, CAB 38/10/76.

[122] Smith, *International Law*, 9.

law, it "is habitually deficient in that coercive side of the term law ..."[123] Also, even amongst the great powers, the recognition that military force was perceived as the final deciding factor and that international law lacked definite means of enforcement short of war also weakened the system.[124]

Finally, even when an agreement was deemed binding, states could find a way to redefine how obligations were to be discharged. In certain respects, this created a greater challenge for effective international law than the risk of open breaches. As no court possessed mandatory jurisdiction to adjudicate on the nature of legal commitments, each state was left to determine how obligations were to be fulfilled. International lawyers often came up with colorable interpretations rationalizing their state's conduct. For instance, in 1877, when Disraeli's government faced the unpopular option of militarily defending the Ottoman Empire or breaching the terms of the Tripartite Guarantee of 1856, the Foreign Secretary Derby instead chose to reinterpret the treaty in a manner relieving Britain of obligation to intervene.[125] By lawyerly reinterpreting and recasting the obligations contained in the agreement, Britain could avoid any duty to Turkey.

In fact, much of Salisbury's opposition to binding engagements arose from indeterminacy of language. He did not oppose onerous obligations so much as vague duties, which could be circumvented, and sought to frame them in such a manner that they would be likely to be upheld.[126] His record as Foreign Secretary indicated that he never disputed that treaties were binding, but insisted on concise obligations so as to prevent parties from evading their duties.

Statesmen still had to please two audiences – one domestic and one international. Maneuvers such as that undertaken by Derby might be more likely to convince the British public, particularly if the obligation was as unpopular as the Turkish guarantee was. But such a course would still leave the international community skeptical. States still had to answer to the international community to the extent that they valued good relations, thus the sanction of international law remained relative to national power and the degree of interdependence of the state in question.

---

[123] Id., 16.

[124] Maine, International Law, 52–53.

[125] See Howard, Britain and the Casus Belli, 112. The Foreign Office avoided the issue of obligations by claiming that Turkey had no right to invoke the provisions; only the other great power parties could activate the casus belli, none of whom had any interest in doing so.

[126] Id., 104, 11–12.

British foreign policy consistently attempted to maintain respect for international law, while functioning within a system dominated by the great powers. Salisbury summarized this position shortly before the Greco-Turkish war of 1897, when responding to Liberal calls to abandon the 1856 treaties negotiated by the powers to protect the Ottoman Empire:

> [T]he federated action of Europe – if we can maintain it, if we can maintain this Legislature – is our sole hope of escaping from the constant terror and the calamity of war, the constant pressure of the burdens of an armed peace which weigh down the spirits and darken the prospects of every nation in this part of the world. ["Hear, hear!"] The federation of Europe is the only hope we have; but that federation is only to be maintained by observing the conditions on which every Legislature must depend, on which every judicial system must be based – the engagements into which it enters must be respected. ["Hear, hear!"] They must not be treated as pieces of waste paper to be torn asunder at will in obedience to any poetical, or rhapsodical, or classical feeling that may arise.[127]

He recognized that the federated action of Europe, by which he meant the great powers, could only slowly reach and act on decisions, and would only act in the national interest, but that this constituted the most feasible means of maintaining international stability through law. While begrudgingly acknowledging any legal character to international law, treaties could not "be treated as pieces of waste paper" if the system was to have any chance.[128]

Breaches of international law were infrequent, although they could have large consequences when they occurred. In fact, it was usually the egregious breaches and the shredding of "scraps of paper" that have gained the attention of historians and the public, not the more numerous, mundane instances of compliance. While international law possessed weak sanctions, it did provide statesmen with a greater degree of predictability

[127] Salisbury, *Hansard* 4th ser., XLVII, 1013, Mar. 19, 1897.
[128] In an earlier piece, he simultaneously warned against overreliance on international law, noted the lack of legal institutions à la Austin, yet acknowledged the role of law as a grammar for international relations and an obstacle to transgressions or in his words, "to many States, less quietly disposed, they diminish the temptations of war." Salisbury, "The Land Question of Ireland: Issued by the Irish Land Committee," *Quarterly Review*, 151, no. 302, (Apr. 1881): 543–544.

in international relations. Not unlike domestic law, international law functions more by creating sufficient predictability for interstate relations to function. Although never deterring all illegal conduct, international law provided enough stability for relations to continue. As a result, enforcement of legal obligations remained an intricate diplomatic pirouette. Dependent upon the international political situation, national strength, and interest in the question at stake, enforcement remained tentative. While international legal theory tabulated numerous rights and duties within the international community, rights which all states recognized in the abstract, it remained another question when such rights were ripe for upholding within a concrete factual context.

Great power legal enforcement had several implications. First, it meant that small powers had very little leverage against the great powers unless they found a stronger ally. Second, among great powers, the system worked best when neutral great powers influenced the conduct of other states. Yet within these constraints, statesmen were able to conceive a practical role for law. Laws of maritime warfare prevented limited wars from dragging in neutral states, while alliances, guarantees, and status quo agreements set boundaries for great power rivalries, and the humanization of land warfare held out the potential that conflicts would be short, sharp, and soon forgotten. By working within existing diplomatic structures and exploiting the contours of the great power system, law could contribute to international security. Law could not solve all problems, but in order for it to play a role, it needed to reflect these underlying power structures. As Mr. Dooley realized, all the biggest crooks *were* on the police force.

CONCLUSION

International law could never fully eliminate banned conduct, and statesmen never expected it to do so. At best it could function as "an obstacle but not a barrier." Only by keeping in mind what international law could and could not do is it possible to understand what British statesmen expected from arms control negotiations at the turn of the century. The historian's perception of international law is central to how arms control initiatives such as the Hague Peace Conferences or the Anglo-German naval arms dialogue are evaluated. If one perceives international law in terms of world courts and international police enforcement, then two interpretations of British arms control initiatives seem logically to follow: Either statesmen who sought arms control were utterly naïve about the realities of world affairs, seeking unrealizable utopian goals, or, alternatively, they were cynical practitioners of *realpolitik*, never expecting agreements to materialize but utilizing negotiations to embarrass foreign competitors and maintain domestic pacifist support. Certainly, foreign policy-makers were at times motivated by naivety and cynicism. Yet this fails to convey the full story.

A broader view of international law must recognize that law could fulfill its function of increasing predictability in international relations in connection with other elements of policy-making. While law could never serve as an alternative to traditional methods of ensuring national security, it could be utilized to bolster a state's position. If the historian keeps in mind the intended uses and limitations of international law, British arms control strategy can be placed in its true context. International law in the nineteenth century provided an instrument for advancing the national interest. Like other elements of national policy, such as economic clout or military power, the efficacy of law was uncertain and often shifting. A state could not base its security planning solely upon international law, any more than a state could rely entirely upon its own arms. But law could play a role in security planning, and contemporary practice of law perceived a central position for legal relationships in upholding the strategic balance of power.

In order for law to serve its function of facilitating stability, it was necessary to set expectations that could be fulfilled. If law attempted to undertake too bold a task, it could not succeed. Moreover, even when attempting to utilize law in more limited negotiations, statesmen had to craft effective regulations that could accomplish national goals. The following two chapters will detail the challenges faced by international law when setting unrealistic regulations, as seen with the quest for disarmament at The Hague in 1899 in Chap. 4, and when setting limited goals, as seen in the emerging area of naval arms control in the early 1900s in Chap. 5.

CHAPTER 4

The First Hague Peace Conference

INTRODUCTION

The First Hague Peace Conference needs to be viewed not simply as the first step in twentieth-century developments, but as a culmination of nineteenth-century trends. For diplomatic historians, the focus is often on the following 15 years, and ultimately the failure of international law to halt the war in 1914. In this view, the Hague Peace Conference was merely a footnote in the story of the road to war, exemplifying the unrealistic and utopian goals of a segment of the population who had sought to limit armaments, set rules for war, and create a system for peacefully resolving disputes.[1] Others note the role of the conference as a starting point for twentieth-century developments in international law and international organization, emphasizing legal precedents set by its conventions and the foundation of an embryonic international judicial system.[2] A fuller exposition of the conference needs

---

[1] Tate, *The Disarmament Illusion*; Marder, *The Anatomy of British Sea Power*, 341 et. seq.; Jost Dülffer, "Chances and Limits of Arms Control 1898–1914," in *An Improbable War. The Outbreak of World War I and European Political Culture before 1914*, ed. Holger Afflerbach and David Stevenson (New York: Berghahn Books, 2004); Davis, *The United States and the First Hague Peace Conference*.

[2] Between 1962 and 1975, Calvin Davis reevaluated his position regarding the First Hague Peace Conference, acknowledging it as a step in the further evolution of international law. Davis, *The United States and the Second Hague Peace Conference*, viii; *see also* Detlev Vagts, "The Hague Conventions and Arms Control," *American Journal of International Law* 94, no. 1 (2000): 31–41.

© The Editor(s) (if applicable) and The Author(s) 2016
S.A. Keefer, *The Law of Nations and Britain's Quest for Naval Security*, DOI 10.1007/978-3-319-39645-3_4

to place it in the context of its past, as one of a series of nineteenth-century conferences designed to codify international law. While the stir created by the Czar's proposal increased popular expectations of the gathering, and politicians acknowledged the historic significance of the conference, responsible diplomats had low expectations and perceived it as a political maneuver. Moreover from prior experience, statesmen predicted specific coalitions of states, and planned the conference on these expectations.

At The Hague in 1899 the general lack of interest in arms limitation doomed the topic. Even if the political will had been present, the framing of the proposals as general disarmament, rather than limited arms control, diminished the likelihood that anything significant would be accomplished. The defining of the project as disarmament pigeonholed it with earlier proposals, posed for political capital more than practical results. While the original program spoke only of limited steps, the broad scope of the project, together with popular anticipation that the conference would yield great results, increased the political stakes. Unlike its predecessor at Brussels in 1874, statesmen were obliged to have concrete results by the close of the conference, rather than merely drafting a working text for future study.

The Hague agenda items relating to the rules of war immediately evoked unresolved issues from 1874. The 1874 conference was perceived as a model for political alignment in 1899. The Belgians were particularly concerned that Britain would not renew its leadership role in representing the interests of small countries. However, Great Britain at both conferences sought to organize a coalition of small powers to avoid the creation of a "code of conquest." Major-General Sir John Ardagh framed the British position on the laws of war within this context. Moreover, the Brussels Conference established a working method intended for the Hague Conference that has been somewhat obscured in hindsight. The Brussels Conference was more a forum for airing opinions than for the negotiation of binding instruments. Indeed, the conference was initially inspired by nongovernmental organizations seeking further codification before the proposal was taken over by governments. At Brussels, the final protocol of the conference was signed by all the delegates as an accurate summary of their discussions, then sent home for further deliberations on whether it would be codified as a binding treaty. The British delegate signed the document under this understanding, as Great Britain opposed much of the code and ultimately ended the project by refusing to sign or ratify a binding agreement the following January.

The Hague Conference was initially conceived as a forum for discussing views on how arms could be limited, rather than for the immediate goal of limiting armaments. It was in part for this reason that political questions were to be excluded. The conference organizer, Russia, envisioned that the best methods of limiting armaments could be discussed in abstract, then experts could work out the details and present governments with a formal proposal for a binding treaty after the conference. Like the earlier gathering in 1874, the goal was to produce a general statement which might later be used to craft a binding treaty. However, the 1899 Conference received far greater publicity and roused public expectations that the drafts produced at the conference would eventually become binding agreements, ultimately limiting candid discussions of the issues.

The proposals followed the pattern of earlier efforts in 1816, 1831, and in the 1860s. Like these calls by Russian Czar Alexander I, French King Louis Philippe, and French Emperor Napoleon III, respectively, disarmament was a response to the threat of unrest posed by excessive government expenditure. The First Hague Peace Conference differed from these other initiatives in the manner of the announcement. The Russian Circular of 1898 was a diplomatic bombshell even to Russian ally France. Despite the public clamor, the 1898 circular did not differ greatly from previous initiatives. Disarmament had been a common political tool used for both domestic audiences and the international community. Differences in opinion could be used to embarrass dissenting nations, while common positions on armaments signaled broader consensus on diplomatic issues.[3]

In terms of specific armaments proposals, the Hague Peace Conference seemed poised to follow the precedent set at St. Petersburg in 1868 with the British government anticipating a refinement of earlier limitations on needlessly cruel weapons. In 1898, the advent of quick-firing artillery led Russia to seek a moratorium to spare the industrializing country the expense. As in 1868, the British negotiators were reluctant to relinquish technological advantages, and both the Admiralty and the War Office opposed nearly every limit on the agenda. However, the Admiralty was willing to advocate limits that would bolster its strategic position. Notably,

[3] The French disarmament overtures toward Prussia in 1870 are a case in point. Napoleon III made these initiatives both to please a domestic audience in the evolving Liberal empire by attempting to limit the burden of armaments and to signal a broader Anglo-French relationship to a hostile Prussia. J. L. Herkless, "Lord Clarendon's Attempt at Franco-Prussian Disarmament, January to March 1870," *Historical Journal* 15, no. 3 (1972).

Salisbury's government undertook a previously unpublished and unreported secret naval arms control initiative with Russia shortly before the Hague Conference. Thus, British opposition was never complete.

By placing the First Hague Peace Conference in the context of earlier legal reform and prior arms limitation proposals, the expectations held by British diplomats can be more fully understood. Instead of interpreting the results merely as a repudiation of any legal regulation of armaments, the gathering reflected a lack of common interest at that time as well as the inherent difficulty in disarmament. In this context, concerns expressed at The Hague regarding the limitations of national sovereignty and the utopian requirement of an international police force should be reassessed. These reservations centered upon objections to disarmament, while diplomats still acknowledged less radical arms limitations could be enshrined in law. However, these assumptions that law could serve a role were rarely made explicit, and can best be gleaned from long-standing state practice.

Law could play a role in regulating armaments, but the most successful measures in the nineteenth century were limited arrangements, while grand attempts at general disarmament failed. Agreements like the Black Sea Treaty indicated a need for provisions to be easily verified, an impossible condition for a general armament treaty binding the majority of the nations of the world. Limited treaties did not draw the same criticism regarding enforcement mechanisms. Bilateral agreements, like the Anglo-French or the Anglo-American treaties, provided an easier format for limiting arms than general multilateral gathering like that at The Hague. The experience in 1899 showed that arms control could play a role in foreign policy planning, but that much also depended on how much was expected from law.

INTERNATIONAL LAW AND GENERAL DISARMAMENT

Disarmament posed greater challenges for international law than did arms control. As a result, scholarly works on general disarmament were theoretical, often based on the hypothesis that the creation of some form of international police power was possible. Arms control, or the limitation of only certain categories or levels of armaments, left the parties with means of self-defense. In contrast, general disarmament required states to sacrifice their ability to defend themselves. As a legal question, general disarmament also eliminated this ultimate means of enforcing disarmament obligations. In order to ensure security and enforcement, theoretical

writing on general disarmament focused upon the radical reorganization
of international society. The theoretical nature of this writing clearly distinguished these works from other scholarly works describing the existing
international system.

General disarmament remained a vaguely defined concept throughout
the era, sometimes referring to the complete abolition of weaponry, but
often just entailing a substantial reduction in military forces. At its core,
disarmament required different methods of enforcement. Limited arms
agreements functioned within the existing system of international law,
through traditional methods of state enforcement. General disarmament
presupposed a radical shift in international relations, either through more
peaceful relations or through deeper international integration. The successful arms control initiatives of the nineteenth century generally did not
aim to fundamentally alter international relations and were predicated on
continuing interstate competition. Arms control merely sought to channel
competition away from destabilizing activities to sustainable interactions.

However, the terminological ambiguity contributed to a muddled
debate. While Europe had ample arms control precedents from which
to develop new limitations, general disarmament shifted international
law onto entirely new grounds. While precedents hinted at means of sur-
mounting hurdles of national sovereignty, accurate comparisons of armaments, verification, and enforcement, these issues had only been handled
in limited agreements. When statesmen discussed general disarmament,
these questions were reopened. The problem was compounded by a general lack of interest in disarmament. Statesmen like Salisbury, who were
sufficiently familiar with international law, could conflate arms limitation
proposals with general disarmament and thereby eviscerate them. By arguing that an international police force or the cession of national sovereignty
would be required, despite having precedents indicating the contrary,
arms control could be killed by criticism applicable to disarmament.

*   *   *

Given the great complexities involved in measuring comparative armaments, and the unrealistic cession of sovereignty required by most
schemes, academic international lawyers entered the debate ambivalently.
At the 1887 meeting of the Institute of International Law in Heidelberg,
when Belgian attorney Gustave Rolin-Jaequemyns raised the question, he
drew the wrath of many members who feared that discussions of such

utopian proposals would bring ridicule to the field of international law.[4] General disarmament directly contradicted established conceptions of sovereignty.[5] Disarmament contradicted the fundamental duty of a sovereign state to defend itself through all means at its disposal. The organization refused to directly debate the topic at their annual gathering, although several opinions were recorded which indicated the state of legal theory.

The co-founder of the Institut de Droit International, Rolin-Jaequemyns asked whether two or more states could limit their ability to arm themselves by treaty, whether such an agreement bound them, and what enforcement measures such an agreement required.[6] After discussing the duty of a state to defend itself and the exposed position of an unarmed state in the midst of its armed neighbors, he answered:

> If it is suicidal for a nation to remain unarmed in the midst of armed neighbours, is it not another method of suicide for a group of nations, united by a common civilization, to allow themselves to be carried away in a body, in a mad rush to cast a constantly increasing portion of their money, credit, physical and intellectual activity each year into the ever-expanding gulf of military expenditures and armaments?[7]

Scottish professor James Lorimer provided an answer to these questions, invoking concepts of arms control. He held that no arms limitation would succeed if it reduced the relative strength of a state compared to its neighbors. Thus, any convention should emphasize proportional reductions.[8] This in turn would institutionalize the status quo, locking national military strength at current levels. In order to create a workable agreement between states with vastly different national characteristics, Lorimer held that governments should regulate expenditure on armaments, rather than reduce

---

[4] Wehberg, *Limitation of Armaments*, 12.

[5] *See, for example,* the German debate over the status of international law in relation to national sovereignty, *in* Koskenniemi, *The Gentle Civilizer of Nations*, 179–228.

[6] M. Gustave Rolin-Jaequemyns, "Limitation conventionelle des dépenses et des effectifs militaires," *Revue de droit international et de législation comparée* 19 (1887): 400.

[7] Proposition of Mr. Rolin-Jaequemyns, *as quoted in Documents Relating to the Program of the First Hague Peace Conference,* 8; M. Gustave Rolin-Jaequemyns, "Limitation conventionelle des dépenses et des effectifs militaires," 403.

[8] James Lorimer, "La Question du désarmement et les difficultés qu'elle soulève au point de vue du droit international," *Revue de droit international et de législation comparée* 19 (1887): 474.

the strength of armies or navies. This would remove the need for excessive international interference in domestic affairs required for the verification of numerical troop limits.[9] Regarding enforcement, Lorimer admitted that at present no international mechanism existed which could guarantee observance of such a treaty. Only a coalition of states could enforce treaty obligations.[10] While Lorimer noted that international law had to work within the confines of the existing diplomatic system, he ultimately championed the ideal of disarmament, using it as an argument for developing a strong international legal system with judicial, executive, and legislative institutions.

Concluding the 1887 debate, Count Leonid Kamarowski, professor of international law at the University of Moscow, argued that law provided the only way to solve the dilemma of an arms race, as no state could limit its armaments alone. As the development of international law had not progressed to a point where states could achieve effective limitations, a series of preliminary conferences in which diplomats laid out their positions on arms control followed by a final congress would provide the most effective means of advancing this area of international regulation. Obligations of limited duration would allow the testing of ideas, and serve as confidence-building measures.[11] Like Lorimer, Kamarowski noted that the contemporary international legal environment could sustain arms control, but not disarmament. He also used this as a starting point to argue for an international police force and a strong legal system. While he carefully defined disarmament as merely the reduction of military forces to actual requirements, the legal institutions he desired placed his scheme in the more utopian category of disarmament.

There were several other legal works on disarmament in the period, which also sought radical international changes as prerequisite. In 1894 Raoul de la Grasserie, a French judge at the court of Rennes, called for complete disarmament over an extended period. Each nation would proportionally disarm, initially three-fifths of its active armies in a preparatory period, and then the remaining two-fifths under international supervision. An international court would fix the size of each national army, allotting troops for the purposes of securing internal order and serving in an international army. Ultimately, an international government and court, reinforced with an arbitration system and backed by this international army,

<hr />

[9] *Id.*, 475.
[10] *Id.*, 476.
[11] Kamarowski, "Quelques réflexions sur les armements croissants de l'europe," 482–84.

would keep peace across the world.[12] The scheme assumed that states would relinquish control of national defense to an international organization and accept severely curtailed freedom of action in international relations. This utterly unrealistic view completely ignored the problem of gaining state acceptance, as well as the practical difficulties of setting appropriate levels of armed forces.

The mechanics of disarmament also proved daunting, as agreement was needed on how to measure military strength. The many factors in determining national strength included not only the size of armies, but also the training of troops, length of military service, industrial capacity, and infrastructure, not to mention geographical differences such as defensive rivers and mountain barriers. American lawyer Dudley Field proposed a limit of one soldier per thousand inhabitants.[13] French professor Alexandre Mérignhac noted that strict proportional limits favored states with larger populations, allowing Germany a larger army than France; he argued instead that peacetime strength at the time of entering the agreement formed a fairer basis.[14] Kamarowski held the total numbers depended on "indices of *real life*," including the number of soldiers needed for domestic security, and for defending colonies and extra-European territory.[15] Lorimer noted that in setting limits colonial soldiers, recruited

[12] Raoul de la Grasserie, *Des Moyens pratiques pour parvenir à la suppression de la paix armée et de la guerre* (Paris: Ancienne librairie germer baillière, 1894), 91–93.

[13] David Dudley Field, *Draft Outlines of an International Code* (New York: Baker, Voorhis and Co., 1872), 367. This effectively amounted to disarmament. While the American Army could still expand under this proposal, other militaries would be reduced to a level only sufficient for internal security. For instance, at this ratio, the peace footing of the German Army of 1899 would have been reduced from 479,229 to 52,000, while the French Army of that year would decline from 547,515 to 38,000. Data drawn from Carroll D. Wright, *The Statesman's Yearbook: Statistical and Historical Annual of the States of the World for the Year 1899* (New York: Macmillan Co., 1899), 511, 24, 76, 90.

[14] Alexandre Mérignhac, *Traité théoretique et pratique de l'arbitrage international* (Paris: Librairie du Recueil Général des Lois et des Arrêts, 1895), 512–13. In 1898, a retired German Lieutenant-Colonel, Rogalla von Bieberstein, agreed that a proportional reduction of troops should account for the need of smaller countries to arm a larger proportion of their population. Rogalla von Bieberstein, *Proposals of Rogalla von Bieberstein*, Zukunft Dec. 3, 1898, *reprinted in* Wehberg, *Limitation of Armaments*, 59–60. Germany, of course, faced a Franco-Russian alliance at that time, in which the far more populous Russian nation greatly outnumbered Germany.

[15] "[L]es indications de *la vie réelle*." [Italics in original.] Kamarowski, "Quelques réflexions sur les armements croissants de l'europe," 484.

from foreign territory and neither paid nor trained to European standards, should not count as the equal to European soldiers.[16] International lawyers also discussed and disputed the value of limiting service length and recruitment age.[17] Naval armaments proposals were less developed, some like Field claiming there was no need to limit construction of warships, for while not quite defensive in their nature, "they are limited in their operations."[18] On the other hand, H. William Blymyer, in presenting his plan for disarmament to the Universal Peace Congress of Berne in 1892, sought the prohibition of any new ship over 3000 tons.[19]

Academic disarmament projects differed from contemporary practice in their advocacy of a broad international government, a proposal unlikely to find acceptance amongst the great powers. Arms control treaties negotiated prior to 1899 had more immediate goals – reducing expenditures and lowering the risk of war – and were designed to function in the existing international system. Academic disarmament projects envisioned a heretofore unprecedented scale of international organization and stability. Many like Kamarowski saw the ultimate answer in an international police force or even more cumbersome arrangements.[20]

Realistically, international law could not directly challenge conventional conceptions of sovereignty. Academicians' focus on concepts of general disarmament complicated matters, as the radical utopian nature of proposed world federations damaged the credibility of international law. When the young Russian Czar Nicholas II issued his call for a conference to discuss the "possible reduction of the excessive armaments which weigh upon all nations," statesmen faced the dilemma of obliging the young ruler while not fettering their nations with unworkable projects.[21]

---

[16] Lorimer, "La Question du désarmement," 475.

[17] See Mérignhac, *Traité théoretique et pratique de l'arbitrage international,* 513–14; A. Souchon, "La Question du désarmement," *Revue générale de droit international public* 1 (1894): 518.

[18] Field, *Draft Outlines of an International Code,* 368. American Captain Mahan, an influential advocate of sea power as well as a delegate to The Hague in 1899, adopted the argument of Field, noting that navies were ineffective instruments of aggression. Mahan, *Armaments and Arbitration,* 67.

[19] H. William Blymyer, Mémoire sur la sanction des arbitrages, *as cited in The Limitation of Armaments,* at 73–74.

[20] Kamarowski, "Quelques réflexions sur les armements croissants de l'europe," 484–85.

[21] Count Mouravieff, *Circular Note of Count Mouravieff to the Diplomatic Representatives Accredited to the Court at Petrograd,* December 30, 1898/January 11, 1899, *as quoted in Documents Relating to the Program of the First Hague Peace Conference,* 1–2.

Ultimately, the course of action advocated by Kamarowski and Lorimer was pursued at the 1899 Hague Conference. The gathering was to be the first of a series of conferences to gain experience in limited reductions of armaments, but with far broader goals.

CALLING OF THE HAGUE CONFERENCE OF 1899

Since the issuance of the first circular of 1898, scholars have questioned the Czar's motives. The call came as a surprise to the European powers, even to Russia's ally France, whom statesmen assumed would have been consulted prior to issuing such a circular.[22] The recent acquisition of quick-firing artillery by Germany and Austria-Hungary probably initially played a major role.[23] The Russian Minister of War, Aleksei Kuropatkin, suggested a bilateral arrangement with Austria-Hungary to postpone the exorbitant expense of supplying the Russian Army with this new gun. However, while financial concerns provided an initial impetus for discussing armaments, the sincerity of the Czar in seeking to halt the arms race should not be underestimated.[24]

Russian policy drew on precedents dating to the beginning of the nineteenth century, when Czar Alexander I had called for a system of stability and peace through international law at the height of the Napoleonic Wars.[25] The nineteenth century provided precedents for the calling of peacetime conferences to discuss the rule of international law in regulating war. Conferences leading to the Geneva Conventions of 1864 and 1868, as well as the St. Petersburg Conference of 1868 and the Brussels Conference of 1874, were all called to discuss military issues, although questions of the laws of war played more of a role than disarmament.[26] Notably, Czar Alexander II called two of these four conferences.[27] As a further parallel, the Russian call for the 1868 St. Petersburg Conference also followed the development of a new weapon, an exploding bullet introduced by the czarist army.[28] Therefore, when the industrially underdevel-

---

[22] Sir E. Monson to the Marquess of Salisbury, 1 September 1898, *in* Correspondence Respecting the Peace Conference Held at the Hague in 1899, FO 412/65, (1898–1900).

[23] Morrill, "Nicholas II and the Call for the First Hague Conference," 298–99.

[24] *Id.*

[25] Choate, *The Two Hague Conferences*, 3–4.

[26] Scott, *The Hague Peace Conferences of 1899 and 1907*, Vol. 1, 18–19.

[27] *Id.*, Vol. 1, 23.

[28] *Id.*, Vol. 1, 21.

oped empire faced the introduction of another technologically advanced weapon into world arsenals, a call for a limit could provide a solution as it had in the past.

However, the Russian Council of Ministers soon widened the plans from a bilateral discussion with the Habsburg Monarchy to a general multilateral discussion on the limitation of armaments. The shift to a multilateral conference reflected concerns within the Russian government about the political repercussions of making a direct request to Austria-Hungary, whose government would surely disfavor a negotiation excluding its ally Germany.[29] Additionally, a call made to Austria-Hungary alone would demonstrate Russian weakness.[30] The limited goal of regulating a single type of military ordnance suddenly expanded into a scheme to limit overall military expenditures.[31] Conversely, while political considerations required a discussion among more states, the expansion of the agenda to more topics made it less politically feasible.

In the initial conference call in the summer of 1898, the Czar sought an international discussion on "means of ensuring ... peace, and above all of limiting the progressive development of existing armaments."[32] Like the 1874 Brussels gathering, the conference was initially intended to generate ideas rather than to reach legally binding conclusions, possibly codifying principles of general disarmament in an informal and non-binding protocol. The parties would have greater liberty to openly discuss possibilities of arms limitation without committing themselves to any firm position.[33] The resulting document could then be circulated among the powers and a formal legal agreement reached.

By the winter of 1898–1899, international developments dampened the Czar's initial enthusiasm for disarmament, and the need to prevent the failure of a conference called solely for this purpose led to the inclusion of other issues in a second circular of December 30, 1898.[34] This circular stressed the tentative nature of its agenda, merely calling for "a preliminary exchange of ideas between the Powers," and expanding the topics from arms limitations to include "the possibility of preventing

---

[29] Morrill, "Nicholas II and the Call for the First Hague Conference," 301–03.
[30] Davis, *The United States and the First Hague Peace Conference*, 45.
[31] Morrill, "Nicholas II and the Call for the First Hague Conference," 304–05.
[32] Count Mouravieff, *as quoted in Documents Relating to the Program of the First Hague Peace Conference*, 1.
[33] Scott to Balfour, Sep. 3, 1898, No. 9, and Sep. 1, 1898, No. 19, *in* FO 412/65.
[34] Davis, *The United States and the Second Hague Peace Conference*, 9–10.

armed conflicts by ... pacific means."[35] The new circular added arbitration and the completion of two earlier non-ratified documents – the 1874 Brussels Declaration on the rules of war and the 1868 Geneva Convention extending humanitarian rules to war at sea. If the states could not reach agreement on disarmament, perhaps a few accomplishments in the field of international arbitration would prevent the conference from appearing a complete failure. Of the eight topics included for discussion in the circular, the first four addressed armaments, specifically seeking (1) "non-augmentation ... of the present effective armed land and sea forces, as well as war budgets" and a study of future reductions, (2) "[i]nterdiction ... of new firearms ... and of new explosives," (3) "[l]imitation of the use ... of explosives of a formidable power ... and prohibition of the discharge of any kind of projectile or explosive from balloons or similar means," and (4) "prohibition of the use ... of submarine or diving torpedo boats ... [and] agreement not to construct in the future war-ships armed with rams."[36]

In order to focus the conference upon technical issues of disarmament, the Czar's circular forbade the discussion of political questions as well as any topics not specifically listed. Diplomats could avoid being sidetracked by discussions on Alsace-Lorraine, the Boer states, or any other hot issues of the day. The Czar advised that a great power should not host the conference, but rather a smaller state should do so, so as to prevent undue influence on the debates.[37] The Netherlands accepted sponsorship and issued invitations for the conference to be held at The Hague, in May of 1899.[38] Significantly, the circular as addressed to "Representatives Accredited to the Court at Petrograd" barred states without accredited representatives in Russia, i.e. the majority of Latin American states.[39] Invitations included European states, as well as Brazil, China, Japan, Mexico, Persia, Siam, and

[35] Count Mouravieff, *as quoted in Documents Relating to the Program of the First Hague Peace Conference*, 2–3.

[36] *Id.*, 3.

[37] *Id.*

[38] W. H. de Beaufort, *Circular Instruction of the Netherland Minister for Foreign Affairs to the Diplomatic Representatives of the Netherlands*, April 6, 1899, *as quoted in* James Brown Scott, ed., *The Hague Conventions and Declarations of 1899 and 1907* (New York: Oxford University Press, 1915), xviii–xix.

[39] *Documents Relating to the Program of the First Hague Peace Conference*, 2. In addition, pre-conference diplomacy bypassed minor hurdles when the Boer states and the Papacy sought invitations, opposed by Great Britain and Italy, respectively.

the United States. The exclusion of Latin America appeared particularly arbitrary in retrospect, as the Russian government extended invitations to Luxemburg, Montenegro, and Siam, all states with insignificant militaries and no accredited representatives in St. Petersburg.[40]

The prevailing opinion of the great powers held that the conference would yield few concrete results.[41] Many leaders raised doubts about the sincerity of Russian aims. The offer to limit military expenditures appeared planned to allow Russia time to develop its economy in peace before beginning a military buildup.[42] France lacked interest in the project, as an arms agreement might prevent it from retaking Alsace-Lorraine by force. Moreover, the Russians had failed to consult France before issuing the circular, raising speculation that the Czar was abandoning its ally.[43] The United States accepted the invitation, but as its peacetime army was far smaller than the European armies the Americans did not expect any limitation on their military. Both Italy and Austria-Hungary opposed arms limits, and Japan would only accept a limit after its fleet had increased to the level of the great powers. Germany sought to prevent Russian embarrassment at the conference, but did not wish to hinder its ability to arm itself.[44] Friedrich von Holstein, counsellor at the German Foreign Ministry, approved of German participation at the conference, believing only a broad multilateral discussion by all the powers could achieve any results and that "the idea of disarmament will not die."[45] This view reflected the general European resignation to attendance at the conference, intermingled with concerns for possible entanglements in unmanageable disarmament schemes.

[40] Scott, *The Hague Peace Conferences of 1899 and 1907*, 47.
[41] See, for example, Rumbold to Salisbury, Sep. 14 1898, *in* FO 412/65; *see generally* Davis, *The United States and the Second Hague Peace Conference*, 6.
[42] See, for example, Lascelles to Salisbury, Dec. 22 1898, *in* FO 412/65; Milbanke to Salisbury, May 12 1899, *in* FO 412/65.
[43] Rumbold to Salisbury, Sep. 14, 1898, No. 23, *in* FO 412/65. Moreover, France had invented the 75 mm quick-firing gun that the initiative aimed at stifling. The author thanks David Stevenson for raising this point.
[44] Tate, *The Disarmament Illusion*, 277–78. While most of the smaller powers generally approved of arms reductions, in its semi-official newspapers Serbia candidly expressed a desire to expand its borders in a general European war. "We live in the hope of getting something for ourselves out of the general conflagration, whenever it takes place." Macdonald to Salisbury, Sep. 15, 1898, *in* FO 412/65.
[45] Rich, *Friedrich Von Holstein*, Vol. II, 603.

BRITISH PREPARATION FOR THE HAGUE CONFERENCE

At the St. Petersburg Conference in 1868, the British had opposed technological limitations. In 1899, the Russians were seeking two types of limitations – a quantitative limitation on troops or military budgets and a qualitative limitation on new technology. Given prior experience, the Russians could have anticipated that qualitative restrictions would be unpopular with Salisbury's government. The British also largely opposed quantitative limitation, refuting the concept of disarmament in planning documents prior to the conference. Arguing that an international police force could not be created, the Admiralty and War Office held that disarmament could not be discussed fruitfully. Yet the British government was not wholly opposed to arms control, and secretly offered a naval limit to Russia. The government also favored limited regulations that would cement British naval predominance, such as banning naval mines, torpedoes, and submarines, or general naval program reductions which would preserve its relative superiority. However, the British exceptions were not predicated on schemes of world government, and could be realized under existing circumstances.

The second Russian circular was partly motivated by a desire to isolate the British, by proposing topics expected to be unpopular with Britain.[46] If Britain refused to attend, or obstructed discussions, the island nation could be isolated from the continental powers, while Russia would benefit from a diplomatic regrouping. However, the British foiled Russian schemes by accepting the Russian agenda. The British government still opposed nearly every element listed for discussion, yet sought to avoid becoming the scapegoat for the failure of the program. While British skepticism about general disarmament reflected real concerns about the legal challenges, this position ignored the ample experience Britain had in arms limitation and security-related law. This knowledge would have demonstrated that law could play a role in shaping the security environment without the creation of a utopian world government. Like technical arguments, international law could be utilized as another excuse for not accepting unwanted arms limitations.

Prime Minister Lord Salisbury shaped the British bargaining position. Fresh from a diplomatic victory at Fashoda, which affirmed the value of sea power, Salisbury appeared reluctant to limit this potent weapon. Like

---

[46] Davis, *The United States and the First Hague Peace Conference*, 50–51.

many international observers, he argued that the expense and the destructiveness of war deterred conflict.[47] Salisbury selected delegates likely to vigorously oppose disarmament, most notably Admiral Jackie Fisher.[48] Fisher later wrote of his experience at The Hague, claiming "every treaty is a Scrap of Paper!"

> The Essence of War is Violence.
> Moderation in War is Imbecility.
> You hit first, you hit hard, and keep on hitting ....
> It's perfect rot to talk about "Civilised Warfare!"
> You might as well talk about a "Heavenly Hell!"[49]

There was little interdepartmental coordination before the conference, although this differed little from previous gatherings. The Admiralty only learned of the 1868 St. Petersburg Declaration after it was signed. Moreover, the failure to consult other departments during submarine cable negotiations in the 1880s led belatedly to a complete reversal on policy, unfortunately only after a convention had been signed.[50] However, Admiralty and War Office opinions were canvassed prior to the gathering, and both departments sent experts to accompany the British delegation at The Hague.

Salisbury questioned the value of disarmament, fearing a limit on armed forces could be circumvented, as Prussia had done after the Treaty of Tilsit in 1807. Troops could be trained while remaining unarmed, ready to organize in case of war. Likewise, he pondered whether vessels could be built, exclusive of armament, to be fitted in case of emergency.[51] In

---

[47] Salisbury to Scott, Oct. 24 1898, *in* FO 412/65.

[48] Tate, *The Disarmament Illusion*, 289–90.

[49] John Arbuthnot Fisher, *Records by Admiral of the Fleet Lord Fisher* (London: Hodder and Stoughton, 1919), 75–76.

[50] Colonial Office to Foreign Office, Nov. 1, 1887, *in* Correspondence Respecting the Protection of Submarine Cables in Time of War, FO 412/22 (1886–1887).

[51] This was a dubious proposition by the turn of the century, although it should not have been expected that an elder statesman would have been aware of the impracticality of improvising warships, other than auxiliary cruisers. Warships were specially constructed so as to bear the weight and stresses of heavy armaments and armor, and often had their engines configured below the waterline, all in a manner that would render them ill-suited for peacetime purposes. *See* Captain Ottley, Memorandum on the Question of Contraband of War in its Relation to Ships Sold by a Neutral to a Belligerent, Appendix 11 *in* Report of the Inter-Departmental Committee appointed to consider the Subjects which may arise for Discussion at the Second Peace Conference, Apr. 11, 1907, CAB 37/87/42 (1907) at 80–81.

order to verify compliance with such an agreement, an "inspecting and restraining power" would be necessary, which would need to be created before any military limits could be discussed.[52] An international police force would be needed to enforce these obligations both in peace and in war, an impossible task.

The argument, while touching upon real concerns, was disingenuous. By placing the emphasis on creating an international organization prior to discussing any arms limitation, Salisbury could ensure that no serious discussion on unwanted topics took place. Yet this statesman had knowledge of prior arms limitations operating without a police force, concurrently renegotiating the Rush-Bagot Agreement with the United States while preparing for the Hague Conference, and more generally he was familiar with the functioning of international law.[53] While limitations of land forces might be violated relatively easily, it would be much more difficult to hide a large-scale violation of a naval arms limit long enough to significantly alter the naval balance, and almost impossible to obscure a violation large enough to alter the strategic balance against the British Navy. Major warships took at least two to three years to complete, and British policy traditionally relied upon its faster shipbuilding capacity to counter moves of foreign navies once uncovered.

The fighting services took their cue from Lord Salisbury. Major-General Ardagh presented the War Office's position in a key memorandum. He believed that the "perpetual see-saw of superiority works for peace" by making states unwilling to go to war while rearming.[54] Echoing arguments made at St. Petersburg in 1868, Ardagh held that Britain, with its smaller population, relied upon technology to maintain its position as a great power. A limited agreement on new technology, such as the ban on exploding bullets, could only succeed if it did not alter the outcome of war. In 1868, the ban on exploding bullets had been approved, and had been maintained as the ammunition had never become integral to military tactics. According to the major-general, a broader interdiction on all technologies would fail for the practical reason that states would eventually find it in their interest to develop new weapons. Moreover,

---

[52] Salisbury to Scott, Feb. 14, 1899, *in* FO 412/65.

[53] See Chap. 5 for renegotiation of the Rush–Bagot Agreement.

[54] Sir John Ardagh, Restrictions on Employment of High Explosives, Appendix No. 9, *enclosure in* War Office to Foreign Office, May 17, 1899, *in* FO 412/65.

Ardagh skillfully built a humanitarian argument in favor of new technologies. Tracing the length of wars and casualty rates over several centuries, he noted that as firearms had improved and became increasingly lethal, wars had become shorter while tactics had adjusted and actually reduced battlefield deaths. This downward trend in casualties could be arrested if new technologies were not allowed to develop.[55]

In a related argument, Ardagh stressed the imperial necessity of technology in "savage warfare." If the more advanced states no longer harnessed their technological innovations to defense, the backward states would gradually achieve the same technological level. Britain could not maintain its great empire if it had to put down uprisings by local inhabitants armed with the same quality weapons, and ultimately the safety of the imperial powers would be imperiled by the "uncivilized races."[56]

Ardagh was conversant with international law and an able delegate for the Hague assignment. His memorandum and other papers indicated he had an understanding of basic international law. Like Salisbury, he raised questions both about the enforcement of disarmament, and the difficulty in defining a measure of military strength. However, he also recognized the role of neutral powers in maintaining international law, in accordance with prevailing theory. His protests against international law must be balanced with his practical awareness of how agreements could be enforced.

Ardagh advanced a thoughtful argument regarding the superiority of informal understandings. Instead of completing the Brussels Declaration and forming a rigid multilateral code regulating wartime conduct, states could reach non-binding bilateral agreements to honor rules of war at the outset of a conflict. The rules could be incorporated in national military codes, which would allow greater flexibility while still providing protection of humanitarian values in war. More importantly, this method would avoid claims of violation of legal agreements. Ultimately, he opposed every point on the Czar's agenda, with the exception of arbitration, on which he expressed no opinion, finding all restrictions on war or weaponry to be impossible.[57]

---

[55] Sir John Ardagh, Draft of Instructions for Peace Conference 1899, at 5–6, *in* Ardagh Papers, PRO 30/40/15, (1899).

[56] Ardagh, Memorandum, *enclosure in* War Office to Foreign Office, May 17, 1899, *in* FO 412/65.

[57] *Id.*

The navy even opposed arbitration. Like the War Office, the Admiralty dissented from nearly the entire Hague agenda.[58] Real disarmament would require international inspection. Moreover, disarmament would be impossible until outstanding political differences had been resolved under the watchful eye of an international police force, an utterly unrealistic expectation. In a style of writing sure to catch Fisher's fancy, the key Admiralty memo paraphrased a recent article in the *Fortnightly Review*:

> Disarmament is impossible without a durable peace.
> Durable peace requires the adjustment of all differences.
> Adjustment is impossible without a force to enforce decisions.
> Such a force does not exist.[59]

Therefore, according to the logic, disarmament was impossible.[60] Technically, it would also be impossible for officers from two different navies to agree on how to measure effective forces. Echoing War Office arguments, the Admiralty stressed the need for technological naval superiority to win wars against less advanced "savage" nations, and argued that modern weapons made war more humane.[61]

While the Admiralty categorically refuted the possibility of disarmament, it expressed an interest in arms limitations that would preserve British strategic superiority. The Admiralty approved a possible ban on

[58] The Admiralty, unlike the War Office, even recognized the dangers posed by compulsory arbitration. As the Navy planned to utilize peacetime preparedness to launch a rapid strike at the beginning of hostilities, the Admiralty feared that arbitration would drag out a dispute long enough for an opponent to mobilize their fleet, destroying the British advantage in preparedness. Admiralty to Foreign Office, May 16, 1899, *in* FO 412/65. Fisher noted that while on land the first pitched battle might not occur until the twelfth day, at sea, the first great naval action could take place on the twelfth hour of war. Fisher, Memorandum, July 22, 1899, *enclosure in* Pauncefote to Salisbury, July 26, 1899, *in id.*

[59] Diplomaticus, "The Vanishing of Universal Peace," *Fortnightly Review* 65, no. 389 (1899): 877; *see* Notes on the Subjects to be Dealt with by Peace Conference, May 10, 1899, *in* Peace Conference, (1899–1900), ADM 116/98. Diplomaticus was purported to be Alfred Austin, poet laureate and friend of Salisbury. Howard, *Britain and the Casus Belli*, 157.

[60] Analysis did not solely concern the absence of an international police force, but also the lack of interest among the great powers. "The fact is that after a long peace each Power is prepared to fight for what it considers its legitimate aspirations. It will only yield when exhausted by war." Notes on the Subjects to be Dealt with by Peace Conference, *supra* note 59, at 1. But the lack of legal enforcement was seized upon as a sufficient reason to oppose disarmament.

[61] Admiralty to Foreign Office, May 16, 1899, *in* FO 412/65.

submarines, as well as on mines and torpedoes.[62] Submarines posed a particular threat to the British Navy, one that the Navy was then only beginning to recognize. Britain depended on its battleship fleet for command of the sea, and the cheap new submersibles held out the prospect that small nations could thwart that maritime control.

The British delegation to the Hague Conference received no formal instructions stating an official position on disarmament, but were referred to the memoranda created by the Admiralty, the War Office, and Lord Salisbury. At the conference, the delegates utilized general arguments against disarmament, based on the needs of smaller powers to utilize advanced technology, the need of "civilized" states to maintain advantages over "savage" nations, and the unrealizable requirement that international law provide a fail-proof control.

BRITISH NAVAL ARMAMENT LIMITATION OFFER TO RUSSIA

The Admiralty also made a practical suggestion about limiting naval armaments just prior to the Hague Conference, directly offering a naval arms limit with Russia. Russian naval expansion had added to traditional Admiralty preoccupation with France. In the 1890s, French naval policy had been hamstrung by rivalry between the *Jeune Ecole* and traditionalists, causing naval policy to gyrate between battleship and armored cruiser programs.[63] While the armored cruiser posed a new threat to British naval dominance, there was a slowing in the pace of French battleship construction. Yet the overall increase in the pace of construction created greater pressures for the Admiralty to maintain the two-power battleship standard, with unofficial calls for arms talks or a preemptive strike.[64] Meanwhile, the newer armored cruisers cost nearly as much to build as a battleship, cost more to maintain in service due to larger crews, and British policy aimed to match cruiser construction at a two to one level over its next two rivals, rather than the lower two-power standard in battleships.[65] These

---

[62] Notes on the Subjects to be Dealt with by Peace Conference, *supra* note 59, at 3–4.

[63] *See generally*, Theodore Ropp, *The Development of a Modern Navy: French Naval Policy, 1871–1904* (Annapolis, Maryland: Naval Institute Press, 1987).

[64] Marder, *The Anatomy of British Sea Power*, 313, 44–45.

[65] Nicholas A. Lambert, *Sir John Fisher's Naval Revolution* (Columbia, SC: University of South Carolina Press, 1999), 20–23.

pressures overlapped with the Fashoda crisis and the attendant risk of war with France in the autumn of 1898, as well as the German and Russian seizure of naval bases in China, signaling a more intense phase of East Asian colonial rivalry.[66]

In response to increase in Russian battleship and French armored cruiser construction, in 1898 the Admiralty announced an extraordinary building program of four battleships and four large cruisers, and anticipated that an additional two or three supplementary battleships would be required in the 1899 estimates.[67] Additionally, on the urging of the Cabinet, First Lord of the Admiralty Goschen suggested a naval agreement with Russia: "Such a hint might test the sincerity of Russia, and at the same time afford a proof of our sincerity."[68] Through Charles Scott, British Ambassador in St. Petersburg, Goschen proposed the cancellation of the two supplementary battleships planned for 1899 in return for a Russian undertaking not to commence additional battleships beyond the four ordered the previous year.[69]

The secret initiative occurred simultaneously with the annual presentation of naval estimates in Parliament, in which Goschen offered to reciprocally reduce naval construction. When introducing the estimates, Goschen asserted that "I have now to state on behalf of Her Majesty's Government that similarly, if the other great Naval Powers should be prepared to diminish their Programme of ship building, we should be prepared on our side to meet such a procedure by modifying ours."[70] The offer was made on the assumption that the relative size of the British Navy would be maintained, and that the other "great Naval Powers" would all agree to such a limit, which the First Lord listed as France, Russia, the United States, Japan, Italy, and Germany.

Goschen made the announcement while explaining an increase in British naval expenditure, one which he held to be due to the rise of new naval powers, Germany, the United States, and Japan, as well as on account of an increase in Russian construction. While the introduction of

[66] Marder, *The Anatomy of British Sea Power*, 302, 20.
[67] Goschen to Salisbury, Mar. 1, 1899, Salisbury Manuscripts, Vol. 93, No. 47, ff. 101–105. Ultimately, the British *Duncan* class vastly outclassed their intended Russian rivals of the *Peresviet* class. Oscar Parkes, *British Battleships: "Warrior" 1860 to "Vanguard" 1950, a History of Design, Construction and Armament* (London: Seeley Service & Co., 1957), 416.
[68] Goschen to Salisbury, Mar. 1, 1899, Salisbury Manuscripts, Vol. 93, No. 47, f. 105.
[69] Scott to Salisbury, Mar. 9, 1899, Salisbury Manuscripts, Vol. 129, No. 61, ff. 181–185.
[70] Lord Goschen, *Hansard* 4th ser., LXVIII, 323–324, Mar. 9, 1899.

new naval competitors complicated the British situation, Goschen based the Admiralty program upon construction rates in France and Russia, the two leading naval powers. Moreover, he noted the precarious nature of the peace in the preceding autumn during the Fashoda Crisis. Thus, the offer was not predicated on an optimistic view of current international relations. While Goschen may have been motivated partly by a desire to justify increasing expenditure and lacked optimism about the realization of this public offer, it was noteworthy in acknowledging that a limit was possible.

Ultimately, the Russian foreign minister Muraviev refused the British offer, claiming that both states could continue to complete their programs prior to entering into a general limit at The Hague. The Russian diplomat also claimed that his country needed to build the battleships to match additional Japanese construction in the Far East.[71] A bilateral initiative failed to address the full contours of naval arms competition. While fruitless, the episode indicated that the Cabinet approved of some forms of arms limitation, and that Salisbury was willing to negotiate such an agreement. Salisbury's interests in arms limitation extended only as far as a numeric limit on new battleship construction with Russia, or at most with the other great powers. When this proved impossible, his administration lost interest in most of the remaining forms of arms limitation.

This previously unreported episode of secret diplomacy directly contradicted Salisbury's publically proclaimed opposition to arms limits. Salisbury opposed plans for broad global disarmament as unworkable, but his government's initiative indicates that he accepted limited agreements among the great powers. While Salisbury generally rejected the Czar's program, he did not completely oppose limitations, nor believe arms control to be inherently unworkable. Opposition to arms limitation in the Salisbury government needs to be viewed with this in mind, as it was never absolute.

GREAT BRITAIN AND DISARMAMENT AT THE HAGUE

The First Hague Peace Conference opened on May 18, 1899, with the assembled delegates of 26 nations. The work of the conference was divided into three commissions, the first dealing with armament questions, the second discussing the rules of war, and the third handling arbitration. The First Commission on disarmament subdivided into two subcommis-

---

[71] Scott to Salisbury, Mar. 10, 1899, Salisbury Manuscripts, Vol. 129, No. 63, f. 89.

sions, one for military questions and the other for naval topics. Despite widespread skepticism, the commission seriously and quickly initiated its work on disarmament. While subsequently viewed as a first-class funeral for disarmament, negotiations focused on the initial steps needed to halt the arms race.[72] Like the 1874 Brussels Conference, the stated purpose of the gathering was to provide a preliminary discussion of theoretical questions. After developing principles related to disarmament, the powers would ideally take concrete steps to disarm. There was political pressure to produce real achievements, although the addition of arbitration at the conference would hopefully obscure failures in arms discussions. Like the 1874 Brussels Conference, the stated goal was only a non-binding discussion, although in 1899 political expectations were higher. Thus, the gathering opened with both a lack of enthusiasm for disarmament and an obligation to achieve something tangible.

The Russians made most of the proposals, as they had called the conference and had placed armaments on the agenda. However, Russian interest had since waned, and their leadership wavered, as Russian delegates sometimes vigorously, sometimes half-heartedly raised armament issues.[73] Among the other great powers, the French raised serious naval proposals, while the British and Americans drafted propositions as a counter to a restriction on bullets. Among the smaller powers, the Netherlands offered several ideas. Beyond this, few concrete suggestions were made for halting the arms race.

The Russian delegate stressed that the parties were only discussing abstract principles, and that what was at stake was only a minor limit on armaments rather than disarmament.[74] The debates surrounding

---

[72] Davis, *The United States and the First Hague Peace Conference*, 122.

[73] Admiral Fisher related one incident during negotiations on banning submarines, a debate in which some parties were cautiously refusing to commit themselves. As the admirals gathered around the table one by one gravely shook their heads and explained why they could not support the proposal, the Russian naval delegate likewise reserved his opinion. Fisher had to inform the Russian delegate, amidst general laughter, that he had abstained from his own government's proposal, at which point the Russian changed his mind – but only if everyone else accepted the limit. Fisher, Memorandum, Enclosure No. 1, in Pauncefote to Salisbury, May 31, 1899, *in* FO 412/65.

[74] "Is it necessary for me to declare that we are not speaking of Utopias or chimerical measures? We are not considering disarmament. What we are hoping for, is to attain a limitation – a halt in the ascending course of armaments and expenses." Staal, June 23, 1899, Scott, ed., *1899 Proceedings*, 301.

the Russian proposals raised a number of contentious points. The parties argued over the wisdom of limiting advanced industrial technology to warfare, the difficulties of quantifying military strength, and finally over what type of international institutions would be necessary to oversee disarmament.

Land Armaments at The Hague

The subcommission dedicated to land armaments started with the easiest questions, beginning with small arms, and moved progressively towards more difficult topics, including limits on armies and military budgets. The general goal was to limit expenditure associated with new weaponry, as the introduction of every new weapon necessitated the wholesale replacement of existing inventories.[75] But such a goal logically required wide-scale limitation of military technology. The subcommission also discussed possible means of limiting the evolution of small arms, machine guns, explosive powders, and the new quick-fire artillery. Additionally, experimental and exotic technologies such as aerial bombardment, poison gas, and expanding bullets were reviewed. The assembly even questioned whether future advances in chemistry and electricity should be considered.[76]

Subcommission President Beernaert opened discussions on small arms, seeking specific proposals, as well as general criteria for limiting them. The Russian and Dutch delegates each arrived at the second meeting with their own agendas. The Russians advocated setting a minimum bullet caliber and weight, initial velocity, rate of fire, and prohibiting both expanding bullets and automatic loading rifles.[77] Similarly, the Dutch sought to prevent changes in rifles, by freezing the then-current technological specifications.[78] In the past half-century, muzzle-loading rifles had been replaced

[75] Gilinsky, June 23, 1899, *Id.*, 302–03.
[76] Beernaert, May 31, 1899, *Id.*, 347–48.
[77] Barantzew, May 29, 1899, *Id.*, 337. The Russians also advocated a minimum rifle weight, which the German delegate later weakly opposed, claiming humanitarian benefits for soldiers who would be less burdened by heavy weaponry. Schwarzhoff, May 31, 1899, Scott, ed., *1899 Proceedings*, 346. However, he did admit that any decrease in gun weight would probably be compensated by carrying more ammunition. Schwarzhoff's argument typified expert opposition to arms proposals by assertions of the insuperable complexity of all problems – he claimed that the proposal did not specify if rifle weight included bayonets or a full magazine of ammunition – all questions that could be simply resolved had political will been present.
[78] Den Beer Poortugael, May 29, 1899, Scott, ed., *1899 Proceedings*, 337.

by breech-loaders, and rates of fire had increased. At the same time, bullet caliber had decreased in order to accommodate larger quantities of ammunition.[79] By limiting these trends and fixing a standard, the proposal sought to eliminate the incentive to replace small arms regularly.

Colonel Gross von Schwarzhoff, the German military delegate, raised numerous cogent arguments against the proposed restriction. Schwarzhoff's participation relieved the other delegations of the need to oppose disarmament vigorously, as his outspoken opposition claimed for Germany the onus of scuttling talks that no one truly wanted. He noted the inherent difficulties in limiting some weapons characteristics, such as rate of fire, which largely depended upon training. He also raised more general concerns regarding the need to make proposals specific. The Russian and Dutch proposals both spoke of limiting substantial "improvements" in firearms without specifying what would constitute such a change.[80] Dutch delegate den Beer Poortugael also requested that vague wording be made more specific, opposing ambiguous proposals that allowed states with antiquated rifles to bring them up to the latest standard.[81] It was unclear when a change would be considered a minor modification and when it was a major improvement. Ultimately, the small-arms proposal failed despite Dutch pleas that the gathering accomplish something concrete.[82]

The Russians also called for a halt to technological improvements in artillery, with the express purpose of allowing less-advanced states to catch up with their industrialized neighbors.[83] While no one directly raised the argument, this technological leveling would eliminate advantages on which other great powers depended. The proposal failed by a nearly unanimous vote. Even the Russian delegate, apparently to avoid the appearance of

---

[79] John Ardagh, Memorandum, *enclosure in* War Office to Foreign Office, May 17, 1899, *in* FO 412/65, at 82.

[80] The Dutch proposal stated that "[t]he improvements permitted shall be of such a nature as not to change either the existing type or caliber." Den Beer Poortugael, May 31, 1899, Scott, ed., *1899 Proceedings*, 345.

[81] Den Beer Poortugael, June 7, 1899, *Id.*, 350–51.

[82] "[I]f we place not a single restriction on the ruinous transformation of armaments, we shall forge weapons for the enemy common to all Governments, for those who wish to revolutionize the established order of the world and who will not hesitate to scatter among the people venomous germs and a doubt as to the sincerity of the Governments whom we represent." *Id.*

[83] Gilinsky, May 29, 1899, Scott, ed., *1899 Proceedings*, 339.

isolation on the issue, did not vote in favor of it, despite this being the Czar's initial goal for the conference. Similarly, Russian plans to limit the introduction of new types of explosives failed after it was explained that the limit would require states to share formulas to ascertain that alterations would not be made. The chemical composition of explosives was a closely guarded secret and states would not willingly share such information with rivals.

The small-arms proposal opened up a broader debate on the limits of international law. Den Beer Poortugael inadvertently raised the question when trying to persuade delegates to accept the Dutch small-arms proposal. When explaining how parties could be prevented from impermissibly changing their firearms, he quoted the famed international lawyer from the 1874 Brussels Conference, Baron Jomini, as saying "[i]t would be a wrong to the contracting parties to imagine that they could have the intention of not abiding by their agreement."[84] Schwarzhoff noted that the vagueness of the proposals would foster misunderstandings. Demanding clarity was not a question of bad faith, but of what improvements constituted radical transformations. Ardagh also noted that such limitations could not be verified easily, as states could build prohibited rifles in state arsenals and distribute them on the outbreak of war.[85]

This discussion highlighted challenges relating to international control. Some delegates sought a judiciary to adjudicate breaches, and an executive to enforce judgments. The Russian delegates noted that international control simply did not exist, even in the case of commercial conventions. Nor could it realistically be expected that the gathering could create such an institution. Even in 1899 statesmen acknowledged that by raising the question of control, the whole discussion could be derailed through the creation of an insurmountable difficulty.[86]

---

[84] Den Beer Poortugael, June 7, 1899, *Id.*, 351.
[85] Ardagh, June 7, 1899, *Id.*, 352–53.
[86] Raffalovich and Gilinsky, June 7, 1899, *Id.*, 353. These statements by Raffalovich claiming that states could rely on the good faith of other parties could be seen as naïve, but the better explanation is that this was an attempt to diplomatically maneuver states into an agreement. It is not unreasonable to assume that statesmen might find it more inconvenient to admit that governments were capable of dishonesty than to accept an agreement, considering the great lengths delegates went to find technical reasons not to limit arms rather than admitting that limits were not wanted.

120   S.A. KEEFER

General Limitation Debates at The Hague

These same themes marked the general disarmament debates in the parent First Commission. Broader topics were reserved for the full commission to debate. Russia made several proposals to halt the continental arms race, including limiting the number of troops, halting technological innovations, and restricting military budgets. Russian delegates clearly indicated they did not intend general disarmament, seeking only to halt the continual increase of military forces.[87] Russia sought a freeze on troop levels for a period of five years, in order to test the principle of arms limitation. If the project succeeded in changing the arms race dynamic, then further conferences could actually reduce armaments.[88] However, the Russian proposal expressly excluded colonial forces, on the grounds that they were necessary for local policing and defensive duties. While the Russians claimed that these forces did not alter the balance in Europe, including their Siberian armies as colonial troops conveniently ignored the fact that these soldiers could quickly return to fight in the west.

Colonel Schwarzhoff again opposed the Czar's project, eloquently pointing out the complexity of the situation. He quickly noted that there could be no guarantee that Russia would not recall troops stationed in Asia. Moreover, relative military strength depended on far more than troop numbers, and included the level of training, length of service, overall military organization, railroad networks, and the number and placement of fortresses. Each state organized its defenses based upon its individual character, history, traditions, economic resources, geographic situation, and political policies. Any reduction in one part of national defense could lead to increases in other areas. For instance, a limit on troops could translate into financial savings that would be available for improving the national rail network, effectively increasing the military strength of a state like Russia that lacked a modern transportation infrastructure. "I believe that it would be very difficult to replace this eminently national task by an international agreement. It would be impossible to determine the extent and the force of a single part of this complicated machinery."[89]

---

[87] Staal, June 23, 1899, *Id.*, 301.

[88] Gilinsky, June 23, 1899, *Id.*, 304–05.

[89] Schwarzhoff, June 25, 1899, *Id.*, 309–10. *See also* Memorandum from General von Schwarzhoff, June 26 1899, in Johannes Lepsius, Albrecht Mendelssohn Bartholdy, and Friedrich Thimme, eds., *Die Grosse Politik Der Europäischen Kabinette, 1871–1914: Sammlung Der Diplomatischen Akten Des Auswärtigen Amtes*, 40 vols. (Berlin: Deutsche Verlagsgesellschaft für Politik und Geschichte, 1922–1927), Vol. XV, 200.

Schwarzhoff questioned the central premise of the gathering, providing a weaker argument against the proposed five-year budgetary ceiling. Although the Germans already had a five-year budgetary law, it did not coincide with the five-year period proposed by Russia. This, according to Schwarzhoff, presented an insurmountable obstacle.[90] Other states raised issues concerning military organization and the relative size of forces. Disarmament was generally predicated upon the status quo, disadvantaging nations that were already maintaining limited armies. Similarly, the United States delegation noted that its military was much smaller than those of European states, especially as a percentage of population. Therefore, the United States would "refrain from enunciating opinions upon matters into which, as concerning Europe alone, the United States has no claim to enter" as "their size can entail no additional burden of expense upon [other nations], nor even form a subject for profitable mutual discussion."[91]

The Russians argued that a temporary agreement would allow arms to be limited without seriously risking national security. The Hague negotiations were framed as a preliminary examination, allowing an abstract discussion of principles. Despite the assurances that discussions were only theoretical, the underlying tenor of the Russian proposals favored disarmament. Many participants questioned Russian sincerity, and, more importantly, the great powers did not generally desire arms limitation. When the Czar's grand proposal came up for a full discussion, no state offered any suggestion as to how it could be put into effect. Sparing the Russians the embarrassment of a vote, the Commission President deemed the silence an adequate answer, and referred the topic for further study.[92] The parties agreed to place a resolution in the final act of the conference, which read "[t]he Commission is of opinion that the restriction of military charges, which are at present a heavy burden on the world, is extremely

---

[90] Scott, ed., *1899 Proceedings*, 310. Professor of International Law at the University of Marburg, Walther Schücking, easily refuted this claim, noting that the treaty ratification process would necessarily involve the Reichstag, which could amend its prior legislation to conform with new obligations. Schücking, *The International Union of the Hague Conferences*, 330–31.

[91] U.S. Dep't of State, *Papers Relating to the Foreign Relations of the United States with the Annual Message of the President 1899* (Washington: Government Printing Office, 1901), 515.

[92] Beernaert, June 30, 1899, Scott, ed., *1899 Proceedings*, 315–16.

desirable for the increase of the material and moral welfare of mankind."[93] While resolutions could include binding obligations, this one contained no expression of duty, stating only the principle that the arms race posed a burden on humanity.

The British delegation maintained a low profile. While Ardagh took a central role in the expanding bullets discussions, and Fisher vigorously participated in naval armament discussions, in the general arms discussions there was no need to wreck the Czar's proposals. Although the British delegation had been prepared to raise stronger objections to the Russian program, the Germans carried the burden for them.

Naval Armaments at The Hague

The discussions on naval limits witnessed a repetition of now-common themes. The British delegation supported weapon bans deemed favorable to British interests while still proclaiming the impossibility of regulating areas deemed unfavorable. The first set of naval topics included a limitation on naval ordnance and new explosives.[94] Russian naval delegate Scheine called for a prohibition on "new types" of artillery. Scheine also contemplated limitations on automatic reloading mechanisms, novel means of using explosives, as well as other experimental weapons such as pneumatic artillery.[95] He summarized the great changes from smooth bore to rifled cannon and from muzzle-loaders to breech-loaders, noting how each advance required costly rearmament, and then expressed misgivings that the introduction of new quick-firing artillery would cause similar disruptions. Scheine divided naval artillery by size, then sought a limit on modifications to heavy cannons between 120 and 430 mm. The initial Russian proposal called for an upper limit of 200 mm for quick-firing ordnance and

---

[93] "Final Act of the Peace Conference, July 29, 1899," *American Journal of International Law* 1, no. 2 Supplement (1907): 103.

[94] Changes in explosives were having a revolutionary effect on naval ordnance in the 1890s, as new smokeless powders allowed artillery to fire at longer ranges. This led to the evolution of intermediate caliber guns in battleships and then ultimately to the all-big-gun ship, the *Dreadnought*, rationalizing gunlaying and exploiting longer ranges. *See* Marder, *The Anatomy of British Sea Power*, 520–21; Jon Tetsura Sumida, *In Defence of Naval Supremacy: Finance, Technology and British Naval Policy, 1889–1914* (London: Routledge, 1989), 46–51.

[95] The only warship to carry pneumatic artillery was the experimental American dynamite-firing *Vesuvius*.

an overall ceiling of 430 mm for ordinary cannon.[96] The 430 mm limit was slightly below the largest naval ordnance then afloat, the "monster guns" featured in Italian battleship designs in the 1880s. Since that time, the cult of the monster gun had declined as newer explosives had allowed much smaller guns, with far higher rates of fire, to exceed the penetrative power of the older artillery.[97] The British Admiralty noted that they had no intention of building warships with 430 mm guns as the weapons were obsolete, yet would not relinquish the future right to build larger guns.[98]

Opponents seized on the proposed limitation of technology, noting that what constituted a "new type" of artillery remained vague. Moreover, Admiral Fisher claimed the advanced states needed the latest technologies in order to maintain their position over "less civilized" nations.[99] Fisher claimed that a "committee of control" would be necessary to enforce Scheine's propositions, constituting an unacceptable sacrifice of national sovereignty. Scheine countered that a simple conventional pledge would be sufficient, and noted that the brief three-year period of the naval proposals would allow the concepts to be tested. While Scheine and French Admiral Pephau provided firmer texts, these did not overcome objections, mainly from German quarters, that the regulations were unenforceable.[100]

American Captain Mahan attacked the proposed regulations, noting that gun power was inextricably linked to armor strength, and then disingenuously suggesting that the only way to limit guns was to simultaneously limit armor. Possibly failing to recognize the Captain's sarcasm, the subcommission president van Karnebeek roundly praised him for suggesting a new avenue for arms limitation and added the topic of armor

---

[96] Speech of Scheine, May 29, 1899, Scott, ed., *1899 Proceedings*, 362–63. Quick-firing ordnance had been adopted in warships from the late 1880s onwards in order to counter the rising threat of torpedo boats, as older artillery had proven unable to counter the rapidly moving craft. *See* Sumida, *In Defence of Naval Supremacy*, 39–40. The new quick-firing system had been successively applied to larger ordnance up to about 15 cm by the late 1890s.

[97] Gardiner, *Conway's All the World's Fighting Ships, 1860–1905*, 6.

[98] R. Custance, The Propositions of Admiral Pephau, June 2, 1899, *in* ADM 116/98.

[99] Fisher, May 26, 1899, Scott, ed., *1899 Proceedings*, 360.

[100] The French proposal defined "radical transformations" as "similar to that by which the muzzle loader was replaced by the breech loader." Pephau, May 29, 1899, *Id.*, 363. The German delegate noted that "it might be adopted without binding one's self. It is very ably conceived and its terms enable anything to be inserted in it that is desired." German Delegate [Siegel], June 5, 1899, Scott, ed., *1899 Proceedings*, 370.

limitation to the discussion.[101] Not to be outdone, Mahan took the argument a step further and claimed that the only way to limit armor would be to place unacceptable prohibitions on domestic steel-manufacturing processes. Disavowing any intention of limiting armor, he asserted the impossibility of banning new industrial processes.

Ultimately, the Russian gun proposals failed to generate support and were quietly referred to national governments for further study. While the British delegation claimed that lack of international supervision made the gun proposals unworkable, these objections did not prevent them from supporting Russian proposed limitations on the use of rams and submarines.[102] Russian delegate Scheine weakly supported his government's proposals, providing an escape clause by demanding a unanimous ban on submarines. This was a level of adherence not required for other arms limitations. Fisher promptly contradicted Scheine, claiming that only a great-power ban was needed to ensure Great Britain's support.[103]

Like the torpedo boat, the submarine was viewed as the weapon of weaker naval powers. In 1899, the technology was in its infancy and appeared suitable only for coastal and harbor defense, but still held the prospect of providing an inexpensive alternative to battleship fleets. Smaller nations were less willing to ban submarines, while larger naval powers were more willing to limit the technology. Germany, Italy, Japan, and Russia all expressed an interest in a universal prohibition, but France, with its *Jeune Ecole* tradition of torpedo boats and coastal-defense battleships, wanted to keep submarines legal. The United States, which along with France had invested in submarine technology, also sought to maintain their legality. Austria-Hungary, along with Turkey, and the nominal advocates of arms limitations the Netherlands and Sweden, sought to keep submarines legal, claiming the weaponry was merely defensive in nature.[104] When the topic reached a final vote in the full commission, ten states voted in favor of a ban while nine voted against, but many of those voting in favor attached reservations requiring unanimity, and the measure failed.[105]

---

[101] Mahan and Karnebeek, May 29, 1899, Scott, ed., *1899 Proceedings*, 363.

[102] Terminology was inexact at this point, with various delegates referring to "diving or submarine torpedoes," or "submarine torpedo boats," when referring to submarines.

[103] Fisher, May 31, 1899, Scott, ed., *1899 Proceedings*, 367.

[104] *See* discussions of May 31, 1899, *Id.*, 367–68.

[105] Fourth Meeting of First Commission, June 23, 1899, *Id.*, 299.

The conference also considered a ban on the construction of war vessels with rams. As in the submarine debate, states split along lines of interest, with Great Britain willing to ban the weapon if all the great powers agreed. Again, the smaller powers opposed this limitation and the proposal failed to receive general support. In contrast to the submarine, a potential weapon of the future, the days of ramming had long passed.[106] A ban could have been enacted without radically altering naval armaments or relative naval strength, yet opposition remained fierce. This indicates that states reached agreements only after full discussion of the potential value of weapons, making the resulting arms declarations more than token achievements.

The final naval topic raised was a budgetary limit on naval forces. As a last-ditch effort at reaching some agreement, Scheine proposed that states fix their annual naval budgets for a three-year period, freely communicating this information with the other parties. Once this information had been exchanged, no further alteration would be allowed. The proposal would allow budgets to be linked to foreign expenditures, and as each state set its own limits, would be less intrusive on sovereign prerogatives. Several delegates questioned how the proposal would work, fearing that it would be difficult to set a budget without knowing what others were planning. Scheine replied that if one state set a budget that was dramatically higher than past expenditures, other states could proportionally increase their budgets in response, thus contemplating at least a two-stage process with provisional budgets being adjusted after information was received from other states.[107] Again, Germany rallied opposition to the proposal, noting that its budget was already set by law, providing information for all states, thus "what is demanded already exists."[108]

* * *

The naval discussions highlighted the manner in which technical and legal arguments were used to prevent unpopular bans from being enacted.

---

[106] Marder, *The Anatomy of British Sea Power*, 166, fn. 37. The 1866 Battle of Lissa had apparently confirmed the value of the ram in naval warfare. The lack of wartime experience in a time of great technical change led to an exaggerated opinion of naval ramming, but by the 1890s potential battle ranges had progressed too far for ramming to occur. Stanley Sandler, "The Day of the Ram," *Military Affairs* 40, no. 4 (1976).

[107] Scheine, June 26, 1899, Scott, ed., *1899 Proceedings*, 377–78.

[108] Siegel, June 26, 1899, *Id.*, 378.

Contemporary legal arguments need to be viewed in this light. The British claimed that lack of an international police force made a gun limitation absolutely impossible, yet they had no similar qualms about submarine limitations. The unwieldy multilateral conference also provided an excuse for inaction, as states demanded unanimous acceptance of limitations, recognizing the impossibility of achieving consensus. Britain's position on submarines and rams exposed the fallacy of this position, as the world's greatest naval power, when it truly sought an arms limitation, recognized that only a ban on the great powers was essential. Moreover, Fisher later admitted that he exaggerated some of his positions at The Hague.[109] Ultimately, technical and legal arguments were utilized as justifications for disposing of unpopular arms topics, leaving armaments unregulated and public opinion mollified by asserting the impossibility of taking action.

It was the qualitative proposals, rather than the quantitative ones, that garnered most attention at the conference. The Czar's proposals tended to focus upon the effect of new technology on weapons acquisitions, thus limitations sought to halt the advance of new inventions. This approach was problematic, as not only were states generally unwilling to limit technology, but even when there was an interest in doing so it proved too difficult to define and restrict unknown future changes. For instance, while naval delegates were discussing limiting obsolete weapons like rams, the British Navy was conducting its first experiments with wireless telegraphy, a technology which would utterly change British force dispositions in the next decade and arguably constituted a major military advance.[110] While dual-purpose technologies such as steelmaking and wireless telegraphy were innovations that were too useful to civilization to allow them to be banned, the inability to predict how a seemingly benign technology could be employed militarily was a significant difficulty.

The alternative lay in quantitative restrictions. Proposals to limit troop numbers or budgetary outlays were unenthusiastically discussed. The most significant proposal for naval arms limitation, the quantitative limit

---

[109] Fisher to Esher, Apr. 25, 1912, *in* Arthur J. Marder, ed., *Fear God and Dread Nought: The Correspondence of Admiral of the Fleet Lord Fisher of Kilverstone, Vol. II Years of Power, 1904–1914* (Oxford: Alden Press, 1956), No. 364, at 453–454.

[110] "The Naval Manoeuvres," *The (London) Times*, July 17, 1899, at 7. On the role of wireless telegraphy and British naval strategy, *see* Nicholas A. Lambert, "Transformation and Technology in the Fisher Era: The Impact of the Communications Revolution," *Journal of Strategic Studies* 27, no. 2 (2004).

offered in Parliament by First Lord Goschen in March, was not even mentioned at The Hague by either British or foreign delegates. The tense state of relations in Europe prevented most states from seriously considering fundamental limitations on military force levels.

A memorandum prepared at The Hague by Charles à Court, a military expert attached to the British delegation, provided a British perspective on the situation. On land, the question revolved around the largest military power, Germany. The refusal of Germany to consider army limitations doomed the proposals, as smaller countries could not safely limit their armaments in the face of German intransigence. At sea the situation was the reverse. Absolving the British of any responsibility, à Court claimed that the smaller naval powers drove this arms race dynamic. He argued that Britain was willing to limit naval armaments, if the other great powers were willing to accept an agreement. Neither Russia nor France would single-handedly fight Britain at sea, nor agree to a limit while Britain maintained naval supremacy. The rise of Japan, Germany, and the United States complicated calculations. None of the rising naval powers would willingly limit their forces until they had attained the level of strength of the next highest ranking navy.[111]

Fundamentally, most states still perceived that armaments increases could improve their security more than arms limitation. International law lacked sufficient strength for states to place their full trust in this institution, particularly when disarmament was under discussion. In order for law to play a role, the arms limitation goals needed to be less ambitious, and confidence in law needed to be increased. In spite of this, legal arguments against arms limitation had a disingenuous quality, like similar arguments of insurmountable technological complexity. Had the political will been present, these difficulties could have been overcome, as demonstrated at the Washington Conference in 1921–1922.

Armaments Declarations at The Hague

Despite failures in other limitation debates, the First Hague Peace Conference did decide on three binding declarations limiting largely new and untried armaments. These included bans on aerial bombardment, on shells whose main purpose was to disperse poisonous gas, and

---

[111] Charles à Court, Note on the Limitation of Armaments, *enclosure in* Pauncefote to Salisbury, July 31, 1899, *in* FO 412/65.

on expanding bullets, of which the dum-dum was the most famous type. While aerial bombardment and poison gas generated little discussion, the dum-dum bullet declaration was directed against ammunition used solely by Great Britain, resulting in heated discussions.[112]

Expanding bullets were not listed on the Czar's program but had been raised as a possible means of limiting armaments by the Swiss and Dutch delegations at the first meeting of the military sub-commission. While preparing for the conference, Major-General Ardagh alluded to the subject when he correlated decreasing bullet size with improved weaponry effectiveness. As firearms evolved from muzzle-loaders to breech-loaders, and then into repeating rifles with magazines, bullet sizes had correspondingly decreased.[113] As this evolution continued, British military experts feared that smaller bullets would have less effect on their targets. In the Chitral Campaign in India in 1895, veterans claimed that the .303 caliber bullet of the 'Lee–Metford' rifle was insufficient to stop determined foes.[114] In response, the British had developed bullets that expanded upon hitting a target.[115] Hyphenate term as earlier? which term are you referring to? Generally yes, hyphenation should be consistent. Should this be styled as 'Lee–Metford' with an en rule? Yes, this should have an en dash. Good catch.

According to critics, expanding bullets caused excessive injury as a soldier could be put out of combat merely by being struck by an ordinary bullet. Other delegations raised the standard of excessive injury set in the

---

[112] The following discussion on expanding bullets is derived from an earlier article, Scott Keefer, "'Explosive Missals': International Law, Technology, and Security in Nineteenth-Century Disarmament Conferences," *War in History* 21, no. 4 (2013): 445.

[113] The percussion musket used up until the Crimean War, the "Brown Bess," was .753 inch caliber and fired a round per minute, the muzzle-loading Enfield was .577 caliber, the breech-loading Martini-Henry was .45 caliber, and the magazine Lee–Metford rifle was .303 caliber with a rate of fifteen rounds per minute. The Maxim gun increased the rate of fire exponentially to 500 rounds per minute. Ardagh, The Duration of Wars, from the 14th to the 19th Centuries, in particular reference to Improvements in Destructive Agencies, App. No. 6, *enclosure in* War Office to Foreign Office, May 17, 1899, *in* FO 412/65, at 97–98.

[114] Ardagh claimed that soldiers pierced by smaller bullets had been able to continue unhindered to the hospital. Pauncefote to Salisbury, June 15, 1899, *in* FO 412/65.

[115] These bullets had a solid lead core partially covered by a nickel envelope up to the tip of the bullet. The opening in the nickel envelope allowed the soft lead to expand and break into fragments. As Ardagh pointed out at the conference, all older bullets, such as those still used by the British Army's Snider rifle, lacked the nickel envelope over the lead bullet, and therefore also expanded. *See* H. Brackenbury, Memorandum *enclosure in* War Office to Foreign Office, June 22, 1899, *in* FO 412/65.

1868 St. Petersburg Declaration. In response, the British delegate stressed the need for greater stopping power in the context of "savage warfare" in the colonies. Ardagh argued that while "civilized" soldiers would lie down and wait for the stretcher-bearer upon being hit by a small bullet:

> your fanatical barbarian, when he receives wounds of a like nature, which are insufficient to stop or disable him, continues to dash on, spear or sword in hand, and before you have had time or opportunity to represent to him that his conduct is in flagrant violation of the understanding relative to the proper course for a wounded man to follow, he may have cut off your head.[116]

Both Ardagh and Fisher repeatedly distinguished between "civilized" and "savage" warfare, where other delegations had been silent. But Ardagh's claimed need for more powerful bullets against savages went beyond acceptable standards, and drew the rebuke of the Russian delegate, who claimed the humanitarian spirit did not allow such invidious distinctions.[117] However, privately other delegations cynically acknowledged the British division between civilized and savage. In much the same off-hand manner as neighbors swap recipes, the Dutch delegate claimed their army had been happy with the effects of fully mantled bullets when fighting their "savages," as these had the penetrating power necessary for reaching foes sheltering behind improvised stockades and in jungles.[118] While the British couched their need for expanding bullets in the context of "savage warfare" in the colonies, the unstated purpose was the intent to use similar bullets in European warfare, possibly to break up cavalry or bayonet charges.[119] The dum-dum bullet, referring to a type made in the eponymous Indian town, was merely the most famous expanding bullet, as the British made similar ammunition in domestic arsenals for European conflicts. At the conference, Ardagh studiously avoided all

---

[116] Ardagh, Memorandum respecting Expanding Bullets, *enclosure in* Pauncefote to Salisbury, June 15, 1899, *in* FO 412/65.

[117] Raffalovich, May 31, 1899, Scott, ed., *1899 Proceedings*, 343.

[118] Ardagh, Memorandum, *enclosure in* Pauncefote to Salisbury, July 10, 1899, *in* FO 412/65. While the Dutch delegate was seeking British adherence to a declaration against expanding bullets, and may have made the claim merely to persuade Ardagh, it reflected common views on the necessity of superior weapons to maintain European predominance.

[119] Ardagh, Memorandum respecting Expanding Bullets, *supra* note 116.

mention of these other expanding bullets, as they belied claims the ammunition was solely designed for imperial conflicts. Had he wanted to, he
could have made stronger arguments by noting that the dum-dum bullet
did not inflict the traumatic injuries of the Tübingen bullet – a type used
in a medical study on the effects of expanding bullets, which was often
referred to in discussions at The Hague. However, as other expanding
bullets in British domestic arsenals mirrored the effects of the Tübingen
bullet, Ardagh remained silent.[120]

More pointedly, the proposed regulation would only have applied reciprocally. The British could have continued to use the bullets against its colonial
subjects as they acquired no rights as signatories. Had their concern solely
been with colonial subjects, a ban similar to the St. Petersburg Declaration
should have been acceptable as it had been in 1868. The fact that the British
continued their opposition to the declaration in spite of the provision of
reciprocity indicates that their real concern was with using expanding bullets against European enemies, not in colonial insurrections, an interpretation which Ardagh explicitly confirmed. Ardagh, after noting the dubious
humanity of using dum-dum bullets in colonial warfare, reflected:

> On the other hand, there is at least some reason to doubt whether the pres-
> ent English pattern of bullet entirely fulfils the requirements of a bullet for
> even civilized warfare. But for this doubt, I should have been content to
> admit the application of the restriction as a supplement to the Convention
> of St. Petersburgh [sic], which, as it is only binding upon those who have
> acceded to it, would have excluded savage warfare ...[121]

The British delegation may have been opposed to a limit for other reasons, including concern that any general agreement would tend to delegitimize British use of dum-dum bullets in colonial wars, regardless of

---

[120] Second Supplementary Note by Major-General Ardagh on Small-arms Bullets, *enclosure
in* Pauncefote to Salisbury, June 27 1899, FO 412/65.
[121] Ardagh, Memorandum respecting Expanding Bullets, *supra* note 116. He went on to
note that "... even though a complete and unperforated envelope were to be accepted as a
binding condition, it should not be beyond the ingenuity of the inventor to design a projectile which, while it conformed to the letter of this condition, might nevertheless produce a
wound sufficiently severe to satisfy practical requirements." *Id.* Thus, technological innovation was expected to eventually bypass treaty restrictions.

British abstention.[122] In fact, such considerations played a role in the ultimate British adherence to the declaration in 1907.[123] Yet the desire to use expanding bullets in European wars provided the decisive reason for British opposition.

Despite British opposition, the conference voted to ban "the use of bullets which expand or flatten easily in the human body, such as bullets with a hard envelope which does not entirely cover the core, or is pierced with incisions."[124] The precision of the language caused some misgivings, as the American delegation claimed that it would be better to codify the general principle that all bullets causing excessive harm should be banned. As the specificity of the declaration would make it easier to circumvent, the Americans proposed an alternative declaration enlarging upon the general principle espoused in the St. Petersburg Declaration. However, other delegations countered that a general principle would be easier to breach, as there would be no clear definition of what "excessive injury" encompassed. This lack of clarity would merely lead to recrimination and embittered relations. Thus the assembly decided upon a specific formula, even if the declaration only removed one weapon from the world's arsenals.

In comparison to the debates on expanding bullets, the two other armaments declarations regulating poison gas and aerial bombardment followed non-contentious debates. Only American Captain Mahan raised serious objections to banning poison gas, claiming that:

[122] Turn of the century international lawyers disagreed on whether treaties signed in a general conference bound even non-signatories, some reformers claiming that a law-making conference such as that at The Hague forged rules for the entire world community. See Lawrence, *The Principles of International Law*, 101 *et seq*. The traditional, and prevailing, view held that only signatories to agreements were bound by their terms. Oppenheim, *International Law: A Treatise*, vol. I, 23–24.

[123] "A Declaration signed by perhaps over thirty Powers carries some weight and, by the action of public opinion, is a strong factor in inducing other Powers to join it. This is conclusively proved by our own action in regard to expanding bullets, for, though we refused to sign, His Majesty's Government considered it necessary to abolish the Dum-Dum and Mark IV bullets in consequence of the Declaration, and we have now, at the eleventh hour, signed it." Memorandum by Sir Edmond Elles, *enclosure in* Fry to Grey, 13 Aug. 1907, No. 48, FO 412/88, Further Correspondence Respecting the Second Peace Conference at the Hague, (August 1907).

[124] "Declaration Concerning Exploding Bullets, July 29, 1899," *American Journal of International Law* 1, no. 2 Supplement (1907): 155–157.

... it was illogical, and not demonstrably humane, to be tender about asphyxiating men with gas, when all were prepared to admit that it was allowable to blow the bottom out of an ironclad at midnight, throwing four or five hundred into the sea, to be choked by water, with scarcely the remotest chance of escape.[125]

Mahan remained adamantly opposed to a ban on poison gas, on principle rather than out of national interest.[126] The final regulation banned shells "the object of which is the diffusion of asphyxiating or deleterious gases."[127] In providing the British view in the naval subcommission, Fisher expressed no opposition to the ban on poison gas, but the Admiralty, together with the War and Foreign Offices, overruled him.[128]

Finally, the conference placed a limit on aerial bombardment. Ardagh considered aerial bombardment in the same light as other technological advances, seeing only the potential for new weaponry to limit the expense and devastation of war. Noting the length of the siege of Paris in 1870–1871, Ardagh claimed that most deaths during the siege resulted from starvation rather than bombardment. While the Prussian bombardment had been relatively ineffective, Parisian morale was shattered. If an inaccurate bombardment could quickly end a siege, reasoned Ardagh, precision-targeted aerial bombardment could rapidly bring even a determined garrison to terms, sparing the lives of civilians in the process.[129]

[125] Scott, *The Hague Peace Conferences of 1899 and 1907*, Vol. II, 37.

[126] Ardagh speculated that the Americans must have been planning a poison gas shell, but while the technology had been available since the Civil War, no weapon was forthcoming. See F. Stansbury Haydon, "A Proposed Gas Shell, 1862," *Journal of the American Military History Foundation* 2, no. 1 (1938).

[127] "Declaration Concerning Asphyxiating Gas, July 29, 1899," *American Journal of International Law* 1, no. 2 Supplement (1907). Discussions had raised the issue of whether shells that incidentally discharged noxious gases were prohibited, which was answered in the negative. This definition contributed to the early chemical weapons used in the First World War, which featured chemical agents in shrapnel shells. As these shells had a dual purpose of scattering shrapnel and spreading chemical gas, they were argued to be in conformity with the requirements of the Hague Declaration.

[128] See Memoranda, Enclosure No. 4, *in* War Office to Foreign Office, Oct. 11, 1899, *in* FO 412/65.

[129] Ardagh was prescient in his predictions: "That the discharge of high explosives from aerial machines will constitute the most formidable method of warfare yet known is probable, and that the balloon, and possibly the kite, as engines of destruction, will form part of the armament in the next war which is waged between any two first-class Powers is not unlikely." Ardagh, Restrictions on Employment of High Explosives, Appendix No. 9, *in* War Office to Foreign Office, May 17, 1899, *in* FO 412/65.

As in the 1868 discussions of "explosive missals," the 1899 gathering suffered from a lack of practical experience or precise terminology. As the British and other delegations were unclear about the future evolution of aerial technology – which in 1899 did not include heavier-than-air craft – their members referred to both balloons and kites as the subject of their deliberations.[130] It proved difficult both to frame regulations as well as to judge the necessity for limiting aerial warfare before it had been attempted in a systematic way. Many shared the humanist sentiment expressed by Dutch delegate den Beer Poortugael when he asked "[d]oes it not seem excessive to authorize the use of infernal machines which seem to fall from the sky?"[131] Yet more delegates agreed with his assessment that technology could easily make such weaponry possible. Without knowing the direction technology would advance, the conference decided on a five-year ban, allowing reconsideration of the question once the technology had sufficiently matured.

The British delegation withdrew its objections to the aerial bombardment prohibition in order to gain American support in defeating the expanding bullet ban, a matter that was far more important to the British military.[132] However, the British delegation continued to shape the development of regulations through its opposition to them. The delegations had initially planned on incorporating all three armament declarations either in a protocol to the 1868 St. Petersburg Declaration or in a single treaty instrument. It became clear that British opposition to two of the three declarations would result in the island nation's refusal to ratify a document containing all these provisions, so the final declarations were completed as separate, independent, treaties. Ultimately, Great Britain, alone among the 26 nations at the conference, refused to ratify any of the three declarations.[133] Of the other great powers, only the United States also chose to abstain from some of the declarations, fulfilling earlier predictions

---

[130] The uncertainty about future technology led to a very general and vague regulation. The imprecision of the language led the Romanian delegate to seek clarification on whether the declaration forbade high-angle mortar fire. Coanda, June 22, 1899, Scott, ed., *1899 Proceedings*, 281.

[131] Den Beer Poortugael, May 29, 1899, *Id.*, 341–42.

[132] Declaration respecting the shooting or dropping Projectiles or Explosives from Balloons or other novel analogous contrivances, Enclosure No. 4, *in* War Office to Foreign Office, Oct. 11, 1899, *in* FO 412/65.

[133] The British changed course at the Second Hague Conference, ratifying bans on all three weapons systems. Scott, ed., *Hague Conventions*.

that armaments questions could differentiate the two powers from the other states at the conference.

CONCLUSION

The limits of international law were starkly highlighted during the First Hague Peace Conference in 1899. Sovereign nations refused to accept grand disarmament proposals predicated on a radical revision of the international system, through such means as the creation of an international police force. Yet without provisions for a police force, delegations professed themselves unable even fruitfully to discuss arms limitations in the abstract. While these opinions were widely stated, they belied a certain disingenuousness. Salisbury, Fisher, and Ardagh all participated in the renegotiation of the Rush–Bagot naval arms agreement in the late 1890s and had practical experience in maintaining a relatively successful ninety-year-old arms treaty.[134] Like technical objections to limitations, legal objections were highlighted in order to dispose of a subject that not one of the great powers truly wanted to discuss. This political opposition, more than technical objections, ended disarmament initiatives in 1899. Britain advocated and opposed specific weapons limitations based upon its strategic position, rather than out of concern for humanitarian principles. Its approach to international law indicated a pragmatic assessment of the advantages and liabilities of treaty restrictions. Its opposition to disarmament based on claims of impossibility must also be viewed as an argument designed for public consumption.

Had statesmen been truly interested in checking the arms race, they might have focused on more pragmatic means. Had they focused upon arms control, utilizing the existing legal system and based on an expectation of continued interstate competition rather than a fundamental change in international relations, limitation might have proved possible. Certainly, Britain, in spite of its overall opposition to disarmament, was willing to regulate specific naval weapons posing a threat to its position. Moreover, the Admiralty had publicly expressed a willingness to limit construction programs if the other great powers followed suit, and privately made a concrete offer to Russia. These were dangerous offers to make had they been purely bluff. Like the prohibitions of specific naval weapons,

[134] See following chapter.

Britain was willing to accept limits that would not be predicated upon cumbersome, and wholly hypothetical, international machinery such as an international police force.

The large multilateral format of the Hague conferences proved problematic for negotiations, while a general limitation of armaments required each state to reassess its position relative to all its competitors, rendering bilateral discussions incomplete. The challenges of limiting the continental arms race proved too large, and political will utterly lacking, to take such a step. Yet arms control was possible, but depended on the circumstances of the political relationship in question as well as the characteristics of the weapons system being regulated. Naval arms control could succeed in a manner in which land restrictions could not, if crafted around existing political relationships and the structure of the international political system. Three years after The Hague, an arms race at the opposite end of the globe was successfully ended through an arms control treaty. Naval weaponry was regulated, Britain played a central role, and Ardagh participated as a legal expert.

CHAPTER 5

Naval Arms Control and Regional Negotiations: Precedents, Issues, and Implications

After the fanfare accorded disarmament, the failure of arms limitation initiatives at The Hague in 1899 obscured the positive role that law had played. While lack of interest amongst the great powers doomed disarmament, the large multilateral setting of the negotiations undermined the quest for realistic solutions. A general multilateral disarmament agreement, as was popularly expected to be a result of the Hague Conference, required novel legal institutions to monitor and enforce obligations. However, the British government recognized that arms limitations had precedents and could contribute to security within the existing international legal framework. In the nineteenth century, Britain had repeatedly regulated naval armaments, and by 1900 the British increasingly had reason for seeking security through a limitation of the naval arms race.

In the late 1890s, in addition to the traditional British rivalry with France and Russia, overall naval construction had accelerated, with the United States and Germany both pushing their navies into the top tier of naval powers. In previous decades, the British contended with two to three larger naval powers, usually with France and either Russia or Italy as the next two largest powers. Now all the great powers were involved in the competition, with even Austria-Hungary and Japan contending in the 1900s. A challenge which could have previously been handled through bilateral negotiations, while maintaining a wary eye on the third naval power, now involved at least four foreign powers. While naval historians debate the British focus on either a Franco-Russian or German threat, let alone the relative utility of battleships, the rise of numerous powers inevitably increased the complexity of diplomatic negotiations among politicians who perceived the competition in terms of battleships.[1]

While one of the British Hague delegation's arguments in 1899 focused on the impracticality of disarmament, the Foreign Office had substantial experience utilizing international law in shaping the security environment, including arms limitation. Thus, the opposition to disarmament expressed at The Hague was only an incomplete reflection of the British position. The British government recognized that arms control could work and had been used with success in the past. Prior to his participation at the 1899 Hague Peace Conference, Major-General Ardagh had come into contact with arms limitation obligations. Ardagh was involved in a major inter-agency review of Canadian defenses in the late 1890s, which focused on the defense of the Great Lakes region at a time when the Rush-Bagot Agreement was being renegotiated.

Ardagh also contributed to the peace negotiations that ended the 1897 Greco-Turkish War, charting potential boundary changes and their strategic significance.[2] This experience, similar to his later role in the Argentine-Chilean negotiations, involved the resolution of a boundary conflict while related negotiations involving naval power were conducted. It provided Ardagh with exposure to discussions involving the prospective limitation of armaments, two years prior to the Hague Conference and further indicated that naval arms control was seen as feasible, albeit not desired by Britain in this case.

Greece had initiated the war in 1897 in order to liberate Crete, hoping that Ottoman military power would prove hollow. The Turks won the land campaign, driving the Greeks back in Thessaly, but the Greek Navy dominated the Aegean, allowing volunteers and supplies to aid in the liberation of Crete. The Greek Navy had been expanded in the

---

[1] More recently, on the comparative Franco-Russian and German threats, *see* Matthew S. Seligmann, "Britain's Security Mirage: The Royal Navy and the Franco-Russian Naval Threat, 1898–1906," *Journal of Strategic Studies* 35, no. 6 (2012): 861. Seligmann accepted the revisionist view regarding relative Admiralty concern with submarines and torpedo flotilla craft rather than battleships, but held Germany to be a more significant factor in these concerns. Seligmann, *The Royal Navy and the German Threat, 1901–1914: Admiralty Plans to Protect British Trade in a War against Germany*, (Oxford: Oxford University Press, 2012), 171.

[2] Ardagh, Memorandum on Hostilities between Turkey and Greece, Mar. 23, 1897, FO 881/6907 (1897); Ardagh, Turco-Greek Frontier Strategical Rectification, June 30, 1897, *in* Ardagh Papers, Memoranda and Reports, PRO 30/40/14, (1896–1901) at 240.

early 1890s with the addition of three coastal-defense battleships, giving Greece a credible force in the Eastern Mediterranean.[3] Because of the role played by the Greek Navy in the brief conflict, the negotiating parties initially considered stripping the fleet, or at least its main units, from Greece. Britain opposed this action, on the grounds of strategic interest rather than any legal grounds, and the demands were dropped.[4] Ardagh remained abreast of the strategic issues involved in Greco-Turkish relations and likely would have had knowledge of possible peace terms, including naval arms limitation. In spite of his opposition to disarmament in 1899, the Director of Military Intelligence witnessed the practical applications of arms limitation.

Unique aspects of naval construction provided opportunities for naval arms control. Not every weapons system was alike, however. Ease of verification of force levels was central to arms control, and it was easier to monitor battleships than troop levels. Moreover, different negotiating formats were more likely to create effective agreements. Statesmen did not view arms control as an impossibility after The Hague gathering, but recognized that it had to be crafted around realistic objectives and the realities of technology and politics.

Naval arms control enjoyed a remarkable success in this period, ending a crisis between Argentina and Chile. The 1902 agreement between the South American neighbors, brought about largely through British intervention, demonstrated the role law could play in maintaining security. While the Hague Conference provided an example of unworkable concepts of disarmament, the Latin American Pacts of May suggested the possibilities of arms control. Moreover, renewed Anglo-American discussions about the Rush-Bagot Agreement provided successive British governments with experience of introducing naval arms limits. This chapter will detail British involvement in the Pacts of May and the 1890s–1910s Great Lakes negotiations, then turn to larger themes raised by naval arms control.

---

[3] Zsis Fotakis, *Greek Naval Strategy and Policy, 1910–1919* (London: Routledge, 2005), 14–15. The addition would have allowed Greece to even challenge the Hapsburg Navy on reasonable terms. Fotakis, *Greek Naval Policy*, 11.

[4] Monson to Salisbury, May 7, 1897, No. 147, *in* Further Correspondence Respecting the Affairs of South-Eastern Europe, FO 881/6994 (May 1897); Michel Lhéritier, *Histoire Diplomatique De La Grèce De 1821 a Nos Jours*, Vol. IV (Paris: Les Presses Universitaires de France, 1926), 410.

ARGENTINE-CHILEAN NAVAL ARMS RACE

The Argentine-Chilean dispute accompanied the rise of the two nations and the coalescing of a regional balance of power system in South America. By the late nineteenth century, South American diplomacy had evolved into a diagonal system, with a Pacific rivalry between Chile and Peru interacting with an Argentine–Brazilian rivalry in the Atlantic.[5] As Chile and Argentina gained prominence and increasingly competed for dominance, their diplomats conspired with each other's enemies, increasing regional instability.

Chile's power dramatically increased through the 1879–1883 War of the Pacific, in which this nation decisively wielded sea power to defeat Peru and Bolivia.[6] Chile gained the nitrate-rich coastal provinces of Tacna and Arica, providing an important revenue source while also earning the lasting enmity of its vanquished foes. Chile gained the reputation as the "Prussia of South America," an analogy furthered by the eternal Peruvian and Bolivian quest for the lost provinces, as a regional Alsace-Lorraine.[7]

Meanwhile, Argentina, which had a comparable population in 1870, underwent significant peaceful development as a destination for European capital and immigrants. By 1900, Argentina had a population 50°percent greater than Chile's, as well as three times the level of foreign trade, and growth trends indicated a further widening of the gap.[8] Given regional tensions and insecurity, Argentine fears grew that Chile would launch a preemptive strike before the disparity was insurmountable. In the 1890s, Argentine-Chilean tensions reflected a struggle for regional dominance. Ongoing boundary disputes provided an endless source of friction, raising the prospect of war in repeated crises from 1898 onwards.

An increasingly intense naval arms race reflected these tensions. The rugged terrain of the Andes made large-scale land warfare difficult, while the War of the Pacific indicated the possibilities of naval conflict.[9] In the

[5] Robert N. Burr, "The Balance of Power in Nineteenth-Century South America: An Exploratory Essay," *Hispanic American Historical Review* 35, no. 1 (1955).

[6] Donald E. Worcester, "Naval Strategy in the War of the Pacific," *Journal of Interamerican Studies* 5, no. 1 (1963).

[7] Moreover, Chile furthered the image by employing German military instructors and adopting the spiked Prussian helmet for the army.

[8] Grant, *Rulers, Guns, and Money*, 131.

[9] In that war, instead of a direct overland assault, Chilean ironclads fought and defeated their Peruvian adversaries, then exploited command of the sea to undertake a direct naval

early 1890s, Chile possessed clear naval superiority over Argentina, adding a battleship and two small cruisers in 1893.[10] The two states embarked on both a qualitative and a quantitative arms race, purchasing protected cruisers, then more powerful armored cruisers during the 1898 war scare. The two fleets increased dramatically during the arms race, reaching a fever pitch in 1901–1902. Purchases arranged in the last six months of the competition alone would have expanded the tonnage of the Argentine and Chilean navies by 88°percent and 50°percent, respectively.[11] The Chilean fleet doubled in size over the decade, while the Argentine navy nearly quintupled.

As in European geopolitics, conference diplomacy masked strategic maneuvers. During a 1900 war scare, Peru and Bolivia exploited an upcoming Pan-American conference to advocate the principle of universal obligatory arbitration to force Chile to arbitrate its border. Like Germany before the Second Hague Peace Conference, the Chilean government was concerned that the gathering could be used to spring a diplomatic trap.[12] At the 1901 Pan-American Conference held in Mexico City, Chile appeared

---

invasion of Lima, followed by an advance inland. Worcester, "Naval Strategy." Mahan formulated his theories of sea power while stationed at Lima, Peru during the conflict. Larrie D. Ferreiro, "Mahan and the 'English Club' of Lima, Peru: The Genesis of the *Influence of Sea Power Upon History*," *Journal of Military History* 72 (2008).

[10] Chile could even challenge the United States in South American waters. A. T. Volwiler, "Harrison, Blaine, and American Foreign Policy, 1889–1893," *Proceedings of the American Philosophical Society* 79, no. 4 (1938): 641–42.

[11] Total tonnage of the two fleets were as follows:

	Chile	Argentina
1891	24,190	11,734
1896	38,957	25,240
1898	46,207	46,692
1900	50,530	53,532
1903[a]	76,056	100,782

[a] 1903 figures represent probable levels had purchases made at the height of the arms race been completed. George von Rauch, *Conflict in the Southern Cone: The Argentine Military and the Boundary Dispute with Chile, 1870–1902* (London: Praeger, 1999), 150–54

[12] The European governments followed the conference closely, so the diplomatic lesson would have been known to Germany. Moreover, some evidence suggests that Germany sought to prevent the conference from accomplishing its goals. A. Curtis Wilgus, "The Second International American Conference at Mexico City," *Hispanic American Historical Review* 11, no. 1 (1931): 43–44.

nearly isolated, with the majority of South American states supporting compulsory arbitration of past disputes, and Chile advocating only mandatory arbitration of future disputes. Ultimately through diplomatic maneuvering, Chile persuaded Ecuador and Columbia to adhere to its view, but nonetheless appeared beleaguered and alone, suffering a diplomatic defeat.[13]

The strategic situation paralleled the later Anglo-German rivalry in several respects, including the existence of both qualitative and quantitative competition,[14] and the use of both formal and informal arms control. Chile repeatedly sought a free hand by affirming peace with its northern neighbors to allow a focus on its southern border, and by reaching a détente with Argentina that would force Bolivia and Peru to accept their existing borders. Moreover, the relative Chilean decline intensified pressures with its government recognizing it had a window of opportunity to act before the Argentine Navy became too strong. The possibility of a preemptive strike by Chile was as at its greatest in 1897–1902 as it faced a closing window of opportunity. The Chilean posturing mirrored later policy debates within British and German circles as to the possibility of resolving the arms race through a unilateral strike. Finally, the resolution of the Latin American arms race highlighted the potential role of international law in addressing strategic uncertainties and mistrust.

Chile's financial situation deteriorated steeply in early 1898. Banking authorities indicated the state was spending around £445,000 per month maintaining its military on active status, with cash reserves dwindling to £593,000 by April.[15] By July, Chilean finances had collapsed, causing a run on the banks, and by August, the Chilean economy was at a standstill. The freezing of credit and the lack of money led stores to close and left workers unpaid, further fueling animosity and increasing the military's determination to act.[16] In response, the Chilean government removed its

---

[13] *Id.*: 34; Robert N. Burr, "By Reason or Force: Chile and the Balancing of Power in South America, 1830–1905," *University of California Publications in History* 77 (1965): 228–44.

[14] As noted by von Rauch, *Southern Cone*, 184.

[15] Gosling to Salisbury, Apr. 2, 1898, *in* Chile – Diplomatic, FO 16/316, (1898) at 53.

[16] Gosling to Salisbury, Aug. 1, 1898, *in* Chile – Diplomatic, FO 16/317, (1898) at 108. In June, a Chilean newspaper calculated the relative balance of strength of the two navies, finding that Chile still retained a sufficient margin of force to attack. Using an undefined "coefficient" to determine the strength of major fleet units, it arrived at the conclusion that Chile maintained a 510:457 superiority over its rival, although recent acquisitions of armored cruisers favored the latter state, accounting for 100 and 300 points of the respective totals. Gosling to Salisbury, June 28, 1898, *in* FO 16/316, at 203.

currency from the gold standard, and ordered the printing of $50 million. In order to bolster confidence in currency markets, the law creating the new currency required that Chile begin stockpiling gold in order to redeem the paper currency for gold in January 1902.[17]

After leading their countries to the brink of war, the presidents of Argentina and Chile sought to rebuild their relations. The northern border question was resolved by early 1899, and Presidents Errázuriz and Roca planned a significant diplomatic gesture to confirm their reconciliation. The two national leaders boarded their flagships and each led a naval squadron to the Straits of Magellan, where dignitaries from both states toasted their friendship. During the four-day visit, each took turns regaling and hosting the officers of the other navy at balls and dinners held on deck and ashore at Punta Arenas. While the gathering signaled a détente allowing an easing of finances in both states, no fundamental breakthrough occurred, and no armament agreement was reached.[18]

* * *

The large British commercial interests in Argentina and Chile propelled Britain to take a central role in resolving the dispute. The British government recognized that war would potentially have disastrous effects on British investments, and, because of the increasingly interlocked balance of power system, would likely spill over into neighboring South American states.[19] An Argentine-Chilean war would have given Peru and Bolivia the opportunity to profit from the Chilean distraction by attacking in the north. Brazil would have an interest in preventing Argentina from becoming too strong, and would therefore intervene on behalf of Chile. If Peru intervened, Chile hoped it could gain support from Ecuador and Columbia, both of whom had border issues with Peru. If such an escalation seems unrealistic in retrospect, one only need look at expansion of

---

[17] Gosling to Salisbury, Aug. 3, 1898, *in* FO 16/317, at 113.
[18] Gosling to Salisbury, Mar. 1, 1899, *in* Chile – Diplomatic, FO 16/324, (1899) at 48.
[19] Ardagh reflected on this risk in advocating Britain shoulder the immediate expenses of surveying the border. "That alone would be a great gain, when the large financial interests of Great Britain in both Chili and Argentina are considered. We must also reflect that if war broke out between those countries, it is not improbable that the conflagration might extend over adjacent states, so, on the whole, the extra cost of a Survey Party would be a well spent insurance." Memo by Ardagh, Chili–Argentine Arbitration Tribunal, Dec. 28, 1901, *in* Argentina–Chile Boundary Arbitration, FO 16/356, (1896–1902) Part II, at 372.

war in 1914. Given the potential for escalation, the British government perceived a necessity to defuse the crisis.

Moreover, Robert Burr has argued that Great Britain needed to reaffirm its regional presence in South America following the Hay–Pauncefote Treaty with the United States.[20] Britain had relinquished its central role in the region by acknowledging American predominance in the Caribbean, and wanted to reassert its position in South America. At the turn of the century, a perception of British decline existed in Latin America, with many in the region viewing early British defeats in the Boer War as a signal of the limits of the island nation's power.[21] The smaller Latin American nations increasingly sensed a shifting of power, with the prospect that they could someday fend off the great powers. British involvement in resolving the regional tensions held the prospect of enhancing British prestige.

Britain initially became involved in the crisis with respect to Argentine-Chilean boundary delimitation, with the parties delaying final settlement into the 1890s, when increased activities in the region brought the parties into confrontation. In 1896, the two nations agreed in theory to arbitrate parts of their dispute, with the British sovereign acting as the arbitrator. When crisis flared up in 1898, Salisbury's government accepted the role, recognizing the risk open conflict would cause to Britain's commercial interests in the region.[22] According to Foreign Office records, the only time in modern history where the British sovereign had acted as an arbitrator in an international dispute occurred more than half a century previously when Queen Victoria arbitrated a dispute between France and Mexico in 1844.[23] The Foreign Office saw arbitration as a thankless and dangerous task and approached the duty warily.[24] Given this degree of caution and the rarity of British arbitration of international disputes, the government's acceptance of the role is noteworthy. A dangerous task was undertaken only because it was outweighed by the risk of war.

---

[20] Robert Burr, "By Reason or by Force," at 248.

[21] Cusack-Smith to Lansdowne, Jan. 19, 1901, *in* Chile – Diplomatic, FO 16/331, (1901) at 55.

[22] Barrington to Villiers, July 13, 1898, *in* FO 16/356, Part I, at 22.

[23] Memorandum by Oakes, Chile–Argentine Arbitration, Nov. 7, 1902, *in* Argentine–Chile Boundary Arbitration, FO 16/357, (1902) at 399.

[24] "There is always some danger – especially in S. & C. America – of difficulties arising if our diplomatic or Consular officers are permitted to arbitrate." Foreign Office Memo, Aug. 26, 1901, *in* FO 16/331, at 316; "It would be a thankless and unsatisfactory office to judge from past history ..." Cusack-Smith to Lansdowne, Aug. 26, 1901, *in* FO 16/331.

Even after the parties accepted arbitration, the case proceeded exceedingly slowly. The parties initially submitted the relevant documents to the arbitrators, but Chile included a memorandum stating its case. Argentina requested the right to reply to the Chilean statement, taking 23 months to prepare its argument. As the crisis was reaching a fever pitch in late 1901, Chile had already taken seven months in preparing its own counterargument, and it could be expected Argentina would take at least as long to respond, dragging the case on through 1902 despite the growing risk of war.[25] The British organized a three-man arbitral panel, including Major-General Ardagh, as a military officer of high rank, Thomas Holdich, a renowned geographer with experience in surveying operations, and Lord Macnaghten, an eminent jurist.

Meanwhile, tensions between the parties continued to mount. In 1901, both sides took actions in the Andes which were viewed as encroachments by their neighbor – Chile building roads in the mountains, and Argentina stationing police forces in the disputed territory. By December, Argentina broke off relations with Chile and war appeared imminent.[26] Chile mobilized its national guard and halted railroad traffic to concentrate troops. The Chilean Minister sent mixed signals to British Consul Cusack-Smith. Cheerily claiming that despite the concentration of troops he expected negotiations to proceed peacefully, he simultaneously asked for British good offices to resolve the matter.[27]

While the immediate problems were patched over, William Barrington, British Minister Plenipotentiary in Buenos Aires, warned that "[a]s matters stand, slight friction might lead to war;" while the same day the British consul in Valparaiso believed "Chili [sic] would welcome rupture though will probably not provoke rupture."[28] Argentina expressed exasperation at what it perceived to be Chilean breaches of an informal arms control agreement, and impatience to

---

[25] Cusack-Smith to Lansdowne, Dec. 23, 1901, *in* FO 16/356, Part II, at 367.

[26] Argentina maintained that while it called its ambassador home in the midst of the crisis, Chile continued to be represented in Buenos Aires, so there was never a complete rupture. Barrington to Lansdowne, Dec. 22, 1901, *in* FO 16/356, Part II, at 352. However, the underlying message of such an action taken at the height of a crisis, clearly indicated a break in relations.

[27] Cusack-Smith to Lansdowne, Dec. 12, 1901, and Dec. 13, 1901, *in* FO 16/356, Part II, at 339, 341.

[28] Barrington to Lansdowne, and Cusack-Smith to Lansdowne, both Dec. 22, 1901, *in* FO 16/356, Part II, at 352, 353.

end the wasteful expenditure on armaments. President Roca held that "[h]e was quite alive to the disastrous results inseparable from war should such a calamity ensue, but the armed peace, which was the present state of the relations between the two Countries was very onerous and could not go on indefinitely."[29]

The British legations in Buenos Aires and Valparaiso sent a flurry of telegrams attempting to avert war. At the New Year, after daily telegrams had been sent from both capitals throughout the previous month, an eerie silence sparked fears that war had broken out. Both King Edward VII and Prime Minister Salisbury had their holidays interrupted as the government sought to respond to the crisis, indicating the severity of the situation and the importance of the matter to Britain.[30]

Shocked into action, the Foreign Office recognized that more direct involvement would be needed to defuse the crisis. Up to this point the British government had shown reluctance to directly offer good offices without the request of both parties, and Argentina had consistently opposed British intervention due to the public outcry that would result. The perpetually postponed border survey, stalled pending the filing of final arguments by the parties, was immediately ordered into action. Legally unripe, as the parties had not completed their arguments, the survey party was innocently renamed a "commission of enquiry." Despite the lateness of the season, with good mountaineering weather expected only until April, the survey party sailed from England in January with the express goal of cooling passions by demonstrating some sign of progress on the border question.[31]

The Foreign Office issued draft telegrams to its legations to be sent to both capitals in the event of hostilities, indicating British action if war broke out.[32] The legations in Buenos Aires and Valparaiso had already been ordered to communicate directly with one another, in order to save time and provide a second channel for Argentine-Chilean negotiations.[33] In December 1901, and again when negotiations reached their peak in

[29] Barrington to Lansdowne, Dec. 27, 1901, *in* FO 16/356, Part II, 381.

[30] Lansdowne had prepared a course of action if war appeared imminent, which specifically required approval of the King, who was at Sandringham, and Salisbury, holidaying at Hatfield. They were duly contacted on December 30 when it was feared war had broken out. Viliers to Salisbury, Dec. 30, 1901, *in* FO 16/356, Part II, at 397.

[31] Holdich to Viliers, Jan. 6, 1902, *in* FO 16/356, Part III, at 453.

[32] Draft Telegram, undated, *in* FO 16/356, Part II, at 401.

[33] Foreign Office to Cusack-Smith, Dec. 12, 1901, *in* FO 16/356, Part II, at 338.

April and May 1902, almost daily messages were sent by telegraph in duplicate between the Foreign Office and the two legations. Given the cost-paring nature of the Foreign Office, which required authorization for the smallest expenses, and the tendency of the legations to explicitly justify the sending of any telegram, the acceptance of this extraordinary expense was significant.[34]

The competition had reached a fever pitch in these months. Argentina had previously warned Chile that any naval acquisition would be matched, establishing a tacit agreement on naval weaponry. In early 1902, Chile purchased the recently completed protected cruiser *Chacabuco* and three destroyers to redress its declining strategic position under the guise of replacing outdated ships. Argentina perceived this as a direct threat, as such warships would have no additional value in a conflict with Peru or Bolivia. In response, Argentina authorized the immediate purchase of a pair of more powerful armored cruisers.[35] Seeing its strategic situation slipping hopelessly away, Chile made an even bolder move, ordering a pair of 11,800-ton second-class battleships.[36] Each battleship was nearly half as large again as any previous acquisition by either navy, signaling a major escalation in the race.

The British brought financial pressure to bear upon the two countries, indicating that no further credit would be forthcoming to finance the purchase of warships. Privately, international bankers, including representatives of Barings Brothers, who had significant interests in Argentina, Rothschilds, with a major presence in Chile, and the Argentine financier

[34] Boyce has calculated that the expenses for the exchange of two ten-word telegrams between Australia and Great Britain, further away than Chile, but still a comparable distance, cost the equivalent of several weeks' wages for the average worker. While the government received reductions in return for subsidies, the cost was still extraordinary. Robert W. D. Boyce, "Imperial Dreams and National Realities: Britain, Canada and the Struggle for a Pacific Telegraph Cable, 1879–1902," *English Historical Review* 115, no. 460 (2000): 45, 66. This was at a point when fiscal restrictions were so tight, the Chilean legation even asked permission to purchase a flag to replace the weather-beaten Union Jack hanging in front of their office. Gosling to Salisbury, Mar. 7, 1898, *in* FO 16/316, at 36.

[35] Barrington to Lansdowne, Apr. 24, 1902, *in* FO 16/357, at 51.

[36] Chilean authorities had already held a lengthy meeting with British naval architect Sir Edward Reed in December, resulting in the order of the two vessels in Britain. Cusack-Smith to Lansdowne, Dec. 23, 1901, *in* FO 16/356, Part II, at 354. The vessels were specially designed for Chile, for delivery in twenty months. Lowther to Lansdowne, Apr. 8, 1902, *in* FO 16/ 357, at 17.

Ernesto Tornquist, went further by seeking direct British facilitation of arms control negotiations, and by stating their unwillingness to lend any more funds.[37] However, the Chileans had their gold conversion fund. Following the currency collapse and financial law of 1898, revenues had been raised to convert $50 million in printed money to gold by the end of 1901, but successive governments found the temptation of the fund too great to resist.[38] As the new year began with crisis, the gold standard was not restored, and the Chilean government held this fund of ready cash as a weapon in its conflict with Argentina.[39]

In the meantime, Argentina countered the Chilean purchase of second-class battleships with a pair of 14,850-ton first-class battleships. Representing a further qualitative escalation of the arms race, these would have been the only first-class battleships possessed by a Latin American power. In reality, both the Argentine and the Chilean governments recognized the need to end the arms race. Chilean financial markets reacted poorly to rumors that the gold conversion fund might be raided, making further purchases unlikely.[40] At the same time, Argentine President Roca acknowledged the "paralyzing effects" on credit caused by the arms race expenses, admitting that no further loans were available and his country could only continue by a fresh issue of paper money as well.[41] Still, Chile was wary of making direct offers to Argentina, and initiatives were perceived as a sign of weakness by the Argentine press.[42] More centrally, a deep-rooted mistrust of Chile required a firmer agreement than either the presidential meeting of 1899 or informal arms control had provided. Back-channel negotiations through the British legations allowed a compromise to be arranged without exposing negotiations to the sensationalist press. The utilization of a binding agreement provided greater confidence to both parties.

---

[37] Barrington to Revelstoke, Mar. 25, 1902, *in* FO 16/356, Part III, at 600. On the banking presence in Chile and Argentina, see Gustavo Ferrari, *Conflicto Y Paz Con Chile (1898–1903)* (Buenos Aires: Editorial Universitaria de Buenos Aires, 1968), 56.

[38] Cusack-Smith to Lansdowne, June 18, 1901, and Nov. 18, 1901, *in* FO 16/331, at 138, 236.

[39] Lowther to Lansdowne, Apr. 8, 1902, *in* FO 16/357, at 12.

[40] Lowther to Lansdowne, Apr. 3, 1902, *in* Chile – Diplomatic, FO 16/336, (1902) at 70.

[41] Barrington to Lansdowne, Apr. 10, 1902, *in* FO 16/357, at 29.

[42] Barrington to Lansdowne, Mar. 7, 1902, *in* FO 16/356, Part III, at 589.

THE PACTS OF MAY

Great Britain played a central role brokering the treaties that ended the arms race, by serving as a channel for communication, by threatening the closure of financial markets, by agreeing to arbitrate future disputes between the parties, and by acting as a source of enforcement for the resulting Pacts of May.[43] The Pacts of May involved a comprehensive solution of outstanding problems. In addition to signing an arms control agreement, the parties completed a general arbitration agreement, a mutual declaration of non-intervention in political disputes, and a mutual declaration agreeing to appoint a British expert to complete the actual border delimitation reached through British arbitration. Through international legal instruments, backed by British prestige, the two neighboring states had the confidence to securely limit armaments.

The negotiations leading to the arms control agreement featured many of the methods of arms limitation utilized in later naval agreements. The final agreement incorporated qualitative and quantitative limitations, fleet tonnage ceilings, and numeric ship balances. The parties also showed an understanding of the problems of control and monitoring, opting against a complex formula in favor of a straightforward and easily verified agreement.

The immediate question related to halting the delivery of recently purchased warships. The Argentine government sought an actual reduction in naval expenditures and suggested that each side sell the two most recently ordered warships – the two armored cruisers building for Argentina at the Ansaldo naval yard in Italy, and the two battleships ordered by Chile from Vickers. Chile feared that the naval ratio would continue to favor Argentina, and sought to keep these new battleships while possibly discarding older warships. Chile offered that each side purchase one of the battleships while cancelling the cruisers.[44]

It appeared that negotiations had reached an impasse. It was at this point that Argentina made its order for the pair of first-class battleships,

---

[43] The British role was expressly stated in the preamble to the resulting naval arms control treaty. "Convention between Chile and the Argentine Republic Respecting the Limitation of Naval Armaments, May 28 1902," *American Journal of International Law* 1, no. 3 Supplement (1907). [*hereinafter* 1902 Chilean-Argentine Convention].

[44] *See* Barrington to Lansdowne, May 17, 1902, *in* FO 16/357, at 90.

and in reply Chile threatened to order a first-class battleship of its own.[45] However, the British prodded the parties forward, demanding a halt to the arms race. The Foreign Office explicitly instructed its agents in both capitals to insist that no further armaments be purchased, to "invite from them an undertaking that they will not engage in abnormal expenditures upon naval and military measures" and "[e]xplain that this friendly warning is one we cannot allow the Argentine/Chilian [*sic*] govt. to disregard."[46] Given Britain's leverage as weapons exporter and lender, the parties had little choice but to continue the talks. The negotiations which had already been conducted through British agents, were now ordered to continue at British insistence.

As in the Anglo-German naval arms race later in the decade, the issue of linking arms control to a larger political settlement was discussed. In addition to immediate questions of naval armaments, the powers had to wrangle with larger questions of a regional balance of power. Connected to this issue was the larger question of aggressive behavior if neutrality had been pledged in regional disputes. Chile sought arms control as part of a comprehensive settlement, including an agreement obliging Argentina to arbitrate any future disputes, and an undertaking of neutrality in any controversies involving third parties. By binding Argentina to neutrality in continental affairs, Chile could finally resolve its border issues with Peru and Bolivia. Argentina, for its part, preferred to negotiate an arms deal first, while negotiations on arbitration and neutrality could continue afterwards. Argentina feared that a treaty obligating detachment would provide Chile with a *carte blanche* to undertake further aggression against its northern neighbors.[47] A declaration of neutrality would be tantamount to making Bolivia a Chilean satellite.

The Argentine government desired arms control, with President Roca asking "how far Chile will go towards disarmament."[48] Argentina offered to cancel both the two battleships and two armored cruiser orders it had pending in return for halting the two Chilean battleships. Argentina sought to leverage a larger paper program in gaining Chilean acceptance of arms control, by offering to cancel two ships under construction and two planned

---

[45] Barrington to Lansdowne, Apr. 19, 1902, and Lowther to Lansdowne, Apr. 20, 1902, *in* FO 16/357, at 41, 45.

[46] Draft Telegram, Apr. 21, 1902, *in* FO 16/357, at 47.

[47] Barrington to Lansdowne, Apr. 24, 1902, *in* FO 16/357, at 51.

[48] Barrington to Lansdowne, Apr. 30, 1902, *in* FO 16/357, at 63.

ships in return for two Chilean vessels. At the same time, Roca depended upon the moral support of Britain to ensure observance of any agreement. Great Britain occupied a unique position in this regard, as Chilean ships were being built in a private British yard.[49] Enforcement of the treaty was critical. Britain wielded significant influence in regional politics, assuming the role intended for an international police in monitoring disarmament.

Chilean President Riesco responded that Chile could go as far as actual naval reduction, beyond cancelling current orders, but only if Argentina agreed to a statement of neutrality regarding Pacific questions. A refusal would be deemed "an admission of determination to interfere in Pacific questions."[50] A telegram was immediately sent back from Argentina, disclaiming any interest in Pacific questions, but also expressing reluctance to put this in writing, fearing that arbitration of future disputes might signal an intention to ignore future Chilean aggression.[51]

Chile desired that the parties reach an equilibrium in tonnage, fearing permanent naval inferiority if the current force ratio was enshrined in a treaty. Chile offered to negotiate in London, and, failing any decision, would let the Admiralty decide on the relative forces to be maintained by each party.[52] Argentina had persistently objected to a larger British role in the parties' dispute, and could not accept the infringement upon sovereignty of allowing a foreign government to dictate the size of their navy. Moreover, Argentina raised relevant questions about the complexity of the Chilean proposal, preferring instead to simply cancel current contracts. Even the cancellation of current orders would create headaches for the parties, as the contracts specified indemnities if the purchases were not completed. However, the goal of actual reduction would naturally result as older ships were gradually retired, and the cancellation of current orders could be accomplished by sale to third parties, obviating any financial loss to the parties. This would relieve the parties of the challenges of verifying compliance with any agreement, and obviate the need for any complex formula of naval parity to be reached.[53]

---

[49] The Foreign Enlistment Act of 1870 forbade the sale of warships to belligerents, but the law did not apply in time of peace. Nonetheless, the British government exercised significant influence over the sales by private firms, as seen in their seizure of dreadnoughts being built for Turkey in 1914.

[50] Lowther to Lansdowne, May 1, 1902, *in* FO 16/357, at 65.

[51] Barrington to Lansdowne, May 2, 1902, *in* FO 16/357, at 69.

[52] Lowther to Lansdowne, May 20, 1902, *in* FO 16/357, at 100.

[53] Barrington to Lansdowne, May 21, 1902, *in* FO 16/357, at 101.

Ultimately, Argentina agreed to negotiate on the remaining issues simultaneously, although expressing doubts that agreement could be quickly reached. On this basis, the parties decided to limit naval armaments on a trial basis, for a period of five years. In a five-article agreement, the Chilean-Argentine Convention of 1902 froze armament levels and advocated further reductions. The treaty provided for the sale of warships under construction and the dismantling of existing vessels. Article I provided the main regulation, explicitly referencing the need for a "just balance" between the naval forces of the two states to be achieved by reduction.[54] Beyond the cancelation of current warship orders, the parties agreed to negotiate a further reduction within 12 months. The treaty forbade any increase in naval armaments for five years, unless 18 months' notice was given to the other party.[55] It was left unclear whether the parties were obliged to give 18 months' notice prior to acquiring a warship, or prior to ordering the construction of a new vessel, which could take two or more years. Instead of a detailed agreement discussing tonnage, artillery, or the number of warships, the treaty generically bound the parties with regard to naval armaments, satisfying Argentine concerns regarding negotiations becoming bogged down in details.[56] Submarines, a new weapon of uncertain value, were excluded from regulation along with coastal artillery and other harbor defenses.

The bilateral agreement also addressed larger questions relating to the regional balance of power, recognizing the role of the naval race in exacerbating tensions over the boundary question.[57] Specifically, it forbade the parties from selling warships to third parties "having questions pending" with either state. This provision prevented the continuation of the arms race through proxies and explicitly recognized the larger context of their rivalry.[58] Moreover, a mutual declaration of non-intervention was attached as a preliminary protocol to the arbitration agreement signed contemporaneously with the arms control treaty. In the declaration, Argentina pledged non-interference in the external affairs of other countries, while Chile confirmed it had no plans for territorial expansion, "except such as resulted from the fulfillment of Treaties at present in existence or which might

---

[54] 1902 Chilean–Argentine Convention, Art. I.
[55] *Id.* Art. II.
[56] *Id.* Art. II.
[57] *Id.* Art. I.
[58] *Id.* Art. III.

hereafter be concluded ..."[59] Both statements confirmed the Chilean right to negotiate a final settlement with Bolivia and Peru, without the specter of Argentine intervention.

The two states ratified the agreements during the southern hemisphere's winter, but not without internal dissent. Explanatory notes and protocols were exchanged at the May signing, modifying the original agreement to assuage nationalist feelings. An explanatory protocol, concluded in July "in order to remove the slight doubts that have arisen," further defined spheres of influence. Additionally, the protocol confirmed that the parties had the right to exercise "natural defense" in their respective regions, Argentina in the Atlantic, and Chile in the Pacific.[60] In this document, the parties agreed that the implementation of existing treaties could not be subject to arbitration, reaffirming Chile's desire to settle its northern boundary questions without Argentine interference. Moreover, Argentina was reluctant to reduce its extant fleet, and the Explanatory Protocol held that the creation of a "just balance" required no further sale of ships, and could be accomplished by disarming ships retained by each side.[61] While the Chilean Congress passed the treaty as modified by the protocol and notes, there was some dissent from the resulting agreement. The original treaty forbade any further purchases, while the July protocol eviscerated the obligation to reduce existing fleet levels. The Chilean navy was not allowed to increase its armaments while Argentina was not required to decrease its navy, thus de facto Argentine naval superiority might be codified by the treaty.[62]

After the initial indignation receded, Chile valued the newly enshrined entente with Argentina too much to disturb the settlement. While Chile had not regained naval parity, Chile had assured peace with Argentina, allowing a stronger negotiating position from which to conclude negotiations with Peru and Bolivia. British arbitration of the Argentine-Chilean boundary was completed at the end of 1902, providing a settlement of the border question. The ultimate award granted Chile 54,000 square kilometers of disputed territory and Argentina 40,000 kilometers.[63]

---

[59] "General Arbitration Treaty between the Argentine Republic and Chile, May 28, 1902," *American Journal of International Law* 6, no. 2 Supplement (1912).

[60] Explanatory Protocol, ¶ 2, *annexed to* 1902 Chilean-Argentine Convention.

[61] *Id.* at 2.

[62] Lowther to Lansdowne, Aug. 10, 1902, *in* FO 16/357, at 281.

[63] *See* Speech by Serrano Montaner, on the Arbitration Award, *enclosure in* Lowther to Lansdowne, Dec. 14, 1902, *in* FO 16/357, at 505.

After the announcement of the arbitration award in November of 1902, the parties finalized their naval reductions. The May treaty had required the parties to meet within one year to set the "just balance," anticipating a systematic reduction of their navies. Meeting in Buenos Aires, the parties reached a further agreement in January 1903. In this supplementary treaty, the just balance, "discreta equivalencia," included the previously discussed sale of the two armored cruisers building for Argentina and the two battleships under construction for Chile.[64] The agreement specified that the warships could not leave their dockyards without the joint agreement of both parties. Great Britain was given a monitoring role, as the ships were formally put at the disposal of the British government.[65] If the ships remained unsold, they could not be reincorporated into their navies.[66] To further adjust the naval balance, Chile was required to disarm its battleship *Capitan Prat* while Argentina disarmed two armored cruisers, the *Garibaldi* and the *Puerredon*.[67] Disarmament was defined as removing the ships from a state of readiness, mooring them in a basin, discharging the crews beyond men needed for preservation, and landing all coal, powder and ammunition, small artillery, torpedo tubes and torpedoes, electric search-lights, boat, and stores.[68] Neither party could rearm the disarmed warships without giving 18 months' notice.[69]

The Chilean public expressed some regret at the arrangement, but most recognized the need for an agreement. The supplementary agreement did not require congressional sanction, thus would not be scrutinized as thoroughly as the original Pacts of May. While the arms race was halted, a mild blowback effect did result: Chile utilized funds from the sale of the battleships to complete a dockyard at Talcahuano.[70]

Britain accepted its role under the agreement and the parties jointly authorized the sale of the four warships. Ultimately, Britain purchased the

---

[64] "Agreement Concluded and Signed between the Argentine Republic and Chile, Giving Effect to the Terms of the Convention of May 28, 1902, for the Limitation of Naval Armaments, January 9, 1903," *American Journal of International Law* 1, no. 3 Supplement (1907): Art. 1.

[65] *Id.* at Arts. 2, 3, & 7.

[66] *Id.* at Art. 1.

[67] *Id.* at Art. 4.

[68] *Id.* at Art. 5.

[69] *Id.* at Art. 6.

[70] Lowther to Lansdowne, Jan. 8, 1903, *in* Argentine–Chile Boundary Arbitration, FO 16/358, Part I, (1903–1905), at 5.

two battleships in order to prevent their acquisition by a rival navy, and Japan bought the two armored cruisers, shortly before its 1904–1905 war with Russia. Because of differences in armament and speed, the battleships did not fit tactically with other British battleships,[71] providing a reason not to purchase privately built battleships in the future, when the possible sale of Brazilian dreadnoughts was raised. Chile and Argentina jointly undertook negotiations for the sale of additional warships, with no result.[72] The Latin American crisis had been resolved, but the larger armaments competition remained.

THE PACTS OF MAY AND REGIONAL COMPETITION

Ultimately, both parties upheld the treaty and the war scares evaporated. The Foreign Office did not forget the lessons learned, passing them on to the new Liberal government of 1905. Earlier that year, the British role in resolving the arms race was raised in the House of Commons, and remained part of the ongoing debate surrounding arms reduction. William Randal Cremer, Liberal member for Haggerston and noted arbitration advocate, requested information on the Argentine-Chilean naval arms treaty. As the Latin American arms agreement had been accompanied by an arbitration treaty, Cremer asked about possible arms reductions with the French based on Britain's existing arbitration agreement with its Gallic neighbor.[73] In preparing the government's reply, the Foreign Office circulated a memorandum detailing the naval agreement and the British role in resolving the arms race.[74] Cremer's exchange with Prime Minister Balfour highlighted radical Liberal desire for arms limitation, especially as the call for a Second Hague Peace Conference had been issued the previous autumn. The Latin American model, as well as the British role in resolving it, was part of the Liberal Party's frame of reference prior to assuming office that winter.

In addition, the Argentine-Chilean model was raised in connection with a new arms race brewing in South America. In 1906, Brazil embarked on a program of naval expansion following the loss of an ironclad in a harbor

---

[71] Gardiner, *Conway's All the World's Fighting Ships, 1860–1905*, 39.

[72] Haggard to Lansdowne, Mar. 25, 1904, *in* FO 16/358, Part III, at 428.

[73] Cremer, *Hansard* 4th ser., CXLVII, 867–869 June 6, 1905.

[74] Memorandum, Arbitration and Disarmament Treaty between Argentina and Chile, June 5, 1905, *in* FO 16/358, Part III, at 448. The memorandum updated a document that had been previously circulated in the Foreign Office in 1903.

explosion.[75] Seeking to regain the naval preeminence it possessed before the rise of Argentina, Brazil ordered three 13,000-ton battleships from Armstrong, threatening to reignite regional naval competition.[76] As with the Argentine-Chilean race, borders and the regional balance of power underlay the acquisitions as much as the prestige of naval preeminence. Brazil was negotiating a border issue with Bolivia, while the Bolivians were receiving diplomatic assistance from Argentina. Believing that Argentina would never directly challenge them if they possessed naval superiority, the Brazilians sought to regain their former position.[77] As a possible additional motive, Brazil possibly sought an alliance with the United States, and hoped to bargain from a position of regional preeminence.[78] National interest also coincided with political ambition. The British minister pleni-potentiary concluded that private interests played a significant role in the arms contracts, rather than any immediate differences with Argentina.[79]

Argentine financier Tornquist, assisted by Revelstoke and Baring, again sought back-channel negotiations to resolve the issue, meeting on ship-board with William Buchanan, American delegate at the recently con-cluded Rio de Janeiro Pan-American Conference. Tornquist, speaking on behalf of the Argentine president, and the American diplomat negotiated a compromise involving the transfer of warships between Argentina, Brazil, and Chile. Brazil would cede two of the three proposed battleships, one each to Argentina and Chile, and in return would receive two Argentine and one or two Chilean armored cruisers.[80] Buchanan suggested that Chile could play a pivotal role in convincing Brazil, if Chile stood by Argentina. In this manner, Brazil could rebuild its naval position while maintaining rough naval parity with the other two powers. Chilean President Alcorta agreed with the plan, but Buchanan was unable to convince Brazilian President Rio Branco of its wisdom.[81] Buchanan attempted to persuade Britain to intervene by utilizing its financial position to press the countries

[75] Grant, *Rulers, Guns, and Money*, 149.
[76] Dering to Grey, July 25, 1906, *in* Brazil, FO 371/13, (1906).
[77] Barclay to Grey, Oct. 5, 1906, *in* FO 371/13, at 246.
[78] Baring to Mildmay, Oct. 12, 1906, *enclosure in* Minutes, Nov. 28, 1906, *in* FO 371/13, at 284.
[79] Barclay to Grey, Oct. 15, 1906, *in* FO 371/13, at 250.
[80] Confidential Negotiations with regard to the Brazilian Naval Armaments, *enclosure in* Minutes, Nov. 28, 1906, *in* FO 371/13, at 257.
[81] Tornquist to Buchanan, Sep. 28, 1906; Buchanan to Tornquist, Oct. 5, 1906, both *enclosures in id.* at 261A, 268.

to accept negotiations, specifically mentioning the British course of action in 1902,[82] but with no success.

Sir Edward Grey reviewed the correspondence regarding this initiative, while the United States and Great Britain were both negotiating on a common armament platform prior to the Second Hague Peace Conference, and renegotiating the almost ninety-year-old Rush-Bagot Agreement. These South American proceedings must have interested Grey. The Latin American arms races and negotiations not only had an impact upon the naval race in Europe, but also provided evidence of the directions in which arms races evolved and could be ended. After the abortive negotiations, Brazil rapidly switched its battleship orders to dreadnoughts, Britain's new super-battleship.[83] As no other navy possessed such powerful weapons, the acquisition by Brazil conveyed a potent political message and could potentially influence the European arms balance. The Argentine-Chilean arms control treaty was raised again at The Hague, and provided a model for British arms control negotiations following the 1907 Hague Conference.

* * *

The British role in the 1902 Argentine-Chilean negotiations provided a precedent for later discussions with Germany. Both negotiations highlighted a number of similar issues. These included the timing of political and arms agreements, whether neutrality allowed one state to pursue further aggression on the continent, the replacement of old ships to mask expansion, and the role of third parties in shifting the naval balance. Just as Mediterranean concerns made a bilateral deal difficult for Great Britain and Germany, the role of Peru and Brazil made a bilateral deal difficult for Argentina and Chile. However, Argentina and Chile accounted for this in the treaty by preventing arms sales to third parties.

The Argentine-Chilean and the Anglo-German disputes differed in a more significant way. The Latin American powers could not violate the arms agreement without the complicity of one of the great powers, as they could not build their own battleships. Verification and enforcement were simplified by the fact that British bankers funded naval expansion, and Britain's naval yards were the main suppliers of warships. The Anglo-German naval arms race differed in that the two states built their own

---

[82] Baring to Mildmay, Oct. 12, 1906, *enclosure in id.*
[83] O'Sullivan-Beare to Grey, Nov. 10, 1906, *in* FO 371/13, at 291.

warships. The lack of similar enforcement tools did not mean arms control was an impossibility in Europe, merely that other methods than international enforcement were required. In Europe, verification became essential, with exchanges of information taking a larger place in negotiations.

In 1902, a legal agreement was necessary as détente and informal arms control did not fundamentally improve confidence. The episode provided a material lesson to the British, indicating the need for a simple, easily verifiable agreement to increase confidence among the parties. The lesson was not wasted, as the British approach to arms control in the decade prior to the First World War indicated a cognizance of these preconditions, and the Foreign Office framed initiatives around them.

REVISION OF THE RUSH-BAGOT AGREEMENT

The Foreign Office contended with another regional arms control treaty in the 1890s and 1900s – the Rush-Bagot Agreement. As with the Argentine-Chilean negotiations, discussions centered around easily verifiable obligations and the confidence which could be gained from them. Circumstances on the Great Lakes changed greatly between the 1860s and the 1890s. The completion of the Welland Canal on the Canadian side allowed the British to circumvent the agreement in an emergency, by sending in ocean gunboats.[84] Moreover, America perceived a greater risk to its growing cities in the region. In the early nineteenth century, the area had been wilderness, but was now populated with some of its richest industrial metropolises, including Chicago, Milwaukee, and Detroit. The volume of trade in the Great Lakes rivaled that passing through the Suez Canal.[85] American naval planners increasingly worried about both undefended trade on the Great Lakes and the risk of bombardment of undefended cities.[86] The agreement increasingly appeared to favor British at the expense of American interests. On the other hand, America's perceptions of the dangers of its position were more than compensated by its ability to overwhelm Canada. Increasingly, American strategic calculations centered upon the "Canadian

[84] C. Barter, Shipbuilding on the Great Lakes and the Treaty of 1817, Apr. 27 1892, *in* FO 5/2598.

[85] "A Ship-Building Port," *The New York Times*, Jan. 15, 1892, *quoted in* Shipbuilding on the Great Lakes and the Treaty of 1817, at 38, *id.*

[86] "How to Shell Chicago," *Chicago Tribune*, Dec. 20, 1895, *enclosure in* Vansittart to Salisbury, Dec. 21, 1895, *in* FO 5/2598.

hostage," assuming that in a future conflict the British would dominate the seas while the United States would conquer Canada.[87] By late century, the treaty had become more important to the British. By the 1890s, influential Midwestern Senators sought the termination or modification of the agreement for commercial reasons. With the growth of the post-1890 New Navy, American shipbuilding firms increasingly sought lucrative contracts, but Great Lakes steelyards and shipbuilders were shut out by treaty provisions forbidding the construction of warships.[88] Additionally, the states sought vessels for use in training naval militia.[89] Secretary of State James Blaine suggested the treaty be modified to allow warship construction, with the finished vessels being obligated to leave the lakes. The British repeatedly sought to stall negotiations, fearing that modifications might lead to greater friction and suspicions. The British also worried that modifications would allow the Americans to leave a number of warships half-built, which they could rapidly arm in a conflict with Canada.[90]

Blaine held that the purpose of the treaty was to prevent warships from being stationed on the lakes, and suggested the addition of an explanatory article allowing for warships to be built for service on the oceans.[91] The canal locks exiting the lakes would have provided an absolute size limit on warships that could be built. The matter was not pursued at that time, but American construction of revenue cutters for the lakes, in excess of the 100-ton per vessel restrictions, led to the matter being revived later in the decade.

[87] 1891 Plan of Operations in Case of War with Great Britain, War Portfolios, Navy Department, 1, 8, 13. This 1891 plan called for the arming of merchant steamers on the Great Lakes to circumvent perceived American weakness.

[88] Pauncefote to Salisbury, Apr. 14, 1892, *in* FO 5/2598. By 1890, Great Lakes shipbuilders launched 40°percent more vessels than those of the coasts, and could build ships up to 400 feet in length, longer than the largest American battleships under construction. "Lake Shipbuilders," *Army and Navy Journal*, Jan. 30, 1892, at 395, *in* FO 5/2598. Great Lakes shipbuilders would still be limited by the canal locks, which limited vessels to 240 feet length in order to pass through the locks. *Id.*

[89] In 1890, local dignitaries petitioned the government for a modern warship to replace the antiquated *Michigan* in time for the 1893 Colombian Exposition in Chicago, ultimately having to make do with a full-scale brick replica of an *Indiana* class battleship. Callahan, *Neutrality of the American Lakes*, at 18, fn. 1. The *Illinois*, as it was named, went on to become the headquarters for the state naval militia.

[90] Shipbuilding on the Great Lakes and the Treaty of 1817, at 4, *in* FO 5/2598.

[91] Pauncefote to Salisbury, May 3, 1892, *in* American Lakes: Naval Force to be Maintained by United States and Great Britain, ADM 1/7340b (1897–1898), at 6. Specifically, the

In the summer of 1898, the Foreign Office referred the matter to an Anglo-American Joint High Commission discussing a wide range of Canadian affairs. Lord Herschell, a former Lord Chancellor who had sat on the Venezuelan border commission, headed the British delegation.[92] While recognizing the risks of modifying the treaty, Herschell quickly surmised that the advantages of maintaining the treaty outweighed the disadvantages of changes. As the Commission had a number of contro- verted issues before it, the Great Lakes revision was left to direct negotia- tion between Herschell and Charles Fairbanks, an American Senator from the Great Lakes state of Indiana.[93]

The Americans revived the Blaine proposal, in light of the Spanish– American War being waged that summer. The Colonial Defense Committee (CDC) affirmed Herschell's views, but argued that in return for the right to build warships on the lakes that the Americans must relin- quish the right to maintain them.[94] Fairbanks proposed that no armed ves- sels be kept on the lakes, except for one or two for militia training.[95] The CDC wanted confirmation that revenue vessels not be built as "men-of- war proper." This was in reaction to the recently built American revenue cutter *Gresham* that carried torpedo tubes, a weapon that had not even been in existence in 1817, as well as gun positions capable of mounting guns. The CDC was willing to concede that up to four revenue cutters could be built, of 300 tons apiece, raising the previous limit by 200 tons, but reducing armament to a single six-pound gun.[96]

suggestion was that "any vessel built for the purpose of being used as a Revenue Cruiser or Vessel of War may be constructed so far only as regards the Hull, Masts, Spars etc. but shall not be plated, armed, equipped or rendered available as an armed vessel on the Lakes, and moreover that she shall be compelled to quit the Lakes within a specified time after the completion of her Hull, etc. as being mentioned with a view to her being transformed into an armed vessel at a Port of her nationality on the seaboard." *Id.* at 7.

[92] "Baron Herschell is Dead," *New York Times*, Mar, 2, 1899, at 5.

[93] Herschell to Salisbury, Aug. 29, 1898, *attached to* Nathan, Memorandum by the Colonial Defence Committee, Sep. 16, 1898, *in* Canada: American Warships on the Great Lakes, ADM 1/7474 (1892–1905).

[94] Nathan, Memorandum by the Colonial Defence Committee, Sep. 16, 1898, *in* ADM 1/7474, at 9. Moreover, the parties acknowledged that the current treaty already provided the right to build warships on the lakes, so long as they were not launched and brought into service, in response to circumstances in 1817. Herschell to Salisbury, Aug. 29, 1898, *attached to* Nathan, Memorandum by the Colonial Defence Committee.

[95] Memorandum by the Colonial Defence Committee, *supra* note 93.

[96] *Id.* The nuance between categories of vessels was further stretched when the Colonial Defence Committee minuted that no "men-of-war proper" would be allowed, no "actual

The Americans countered with demands for six revenue cutters, claiming that future increases in population would require more customs enforcement, and arguing that it would be better to anticipate this rather than to modify the agreement regularly. Additionally, Fairbanks sought 900-ton revenue cutters because of severe weather experienced on the upper lakes. Regarding training vessels, Fairbanks noted the heavy demand by individual American Great Lakes states for their own militia vessels, and suggested each party operate two ships of up to 1100 tons weight, carrying six heavy guns up to four inches, as well as eight of an undefined "minor caliber."[97]

Overall, the parties showed a willingness to compromise and by December 1898, a draft agreement had been completed. The British and Americans agreed to maintain no more than two unarmored training vessels, with the Americans accepting lower limits of 1000 tons, and two heavy and four minor caliber guns, the latter still undefined. Neither party could "maintain upon the Great Lakes any naval armament or vessels of war," the term "maintain" acknowledging the right to build ships for the ocean.[98] The agreement was silent as to the number of ships allowed on any single lake, allowing movement as needed. The parties agreed to six revenue cutters of up to 900 tons apiece, mounting a single six-pound gun, merging British and American goals. The treaty met the American desire to build warships for the oceans, with the restrictions that the ships not be "armour-plated, armed, equipped, or rendered available for war" on the lakes, that these ships be removed as rapidly as possible, and that

---

war vessels" could be used for training, while revenue ships would be in a separate category, By December, Herschell had written home for further clarification, as the term "actual war vessels" in his previous instructions had left naval officers in both countries divided as to what this meant. American delegates also pointed out that guns could be kept on shore for rapid conversion of merchant ships into armed merchant cruisers, weakening the potential restriction. Herschell to Salisbury, Dec. 2, 1898, *in* ADM 1/7474, at 62.

[97] Herschell was inclined to accept these demands: "the jealousy of the individual States is such that each will exert great pressure to have a training ship for its exclusive use. And inasmuch as it will probably not be practicable to give what they would regard as their legitimate share of the ship-building trade to the ship-builders, I think this would afford an additional motive for complying with the wishes of the States. Any one who has not lived for some time in this country can, I think, scarcely realize the force of pressure which local interest brings to bear upon the Executive, and how apt they are to yield to such pressure, or how very difficult it is for them to resist it." *Id.*

[98] Given the attention to wording apparent throughout the negotiations, the division between "naval armament" and "vessels of war" would indicate an intent to regulate other weaponry such as mines or torpedoes, as these had been discussed in negotiations.

no more than one would be completed before the previous had left.[99] The parties extended the notice period prior to abandoning the agreement from six months to one year.[100]

British statesmen paid close attention to detail when negotiating with the Americans, indicating that the Foreign Office had considered the full ramifications of an arms control treaty text. The negotiations undoubtedly must have interested Salisbury, not only because he was a participant, but also because of the upcoming Hague Conference. The talks began the day after the Russian Czar had issued his disarmament circular to the European powers, and were concluded only weeks before the Czar definitively set the program for the First Hague Peace Conference. In the Washington negotiations, Herschell explicitly connected the discussion to the European arms race:

> I said that I entirely agreed that it was desirable to avoid the evils of competition in the maintenance of armed forces, and alluded to the state of things existing in Europe, where each nation added to their naval forces in turn to counterbalance the additions made by others.[101]

Salisbury's oft-repeated disavowal of disarmament is best understood as having been made with a mental reservation regarding arms control.[102]

After the draft had been completed, the Canadians cooled on the project, while the Commission became bogged down on other issues and dropped the matter.[103] The United States informally renewed the offer in

[99] Proposal respecting Naval Vessels on the Great Lakes, *enclosure in* Herschell to Salisbury, Dec. 2, 1898, *in* ADM 1/7474, at 63. The term "armour-plated" had been substituted for the simpler American wording "plated" out of concern that the latter would ban the construction of iron-hulled vessels. Herschell to Salisbury, Dec. 2, 1898, *in* ADM 1/7474, at 62.

[100] The United States further suggested that the treaty be promulgated for a set period of years, and then be maintained unless the one year notice was given, although these details were not finalized in the draft. *Id.*

[101] Herschell to Salisbury, Aug. 29, 1898, *in* ADM 1, 7474, at 11.

[102] Not only did Salisbury know of the agreement, but Fisher and Ardagh were both involved in discussions of Canadian defences on the Great Lakes prior to serving on the British delegation at the First Hague Peace Conference. See, for instance, Lake to Fisher, Nov. 17, 1897, and following correspondence *in* ADM 1/7340b; Herschell to Salisbury, Dec. 2, 1898, and Foreign Office to Admiralty, Sep. 1898, *in* ADM 1/7474, at 6, 62.

[103] Colonial Office to Admiralty, Mar. 8, 1905, *in* ADM 1/7474, at 118; Grant-Duff, Armed Vessels on the Great Lakes, Defense and Operational Plans, WO 106/40/B1/15, (Nov. 1907); see also Bourne, *Britain and the Balance of Power in North America*, at 335.

1901, and repeatedly raised the matter over the next decade. While negotiations lingered into the 1900s, the British ignored technical American
violations and sought to maintain the agreement.[104]

Internal British deliberations focused on verification challenges presented by the proposed American construction. By 1906, all American
gunboats entered the Great Lakes through the Canadian-controlled
Welland Canal, making it relatively easy to monitor these vessels. Naval
construction on the lakes would undermine this security, as "[n]o restrictions which would be practically enforceable could prevent the United
States from having large numbers of war vessels on the stocks ready to be
finished off quickly on emergency."[105]

Verification and effectiveness had long been part of discussions on
the Rush-Bagot Agreement. When Blaine raised the matter in 1892, the
Admiralty noted that the Americans could rapidly bring torpedo boats in
by canal. Even if the treaty banned construction on the lakes, the United
States could also built small craft on the rivers flowing into the lakes, with
the construction of the Mississippi River ironclad flotillas in the Civil War
providing a clear precedent.[106] Merchant ships could rapidly be converted
into cruisers. In response, the government sought to verify construction
facilities on the lakes prior to entering into negotiations, reviving this

[104] In 1904, the United States operated three vessels on the Great Lakes, including the
Essex, a 1375 ton vessel, built in 1876. Villiers, Memorandum, Mar. 8, 1905, *in* FO 5/2598,
at 280; Fiddian to Villiers, Mar. 17, 1905, *in* FO 5/2598. In the early 1900s, the British
operated two vessels in the Great Lakes exceeding the treaty limitations, the *Constance* and
the *Curlew*. H.R. Doc. No. 56-471, Feb. 27, 1900, Message of the President of the United
States, War Vessels on the Great Lakes, (1900) at 65. The British were careful to make sure
their vessels were always smaller than their American counterparts, to avoid an arms race.
Villiers, Memorandum, at 283.

[105] Grant-Duff, Armed Vessels on the Great Lakes, *supra* note 103, at ¶12. The War Office
discussed the possibility of conveying torpedo boats and submarines to the lakes via railroads
in time of emergency, and both sides contemplated arming merchant vessels as auxiliary
cruisers. Percy Lake, Naval Action in Defence of the Question of the Great Lakes, Mar. 28,
1896, *in* Sir John Ardagh, Naval Action in Defence of the Question of the Great Lakes, *in*
WO 106/40/B1/5 (1896); G.S. Admiralty Memo on the Defence of Canada, WO 106/40/
B1/10, (Mar. 24, 1905).

[106] Cyprian Bridge, Minutes attached to Naval Force to be Maintained by United States
and Great Britain on the American Lakes, May 20, 1892, *in* ADM 1/7340b, at 34. See also
Defence of Canada: Memorandum by the Admiralty, Feb. 24, 1905, CAB 38/8/13, at 13
on the American construction of "Ninety-Day Warships" during the Civil War. The same
issue of construction on the rivers had also been present in the Black Sea discussions in
1856.

request when the matter rose in the later 1890s.[107] In spite of these challenges, the Admiralty repeatedly defended the agreement.[108]

The services sparred over which of them had primary responsibility for Great Lakes security.[109] In response to American actions, War Office officials wavered over the value of the agreement, with calls for ending the treaty, initiating a Canadian Great Lakes building program, and funding a £20,000,000 strategic canal expansion.[110] There were repeated demands for torpedo boats ready for rapid service on the lakes, as well as an older plan prepared by Fisher to bring them into the lakes by railroad.[111] However, in joint discussions with the Foreign Office cooler heads prevailed. War with the United States was not considered likely, but the treaty was still important. After the Admiralty denied primary responsibility for the defense of

[107] Cyprian Bridge, Minutes attached to Naval Defence of the American Lakes, July 14, 1892, *in* ADM 1/7340b, at 47; Minutes attached to Construction by the United States of Two Steam Revenue Cutters of the 1st Class for Service on the Great Lakes, Dec. 17, 1896, *in* ADM 1/7340b at 78. Moreover, the Admiralty expressed a belief that construction would be difficult to conceal. "If, for example, after a past of comparative neglect of her defences, the Dominion of Canada should suddenly display great activity in the preparation of a flotilla for service on the Great Lakes or in the formation of a permanent military force, other than for the defence of her seaports against a Maritime Power with which Great Britain might be at war, the secret could not be kept." Observations by the Admiralty upon the War Office Memorandum of Dec. 13, 1904, on Defence of Canada, Jan. 6, 1905, *attached to* CAB 38/8/13, at 8.

[108] "It would also be in the power of the Americans, whilst adhering to the letter of the Agreement, to develop naval construction in places comparatively remote from the Lakes and avail themselves of the facilities afforded by existing water communications. Therefore they may be credited with ability to put on the Lakes forces which, in the end, would greatly outnumber any which we are likely able to oppose to them. Still their Lordships are of opinion that some advantages may remain to us if complete abrogation of the Agreement is avoided, though modifications may be introduced into it. They consider that naval requirements would be best met by leaving the United States' government the responsibility for altering or terminating an arrangement which, as long as it is maintained, frees us from demands for naval protection which it might be difficult to resist and which would not be likely to lead to an effective distribution of our forces if complied with." Draft of Cyprian Bridge to Colonial Office, May 31, 1892, ADM 1/7340b, at 37–38.

[109] See, for example, The Defence of Canada, Mar. 17, 1905, *in* WO 106/40/B1/10 (1905); Observations by the Admiralty upon the War Office Memorandum of Dec. 13, 1904, on Defence of Canada, Jan. 6, 1905, attached to CAB 38/8/13, at 12.

[110] Grant-Duff, notes attached to WO 106/40/B1/15.

[111] Extract from Meeting of Committee of Imperial Defence, July 13, 1905, *in* WO 106/40; Transport of Torpedo Boats by Rail to the Great Lakes, Canada, Feb. 28, 1898, *in* ADM 1/7340b.

the lakes, the War Office followed suit, and support for the Rush-Bagot Agreement increased. The growing disparity in force reduced the military options available to Britain. A strong Canadian response would only generate an unwanted arms race. American shipbuilders would have eagerly seized the opportunity to construct warships on the lakes, but lacked the political influence to abandon the treaty on their own. As it was noted when the matter resurfaced in 1912:

> any change must inevitably drag both countries into an absurd waste of money on ship-building: That political pressure would be so great on both sides that this would be unavoidable, and that at all events the Rush-Bagot agreement serves as a brake, and can be produced by the United States as a reason for not giving way to the clamours of the shipyards on the Lakes.[112]

This correspondence highlights the value of treaty law as an obstacle, if not an insurmountable barrier to conduct.

> The fact is that the agreement if not very effectual is still of some value as a brake on shipbuilding. The violation of it by the U.S.A. forms the subject from time to time of rather foolish protests … – foolish because such protests ignore the hopeless weakness of Canada and Great Britain against the U.S.A. if the latter thought it worth while to put out her strength, and because they are practically a challenge to do so.[113]

It was simply best to "let sleeping dogs lie."[114]

Ultimately, the British policy succeeded, as the United States chose not to abandon the agreement, despite Canadian unwillingness to renegotiate. The negotiations reflected not only inter-service rivalry, but also complex relationships with both the United States and Canada. Despite repeated violations on both sides and fundamental changes in circumstances relating to naval technology and the strategic environment, both sides perceived an interest in maintaining the treaty. Great Lakes shipbuilders did not gain the right to build warships for the ocean-going navy until after the First World War, as they were unable to generate enough support to change the law. The violations that did occur were of a limited nature.

---

[112] Lowther to Earle, Feb. 15, 1912, War Vessels on the Great Lakes, CO 537/496, (Mar. 7, 1912). Attached notes indicated Foreign Office approval of Lowther's opinion.
[113] Earle to Lowther, Mar. 6, 1912, CO 537/496.
[114] *Id.*

The Rush-Bagot Agreement took on a different meaning as the century progressed, forming the cornerstone of closer Anglo-American relations, its significance shifting away from naval security to preventing needless rivalry. While law did not eliminate all violations, it stifled greater naval construction, contributing effectively to British imperial security. Notably, both Salisbury and Grey participated in these negotiations while preparing for the two Hague Conferences, Grey also continuing Great Lakes negotiations while discussing an arms limit with Germany after 1907, providing contemporary experience with legal limitation of armaments.

NAVAL ARMS CONTROL IN THE NEW CENTURY: PRECEDENTS AND IMPLICATIONS

The 1902 Argentine-Chilean treaty built upon earlier nineteenth-century negotiations like the Rush-Bagot Agreement, highlighting the possibilities of formal arms control agreements. In 1900, the technological differences between naval and land armaments provided different opportunities for regulation. Naval construction was more easily verifiable, and Britain's dominant maritime industrial position offered an enhanced ability to respond to rivals, making any breaches easily offset.

Effective control and verification were central to the British naval arms limitation treaties of 1787 and 1856. In the 1787 Anglo-French Naval Declaration, the parties sought limitations on naval preparation levels – confirmed through exchanges of information – rather than bolder limitations on overall forces, avoiding a more stringent verification regime because of fears that tensions would increase without increasing confidence. The 1856 Black Sea negotiations witnessed intense discussions of how best to craft verifiable obligations. The Foreign Office championed warship length and size as the benchmark for regulation, after reasoning that other regulations would be difficult to verify and easy to evade.[115] Warship length could be easily determined, and this could then be used to calculate weight, which in turn limited the space available for engines and guns. Both speed and armament proved more difficult to regulate as the armament could easily be altered, and measurement of horsepower

---

[115] In fact, the British consul at the Dardanelles expressed suspicions about Russian warships passing the Straits in 1857, because they were pierced for more guns than their commander disclosed, it being noted that while they were within the size limits, it was impossible to verify the size of guns they carried. FO 881/1825, at 1.

required intrusive inspections. Size limitations provided indirect regulation, by restricting the weight available for heavy engines, and the length
necessary both for long broadside batteries and the fine hull lines associated with high speeds. The size limitations relegated the naval forces to
minor coastal ships, and the advent of heavier ironclad warships further
reduced the value of such small ships. Russian requests for armed transports or stationary hulks were similarly refused out of concern that treaty
violations could be hidden, undermining confidence in the agreement. As
discussed in the second chapter, more complex regulations were avoided
on the grounds that they would prove difficult to monitor and enforce.

When the Foreign Office was called on to recast the Black Sea obligations in 1870, statesmen entertained a wide range of options for limiting
armaments, but narrowed them based upon criteria of effectiveness. These
ranged from the simple expedient of increasing the number or size of warships allowed, to complex plans for matching the Russians with equivalent
ships. The first proposal attempted to prolong the existing treaty, while
allowing for technological changes ushered in with the larger ironclads.
The latter plan was specifically premised on a tit-for-tat theory – if the
Russians understood that every warship they built would automatically be
matched by an allied warship stationed in the Black Sea, Russia would have
far less reason to inaugurate a costly arms race.[116] Austria-Hungary even
proposed the creation of a naval base on Turkish territory as a means of
balancing Russian ambitions.

The difficulties inherent in verification created impetus to craft simple provisions. The Foreign Office had harbored concerns about Russian
violation of the Black Sea Treaty from its signature, fearing that large
ships-of-the-line were illegally being built in Odessa.[117] Complex regulations required either greater intrusion to verify or tacit acknowledgment
that they could not be enforced. For this reason during the 1870 crisis, proposals calling for the British to match Russian forces by sending
equivalent warships into the Black Sea were dismissed. Ultimately, Russian

[116] Buchanan to Granville, Dec. 12, 1870, FO 881/1901.
[117] FO 881/1825, at 2. The Russians inaugurated the Odessa Steam Navigation Company
to provide vessels which could be quickly converted into warships. Palmerston fretted that
Russia could surreptitiously violate the Black Sea Treaty in this manner, but believed preventing it would be impossible. W. E. Mosse, "Russia and the Levant, 1856–1862: Grand Duke
Constantine Nicolaevich and the Russian Steam Navigation Company," *Journal of Modern
History* 26, no. 1 (1954): 40, 46.

objections to any regulations killed these projects, although the Foreign Office had already recognized their impracticality.

The Anglo-French arms race between the 1840s and 1860s provided another source of precedents. The naval race with France centered on the bewildering pace of technological change and its corresponding effect on the naval balance between the two nations. Over the course of two decades, steam propulsion was adopted, first through inefficient and exposed paddlewheels, and then through screw propellers. Solid shot was supplanted by exploding shellfire, and in response ironclad warships were developed. With the advent of each new technology, which the French government eagerly adopted, the naval race took on a new urgency.[118]

In responding to recurrent naval scares and the rapid rise in construction budgets, leading figures in Parliament, including then-Prime Minister Robert Peel, Admiral Sir Charles Napier, and future Prime Minister Benjamin Disraeli, all sought a naval agreement with France.[119] While discussions in Parliament did not culminate in an actual overture to France, Richard Cobden prepared arms control projects. Cobden was an eager advocate of arms limitation for both financial and philosophical reasons. Despite his utopian predilections, the practical nature of his proposals stands out. By eschewing radical pacifist arguments, and focusing upon the practicalities of arms limitation and the continued need for strong national defense, Cobden sought to convince skeptics that arms control was possible.[120] His writings indicated the evolution of thought on the matter and the centrality of verifiable limits. Rather than attempt to anticipate future trends in technology, Cobden claimed the disclosure of extant building programs and inspections would serve to limit the arms race as much as any formal limit.[121] Exchanges of naval information were central to Cobden's

[118] C. I. Hamilton, *Anglo-French Naval Rivalry 1840–1870* (Oxford: Clarendon Press, 1993), 29; McNeill, *The Pursuit of Power*, 225–27.

[119] "The interest of Europe is not that any one country should exercise a peculiar influence, but the true interest of Europe is to come to some one common accord, so as to enable every country to reduce those military armaments which belong to a state of war rather than of peace." Sir Robert Peel, *Hansard*, 3rd ser., LIX, 403–404, Aug. 27, 1841. *See also* Sir Charles Napier, *Hansard*, 3rd ser., CLVI, 989, Feb. 13, 1860; Benjamin Disraeli, *Hansard*, 3rd ser., CLXIV, 1678–1682, July 26, 1861; Richard Cobden, *The Political Writings of Richard Cobden*, Vol. II (London: William Ridgway, 1867), 220–21, 84, 415–16.

[120] Tate, *The Disarmament Illusion*, 32–34. See, generally, Nicholls, "Cobden and the International Peace Congress Movement," 363–64.

[121] Cobden, *Writings*, 432–33.

projects, as they would allow Parliament to defuse naval panics through the provision of accurate information. Naval inspections were proposed on more than one occasion during this period. France offered to allow British observers to visit French naval yards in 1853, and the Admiralty accepted a similar French offer in 1861.[122] An international agreement would assist naval limitations by providing members of Parliament with the information necessary to justify an orderly program of naval construction. Cobden sought no more than this from an agreement, as it would allow him to rein in naval expenditures.

The quest for simple, verifiable agreements raised questions about the criteria used to benchmark limitation. Cobden focused upon readily confirmable numerical counts of warships, rather than more complex formulae. His proposals were based on an assumption of proportional reductions, implicitly refusing to reduce British strength relative to France.[123] However, despite the immediate appeal of such a simplistic solution, Cobden's system tended to ignore numerous factors influencing overall naval strength, and numbers were subject to political manipulation. Cobden and advocates of limitation often counted total national naval forces, undifferentiated by total gun power or size, thus including numerous small British gunboats in the total count, despite their lesser firepower. Naval advocates also countered that France kept vessels in a higher state of readiness, while Britain lacked crews to put its larger number of warships to sea at short notice.[124] Moreover, each side included or excluded warships under construction to fit their arguments. Finally, both sides argued about the relative value given to different types of warships, as evidenced by arguments over whether or not "blockships" should be included in fleet lists. These were old ships of the line converted to steam, but with weak engines which opponents claimed left them slow and unequal opponents

---

[122] Id., 259–60, 399–400. The latter visit fueled a naval panic when it was revealed that France had fifteen ironclads under construction, yet what remained noteworthy was that the information had been shared.

[123] Id., 431. Proposals centered on a bilateral solution to the Anglo-French race rather than a multilateral treaty. This reflected naval competition, as in 1860 Britain possessed 53 steam ships-of the-line with an additional nine blockships, while France operated 35. The next nearest naval competitor, Russia, manned nine steam ships-of-the-line. Data compiled from Jan Glete, *Navies and Nations: Warships, Navies and State Building in Europe and America, 1500–1860* (Stockholm: Historiska Institutionen, 1993), Vol. II.

[124] See debate of July 29, 1859 and particularly the speeches of Cobden, Sir John Packington, and Lord Clarence Paget, *Hansard*, 3rd ser., CLV, 676–728, July 29, 1859.

to purpose-built steam warships.[125] Nonetheless, the arguments raised over naval balances and the suitability of types of limitation indicated a robust debate on the topic, providing statesmen with a pragmatic basis from which to make later proposals. These concepts figured prominently in later arms control negotiations in the twentieth century, finding expression in interwar naval arms control treaties.

*   *   *

An appreciation of naval technology underlay concerns about verification. British policy was based on two premises: that Britain could build more ships, more rapidly, than any potential opponent: and that naval attachés could discover foreign construction before any material shift in the balance of power occurred. Sir William White, Director of Naval Construction from 1886 to 1903, succinctly made this point:

> ... [O]ur resources in shipbuilding, engineering, armour and armament are so much greater than the corresponding resources in any foreign country that the speed at which construction can be carried out is greater than that which can be attained abroad. This fact is the key of the true policy in warship construction for the British Navy. It is always possible for the Admiralty to know exactly what is being done abroad in all classes of ships, to wait until foreign vessels have been laid down, then to complete designs which shall be superior in offensive and defensive power, and to complete the vessels as soon as their possible foreign rivals.[126]

Other leading figures at the Admiralty, from 1860s Sea Lord Viscount Eversley to Fisher, confirmed this long-standing policy.[127]

By mid-century, nations could only improvise minor auxiliary warships in an emergency. The advent of ironclads and the subsequent race to build heavier ordnance and armor further increased the difficulties in rapidly expanding a navy. Even if it had been possible for Russia to alter the Black Sea naval balance in the 1850s by adding a few smooth-bore cannon to

---

[125] Cobden, *Writings*, 299. In reality, the blockships were far more capable than critics originally claimed. Hamilton, *Anglo-French Rivalry*, 27–28.

[126] Sir William White, "Modern Warships," *Journal of the Society of the Arts* 54 (1906): 868.

[127] Lord George Eversley, "Naval Scares," *Contemporary Review* 90 (1906): 632–33; Marder, ed., *Fear God and Dread Nought*, Vol. II, No. 351, at 431.

small war vessels, this type of improvisation could not alter the naval balance in the era of ironclads. The sophistication and specialization of naval weapons favored verification. As long as the ironclad battleship remained the central element in strategic calculations of naval power, these beliefs about verification held true. However, the rapid evolution of technology created uncertainty about the centrality of the battleship, and spawned weapons which could challenge its predominance, most notably the torpedo. But despite concerns about the asymmetrical threat posed by cheap alternatives to ironclads, epitomized by the *Jeune Ecole* espousal of the torpedo boat in the 1880s, the battleship remained the key unit of measurement of naval power.[128]

More recent historiography has questioned the centrality of battleships to Admiralty planning. Jon Sumida has argued that battlecruisers were designed to combine the functions of battleship and armored cruiser, replacing them both, with the resulting fast, long-range vessels also indicating a preoccupation with a global threat rather than a continental German opponent.[129] In fact, at least one German commentator appears to have connected the development of the battlecruiser to British arms control advocacy, speculating that British willingness to limit battleships reflected a decision to shift to building battlecruisers.[130] Additionally, the increasing range of torpedo attack made narrow seas like the Mediterranean and North Sea hazardous for battleships. Nicholas Lambert has argued that this torpedo threat further reduced the utility of the expensive weapons while flotilla craft could have performed a function of sea denial.[131]

However, Lambert still recognized the political role played by battleships in peacetime, also noting that politicians were rarely told the full plans

---

[128] Britain attempted to limit other naval weapons which posed challenges to its battle fleets. British delegates advocated limits on submarines and torpedoes at The Hague in 1899, and also espoused the limitation of naval mines and auxiliary merchant cruisers at The Hague in 1907.

[129] Sumida, *In Defence of Naval Supremacy.*

[130] "[T]he two navies would still have entire liberty to construct not only large vessels but also vessels of another type, perhaps hardly smaller, and that in unlimited number, by which the strength of such a fleet would perhaps become quite different from what it would be expected to be, according to the proportion fixed in the agreement. In fact the English have already placed under construction such an intermediary type, from which I infer that the idea of considering as a basis of the agreement the number of large vessels has already taken a greater hold upon them than upon us." Von Ahlefeld, "A Basis for an Anglo-German Agreement," *Deutsche Review*, May 1912, *as quoted in* Wehberg, *Limitation of Armaments*, 63, 64.

[131] Lambert, *Sir John Fisher's Naval Revolution.*

of the Admiralty.[132] Even if the Admiralty largely disavowed Mahanian expectations of future naval war in terms of decisive capital ship battles, politicians still focused disproportionately on battleships. Annual debates on the naval estimates centered on battleships, by far the most expensive purchases made. The Cabinet discussions on the Mediterranean in 1912 give a clear indication of the views of the Foreign Office on the importance of battleships, with the fear that the removal of battleships from this region could have grave diplomatic repercussions in Italy, Spain, and the Near East.[133] Even if the Admiralty questioned the primacy of the battleship in wartime, it remained the main object of naval arms races and naval diplomacy in peacetime.

The battleships, which formed the foci of naval arms races, took an extraordinarily long time to complete. In the 1870s and 1880s, construction times for foreign warships often exceeded a decade, while the British maintained shorter construction periods.[134] Britain's answer to emerging naval threats, such as French steam-powered warships in the 1840s and 1850s and ironclads in the 1860s, relied on a rapid response from its industrial base. Upon discovering a new challenge, Britain built battleships more rapidly and in greater numbers than its potential competitors. Thus while France repeatedly gained a temporary lead in the naval arms race between the 1840s and 1860s, the British quickly recaptured their position.

Even if Britain could out-build a competitor, the challenge needed to be discovered in time to effectively respond. In this regard, heavy battleships proved an advantage as they were easy to discover. The construction of a large warship was difficult to conceal, particularly in an age when

---

[132] *Id.* at 9, 15, 17–20, 135, 165, 166. Lambert claimed that Liberal politicians had less knowledge about how sea power worked than Balfour and the earlier Unionist government, 165–166. Sumida did point out that Balfour had been informed of the threat posed by torpedoes to battleships in narrow seas, and that Fisher had tried to convince Balfour to replace battleships with battlecruisers. Sumida, *In Defence of Naval Supremacy*, 55, 58. Nonetheless, professional opinion remained mixed about the value of the battleships, with no clear consensus on their obsolescence. Even Fisher recognized that a radical move such as immediately ending battleship construction in 1904 would be rejected by the Admiralty. *Id.* 52–53. There seems to be a clearer consensus among historians that Fisher only selectively shared information with politicians and colleagues, rarely providing anyone with his full plans or opinion.

[133] Thomas G. Otte "Grey Ambassador: The *Dreadnought* and British Foreign Policy," *in The Dreadnought and the Edwardian Age*, Robert J. Blyth, Andrew Lambert, & Jan Ruger, eds. (Farnham, Surrey: Ashgate Publishing, 2011), 70.

[134] Theodore Ropp claimed that France possessed the ability to match British construction times in the 1880s, yet acknowledged that in practice the British completed battleships in around three years while France took ten to twelve. Ropp, *The Development of a Modern Navy*, 59.

naval attachés regularly conducted visits of foreign shipyards. As Cobden noted, "[i]t would be just as possible to build a great hotel in secrecy in Paris, as to conceal the process of constructing a ship of war at Toulon or Cherbourg."[135] Despite attempts at subterfuge by foreign officials, attachés were able to accurately assess foreign construction programs.[136] Other means of securing information were also available, including royal visits, espionage, and publicly available scientific information. Spies were able to smuggle plans for the first ironclad, the *Gloire*, out of France despite heightened security.[137] Another colorful incident was related by the Secretary of the Admiralty, Lord Clarence Paget, who visited the new ironclad as an English tourist, taking a rowboat out to the warship where he measured the height of the battery with his umbrella.[138] When coupled with other intelligence sources, attaché visits provided Britain with the ability to estimate the type, number, and size of ships under construction as well as the rate of progress. Moreover, the Foreign Office and Admiralty relied upon these intelligence sources in strategic planning.[139]

The lengthy construction time, the ability to detect shipbuilding, and British capacity to rapidly build warships in response, made naval arms control feasible for the British. Moreover, Britain's position as the dominant naval power further enhanced its position. If an agreement had been entered into between Britain and a competitor, and the adversary sought to breach the agreement and overtake Britain's position, the adversary would need to undertake a significant amount of construction in a short period of time. The likelihood that this level of construction could be commenced and completed, before British intelligence learned of the breach, was slim. In all likelihood, the competitor would be detected long before a violation could alter the fundamental strategic situation. Ultimately the violator would be left in no better position than before breaching the agreement, while sustaining significant diplomatic damage for an act of bad faith.[140]

---

[135] Cobden, *Writings*, 219–20.
[136] Matthew S. Seligmann, *Spies in Uniform: British Military and Naval Intelligence on the Eve of the First World War* (Oxford: Oxford University Press, 2006), 106–10; *see also* John F. Beeler, *British Naval Policy in the Gladstone–Disraeli Era, 1866–1880* (Stanford: Stanford University Press, 1997), 209; Hamilton, *Anglo-French Rivalry*, 275–77.
[137] Hamilton, *Anglo-French Rivalry*, 275.
[138] Arthur Otway, ed., *Autobiography and Journals of Admiral Lord Clarence E. Paget* (London: Chapman & Hall, 1896), 194–96.
[139] Seligmann, *Spies in Uniform*, 258–60.
[140] See, for example, British discussion of the likely effect of Canadian violations of the Rush-Bagot Agreement. CAB 38/8/13 at 8–9.

This situation contrasted starkly with that for land armaments. Troop levels were inherently difficult to verify, and the great variety of military organizations on the continent made them difficult to quantify and compare. Differences in active and reserve status, level of training, as well as colonial forces and gendarmerie, allowed ample opportunity to evade treaty obligations. Unlike battleships, which took years to complete, an army could be raised in months, if not weeks. Similarly, small arms could be more easily stockpiled and concealed in warehouses. These problems with land arms control were all raised at The Hague in 1899, indicating that limitation of military forces required far more invasive procedures. Any security gained from such an agreement was far less certain. Naval armaments provided an area far more conducive to treaty regulation through effective verification. These premises of naval verification were questioned in the 1909 Dreadnought Scare, but at the turn of the century they provided a valid basis for a limited treaty restricting weaponry, without compromising British naval superiority.

The Foreign Office rarely articulated how it intended its arms control policy to work. However, when considered with Admiralty construction policy, Britain clearly sought to maintain superiority through faster ship-building aided by attaché verification. To complement this policy, Britain also sought limited arms control agreements rather than sweeping disarmament treaties. Certainly British negotiations with Germany after 1907, and the focus on exchanges of information, indicate this policy-making direction.

Whether or not the Admiralty viewed future conflict in Mahanian terms of a North Sea struggle in which numbers of capital ships alone counted, the public and the politicians they elected viewed naval security in these terms. British foreign policy utilized battleships for deterrent and other diplomatic purposes, and the rise of naval competitors reduced their value as diplomatic instruments. As Churchill suggested, peacetime arms competition served as a form of proxy war.[141] Arms control was meant to apply

---

[141] "The most hopeful interpretation which can be placed upon this strange phenomenon is that naval and military rivalries are the modern substitute for what in earlier ages would have been actual wars; and just as credit transactions have in the present day so largely superceded [*sic*] cash payments, so the jealousies and disputes of nations are more and more decided by the mere possession of war power without the necessity for its actual employment." Speech of Mr. Churchill, House of Commons, *Parl. Deb.*, 5th ser., 1912, xxxv, 1573, Mar. 18, 1912.

in times of peace, during which time it would influence foreign calculations as to the relative naval strength and the likely outcome of war. Treaty
regulation of battleships would have allowed Britain to continue to wield
influence as a great power by legitimizing its relative superiority over all
competitors.

CONCLUSION

Prior accounts of arms control initiatives between 1898 and 1914 have
focused on the two Hague Peace Conferences and Anglo-German bilateral
talks. However, British experience in legal negotiations for arms control
extended considerably beyond that, including not only nineteenth-century precedents, but also involvement in brokering the Argentine-Chilean
naval arms control treaty of 1902, offers to negotiate a successor agreement including Brazil in 1906, and renegotiation of the Rush-Bagot
Agreement from the 1890s onwards. Great Britain herself was involved
in two of the most significant naval arms agreements of the preceding
century – the 1817 Rush-Bagot Agreement and the 1856 Russo-Turkish
neutralization of the Black Sea. In these cases, significant strategic interests
were managed through international law.

These agreements differed from the overall European situation with
regard to enforcement. The Great Lakes and Black Sea agreements regulated largely enclosed seas, rendering large-scale violations improbable,
while the South American treaty involved two states incapable of building their own warships and dependent upon British financial markets for
purchasing ships abroad. This made violations nearly impossible without
the complicity of Britain, creating a form of international enforcement
through an actor external to the region. In contrast, the European naval
balance involved numerous states, many of whom built their own warships. Yet in each of these cases, national rivalry and ambition had been
tempered by law, indicating that arms races could be checked by treaty.
Moreover, even these regional agreements possessed limited scope for
actual enforcement, yet through pragmatic regulations had contributed
to stability and security.

The sum total of these experiences in legalized arms control indicated a Foreign Office focus on workable regulations. Effective verification, rather than international enforcement, provided naval limitation
treaties their teeth. Agreements required simplicity, to provide easily
manageable obligations that would be understood and accepted by the

public, and hence more likely to be upheld. When entering a period of prolonged naval activity by all the great powers from the 1890s onwards, Britain had a legal heritage upon which it could draw when fashioning its response. Arms control and international law could, and did, play a role in maintaining the British position in the face of rising competitors.

CHAPTER 6

Preparations for the Second Hague Peace Conference

The Hague Conference

Th' meetin' was opened with an acrimonious debate over a resolution offered be a dillygate fr'm Paryguay callin' f'r immeejit disarmament, which is th' same, Hinnissy, as notifyin' th' Powers to turn in their guns to th' man at th' dure. This was carrid be a very heavy majority. Among those that voted in favor iv it were: Paryguay, Uryguay, Switzerland, Chiny, Bilgium, an' San Marino. Opposed were England, France, Rooshya, Germany, Italy, Austhree, Japan an' the United States.

This was regarded be all present as a happy auggry. Th' convintion thin discussed a resolution offered be th' Turkish dillygate abolishin' war altogether. This also was carried, on'y England, France, Rooshya, Germany, Italy, Austhree, Japan an' th' United States votin' no.[1]

INTRODUCTION

The calling of the Second Hague Peace Conference provided a new opportunity to address naval challenges to Britain's strategic position. However, the general multilateral discussions at The Hague provided cumbersome fora for resolving a problem that up to 1905 chiefly concerned the great powers. The 26 states present at the first gathering were to be joined by Latin American countries, bringing the total number to 44. On the one

[1] Finley Peter Dunne, Mr. Dooley Says, New York 1910 at 204 et. seq. 207–208.

© The Editor(s) (if applicable) and The Author(s) 2016
S.A. Keefer, *The Law of Nations and Britain's Quest for Naval Security*, DOI 10.1007/978-3-319-39645-3_6

hand, Britain faced challenges applying the regional bilateral arms treaty models to a multilateral setting, as a conference of over forty states threatened to bog down discussions. On the other hand, the regulation of some weapons, such as auxiliary merchant cruisers and naval mines, required broader international agreement for effectiveness.

As Mr. Dooley implied above, when regulating armaments and questions of war, the great powers had a disproportionate importance – any agreement which did not reflect their interests would likely fail. The Hague Conferences were lawmaking gatherings, intended to provide rules for the entire international community. The legitimacy of these rules could most easily be achieved by universal participation, yet the most efficient means of securing an effective agreement required focused discussions by the most directly involved states.[2] British diplomacy and preparation for the conference centered on direct great power negotiations, as well as the advocacy of a special role for the great powers in maintaining any armament agreement.

In response to growing naval challenges, the British Foreign Office increasingly employed international law in a number of contexts, seeking to minimize threats. The Anglo-Japanese Alliance, the Anglo-French Entente, arbitration treaties, the modification of maritime rules of war, and arms limitation all served to solidify Britain's strategic position by reducing areas of conflict and setting expectations regarding future conduct. In this context, the arms agreements of 1817 and 1902–1903 were studied for their potential use as models. Britain had experience building limited agreements based on existing diplomatic practices and exploiting opportunities provided by naval construction.

The conference witnessed a broader linkage between arms control and the rules of war. The public and statesmen increasingly recognized the connection between naval arms competition and the manner in which any future naval war might be conducted, providing incentives to modify the latter in order to temper the former. Statesmen argued about whether or not alterations in wartime conduct could reduce the need for armaments, by limiting the use of certain weapons. This, in turn, brought central questions of the efficacy of international law in time of war into question.

The advent of a new Liberal government coincided with preparations for the conference, leading to a greater focus on arms limitations. Arms

---

[2] On tensions between equality and inequality at the Second Hague Peace Conference, *see* Simpson, *Great Powers and Outlaw States*, at 132 *et. seq.*

expenditures had not declined from the plateau reached during the Boer War three years before, and in its election campaign the new government had pledged to rein in the military budget. As the government refined its position on arms limitation and national security, the discussion of goals, concepts, and models of international law became clarified.

The government's central goal lay in a desire to decrease tax burdens while shifting funding to social programs. While humanitarian aspirations motivated many in the pacifist movement, and Liberal statesmen occasionally expressed lofty sentiments in favor of reducing the horrors of war, the official governmental focus remained on the expense of weaponry. Sir Edward Grey specifically stated that the government sought not so much to "limit armaments" as to "limit expenditure upon armaments."[3] The Liberal government did not hope thereby to reduce the risk of war, but to diminish the heavy tax burden which led to a drift toward "revolution and misery."[4]

It must be noted that many members of the Liberal government and civil servants, such as Eyre Crowe, did not support the effort to limit armaments, and even among those who did support the arms initiative, such as Sir Edward Grey, motivations were mixed.[5] It has been written elsewhere that the Liberal government faced an obligation to fulfill an election promise by lowering military expenses, and that the call for arms control was intended as much to appease the radical faction as to achieve any concrete results at The Hague.[6] Even if the effort failed at The Hague, by placing the blame upon Germany, the Liberal government could satisfy its domestic constituency that it had tried to minimize costs. But motivations for major initiatives are often complex, with different justifications being constructed to gain the adherence of different audiences.

---

[3] Grey to Nicolson, Feb. 15, 1907, *in* Gooch, G P, and H. Temperley, eds., *British Documents on the Origins of the War* (London: H M Stationery Office, 1926–1938), Vol. VIII, 207. Grey objected to the use of the term "disarmament," dismissing the goal as unrealistic, while an agreed ceiling on expenditures might be achievable.

[4] Lord Avebury, *Hansard*, 4th ser., CLVII, 1523, May 25, 1906.

[5] Zara Steiner, *Britain and the Origins of the First World War* (London: Macmillan, 1977), 36 et seq.

[6] Sidorowicz, *The British Government, the Hague Peace Conference of 1907, and the Armaments Question*, 1; Moll, "Politics, Power, and Panic: Britain's 1909 Dreadnought 'Gap'," *Military Affairs* 29, no. 3 (1965): 134; Marder, *Dreadnought*, 126; A J A Morris, "The English Radicals' Campaign for Disarmament and the Hague Conference of 1907," *Journal of Modern History* 43, no. 3 (1971): 371.

THE RUSSO-JAPANESE WAR AND THE HAGUE AGENDA

The Russo-Japanese War played a significant role in shaping the British agenda at the Second Hague Peace Conference. Numerous questions involving naval warfare came to prominence during the war,[7] several of which related directly to arms control. The use of naval mines and auxiliary cruisers foretold developing threats to British naval power, which the government hoped to restrain through law. Indirectly, the destruction of the Russian Baltic Fleet at Tsushima, together with the construction of the *Dreadnought*, provided the British with a "window of opportunity" to temporarily reduce naval construction, and bargain for limitations from a position of strength. Finally, proponents of arms control linked the topic specifically to limits on the capture of maritime commerce, noting that other states could not be expected to sacrifice the defense of their trade without receiving guarantees that they would be protected in wartime.[8]

The Admiralty recognized that the Russian use of auxiliary cruisers, or merchant ships converted into warships, posed a threat to British maritime trade.[9] The Russian auxiliary cruisers also violated an existing arms control regime by passing through the Turkish Straits in violation of the 1871 London Treaty.[10] While the ships passed the Bosphorus with their

---

[7] Land warfare presented only minor legal issues, most notably unsubstantiated Japanese claims that the Russians used expanding bullets in violation of the 1899 Hague Declaration. Amos S. Hershey, *The International Law and Diplomacy of the Russo-Japanese War* (London: Macmillan and Co., 1906), 317–18.

[8] Lord Loreburn, Immunity of Private Property at Sea in Time of War, CAB 37/88/58 (n.d., *c.* Apr. 1907), at 5; Pax, "The Exemption from Capture of Private Property," *The (London) Times*, Mar. 30, 1907, at 6 C. Many remained skeptical regarding German claims that they built their navy solely to defend commerce, noting that the battleships the Germans built were unsuited for commerce defense. Marder, *Dreadnought*, 120. At the very least, the true reasons for German naval growth would be exposed by removing the rationale of commerce protection.

[9] The Admiralty expressed particular concern that Germany, utilizing its large, fast, ocean liners, might engage in such conduct. The use of ocean liners posed a unique threat as they could outrun any British cruiser capable of outfighting them. The Germans, like other nations, had provided for these ships to carry artillery. Matthew S. Seligmann, *The Royal Navy and the German Threat, 1901–1914: Admiralty Plans to Protect British Trade in a War Against Germany* (Oxford: Oxford University Press, 2012), 1–2; Marder, *The Anatomy of British Sea Power*, 102–04.

[10] Treaty of London, 13 Mar. 1871, Art. II, *as cited in* Hurst, ed., *Key Treaties*, Vol. II, 467.

guns in their holds, only mounting them on deck after commissioning as warships at Libau in the Baltic Sea, the British legal office held this to be a technical violation of the terms of the 1871 London Treaty.[11] The Russian action raised a question regarding the definition of "vessels of war." This question could not fail to interest a British Admiralty conscious of national dependence upon imported goods, and the latent threat posed by predatory cruisers to British commercial lifelines.[12]

Naval mines posed another threat that the British sought to manage through either an outright ban or application of the rules of war. Naval mines had proven effective in the Russo-Japanese War, at one point sinking or disabling half the Japanese battleship fleet.[13] Moreover, as inexpensive weapons,[14] they would allow small naval powers to pose an asymmetrical threat to the large British battle fleet, similar to the threat of torpedoes. These weapons also constituted a humanitarian issue, as, after the war, mines continued to sink Chinese vessels,[15] and posed huge risks to commerce if major waterways were mined in future wars. As Great Britain possessed the world's largest merchant marine, it might suffer immensely in a conflict even if the British remained neutral, hence the government and public expressed broad support for some limitation on mine warfare.[16]

In preparing for the Hague Conference, government planning reflected an assumption that future wars would be limited, involving two to three great powers, rather than conflicts between grand coalitions of nations.

---

[11] Law Officers of the Crown to the Marquis of Lansdowne, Oct. 29, 1904, CAB 37/72/134 (Nov. 2, 1904).

[12] Avner Offer, *The First World War: An Agrarian Interpretation* (Oxford: Clarendon Press, 1989), 217 et seq.; Avner Offer, "The Working Classes, British Naval Plans and the Coming of the Great War," *Past and Present* 107 (1985): 204–26.

[13] Gardiner, *Conway's All the World's Fighting Ships, 1860–1905*, 216, 21–22. Two battleships were sunk, and a third put out of service for many months.

[14] Two Japanese battleships, valued at around £3,000,000, had been destroyed by a weapon costing £10. Captain Ottley to Fry, Sep. 1, 1907, Enclosure 1 in Fry to Grey, Sep. 2, 1907, *in* Further Correspondence respecting the Second Peace Conference at the Hague, FO 412/89 (1907).

[15] Davis, *The United States and the Second Hague Peace Conference*, 245.

[16] Unionists, Liberals, pacifists and Admiralty all expressed agreement on this issue. *See, e.g.* Submarine Automatic Mines, *in* Miscellaneous, CAB 4/1/52B (Mar. 13, 1905), at 1; expressing Balfour's desire for a ban, *see* Memorandum, Oct. 25, 1905, *in* Correspondence Respecting the Convocation of a Second Peace Conference at the Hague, FO 412/79 (1907).

Neutral great powers would continue to insist on upholding international law, rather than seeing a total breakdown of law in wartime. The Russo-Japanese War confirmed this expectation, as British and American protests against Russian conduct of its maritime war yielded immediate results.[17] When the Russian Baltic Fleet fired upon British fishing vessels in the North Sea, the Czarist government quickly accepted arbitration to prevent the crisis from adding a powerful adversary to the war.[18] As the new government prepared its response for questions that Parliament and the public would undoubtedly raise regarding the utility of international law, it turned to the Russo-Japanese War as a paradigm to which future agreements would be applied. Given recent experience, the government believed that during war, powerful neutrals could enforce bargains reached in peacetime, making it possible to utilize rules of war as a mode of arms control.

DIPLOMACY PRIOR TO THE SECOND HAGUE PEACE CONFERENCE

President Roosevelt called for a Second Hague Peace Conference during the election campaign of 1904, but the powers displayed little immediate interest. Roosevelt timed his circular in a bid to garner the support of pacifists in an election year,[19] and once the election had been won, his interest in the topic waned. Roosevelt's circular had been issued during the Russo-Japanese War, which removed these two great powers from immediate participation. After the conflict ended late in 1905, diplomatic formalities required that the Russian Czar be given the honor of actually calling the gathering, as he had done in 1898. This meant that the conference would be postponed until the Russian government had stabilized its domestic situation. The conference was moved from 1905 into 1906, and

---

[17] John W. Coogan, *The End of Neutrality: The United States, Britain, and Maritime Rights 1899–1915* (Ithaca: Cornell University Press, 1981), 49–51.

[18] Foreign Secretary Lansdowne told the Russian ambassador that conflict had been avoided only with the greatest difficulty and that public opinion could not be restrained if another incident occurred. Lansdowne to Hardinge, Oct. 29, 1904, No. 2, *in* CAB 37/72/137 (Nov. 3, 1904). The British had mobilized the Channel, Home, and Mediterranean fleets, organizing at Gibraltar in order to facilitate their interception of the Russian Baltic Fleet if necessary. Hershey, *The International Law and Diplomacy of the Russo-Japanese War*, 220.

[19] *Id.*, 91–92.

then scheduling conflicts with a gathering of diplomats in Geneva caused a further delay into 1907.

Between 1904 and 1907, statesmen had an opportunity to canvass opinions on arms control, as well as adjust to changes in the geopolitical situation in the world following the Russian defeat in 1905 and the first Moroccan Crisis in 1905–1906. The Anglo-French Entente of 1904 and the destruction of the Russian Navy removed two of the immediate key maritime threats to Britain's position. Additionally, the construction of the British *Dreadnought* altered the pace of the naval arms race, creating opportunities for even more heated competition in battleships. While the immediate Franco-Russian threats receded, the German naval construction program, set down in its Navy Law in 1898, and increased in 1900 and 1906, provided an obstacle to British plans for naval cuts. This whirlwind of change provided the backdrop to the Second Hague Peace Conference, and informed the choices of topics placed on the agenda.

The British appeals to the international community reflected the Liberal desire for financial retrenchment, in order to fulfill an election mandate. Campbell-Bannerman's government had difficulty making the argument for the limitation of arms, as he needed to assure domestic critics that British control of the seas remained secure while at the same time convincing foreign militaries that the British offer would truly result in a meaningful reduction of arms. Predictably, the British Prime Minister received criticism from both domestic and foreign sources. Balfour, the leader of the Unionist opposition, highlighted the dilemma in a domestic parliamentary debate, while Alfred von Tirpitz, Secretary of State of the German Imperial Naval Office, raised the same question from abroad.[20]

While this dilemma did indeed trouble the British government, it was not as insurmountable as later historians have claimed.[21] The British

---

[20] "How will you produce this feeling of implicit belief in the pacific intentions of England when you say, 'We have cut down the Navy Estimates, but the Naval Lords tell us we are fully equal to any two of you, even after the reductions?' … It is sufficient for me to say that the idea that these innocent, naïf, unsuspecting statesmen who are going to join the Hague Conference will be taken in by this noble appeal, is really absurd." Arthur J. Balfour, *Hansard*, 4th ser., CLXII, 110–111, July 27, 1906. Von Stumm to von Bülow, Apr. 25, 1907, No. 7786, *in* Lepsius, Bartholdy, and Thimme, eds., *Die Grosse Politik*, Vol. XXIII, at 51. "[Y]ou the colossus, come and ask Germany, the pigmy, to disarm. [I]t is laughable and Machiavellian." Captain Dumas to Sir F. Lascelles, 9 January 1907, enclosure in Lascelles to Grey, 10 January 1907, Gooch and Temperley, eds., *British Documents*, Vol. VI, at 2.

[21] *See* Morris, "English Radicals' Campaign," 384–85; Tate, *The Disarmament Illusion*, 334–36.

sought an arms control agreement that would assure their continued predominance, but other agreements have similarly enshrined asymmetric strategic relationships.[22] International legal agreements had never been predicated upon symmetry of obligations, as states could accept whatever limits they deemed appropriate. At The Hague in 1907, the British codified several other legal rules that uniquely benefited their strategic position.[23] Campbell-Bannerman may have been too sanguine in his estimation that continued British predominance "implies no challenge to any Single State ... [and is] recognized as non-aggressive, and innocent of designs against the independence, the commercial freedom, and the legitimate development of other States ..."[24] But the task of convincing states to accept an asymmetric bargain did not prevent other similarly uneven agreements from being reached at The Hague. As Britain lacked a large army and hence the ability to subdue any of the continental powers, it was reasonable for the government to expect that these states might be less worried about leaving Britain with a preponderant navy.

Aside from Great Britain, the United States provided the strongest support for arms control at The Hague. This was noteworthy, as the two Anglo-Saxon states had been the most reluctant to enter into the arms declarations at the 1899 Hague Conference, and had been the only great powers not to ratify all of these declarations. The conversion of the two states owed much to domestic developments. While the new Liberal British government hoped to reduce funding of its military, the American government sought to limit unnecessary expenses resulting from weapon obsolescence. Roosevelt's government advocated an active role for military power in foreign policy, but hoped to limit the regular funding battles with a skeptical Congress. President Roosevelt provided uneven support

---

[22] The 1922 Washington Convention and the Nuclear Non-proliferation Treaty both set asymmetric force levels among the parties, the latter agreement creating an absolute two-tier system between nuclear haves and have-nots.

[23] For instance, the development of rules regarding the capture of neutral merchant vessels in wartime continued to benefit nations possessing overseas bases at which these maritime prizes could be adjudicated. The rules did not allow states lacking access to many overseas bases, such as Russia or Germany, to judge the fate of their prizes on the high seas, nor were they allowed to conduct prize court proceedings in neutral harbors. "Convention Respecting the Rights and Duties of Neutral Powers in Naval War, Oct. 18, 1907," *American Journal of International Law* 2, no. 1/2 Supplement (1908): Arts. 4 & 5.

[24] Henry Campbell-Bannerman, "The Hague Conference and the Limitation of Armaments," 1 *The Nation*, Mar. 2, 1907, at 4.

for the concept of arms control, simultaneously advocating a large navy to defend against aggression from "less-civilized" states, while seeking economies to defuse domestic criticism.[25]

The threat of added expenditures became particularly acute with the completion of the British *Dreadnought*. In 1905, the year that the British launched the revolutionary battleship, the American Navy possessed a fleet of 12 battleships completed in the prior decade, and had an additional 13 battleships in varying stages of completion.[26] All 25 of these would need rapid replacing if the *Dreadnought* became the new standard, squandering fully half of the American investment in battleships before their commissioning. Facing domestic constraints on the size of battleships and seeking to prevent a qualitative race before the *Dreadnought* became the new standard,[27] the Roosevelt administration proposed a size limitation.

The American approach only sought to stem a qualitative arms race, as it still allowed states to build any number of battleships.[28] The Americans hoped that Germany would support the proposal, as it would obviate the need to widen the Kiel Canal, which the larger dreadnoughts would require.[29] American hopes were dashed however, as Germany rejected the proposal, the Kaiser noting "Rejected! Every state builds what it wants!"[30] Given German intransigence, and after the British expressed disinterest in this particular form of arms control, the Americans resigned themselves to building larger battleships.

After the failure to gain support on a qualitative limitation, the Americans advocated a naval construction freeze. A quantitative limit, if accompanied by sufficient publicity could shift the onus for its failure

---

[25] Davis, *The United States and the Second Hague Peace Conference*, 122.

[26] Data compiled from Gardiner, *Conway's All the World's Fighting Ships, 1860–1905*, 114, 39–44.

[27] It was not inevitable that the construction of a solitary larger warship would lead to a general increase in size. The Italian Navy had built several revolutionary large battleships in the 1880s without resulting in the setting of a new standard for warship size.

[28] Gleichen to Durand, Sep. 2, 1906, enclosure in Durand to Grey, Sep. 7, 1906, Gooch and Temperley, eds., *British Documents*, Vol. VIII.

[29] Frederick C. Leiner, "The Unknown Effort: Theodore Roosevelt's Battleship Plan and International Arms Limitation Talks, 1906–1907," *Military Affairs* 48, no. 4 (1984): 177.

[30] "*Ablehnen! Jeder Staat baut das was ihm paßt! Geht keinen Andern was an!*" Marginal Note of Oct. 15, 1906, Pourtalès to Wilhelm II, Oct. 13, 1906, Lepsius, Bartholdy, and Thimme, eds., *Die Grosse Politik*, Vol. XXIII.

upon those states which refused to accept the limit.[31] The "mobilization of shame," as such measures have been termed in international law in a later generation, would assist in the realization of their goals. This overestimated the value of public support for arms control, and exaggerated the role of public opinion in decision-making in many states, even perhaps betraying a lack of seriousness in the proposal. The British Liberal government welcomed such an initiative nonetheless, as it would at the very least allow it to justify increases in naval expenditures by placing the blame on Germany, which would undoubtedly reject such an offer.[32] Germany had already obliged the British in this regard, making it known that it would refuse to attend the upcoming conference if armaments were placed on the agenda.[33] An additional motivation for shelving the arms control proposals lay in concerns that their discussion could only worsen international tensions while having no chance of success. Germany sought to prevent a recurrence of its humiliation at the Algeciras Conference the previous year, and viewed the inclusion of arms control as a measure specifically intended to result in its isolation.[34]

The German position on arms control influenced the stance taken by the other great powers, largely due to their inability to reduce defenses while Germany remained aloof. Russia expressed no interest in hampering the reconstruction of its navy,[35] recently destroyed in the 1904–1905 conflict. While Russia needed to rebuild its army, Czar Nicholas II's priority

---

[31] Grey to Durand, Nov. 6, 1906, Gooch and Temperley, eds., *British Documents*, Vol. VIII.

[32] *See* Grey to Knollys, Nov. 12, 1906, *Id.*

[33] Lascelles to Grey, Aug. 16, 1906, *Id.*

[34] *See* Cartwright to Grey, Mar. 2, 1907, *in* Further Correspondence respecting the Second Peace Conference at the Hague, FO 412/86, (Jan. 1906–June 1907); Cartwright to Grey, Mar. 16, 1907, *in Id.*

[35] However, the issue was not as straightforward as the ultimate Russian policy suggests. Following the defeat at Tsushima, the Russian government debated the costs of rebuilding a battleship fleet, given expectations that conflict in Europe would begin prior to the completion of the new fleet, making the investment futile. A significant faction advocated the short-term development of a coastal defense force of torpedo boats and submarines for sea denial in the Baltic. *See* Evgenii F. Podsoblyaev, Francis King, and John Biggart, "The Russian Naval General Staff and the Evolution of Naval Policy, 1905–1914," *Journal of Military History* 66, no. 1 (2002). Had this alternative policy been pursued, it is possible that Russia would not have opposed naval arms control in 1907, given that their interests would have been similar to those motivating the Czar in 1898 – namely, preventing others from gaining a lead over Russia while she geared up her industries and rebuilt her strategic position.

lay with the navy.[36] Russia also emphasized the negative diplomatic consequences of an arms control discussion, and hoped to improve relations with Austria-Hungary and Germany by keeping the topic off the agenda.[37] Russia, nominally organizing the Hague Peace Conference, sent a seasoned diplomat and international legal scholar, Feodor de Martens, to canvas opinion amongst the other European powers on the likely topics to be discussed. While the Russian professor was visiting London, Grey told Martens that the key to the whole question of naval expenditure lay between Germany and Great Britain, and that while the British did not seek to isolate Germany at the upcoming conference, they did intend to reserve the right to raise the question.[38] Grey tentatively suggested that a bilateral agreement between the two countries would suffice, possibly one which would limit expenditure for a five-year period.[39]

Amongst the other great powers, Austria-Hungary echoed its German ally's unwillingness to discuss arms limitations, striving to arm against Italy and Serbia. France had previously expressed only lukewarm support for the British arms initiative, noting that they could not limit land armaments unless Germany took the lead.[40] Moreover, the French could hardly be expected to support a naval arms control agenda in the absence of an overall arms limitation, as it would result in the transfer of funding from the German Navy to the Army.[41] Despite its misgivings, prior to the Martens Mission France acknowledged that it would participate in an arms discussion, not out of any interest in the topic, but in order to assuage domestic public opinion.[42]

---

[36] Stevenson, *Armaments and the Coming of War*, 79.

[37] White to Root, Mar. 1, 1907, in US Dep't of State, *Papers Relating to the Foreign Relations of the United States with the Annual Message of the President 1907*, Vol. Part II (Washington: Government Printing Office, 1910), 1100.

[38] Grey to Nicolson, Feb. 15, 1907, Gooch and Temperley, eds., *British Documents*, Vol. VIII.

[39] *Id.*

[40] Bertie to Grey, May 17, 1906, Gooch and Temperley, eds., *British Documents*, Vol. VIII.

[41] As an article in the *Matin* put it, "it is quite certain that if Germany replaced the construction of four new armoured ships by the organization of four extra army corps, England would not have bothered much about it." *Quotation in* Morgan to Lister, Sep. 9, 1906, enclosure in Lister to Grey, Sep. 10, 1906, *in* FO 412/86.

[42] Grey to Bertie, Dec. 5, 1906, Gooch and Temperley, eds., *British Documents*, Vol. VIII. More practically, Cambon suggested to Grey that instead of airing the question before a large multinational audience, a limited multilateral commission consisting of the great powers would be preferable. Alternatively, he recommended that the British and

The opinions of six of the world's great powers had been expressed at this point, with three opposed to discussion, two in favor, and one on the fence.[43] On the continent, this left Italy, nominally the ally of Germany and Austria-Hungary, but with pro-British inclinations. The previous year Italy had sided against its German ally during the Algeciras Conference, and its reliability as a partner was in question at the time of the Hague Conference.[44] The Italians again surprised their German allies by expressing support for an arms control discussion, and proposing a practical procedure for introducing the topic. Procedural grounds had been raised as a diplomatic means of keeping the question of armaments off the agenda. Italy suggested that armaments be included on the agenda as long as specific proposals, and not merely general discussions, were forwarded.

Under the Italian plan, consideration of concrete proposals would take place in two steps. First, all states would vote to determine whether or not the proposal was worthy of detailed discussion. Only after passing this first hurdle would direct negotiations be undertaken.[45] The Italian proposal would have relegated arms control to the end of the conference, which would have prevented it from playing an effective part in earlier bargains. The Italians hoped that the provision of a veto, which the first step implied, would assuage German concerns.[46] However, this proposal apparently confirmed German fears. While the Italian Foreign Minister claimed to be speaking on behalf of both his and the German government, von Bülow disavowed any prior acceptance of this proposal.[47] Tittoni, for his part, expressed surprise and dismay over the fate of his proposal, although other diplomats felt he contributed to the misunderstanding when springing the project on von Bülow while the latter was vacationing at Rapallo.[48]

Germans compose their differences strictly on a bilateral basis. Grey to Bertie, Feb. 14, 1907, Gooch and Temperley, eds., *British Documents*, Vol. VIII.

[43] Amongst the lesser naval powers, Spain had also expressed its support for the British arms agenda. Grey to de Bunsen, Feb. 28, 1907, *in* FO 412/86.

[44] Cartwright to Grey, Mar. 16, 1907, *in* FO 412/86.

[45] Egerton to Grey, Apr. 5, 1907, *in* FO 412/86.

[46] The British in 1907 interpreted the Italian proposal in this light, recognizing the need to meet domestic criticism by at least discussing arms control at the conference. *See* Foreign Office Memorandum, Apr. 8, 1907, enclosure in Grey to Carter, Apr. 8, 1907, *in* FO 412/86.

[47] Nicolson to Grey, Apr. 10, 1907, *in* FO 412/86.

[48] Lascelles to Grey, Apr. 26, 1907, *in* Sir Edward Grey MSS, German Correspondence, FO 800/61 (1906–1909).

The Tittoni proposal also highlighted different opinions on the role of the community at large in framing international law. Tittoni suggested that concrete proposals should be brought to the conference as a whole, and upon an affirmative vote that the proposals were viable, the great powers would discuss them in greater detail. Grey and Martens had previously agreed that armaments proposals would be handled entirely by a commission of the great powers, who would then pass on their decision to the conference as a whole – the opposite of the Tittoni proposal.[49] Given the disproportionate influence of the great powers, the impracticality of discussions among forty states, and the far greater direct interest of the great powers in the question, their own procedure seemed logical to the British Foreign Office.[50] While the British and Italian plans laid out different procedures, both prescribed a special role for the great powers in settling the matter. The radical equality of states at the international conference would be directly undermined through decision-making by the great powers, but the legitimacy conferred by equality would be sacrificed in order to reach an effective agreement.

As this episode demonstrated, the diplomatic alignments which had been affirmed in 1904–1906 remained tentative. Germany's concern about isolation influenced its response to arms control at the Hague Conference. The official German opposition to any discussion of armaments hardened with the Italian initiative, as previous German views as expressed in the press indicated an ambivalence about the topic.[51] Yet if Germany feared isolation at the Hague Conference, then surely that risk would remain, even without a discussion of armaments, as there were other legal issues to be discussed which could have divided the powers.

Moreover, the risk of German isolation on the specific issue of arms control was overplayed by contemporary diplomats, as Russia also expressed a strong dislike of the topic. Had the issue squarely arisen at The Hague, the three conservative Eastern monarchies of the old Holy Alliance, all opponents of arms control, would have found themselves united against the West, a situation that diplomats in the liberal states would not have welcomed. Additionally, the German government probably feared that if

---

[49] Grey to Bertie, Feb. 20, 1907, *in* FO 412/86.

[50] "It is obvious that, in such a matter as naval and military expenditure, an agreement between the Great Powers is the only method by which any result can be obtained." Memorandum *attached to* Grey to Carter, Apr. 8, 1907, *in* FO 412/86.

[51] *See* Cartwright to Grey, Mar. 16, 1907, *in* FO 412/86.

armaments were discussed despite their opposition, it would appear as though Germany had been coerced into the discussions against its will, lending the appearance of another diplomatic defeat.[52]

Diplomatic considerations loomed large in the background, but an essential element of the story was the perception of international law. German delegates doubted the workability of arms limitation for reasons that did not apply to arbitration or the laws of war, as they were at least willing to discuss these topics. German concerns centered upon the enforcement of international law, and the ever-present risk of circumvention of legal obligations. Moreover, the use of a large multilateral conference as a forum for creating these obligations possessed the drawback that the fortunes of the great powers could be determined by the votes of "forty minor States."[53] German opinion did not believe that security could be enhanced through arms limitation, and that the risk of violations of an agreement would unduly threaten their position.[54] As regarded naval armaments, the British possessed a unique ability to overturn agreements, given that their industry was the leading exporter of warships. German skeptics rightly asked how an agreement could be enforced if dreadnoughts being built for Brazil could be requisitioned by Great Britain in a crisis.[55]

As the German General von Endres put it, paraphrasing Treitschke, in the spring of 1907, "all Treaties are signed with the mental reservation that they will be binding only so long as the situation under which they were created does not materially change. If in a Treaty conditions are imposed upon a State which hamper her welfare and are therefore not entered into voluntarily by her, she is then not only justified, but it is her duty to repudi-

---

[52] *Id.*

[53] *Id.*

[54] "A Law or Treaty is only worthy of its name when there is some power behind it ready to avenge its contravention and to break any State or private resistance to the fulfillment of its terms. Such an end as this the world cannot attain in an appreciable time, and until this time comes the only State that can assert its rights is the State that is strong enough to protect itself. But this strength – this *ultima ratio* – lies in an armed force, and its extent depends on the measure of security that each State enjoys – or otherwise on possible threats from foreign adversaries." The Disarmament Question Before the Opening of the Hague Conference," *Kreuz Zeitung*, Apr. 20, 1907, enclosure in Lascelles to Grey, Apr. 22, 1907, *in* FO 412/86.

[55] The Disarmament Question Before the Opening of the Hague Conference, *Kreuz Zeitung*, Apr. 20, 1907, enclosure in Lascelles to Grey, Apr. 22, 1907, *in* FO 412/86. Moreover, these fears would prove well-founded given British seizure of dreadnoughts under construction for Turkey at the outbreak of the First World War.

ate them at the earliest opportunity."[56] The Germans had a point: *Rebus sic stantibus*, or the doctrine of changed circumstances, had played a central role in Russian abandonment of the Black Sea restrictions in 1870, even if the powers had joined in resasserting the validity of treaties. In contrast to German views, British policy still assumed that law could play a role in constructing state interests, and in constraining state behavior, even if it could not guarantee compliance. Strong neutrals could uphold the law, and the creation of rules would increase the diplomatic costs of violations.[57]

The multilateral negotiations regarding arms control prior to the 1907 Hague Peace Conference produced some of the most varied positions on the issue during the era, and overshadowed the actual discussions at the conference. Conceptually, the discussions pointed to a number of methods of arms control that would be pursued in the following years. Practical measures, such as qualitative limitations on battleship size, were introduced, although they were not to find favor until the 1921–1922 Washington Conference. The idea of a naval construction holiday was raised by the United States, and to a lesser extent by the British, as was a limitation on naval expenditure and the exchange of information as means of building confidence and circumventing an arms race. The French raised the issue of arms control linkage, expressing the fear that a limit in naval armaments would simply lead to an increase in land armaments. Even the Germans contributed to the debate by suggesting that if arms were to be limited, they should be made relative to population size – a move which diplomat Richard von Kühlmann assumed would allot Germany a larger naval force than that granted to Great Britain, and thus ensure that the discussion of limitations would not take place.[58] Implicit in all these discussions was the assumption that the great powers would have a special role in deciding the issue, undermining notions of sovereign equality through an international forum at The Hague. The British government explored these possibilities in depth when preparing for the conference, seeking practical limitations that would enhance British security while recognizing the role of the great powers in the formation of international law.

---

[56] Cartwright to Grey, Mar. 8, 1907, *in* FO 412/86.

[57] *See* discussion in Chap. 3, also The Hague Conference: Notes on Subjects which might be raised by Great Britain or by other Powers, at 9, CAB 38/10/76 (Oct. 26, 1905).

[58] Cartwright to Grey, Jan. 29, 1907, Gooch and Temperley, eds., *British Documents*, Vol. VIII. Edward Grey prepared the rejoinder, noting that the population of British India would more than outweigh the German quota. Marginal Note of Grey, *in Id.*

THE WALTON COMMITTEE AND THE HAGUE AGENDA

The British government prepared for the Second Hague Peace Conference in a more orderly fashion than it had in 1899, demonstrating a greater appreciation of the opportunity to secure a legal foundation for British interests. Prior to the 1899 Conference, Salisbury's government did not extensively prepare British delegates or canvas the relevant departments regarding their interests in the various topics.[59] In contrast, the Committee of Imperial Defence (CID) began preparations for the upcoming Hague Conference in October of 1905, calling for input from various government departments on the topics likely to be raised.[60] Ultimately, in June 1906 the CID commissioned an Inter-Departmental Committee to review the agenda, under the chairmanship of Attorney-General John Walton. Over the next ten months the Inter-Departmental Committee, or Walton Committee, met on 18 occasions, gaining the opinions of the Foreign Office, the Admiralty, the War Office, the Board of Trade, and the Law Officers of the Crown, and issuing its final report on April 11, 1907.[61] The Walton Committee reflected a broader range of opinion than that canvassed prior to the First Hague Conference, providing a firmer basis for planning.[62]

The Walton Committee began its deliberations by requesting opinions on the major topics expected to be covered at The Hague – including the renewal of the 1899 declarations on poison gas, dum-dum bullets, and aerial bombardment – as well as assorted issues related to the laws of war. Initially, the Walton Committee addressed neither arms control nor arbitration.[63] Following the election of the Liberal government, the CID

[59] Hague Conference, Extracts from the Times, FO 881/9328*, (Part 5), (1906), at 2.
[60] The Hague Conference, CAB 38/10/76, at 1.
[61] Report of the Inter-Departmental Committee appointed to consider the Subjects which may Arise for Discussion at the Second Peace Conference, CAB 37/87/42 (Apr. 11, 1907).
[62] Criticism from Lord Chancellor Loreburn that it lacked international legal expertise was unfounded. Lord Loreburn, an outspoken advocate of immunity of private property at sea, claimed that the Committee did not include any experts of international law, unless one included J.S. Risley, an author of a book advocating the repudiation of current legal limits on the conduct of war. Moreover, Loreburn believed that the Committee's final report dismissed most expert international legal opinion as either too academic or out of date. CAB 37/88/58, at 5–6. However, the Inter-Departmental Committee utilized the international legal expertise in the Foreign Office, particularly Assistant Legal Advisor to the Foreign Office, Sir Cecil Hurst. Hurst who drafted key memoranda on arms control, later became the founding editor of the British Yearbook of International Law and President of the Permanent Court of International Justice. Eric Beckett, "Sir Cecil Hurst's Services to International Law," *British Yearbook of International Law* 26 (1949): 3–4.
[63] The Hague Conference, CAB 38/10/76, at 2.

added the topic of disarmament. The Russian Circular issuing the call for the conference did not mention arms control specifically, although it left the choice of topics open to the participating states. This provided the Liberal government with an opening for arms control discussions. The large multilateral format and the discussion of "abstract questions" would allow diplomats to raise subjects without the same fear of being rebuffed as would have occurred in limited meetings of powers, as at the recent Algeciras Conference.[64]

First, the Walton Committee hoped to promote arms control at The Hague through the refinement of existing bans on weaponry. The parties to the 1899 Conference had issued declarations banning aerial bombardment, as well as the use of "projectiles the object of which is the diffusion of asphyxiating or deleterious gases" and dum-dum bullets. The first declaration expired after five years, while the other two, neither of which Great Britain had ratified, remained in force, yet not specifically on the agenda. While the British sought to retain the right to use dum-dum bullets in their "small wars," the Committee now approved the earlier bans in "civilized warfare."[65] As the new Liberal government sought broad arms limits, its revised stance on the 1899 declarations reflected a newfound desire to be viewed as an advocate of arms control. Additionally, the Admiralty actively supported a limitation on aerial warfare, as this method of warfare would harm British interests as an insular power.

The Walton Committee also sought restrictions at The Hague on the use of naval mines at The Hague, if necessary, through the expansion of the rules of war. The CID sought a ban on uncontrolled naval mines as far back as November 1904, with the concurrence of the Admiralty, and the conditional support of the War Office.[66] Should delegates fail to agree on an outright ban on uncontrolled mines, the CID called for rules to regulate their use.[67] The Admiralty, which had previously questioned the utility of treaty limitations on naval armaments, called directly for an

---

[64] George S. Clarke, The Hague Conference: Arbitration and Reduction of Armaments, CAB 38/11/17 (Apr. 20, 1906), at 1.

[65] The Hague Conference, CAB 38/11/20 (May 15, 1906), at 3–4.

[66] Austen Chamberlain, Submarine Mine Defences, *in* Miscellaneous, CAB 4/1/42B (Nov. 13, 1904). The War Office noted that a question might be raised regarding the bombardment of defended places, and whether a defense consisting solely of mines would justify bombardment. CAB 38/11/20, at 4.

[67] CAB 38/11/20, at 4. The Admiralty called for anchored mines to be fitted with devices rendering them harmless if they broke free from moorings, and for unanchored mines to become disabled within a certain period of time after their laying. CAB 4/1/52B, at 2.

international limit on mines, even if it required the convening of a special conference devoted to the topic.[68] Rules of war which limited the type of naval mines states could employ would serve as a form of arms control – by banning those devices that did not meet the qualifications.

The Inter-Departmental Committee also sought to limit auxiliary cruisers through the rules of war. In discussing the right of capture, the Walton Committee noted that very large and fast merchant ships posed a threat to British commerce and to the security of coastal communities exposed to bombardment.[69] The Admiralty raised concerns that an attempt to prohibit the construction of merchant ships capable of conversion to auxiliary cruisers would require far too broad a regulation, sacrificing the British shipbuilding industry.[70] Captain Ottley expanded upon the issue in a memorandum on contraband. While noting that an attaché could easily determine if a ship was designed specifically as a warship, due to configurations of engine rooms and provisions for armored belts and decks, merchant ships intended for conversion could not be distinguished.[71] Domestic law prohibited British subjects from exporting such ships as war material, but other states were not similarly bound. [72] The Walton Committee sought to respond to auxiliary cruisers through definition of ships of war, and by requiring conversion to warships to take place only in national territory, rather than on the high seas.[73]

THE WALTON COMMITTEE AND NAVAL ARMAMENTS

Regarding the larger question of naval armaments, the Secretary of the CID, George S. Clarke, prepared the initial position for the Walton Committee. As the political and military changes of the previous few years allowed Great Britain to pause in its naval construction, Clarke hoped to propose a 10°per-

[68] CAB 4/1/52B, at 1.
[69] CAB 37/87/42, at 7–8.
[70] Admiralty Memorandum on the Subject of a Possible Limitation of Naval Armaments, Appendix 13 *in* CAB 37/87/42, at 88.
[71] Memorandum on the Question of Contraband of War in its Relation to Ships Sold by a Neutral to a Belligerent, Appendix 11, *in* CAB 37/87/42, at 80–81.
[72] The Foreign Enlistment Act of 1870 forbid the British from selling warships to belligerents, largely to prevent a repeat of the sale of *Alabama* type raiders to belligerents, but other states were under no such obligations. Germany had built special merchant ships for conversion to auxiliary cruisers for Russia in the recent conflict. *Id.* at 82–83.
[73] CAB 37/87/42, at 25.

cent reduction in military expenditure over the next three years.[74] In addition, Clarke sought at least a temporary, if not a permanent modification of the two-power standard.[75] As the government sought economy and enjoyed a position of strength, it could reduce expenditure upon armaments pending the results of the negotiations. The government proposed to reduce the construction of heavy armored ships from four a year, as called for in the Cawdor Memorandum, to two battleships in 1907–1908, to be increased to three if efforts at The Hague failed to yield results.[76] Campbell-Bannerman hoped Great Britain could go even further. In a letter to King Edward VII, the Prime Minister noted Admiralty plans to reduce construction to two battleships, stating "if ... there is a substantial and earnest engagement on the part of the great powers to diminish prospective increase it will be for us to consider whether the two ships will be necessary."[77]

The only criticism directed at Clarke's memoranda related to his views on arbitration, indicating general acceptance of his views on arms limitation.[78] Recognizing that several of the powers, including France, Italy, and the United States, welcomed a limit on armaments, and that Russian desire to rebuild its fleet would be tempered by difficulties in shifting funding, the CID recommended that a joint policy be adopted by the parties. German policy appeared the main obstacle, and a clear statement by other nations would at the very least lay clear the responsibility for the arms race.[79] This motivation for arms control discussions reflected Grey's concerns that if the Liberal government could not uphold election pledges to reduce arms expenditures, the blame should be laid at Germany's door.[80] Great Britain could propose a five-year limit on battleship con-

---

[74] *Id.* at 2; CAB 38/11/17, at 2.

[75] *Id.* at 2.

[76] Edmund Robertson, Secretary to the Admiralty, *Hansard*, 4th ser., CLXII, 69–72, July 27, 1906. The outgoing Unionist administration had attempted to fix a regular program of armored ship construction in 1905, which the new Liberal government initially accepted. On the Cawdor Memorandum *see* Marder, *Dreadnought*, 125–126.

[77] Sir Henry Campbell-Bannerman to King Edward VII, July 13, 1906, *in* Cabinet Letters, CAB 41/30/69 (1906).

[78] Minutes, *in* Note on General Points Which Might Be Raised at the Hague Conference, FO 881/9328* (Part 2), (1906). Clarke had called for the mandatory submission of questions including territorial control to arbitration, to which Sir Edward Grey and Sir Charles Hardinge quickly objected, fearing the limitation on sovereignty. *Id.*

[79] CAB 38/11/17, at 3.

[80] Grey to Knollys, 12 November 1906, in Gooch and Temperley, eds., *British Documents*, Vol. VIII, at 98.

struction to replacement tonnage.[81] Even if the British made the proposal
alone, no harm would result to the Imperial position, and it could serve
to increase international confidence in a limit. Clarke also recognized the
linkage between arms control and other areas of international law, including arbitration and the right of capture.[82] Overall, Clarke saw the Hague
Conference as an opportunity to educate international public opinion in
the possibilities for international law to play a role in limiting armaments.[83]

The Foreign Office legal advisor Cecil Hurst also perceived an opportunity to educate public opinion through a temporary arms limit. Hurst, a
trained international lawyer, again noted how a temporary limit on armaments needed to be part of a broader movement towards utilizing law in
foreign relations, the progressive codification of international law.[84] An
agreement only assisted national security if it constituted a "step in the
direction of a more rational state of things."[85] Through the rationalization
of foreign relations via the "mutual coercion by contract," states could
collectively maintain the strategic status quo.[86] In order to resolve the
question of enforcement, Hurst recommended that the agreement include
at least three powers. If one of these three breached the agreement, the
other two could respond, and, jointly, all three could respond collectively
to an offensive action by any non-party. A system of alliances, if coupled
with arbitration clauses, would form the core of an armament agreement.[87]
In this regard, Hurst echoed positions earlier advocated by Lawrence and
other academics, holding that the easiest form of international enforcement would be great power monitoring in their self-interest.[88]

[81] CAB 38/11/17, at 3. The idea of a "battleship holiday" as espoused by Churchill in
1912 echoed this concept. Ultimately, the Washington Treaty of 1922 expanded upon this
method of arms limitation.

[82] *Id.*

[83] *Id.* at 4.

[84] Cecil Hurst, Memorandum on Disarmament, Dec. 1906, FO 881/9328x (Part 12),
(1906), at 1.

[85] *Id.* at 3.

[86] *Id.* At the very least, reasoned Hurst, an agreement would not diminish the strength of any
state, making an attempt more acceptable. The rationale clearly reflected the needs of a status
quo power in maintaining levels of armaments. The agreement should "be merely one for marking time" in armaments, to generate confidence among states in the efficacy of international law
in resolving disputes. *Id.*

[87] *Id.* at 2–3.

[88] *See* Chapter 2; Lawrence, *A Handbook of Public International Law*, 51–52; Lawrence,
Essays, 226–27.

Given Hurst's criteria of reaching "a more rational state" through "marking time" in the relative balance of armaments, certain limitations would prove more profitable. A total limit on construction would fail, as it would cause economic dislocation in the maritime and associated industries, leading to an outcry for the repeal of the agreement. A size limitation would allow competition to continue unabated in other avenues, as would a limitation on the numbers of ships. According to Hurst, only a limitation on expenditure could preserve the status quo.[89]

Hurst's memorandum combined archaic unrealistic goals with pragmatic legal practice. While Hurst's proposal spoke about the older goal of disarmament, and his conception of enforcement through concerted international action harkened back to earlier calls for limitation through an international federation, the actual agreement he advocated constituted an arms control initiative, by seeking only the limitation, rather than the outright abolition, of armaments. Whereas disarmament required strong international institutions and participation by the majority of nations, the agreement detailed by Hurst called for the participation of only several great powers. The method of enforcement reflected the limited goal of altering an international arms dynamic and was to be enforced through existing state practice rather than the creation of a utopian institution. However, this stress on creating a "more rational state" betrayed an archaic goal of eventual disarmament through confidence-building measures such as a status quo agreement on arms.[90]

Hurst's optimism betrayed a certain amount of naivety, both in his faith in the ability of a parliament to check the activities of a government, and in the assumption, which he only partly refuted, that states would enter into such negotiations with the same goal of peaceful progress. His view of the arms race as an irrational manifestation in international politics was shared by other politicians. Grey suggested confidential exchanges of information on construction programs prior to releasing them to parliaments and domestic audiences, to allow statesmen to see how much their plans were driven by those of their neighbors.[91] Hurst's views reflected contemporary

---

[89] *Id.* at 3–4. Hurst did note that a limitation on expenditure would disfavor Great Britain's volunteer force, as a much higher proportion of expenditures went to wages. *Id.* at 4–5.

[90] However, even contemporary commentators remain divided on whether nuclear arms control can only be achieved through nuclear disarmament. *See* Jonathan Schell, "The Folly of Arms Control," *Foreign Affairs* 79, no. 5 (Sep.–Oct. 2000), 22–46.

[91] Grey to Nicolson, May 1, 1907, *in* FO 412/86.

thought on the future of war and international relations, with the belief that aggressive powers could be stopped by the concerted actions of like-minded great powers.[92] Any national leader harboring Napoleonic ambitions would be confronted by powerful neutrals with interests in upholding the status quo. He also echoed then-current views on the relatively greater importance of arbitration or increased international organization in reducing tensions, which would allow natural reductions of armaments.[93]

However, instead of relying upon the intricate working of a grand international organization to uphold his system, he heralded a more limited form of enforcement through self-interest. Hurst emphasized the self-monitoring function performed by economy-minded legislatures, downplaying the risk of cheating in such an agreement.[94] Even if imperfect, such a system could increase the political costs of treaty violations, making them less likely.

* * *

While considering the broad outlines of an agreement, the government still faced the question of the appropriate "yardstick" or "unit of measurement" of disarmament.[95] Even if states agreed to limit their military forces, they needed a means of comparing relative military strengths. Differences in income, geography, population, military organization, and even railroad networking influenced relative capabilities, making a simple quantitative measurement of soldiers inadequate. Regarding naval limitation, various proposals had suggested ceilings on the total number of battleships, gun caliber limits, and battleship size limits. With the construction of the *Dreadnought*, the latter means of limitation – fixing battleship size at an arbitrary level – gained adherents. President Roosevelt suggested that a size limitation on battleships, just below the level of the *Dreadnought*, would

---

[92] See Chapter 2, *infra*.

[93] See for example, K. P. Arnoldson, *Pax Mundi: A Concise Account of the Progress of the Movement for Peace by Means of Arbitration, Neutralization, International Law and Disarmament* (London: Swan Sonnenschein and Co., 1892), 84; Richmond Pearson Hobson, "Disarmament," *American Journal of International Law* 2, no. 4 (Oct. 1908): 743–757.

[94] Memorandum on Disarmament, *supra* note 84, at 4.

[95] Lord Fitzmaurice, Under-Secretary of State for Foreign Affairs, Hansard, 4th ser., CLVII, 1532, May 25, 1906; Military Correspondent, "The Next Peace Conference II: The Limitation of Armaments," *The (London) Times*, July 20, 1906, at 4.

be the best means of halting the naval arms race, as it would prevent competition engendered by replacing existing fleets with ever larger warships.[96] The Admiralty decisively shifted the British negotiating position away from a size limit on grounds of strategic advantage. The British Navy traditionally built significantly larger battleships than those of the other powers, as British service required them to remain on distant stations for longer periods of time. This requirement mandated extra storage space for coal and provisions, and ship designs better capable of remaining on station in all weather.[97] Moreover, the construction of smaller battleships would not yield any savings in expenditures, as three pre-dreadnought battleships would cost more in maintenance than two dreadnoughts.[98] Finally, the Admiralty noted that an increase in size favored Great Britain because other states such as Germany and the United States possessed shallower harbors, limiting their ability to operate larger battleships.[99] In addition to technical reasons against a size limit, the Admiralty claimed that such an agreement would pose a verification challenge.[100]

The Admiralty did not object in the abstract to the limitation of new construction to replacement of existing tonnage, but questioned the wisdom of limitation. Later regulators resolved several of the issues raised by the Admiralty at the Washington Conference in 1921–1922, including the questions of whether or not to include fuel and provisions in allotted ton-

---

[96] Gleichen to Durand, September 2, 1906, enclosure in Durand to Grey, September 7, 1906, in Gooch and Temperley, eds., *British Documents*, Vol. VIII, at 95. The United States had previously made an offer to bilaterally limit battleship size with the British in 1902. *See* Marder, *The Anatomy of British Sea Power*, 116. While the United States cast its 1906 offer in terms of a possible 16,000-ton limit, the size of contemporary American battleships, the Admiralty memorandum considered the disadvantages of a 20,000-ton limit. It should also be noted that the United States built dreadnought battleships on the lower 16,000-ton limit, completing a pair of ships in 1910 that were already under consideration in 1904, the *South Carolina* and the *Michigan*. Robert Gardiner, ed., *Conway's All the World's Fighting Ships, 1906–1921*, 3rd edn (London: Conway Maritime Press, 1985), 105, 12. The American offer of a 16,000-ton limit should be viewed in this light.

[97] Admiralty Memorandum, Appendix 13 *in* CAB 37/87/42, at 88–89. The British generally built battleships around 2,500 tons heavier than those of foreign contemporaries. *Id.* at 88. Lord Eversley, in a debate in the House of Lords, noted that while Great Britain possessed 37 battleships averaging 14,800 tons, France had only four ships of this size, and Germany none. *Hansard*, 4th ser., CLXII, 321–322, July 30, 1906.

[98] Admiralty Memorandum, Appendix 13 *in* CAB 37/87/42, at 90.

[99] *Id.* at 93–94.

[100] *Id.* at 94.

nage, and the fate of old battleships removed from service.[101] The Admiralty made the case that an attempt by a majority of states to impose limitations on a minority at the Conference would merely increase the risk of conflict.[102]

The Walton Committee accepted the Admiralty reasoning against the utilization of a size limitation, holding that the best forms of regulation would include either an overall military expenditure ceiling or an agreement on the total number of warships.[103] The Walton Committee explicitly excluded the possibility of linking naval arms control to a reduction of land forces, a position which would garner little support from France. The Committee made acceptance of any agreement conditional upon adequate means of verification and with an escape clause allowing withdrawal in the case of violation by another party.[104] The Committee concluded by proposing that Great Britain restate the offer of First Lord of the Admiralty Goschen in 1899 and Tweedmouth in 1907, in which they offered to reduce British naval construction programs if the other powers would do likewise.[105]

*   *   *

Between December of 1906 and the final report issued by the Walton Committee in April of 1907, it became clear that a broad naval limitation remained unlikely. The Martens tour early in 1907, in which the Russian diplomat Martens visited the major European capitals in order to clarify the divisions between the powers, highlighted German opposition. At home, the Admiralty sought to retain the right of capture, undertaking a major campaign to convince the Committee of the necessity of this position.[106] This, in turn, would weaken the ability of the British delegates to negotiate for arms control in return for modifications to the rules of war at sea.

After receiving the Walton Committee's final report, the Cabinet engaged in lengthy discussions on the agenda for the Hague Conference. Although the record is fragmentary, continuities emerge between the Walton Committee's final report and the instructions ultimately issued

---

[101] *Id.* at 87, 94.

[102] *Id.* at 87–88.

[103] Limitation of Armaments, *in* CAB 37/87/42, at 19.

[104] *Id.* at 20.

[105] *Id.* at 20–22.

[106] *See* Christopher Martin, "The 1907 Naval War Plans and the Second Hague Peace Conference: A Case of Propaganda," *Journal of Strategic Studies* 28, no. 5 (2005).

by the Foreign Office to the Conference delegation in June. The Cabinet agreed that arms control remained one of the two primary British goals at the conference.[107] The Walton Committee recommended several avenues of arms control, through the direct limitation of naval armaments, through the development of the laws of war, and through the further refinement of earlier weapons bans. While the first goal of a naval arms limitation was not likely to be achieved at The Hague, the remainder of the topics remained upon the agenda.[108] Moreover, the British pursued a limitation of expenditure on naval armaments, the manner agreed upon in the Walton Committee report, through its offer of an exchange of information at The Hague and through its negotiations with Germany following the conference. The exchange of information would assist by informing the powers of the manner in which their defense outlays were related.

The instructions issued to the British delegation at The Hague recognized the difficult political climate. German opposition made it impolitic to bring a detailed proposal, unless it appeared likely to receive a favorable hearing. The Foreign Office requested that its delegates coordinate with the United States, Spain, and possibly Italy, on developing their arms control position, as these states had expressed an interest in the topic. The progressive codification of international law still required that arms control be addressed at The Hague, even if no major accomplishments resulted, to prevent the appearance that the community was moving backwards.[109] The exchange of information proposal in the delegates' instructions would provide a basis for further negotiations, and could assist in limiting expenditures on armaments. This initiative would allow international law, in a very limited manner, to influence armaments policy, even if it did not mandate a direct limitation.

CONCLUSION

Government preparation for the Hague Conference reflected a willingness to creatively legislate solutions to armaments issues. Pre-conference diplomacy reflected concerns that the unwieldy size of the Hague Conference

---

[107] Sir Henry Campbell-Bannerman to King Edward VII, June 5, 1907, *in* CAB 41/31/21 (1907).

[108] Instructions to British Plenipotentiaries, Grey to Fry, June 12, 1907, *in* Gooch and Temperley, eds., *British Documents*, Vol. VIII, at 42, 45–46.

[109] Memorandum, CAB 37/89/63, (May 31, 1907) at 1.

would preclude effective discussions of armaments, particularly when the great powers had a disproportionate interest in the question. Limited multilateral diplomacy among the great powers as variously proposed by Grey, Martens, and Tittoni provided a more effective method, in spite of the expectation that this would prejudice discussion at The Hague, thereby undermining the legal notion of sovereign equality of states.

The Russo-Japanese War raised many issues more appropriately handled by limited regulations, including restrictions of naval mines and auxiliary cruisers. The government planned to utilize a number of limited regulations to check armaments, through the laws of war and possibly an exchange of information. These plans, as developed by the Walton Committee, contrasted sharply with the public and parliamentary assumptions prior to the conference. The types of regulations ultimately envisioned in the British delegation's instructions required different checks and balances than those required for general disarmament. Instead of requiring a supra-national federation vested with enforcement powers, the proposed arms control agreements entailed the support of neutral public opinion. By adopting models of arms control reliant upon neutral diplomatic pressure, the British implicitly assumed that future wars would continue to be limited in scale, with sufficiently powerful neutrals to coerce compliance with the law. These models of international law also highlighted the function that the Foreign Office expected law to play, in helping set expectations for future behavior, while always recognizing that banned conduct could not be eliminated. The government viewed international law not as an answer in itself, but as another tool at its disposal in managing a complex international question.

CHAPTER 7

The Second Hague Peace Conference

Peace Conference: The Opening of Hostilities.[1]

INTRODUCTION

The failure of the Second Hague Peace Conference to resolve the burgeoning arms race between Germany and Great Britain has obscured the real achievement of the gathering. Even before the Second Hague Peace Conference had met, pundits had dismissed the possibility that any disarmament might result from the gathering. As in 1899, no general limitation of armaments resulted, and this issue received even less discussion than at the earlier meeting. Most historians have focused on the paltry results of the general quest to limit overall military budgets or force levels when discussing the law of arms control.[2]

However, the 1907 Conference resulted in several concrete improvements in the international law regulating armaments, refinements that acknowledged the nuanced role played by law in security questions. While these limited regulations were unable to resolve the central questions relat-

---

[1] *The London Times*, as quoted in *Punch, or the London Charivari*, July 10, 1907, Vol. CXXXIII, (1907), at 25. *The Times* article covered discussions on declarations of war at The Hague.

[2] Tate, *The Disarmament Illusion*, 340–45; Dülffer, *Regeln Gegen Den Krieg?* 326–27; Davis, *The United States and the Second Hague Peace Conference*, 215–19; Morris, "English Radicals' Campaign," 391–93.

© The Editor(s) (if applicable) and The Author(s) 2016   203
S.A. Keefer, *The Law of Nations and Britain's Quest for Naval Security*, DOI 10.1007/978-3-319-39645-3_7

ing to the arms race, they did confirm the role of international law in limiting armaments. The acceptance and consolidation of this principle, that states could limit their right of self-defense through international agreement, has since formed the cornerstone of all arms control agreements. Even Germany, which opposed the infringement upon national sovereignty inherent in arms control and which openly expressed doubts about the utility of regulating matters relating to national security, advocated international rules relating to declarations of war. This indicated a tacit acknowledgement that law could play some role in advancing national security. Germany feared a British preemptive strike upon its growing fleet as an alternative unilateral means of arms control,[3] and believed that condemnation by the international community might make such conduct less likely.[4]

Moreover, several noteworthy features of the conference have not been acknowledged by historians. International law evolved in several areas. For instance, at the conference the British championed the abolition of naval mines as well as regulation of the conversion of merchant ships into auxiliary cruisers, both limitations upon a state's ability to arm itself. The powers also forbade the bombardment of one another's great cities, while retaining this tactic against colonial territories. Significantly, both the Americans and British, who previously held the dubious distinction of being the only two great powers to refuse to sign the earlier armaments declarations, now championed arms control.

Through these regulations, Britain exploited the rules of war to further arms limitation goals. Rules of war differed in that they applied in time of conflict while arms control generally applied in times of peace. These two types of regulations required different forms of enforcement, as belligerents, already waging war with one another, had limited additional means to uphold legal claims. Moreover, the rationale for rules of war often included humanitarian goals in addition to pragmatic reasons, whereas states predicated arms limitation solely upon calculations of national advantage. However, rules of war often overlapped with arms limitation when they created restrictions upon the ability of a state to arm itself, as in bans on arming auxiliary cruisers or on types of naval mines.[5]

---

[3] See Jonathan Steinberg, "The Copenhagen Complex," *Journal of Contemporary History* 1, no. 3 (1966).

[4] Whether or not Germany intended to honor law in a future war remained another question. See Hull, *A Scrap of Paper.*

[5] On further overlap of rules of war and naval arms limitation at the Second Hague Peace Conference, see Keith Neilson, "The British Empire Floats on the British Navy" *in* McKercher, *Arms Limitation and Disarmament.*

The Second Hague Peace Conference witnessed a greater British engagement with the international community on questions of law relating to security than at any meeting of the previous half-century. While the British had attended the periodic international conferences in the latter half of the nineteenth century, they had frequently impeded sweeping changes in law, often expressly conditioning their participation on the exclusion of questions relating to naval warfare.[6] Unlike at earlier meetings at St. Petersburg, Brussels, and at The Hague in 1899, in 1907 the British agreed to include numerous maritime questions on the agenda. The changes in military technology since the advent of steam power, as well as decline in the relative British strategic advantage since the mid-century, underlay the new willingness to utilize law. But the evolving British attitude towards the role of law in national security formed the necessary condition for this shift.

Britain's willingness to engage with the international community in setting rules relating to national security can be seen as part of that country's shift away from "splendid isolation." However, Britain's attempt to cement its national position through creation of rules of international law faced great challenges. The field of international law was heavily contested. The final agreements often masked the intense divisions among states, obscuring the sophisticated diplomacy that ultimately produced the compromises. The negotiations leading up to the Hague Conference, as well as discussions at The Hague, showed a volatile, rapidly changing international community.

Geopolitical differences influenced the legal stances taken by powers at the conference. Diplomats often voted against their allies when negotiating rules that would affect them jointly in a future conflagration. Divisions between great powers and minor states influenced positions on armaments, as with the proposed ban on naval mines. Distinctions based on relative power even influenced discussions on judicial procedure, with the great powers seeking a predominant role on any international tribunal just as the smaller, and non-European, states sought confirmation of the principle of equality of states – one state, one vote. Law reflected the political realities of international relations among the great powers, as well as between the great powers and smaller states.

---

[6] Regarding the 1874 Brussels Conference, *see* Derby to Loftus, July 4, 1874, *in* FO 412/16; regarding the 1899 Hague Conference, *see* Davis, *The United States and the Second Hague Peace Conference*, 12–13, 28.

The Second Hague Peace Conference Proceedings

In addition to the often-recounted speech and non-binding resolution offered by Sir Edward Fry, significant, and at times, electric, discussions surrounded the other armaments proposals at The Hague. The issue of naval mines revealed a division between large and small naval powers, as the cheap coastal defense weapons challenged the continued superiority of great power battleship fleets. The possibility that merchant ships could be converted into commerce raiders, and then back into merchant ships, presaged a unique risk to British maritime commerce.[7] Moreover, an imprimatur of legality upon such conduct would undermine the British advantage of possessing a worldwide network of naval bases, as these commerce raiders could seek refuge in neutral ports around the globe depending on whether they flew the naval ensign or a merchant marine pennant. These issues mattered, not as abstract questions of law, nor as toothless concessions to a pacifist constituency, but as issues of sea power.

The British delegation at The Hague coordinated policy with the Foreign Office by submitting daily reports of ongoing sessions, regular memoranda detailing legal issues, and through a back-and-forth correspondence detailing evolving drafts of the conventions. The delegation included seasoned diplomats Sir Ernest Satow and Sir Edward Fry, both distinguished international legal scholars, as well as Senior Foreign Office Clerk Eyre Crowe.[8] The delegation advanced concrete national interests through the use of international law at The Hague. At the same time, it acknowledged the limitations inherent in the law. Not only were the legal issues of immediate consequence to Great Britain, but British statesmen approached these issues with an earnestness and seriousness of mind.

The Arms Limitation Resolution

Even prior to the opening of the conference, the powers had sought to circumscribe the anticipated arms limitation resolution. The great lengths to

---

[7] Matthew S. Seligmann, "New Weapons for New Targets: Sir John Fisher, the Threat from Germany, and the Building of HMS *Dreadnought* and HMS *Invincible*, 1902–1907," *International History Review* 30, no. 2 (2008): 316–17.

[8] Despite leaving considerable records on the Hague Conference and other legal topics, Satow wrote little about arms limitation. While he extensively commented on the immunity of private property, there were few marks on arms control memoranda in his possession. This is not entirely surprising as there were fewer contentious legal principles to decide with armaments as compared to maritime law.

which diplomats went in limiting this tepid document attests to concerns they harbored about its influence. Chancellor von Bülow set the tone a little more than a month before the conference opened, by stating in the Reichstag that "[h]e had been counseled … to take part in the discussion just because it could not have any practical issue, and because by taking part in it he would escape misrepresentation … [After rejecting that course, he held that Germany] will, however, leave the Powers who are sanguine that this particular discussion will prove successful to 'conduct it alone.'"[9]

Before von Bülow's pronouncement, the British had hoped at least to propose an exchange of information on naval programs, but feared that Germany would view such a step as a provocation. In the absence of German participation, there would be no point in bringing a proposal, as none of the other powers could then accept it. Great Britain would then be required to increase its naval construction program, although blame could be placed upon German intransigence. Before abandoning the proposal, however, Grey sought American opinion, as he hoped to coordinate action with the United States on the issue. American Secretary of State Elihu Root suggested that Britain should go ahead with the resolution for the sake of keeping the topic on the public agenda.[10]

The British delegation was instructed to raise the issue at the conference. Satow, in outlining British positions at the upcoming conference, thought the British could offer to freeze military and naval levels at the status quo, "increasing neither the number of men, horses, guns, ships, tonnage, calibre of guns used respectively on land and at sea, on condition that the other Great Powers do the same …"[11] This extraordinary proposal would have combined a number of features later included in naval arms control in the 1920s and 1930s, including gun caliber and warship size, as well as warship numbers. While the Foreign Office questioned Satow's handling of contraband in the memo, no opposition was raised to his statements regarding armaments, although the Admiralty certainly would have raised objections if the proposal seemed likely to succeed.

Certainly, the British delegation at The Hague suffered from internal divisions, due to the diverging interests of the Admiralty, War Office, and Foreign Office.[12] The ban on expanding bullets presented another exam-

---

[9] Untitled, *The (London) Times*, May 1, 1907, at 9, col. E.
[10] Grey to Bryce, May 6, 1907, Gooch and Temperley, eds., *British Documents*, Vol. VIII.
[11] Note by Satow, May 13, 1907, *Id.* Considering Grey's fixation on limitation of military budgets, the absence of this method is interesting.
[12] Crowe to wife, June 15, 1907, Crowe Mss., MS. Eng. D. 2901.

ple. While the British government now accepted the expanding bullet declaration, its military delegates still had reservations and recommended signing it only if the ban was accepted universally. Under discussion in 1907 was an American-inspired proposal to modify the 1899 expanding bullet declaration, by calling for a general ban on all ammunition which caused needless and excessive injuries. The military expressed fears about facing an enemy armed with new bullets of "high stopping efficiency" if Britain lacked the same ammunition.[13] Ultimately, the conference ruled the American proposal to modify the declaration to be out of order, as the topic had not been included on the agenda.[14]

Even in 1907, the army still harbored lingering concerns about the influence of new munitions technology on the military balance. Had the army believed that new bullets of "high stopping efficiency" caused excessive harm without augmenting fighting effectiveness, there would have been no need to employ them against enemies armed with similar ammunition. Possibly, the army believed that the mere possession of expanding bullets would deter their use by a foe, out of fear of reprisals. More likely, the military still believed that high technology munitions might contribute to strength.

The central question of armaments posed a thornier issue, which could not be sidelined by rules of parliamentary procedure. Russia, as convener of the conference, faced a delicate situation as it sought to reconcile the German position, with which it fully agreed, with British insistence upon a substantive discussion of arms control. Fry, the senior British delegate, conferred with American, French, Russian, Italian, Portuguese, Japanese, and Chinese representatives on the question of armaments, agreeing that the conference would confirm the non-binding resolution of the 1899 gathering, but would not raise concrete measures.[15] Russian first delegate Nelidov, elected president of the conference, stressed from the beginning that armaments should not be raised in such a manner as to disrupt the peace. He accepted his duty, endeavoring "to keep peace among us by seeking points of contact and by avoiding everything that might bring out differences of opinion that are too violent" and warning the delegations "let us not be too

[13] Memorandum by Sir Edmond Elles, enclosure in Fry to Grey, July 9, 1907, No. 42, FO 412/87, Further Correspondence Respecting the Second Peace Conference at the Hague (July 1907).

[14] James Brown Scott, ed., *The Proceedings of the Hague Peace Conferences. Translation of the Original Texts. The Conference of 1907*, Volume III, (New York, Oxford University Press 1921), p. 153–4.

[15] Fry to Grey, June 17, 1907, *in* FO 412/86.

ambitious, gentlemen."[16] The Russian diplomat saw armaments as an effect rather than a cause of international tensions, the opposite of Sir Edward Grey's views.[17] To the Russian, the sudden rise of Germany, Japan, and the United States upset the international balance of power, and in response armaments would continue to rise until states achieved a new equilibrium.[18]

Fry coordinated with Nelidov, who in turn brokered begrudging consent from the German delegation, the parties agreeing on the limited goal of a resolution and a British offer for an exchange of information on naval construction.[19] The parties pushed the discussion of the resolution late into the conference, in an August session. Fry spoke on the growth of armaments since the initial conference in 1899, noting that several powers sought to reduce the pace. International law required state consent to this significant constraint on sovereignty, and states had to balance any legal compromise against their duty to defend themselves. However, given the self-perpetuating nature of the arms race, an exchange of information on naval expenditures could educate legislatures on how interrelated their naval programs were.[20] When proposing an exchange of information on behalf of his government, Fry did not specify the actual information to be exchanged, but the proposal included the construction of new ships and their expense. Moreover, he laid the foundation for bilateral negotiations with Germany after the conference. If, as Nelidov suggested, the question was no more ripe for a multilateral solution in 1907 than it had been in 1899,[21] perhaps direct discussions with Germany on the narrower issue of an information exchange might yield fruit.

The conference reiterated the resolution of 1899, noting that "in view of the fact that military burdens have considerably increased in nearly all countries [since 1899] ... the conference declares that it is highly desirable for the

---

[16] Nelidov, June 15, 1907, Scott, ed., 1907 *Proceedings*, Vol. I, 47, 48.

[17] A year later, Grey would fully express his views on the Anglo-German naval arms race, noting that no other issue divided the two states, thus competition in armaments caused the rift, rather than followed it. Memorandum by Grey, Aug. 6, 1908, Gooch and Temperley, eds., *British Documents*, Vol. VI. This same outlook can be seen in the Foreign Office desire for an exchange of information at The Hague, which could alleviate the arms race by demonstrating its self-reinforcing nature, without addressing underlying international tensions.

[18] Fry to Grey, July 16, 1907, *in* FO 412/87. Moreover, Nelidov later stated that Great Britain was merely "giving expression to its own preoccupations," in leading the crusade for arms limitation. Nelidov, Aug. 17, 1907, Scott, ed., *1907 Proceedings*, Vol. I, 92.

[19] Fry to Grey, July 16, 1907, *in* FO 412/87.

[20] Fry, Aug. 17, 1907, Scott, ed., *1907 Proceedings*, Vol. I, 88–90.

[21] Nelidov, Aug. 17, 1907, *Id.*, 93.

governments to undertake again the serious examination of this question."[22] While the hortatory phrase as worded did not create a distinct legal obligation, it affirmed the desirability of ending the arms race as a legal principle. Of all the binding and non-binding documents resulting from the conference, including 13 conventions, two declarations, and five *voeux*, it was significant that this was the only resolution. The use of a resolution instead of a *voeu* in this instance indicated a higher standing for arms control.

Technically, a resolution indicated the existence of a principle of law, while a *voeu* only expressed a non-binding wish, making the resolution a binding agreement.[23] However, the form of expression did not create an obligation to take any steps, only declaring "that it is highly desirable" rather than mandatory, for states to "undertake an examination," the latter phrase consisting of a weak obligation in itself, not even requiring any concrete results.[24] As the conference included the resolution in the final act, as opposed to a separate agreement, such as the declarations and conventions, parties could not refrain from signing it.[25] Nor did it require domestic ratification; it emerged as a perfected legal obligation.[26] While no direct obligation flowed from the arms control resolution at The Hague, by enshrining the desirability of arms limitation as a principle, it laid the basis for future regulation.[27] As an immediate matter, it did nothing to halt the arms race, but it further legitimized diplomatic initiatives to halt arms competition, as calls for direct negotiation could not as easily be openly rebuffed as unfriendly.

[22] "Final Act, Oct. 18, 1907," *American Journal of International Law* 2, no. 1/2 Supplement (1908).

[23] International lawyers generally held that the label of an agreement, whether declaration, convention, or treaty, carried less weight than the actual obligation contained in a document. Oppenheim, *International Law: A Treatise*, Vol. I, Peace 551–52. However, a *voeu* was a specific usage for non-binding statements, and the framing of the arms statement as a resolution was a means of differentiating what would otherwise be a weak obligation from an outright non-binding view.

[24] Scott, *The Hague Peace Conferences of 1899 and 1907*, Vol. 1, 137.

[25] Technically, a party generally had the right to make interpretive declarations and reservations upon the signing of a treaty, which could release them from specific obligations. However, as a practical matter, the inclusion of the resolution in the final act of the conference implied the general consent of the parties.

[26] Scott, *The Hague Peace Conferences of 1899 and 1907*, Vol. 1, 139.

[27] As a point of law, as opposed to the practical question of limiting the pre-war arms race, this should not be underestimated. A similar principle of law, the Martens' clause, which noted vaguely that the means of injuring an enemy are not unlimited, has since developed into a key premise underlying the laws of warfare. "Convention Regarding the Laws and Customs of Land Warfare, Oct. 18, 1907," *American Journal of International Law* 2, no. 1/2 Supplement (1908): Art. 22.

Balloons and Aerial Bombardment

After the arms resolution, the renewal of the 1899 declaration forbidding aerial bombardment has been the most studied arms control precedent of the conference. The earlier ban contained an agreement among the parties to forbid the "launching of projectiles and explosives from balloons, or by other new methods of a similar nature."[28] In 1899, aircraft technology was in its infancy, and military experts were uncertain whether the new weapon would tend to make warfare less humane or more humane. Therefore, the declaration remained in effect only for five years,[29] allowing observers to assess aerial developments in the interim. The obligation expired in 1904 and was submitted to the conference for renewal.

While military advocates saw the unknown potential of airpower as reasons for maintaining state freedom, others perceived a necessity of halting the militarization of the sky before it occurred, justifying a ban at the outset. Lord Reay, of the British delegation, asked "if it is not enough to have two elements in which the nations may give free scope to their animosities and settle their quarrels without adding a third?"[30] As Lord Reay noted, the development of airpower had not progressed so far that states could not limit it. The further development of military aircraft would tend only to increase national reliance upon such weapons, making them more difficult to regulate in the future, and causing a further increase in military budgets.[31] Moreover, the addition of this "third element" would

[28] "Declaration Concerning Aerial Bombardment, July 29, 1899," *American Journal of International Law* 1, no. 2 Supplement (1907).

[29] The declarations regarding poison gas and dum-dum bullets remained in effect until renounced, thus were not on the 1907 agenda.

[30] Lord Reay, Aug. 7, 1907, Scott, ed., *1907 Proceedings* Vol. III, 148. Fortunately, following this pious speech, no one noticed that Great Britain was the only great power non-signatory of the 1899 Aerial Bombardment Declaration.

[31] *Id.* The British were not alone in advocating this stance. Austro-Hungarian delegate Szilássy noted that aerial bombardment in 1907 was "not indispensable" making regulation more practical. Szilássy, Aug. 7, 1907, *Id.*, 146. The regulation of aerial bombardment included an interesting question – did law follow military technology, or could it lead? While the British, Austro-Hungarian, and other delegations believed that law could lead, by stifling a new technology, other delegates believed that law could only follow military developments, and channel conduct into acceptable bounds. Italian delegate De Robilant held that scientific progress could not be halted, "to-morrow we will have armored automobiles armed with rapid fire guns ... and it will become more and more difficult, ... to prevent balloons from being armed in their turn and using their arms." De Robilant, Aug. 7, 1907, Scott, ed., *1907 Proceedings* Vol. III, 150.

pose particular strategic risks to Great Britain, by enabling continental powers to bypass British command of the seas and strike directly against England.[32] Nonetheless, in contrast to their stance at St. Petersburg in 1868, the British government opposed technological innovation.

The emerging norms against aerial bombardment were as much a part of the development of rules of war as they were a part of arms control. The resulting treaty regulated wartime conduct – the "discharge of projectiles and explosives from balloons ..."[33] This overlap led some delegations to prefer regulation of aerial bombardment over an outright ban. By utilizing existing legal norms which prohibited the bombardment of undefended cities, aerial bombardment of military targets would remain legal. The French delegation, in particular, preferred this method,[34] and their diplomats brokered a modification of the rules of land warfare in this regard by adding the words "by any means whatever" after the words "[i] t is forbidden to attack or bombard undefended cities" in Article 25 of the Convention Regarding the Laws and Customs of Land Warfare.[35] This separate regulation created another source of legal obligation, binding non-signatories to the Aerial Bombardment Declaration.[36] However, the Declaration created a broader rule, applying to all aerial bombardment, whether of military targets or undefended cities.

[32] It would be another one to two years before the British public truly awakened to the risks of aerial warfare, and this belated recognition was partly occasioned by the early cross-channel flights by Blériot, partly by belief that bomb-carrying German airships were already prowling over English skies. Alfred Gollin, *The Impact of Air Power on the British People and Their Government, 1909–1914* (London: Macmillan, 1989), 49, 70–71. Nonetheless, the War Office recognized the threat and gave its wholehearted support to international regulation. War Office to Foreign Office, July 8, 1907, *in* FO 412/87.

[33] "Declaration Prohibiting the Discharge of Projectiles and Explosives from Balloons, Oct. 18, 1907," *American Journal of International Law* 2, no. 1/2 Supplement (1908) [*hereinafter* 1907 Hague Aerial Bombardment Declaration].

[34] Renault, Aug. 7, 1907, Scott, ed., *1907 Proceedings* Vol. III, 147.

[35] *See* Amourel, Aug. 14, 1907, *Id.*, 14; "Hague Land Warfare Convention 1907," Art. 25.

[36] 1907 Hague Aerial Bombardment Declaration. The Italian delegate Tornielli expressed the opinion that the use of two separate legal instruments indicated that the general prohibition contained in the rules of war did not cover aerial bombardment and sought express inclusion of a prohibition. Tornielli, Aug. 7, 1907, Scott, ed., *1907 Proceedings* Vol. III, 153. This different interpretation took on practical dimensions following Italian aerial bombardment of Libyan villages in the 1911–1912 Italo-Turkish War. *See* "The Use of Balloons in the War between Italy and Turkey," *American Journal of International Law* 6, no. 2 (1912).

European concerns centered upon the burgeoning German aeronautical technology and the necessity to counter it.[37] Delegates expressed misgivings about their indefensible "aerial frontiers."[38] As a practical matter, the Aerial Bombardment Declaration did not prohibit the construction of military aircraft, nor did it ban other military uses besides bombardment, thus states still needed to prepare aerial defenses.[39] French opposition to the declaration, and support for the rules of war as an alternative, should be viewed with this in mind.

Germany ultimately voted in favor of a further temporary ban, but it could emerge at the end of the active period of the declaration with an extant aerial weapon. Germany also conditioned its vote upon unanimity.[40] This declaration never achieved unanimity, and was notable for the paltry number of states ratifying it. By 1914, only 15 states had ratified it – the United States and Great Britain being the only great powers among them.[41] The Declaration only applied reciprocally, and the entry of a non-signatory into a war terminated any obligations.[42] Given these weaknesses, international law could make only a modest contribution to security.

The British delegation acknowledged these weaknesses when framing its position, recognizing that French and German advances in aviation meant that Great Britain would have to keep pace. International law could not substitute for defense planning. However, the development of international public opinion could contribute to security. Even if France, Russia, and Germany refused to sign the resultant declaration, the new rule would still be in the British interest as a "Declaration signed by perhaps over thirty Powers carries some weight and, by the action of public

---

[37] An Italian delegate actually pointed out that the advances made by its ally Germany were forcing the pace of development. See de Robilant, Aug. 7, 1907, Scott, ed., *1907 Proceedings* Vol. III, 150. Germany possessed an advantage in dirigible aircraft construction, while France led the world in airplanes.

[38] Szilásy, Aug. 7, 1907, *Id.*, 146.

[39] This is not unusual in arms control, and is sometimes referred to as a "no first use" rule. The 1925 Geneva Protocol forbade the use of chemical weapons, while still allowing possession. This served a deterrent function, by allowing states to retaliate if a violation did occur.

[40] Scott, ed., *1907 Proceedings* Vol. III, 149.

[41] Scott, ed., *Hague Conventions*, 223–24. In contrast, Great Britain was the only great power not to have ratified the 1899 declaration. However, all the great powers did sign the Convention Regarding the Laws and Customs of Land Warfare, with only Italy having failed to ratify it by 1914, increasing the likelihood that aerial bombardment would fall under legal prescription in a future conflict. Scott, ed., *Hague Conventions*, 222–23, 36, et. seq.

[42] 1907 Hague Aerial Bombardment Declaration.

opinion, is a strong factor in inducing other Powers to join it."[43] Over time, an international consensus might emerge that could prevent a new weapon from achieving legitimacy.[44]

Not only were states uncertain whether legal guarantees would apply in the case of future conflict, but they also lacked a basic understanding of how aerial warfare might be conducted. Delegates tended to analogize aerial warfare to maritime warfare, and as a result applied ill-fitting legal concepts. De Robilant noted the inapplicability of the 1856 Declaration of Paris to aerial warfare, fearing that "aerial privateers" would descend upon cities.[45] The Italian delegation also expressed concern that because airships other than dirigibles could not be steered while in flight, aerial bombardment by such vessels could not be targeted. De Robilant recommended that only dirigibles be authorized to conduct bombardments, and further specified regulations bringing aeronauts under military supervision, to prevent the development of aerial privateering.[46]

The initial 1899 declaration had been intentionally framed as a five-year regulation in order to allow future law to evolve along with changes in technology. Since that time, only the zeppelin had appeared capable of military application in the immediate future, heavier-than-air craft lacking reliability, range, or payload for military use. However, delegates lacked the comfort with the technological questions necessary to advance new legal concepts, and retained the original wording. The parties did make one significant alteration to the 1907 declaration, lengthening its

---

[43] Memo by Sir E. Elles respecting the Three Declarations of 1899, Enclosure No. 2 in Fry to Grey, Aug. 13, 1907, *in* Further Correspondence respecting the Second Peace Conference at the Hague, FO 412/88, (Aug. 1907). As evidence, the author of this passage noted that Great Britain had been induced to accede to the Expanding Bullets Declaration by weight of public opinion.

[44] Similarly, the customary prohibition on chemical and biological weapons slowly developed during the twentieth century, and despite similar predictions early in the century that these scourges would become hallmarks of modern conflict, their use has been decidedly limited. *See* Scott A. Keefer, "International Control of Biological Weapons," *Nova Journal of International and Comparative Law* 6 (1999).

[45] De Robilant, Aug. 7, 1907, Scott, ed., *1907 Proceedings* Vol. III, 151. However, it should be noted that prior to the First World War, most pilots were self-trained enthusiasts, rather than militarily instructed soldiers, thus might not necessarily fall under military discipline. In the conflicts involving airpower prior to 1914, the pilots were often mercenaries hired following the outbreak of war. *See* Wilmot E. Ellis, "Aerial-Land and Aerial-Maritime Warfare," *American Journal of International Law* 8, no. 2 (1914): 261.

[46] De Robilant, Aug. 7, 1907, Scott, ed., *1907 Proceedings* Vol. III, 151.

effective duration. The new declaration would remain in force until "the close of the Third Peace Conference ..."[47] If statesmen were unprepared to develop new regulations for aerial warfare, they did choose to keep the issue on the international agenda, effectively linking another arms control issue to the progressive codification of international law at The Hague.

Submarine Mines

Submarine mines posed an emerging threat in 1907. Prior to the Russo-Japanese War, mines had only been used for harbor defense, the 1904–1905 conflict pioneering the widespread offensive scattering of mines in enemy waters.[48] The British Admiralty had perceived the danger of submarine mines, and even before the Hague Peace Conference, it had suggested that a special international assembly be devoted to banning the weapon.[49] The Admiralty recognized that a complete ban would be difficult to attain, and as an alternative sought three basic regulations, including provision of devices on automatic mines that would render them harmless in a fixed period, provision of devices that would make anchored mines harmless if they broke loose from their anchor, and a territorial restriction of submarine mines to the territorial waters surrounding an enemy's military harbors. The Admiralty realized that the international community would be less likely to accept the third regulation, but generally hoped to "induce all Europe to fall in with our own humanitarian views ..."[50] This standpoint was based not upon utopian goals but upon an analysis of Great Britain's strategic position. At The Hague, the British delegation adopted this stance, arguing for the island nation's strategic imperatives in the language of humanitarianism.

Captain Ottley, the naval expert attached to the British delegation, summed up his country's official attitude towards arms control, noting that "our attitude towards such questions should be based entirely upon

---

[47] 1907 Hague Aerial Bombardment Declaration.
[48] Ottley to Fry, Sep. 1, 1907, Enclosure 1 in Fry to Grey, Sep. 2, 1907, *in* Further Correspondence respecting the Second Peace Conference at the Hague, FO 412/89, (Sep. 1907).
[49] Submarine Automatic Mines, Mar. 13, 1905, at 1, CAB 4/1/52 B.
[50] *Id.*

their effect upon the influence of sea power."[51] That being said, British proposals were framed with a humanitarian viewpoint, "the indubitable fact that any such restrictions would be specially to the advantage of this country has been purposely kept out of sight."[52] The movement of British fleets had been restricted by the introduction of all types of submarine weapons, and as a belligerent or as a neutral, Great Britain would benefit from a ban on naval mines. This goal would be opposed by smaller naval powers who benefited from the cheap defensive weapon. Therefore, the British delegation would need to stress the humanitarian value in order to overcome opposition.

The effectiveness of a treaty in wartime depended upon the coercion of neutrals as well as the threat of retaliation by belligerents. In peacetime, a treaty would need to be coupled with the public will to enforce it, without creating an overreliance upon legal solutions. The Admiralty remained troubled by the prospects for international law, commenting on Graham Greene's memo that "the existence of an international rule on the subject may give a sense of false security which may be fatal in its effects."[53] Ottley recognized that British security could not be fully assured through a treaty, thus continued vigilance was required.[54] Yet while expressing the misgivings that law might actually detract from security, the Admiralty was unwilling to forgo the potential benefits of a ban, and continued its support.

When the conference opened, Ottley started the first session on naval matters with a strong maiden speech describing the effects on neutral commerce if a heavily travelled strait, such as Gibraltar, Dover, or the Danish Sund, were to be infested with mines. Fully developing the humanitarian chord, he described how the destruction of a large luxury

---

[51] Ottley to Fry, June 21, 1907, Enclosure 1 in Fry to Grey, June 24, 1907, *in* FO 412/86. Ottley also presented a novel proposal to ban the use of torpedoes at night, ostensibly to prevent the occurrence of another Dogger Bank-type incident. However, he noted that Great Britain possessed more submarines than Germany, and that unlike torpedo boats, these vessels could effectively fire torpedoes during daylight. Ottley, Restrictions on the Use of Locomotive Torpedoes at Night, Enclosure No. 2, *in* Fry to Grey.

[52] Ottley to Fry, June 21, 1907, Enclosure 1 in Fry to Grey, June 24, 1907, *in* FO 412/86.

[53] Admiralty to Foreign Office, June 28, 1907, *in* FO 412/86.

[54] "There will always be a lingering doubt in the mind of an Admiral commanding a fleet as to how far he is justified in accepting a mere paper assurance from an enemy, as being really a binding and effective guarantee against a treacherous torpedo attack at night." Ottley to Fry, June 21, 1907, Enclosure 1 in Fry to Grey, June 24, 1907, in FO 412/86.

liner, with a thousand passengers, would constitute an unparalleled catastrophe.[55] The Dogger Bank Incident would pale in comparison. British senior delegate Satow later developed the theme obliquely, averring that even the most balanced neutral would find it difficult not to retaliate.[56] No military necessity could justify such a humanitarian disaster, and the British government presented its proposal to prevent such a risk from materializing.

At the conference, the British raised the most fully developed mine proposal, which formed the basis of discussions. The British plan called for a prohibition on unanchored mines, while Italian and Japanese proposals merely desired that such devices become harmless a certain time after being laid, and a Spanish proposal called for the creation of an international body which could authorize the laying of mines.[57] The Spanish proposal envisioned far greater international regulation than anyone else desired, and quickly disappeared. However, the Italian and Japanese proposals gained traction as alternatives to an outright ban, finding favor among the second-ranked naval powers. Germany also brought a proposal to ban unanchored mines for a period of five years, drawing dissent from its Italian ally.[58] Ultimately, given various experts' opinions on the feasibility of safety devices being attached to mines, the majority of smaller naval states voted to retain legality, while regulating usage.[59]

The other feature of the British proposal to draw strong opposition related to the areas where mines could be strewn. Article 4 of the British

[55] Ottley, June 27, 1907, Scott, ed., *1907 Proceedings* Vol. III, 524.

[56] Satow, Sep. 17, 1907, *Id.*, 381.

[57] *1907 Proceedings*, Vol. III, 526.

[58] *Id.*, 391–92. The British delegation doubted the sincerity of the German proposal, Commander Segrave, a naval expert, claiming that the offer was only made after it was clear that a majority would oppose it. Memo by Commander Segrave, Enclosure No. 1 in Fry to Grey, Sep. 30, 1907, *in* Further Correspondence respecting the Second Peace Conference at the Hague, FO 412/90, (Oct.–Dec. 1907). The United States also unsuccessfully attempted to reintroduce a total ban of unanchored mines. Scott, ed., *1907 Proceedings*, Vol. III, 405.

[59] Scott, ed., *1907 Proceedings*, Vol. III, 405. Article 1 of the final convention prohibited the laying of unanchored mines that did not become harmless after one hour, anchored mines that did not become harmless if they broke free from their moorings, and torpedoes that did not become harmless when missing their target. "Convention Relative to the Laying of Submarine Mines, Oct. 18, 1907," *American Journal of International Law* 2, no. 1/2 Supplement (1908) [*hereinafter*1907 Hague Submarine Mine Convention]. The weapons remained legal as long as they met the safety requirements.

draft proposal limited mining to territorial waters[60] of the belligerents, or up to ten miles from shore batteries or military ports.[61] Rear Admiral Siegel, the German naval expert, noted that in a future war, an enemy might undertake a distant blockade. In order to effectively counter a distant blockade, it might be necessary to sow mines beyond the limits of the territorial sea.[62] In an argument foreshadowing the declaration of a war zone in 1915, the German delegation advanced the concept of the "theater of war" allowing the use of mines anywhere "an operation of war is taking place or has just taken place, or upon which such an operation may take place in consequence of the presence or the approach of the naval forces of the two belligerents."[63] Satow disagreed with a broadening of the area, protesting that vagueness would allow mines to be used anywhere.[64] In the absence of agreement on the point, the final treaty omitted the provision.

In justifying their negotiating stance, the German delegation expressed well-reasoned misgivings that a concise code of the laws of war would not be honored by a state in extreme circumstances. As this would only weaken the entire system of international law, German delegate Marschall argued it would be preferable for law to be vague on these points. Moral obligations would suffice to limit egregious conduct, "[t]he officers of the German navy – I loudly proclaim it – will always fulfill in the strictest fashion the duties which emanate from the unwritten law of humanity and civilization."[65]

Other philosophical questions relating to the juxtaposition of law and war came into focus in the submarine mine discussions. Statesmen questioned whether greater ferocity of war tended to deter states from fighting or whether war should be humanized.[66] As with aerial bombardment, a debate emerged over whether law merely followed technology, or whether

[60] Legal authorities generally defined territorial waters as three miles from the low water mark of the coastline.
[61] Scott, ed., *1907 Proceedings*, Vol. III, 662.
[62] Siegel, Sep. 17, 1907, *Id.*, 380.
[63] *Id.*, 417.
[64] Satow, Sep. 17, 1907, *Id.*, 382.
[65] Marschall, Sep. 17, 1907, *Id.*, 385. On subsequent German conduct in the First World War, *see* Hull, *A Scrap of Paper*, 155.
[66] Satow, Sep. 17, 1907, Scott, ed., *1907 Proceedings*, Vol. III, 381.

technology would follow the law.[67] According to one view, once a weapon had been used, law could no longer successfully prevent its development, while the opposite opinion held that the evolution of technology could be framed by legal regulation.

The resulting convention reduced the humanitarian claims of all the parties to open hypocrisy. Despite the oft-repeated concerns about untethered mines floating the seas to wreak untold havoc upon neutral vessels, the obligations contained in the convention were predicated upon reciprocity.[68] As with the St. Petersburg Declaration of 1868 and Hague Declarations of 1899, this meant that the participation of a non-ratifying belligerent in a conflict would have freed all combatant nations to strew mines, regardless of the consequences to neutrals. If the parties had truly been motivated by concerns about the effects of belligerent conduct upon third parties, the obligations would have been general.

The submarine mine negotiations overlapped with other topics of naval warfare. British delegates successfully prevented minefields from being considered a legally effective form of blockade, a definition that would have altered the rights of neutral merchant shipping in mine-infested waters.[69] On the other hand, the British failed to convince the other delegations that the presence of a minefield before an otherwise undefended city rendered the unfortunate locale liable to naval bombardment.[70] The resulting convention was a decided compromise, failing to meet British goals of banning unanchored mines and limiting the area of mining operations. The preamble to the convention admitted as much, "[c]onsidering that although in the present state of affairs it is impossible to prohibit the use of submarine mines, it is important to limit and regulate such use ....

---

[67] At stake was the question of whether mines could be fitted with devices rendering them harmless within a fixed period of time, or after becoming untethered. Expert opinion was mixed. A Dutch delegate suggested that if the law was set, surely "science will not be slow in finding means to meet it satisfactorily." Röell, Sep. 17, 1907, *Id.*, 417. On the more general question of an outright ban on unanchored mines, it was argued that once a weapon had been used, it could no longer be forbidden. Scott, ed., *1907 Proceedings III*, 404.

[68] 1907 Hague Submarine Mines Convention, Art. 7.

[69] Article 2 contained a provision banning the use of mines "with the sole object of interrupting commercial navigation." *Id.* The phrase "sole object" caused some concern. Like the ban on artillery shells designed for the "sole object" of spreading poisonous gas, it did not prohibit the use of weapons for more than one purpose. Scott, ed., *1907 Proceedings*, Vol. III, 414–15.

[70] 1907 Hague Submarine Mines Convention, Art. 1.

Until such time as it shall be found possible to regulate the matter in such a manner as to offer to the interests involved the proper guaranties ..."[71] the present regulation would have to suffice. The delegates intended the entire matter to be reexamined at the next Hague Peace Conference, giving the convention a duration of seven years, and specifically requiring a further discussion of the matter at that point.[72]

However, the Admiralty did succeed in achieving two of the three aims it had set out in the CID memorandum of 1905, gaining requirements that unanchored mines be fitted with devices rendering them harmless in a fixed period and that anchored mines must become harmless if they broke loose from their anchor, while failing to establish territorial restriction of submarine mines. The government had recognized all along the difficulties in securing agreement on a complete ban, setting realistic legal goals, based upon a thorough understanding of the island nation's strategic needs. Law was never intended as a substitute for defense, but when skillfully crafted could augment national security.

Conversion of Merchant Ships into Warships

The final major arms control issue discussed at The Hague in 1907 related to the conversion of merchant ships into warships. A recent study has indicated that British perception of the threat of converted merchant cruisers played a larger role in policy formation than previously acknowledged.[73] In addition to providing an impetus for the construction of the new battlecruiser, the threat of the converted merchant cruiser spurred the British decision to control these weapons at The Hague.

The issue as formulated at The Hague centered on when and where a merchant ship could be converted into a warship, with delegates generally conceding that a state could legally authorize a conversion of its

[71] *Id.*
[72] *Id.*, Arts. 11 & 12. The specificity of these provisions would prevent the question from disappearing from the Hague agenda, a threat faced by overall arms limitation. On the subsequent British stance towards mines, *see* Hull, *A Scrap of Paper*, 156–157 and Nicholas A. Lambert, *Planning Armageddon: British Economic Warfare and the First World War* (Cambridge, MA: Harvard University Press, 2012) 180–181; Lambert, *Fisher's Naval Revolution*, 271. By 1913, Britain considered using the negative votes by states at The Hague to justify harsh mine warfare against commerce. *Id.*
[73] Seligmann, *The Royal Navy and the German Threat*; Seligmann, "New Weapons," 316–17. *See also* Marder, *The Anatomy of British Sea Power*, 102–04.

own vessels.[74] While the discussion was framed around the legality of war-time conduct, or the laws of war, it affected national armaments and thus formed a measure of arms control. Captain Behr, a Russian naval expert, crystallized the issue, and expressed the matter as a limit to "the right which a belligerent has to increase his naval forces."[75]

Great Britain possessed an unparalleled network of naval bases, provid-ing it with a significant strategic advantage when facing other naval powers. The British had little need for neutral overseas bases, and could afford to deny the use of these ports to all powers. The British went to the conference seeking to reduce the potential threat from fast converted merchant cruis-ers by limiting the circumstances under which a vessel could become a war-ship. For instance, the Russian volunteer fleet based at Odessa would have to transit the Turkish straits as peaceful merchantmen, and could only func-tion beyond the Black Sea if converted on the high seas.[76] By only legally recognizing the conversions that took place in national ports and territorial waters, belligerents would be deprived of the opportunity to enlist cruisers in neutral waters. States such as Germany or Russia, hemmed inside narrow seas and lacking major overseas bases, would have little opportunity to com-mission merchant cruisers, particularly after the British initiated a blockade. Absent such a restriction, these states could fully avail themselves of all the ports of the world in their *guerre de course* against British commerce.

The German delegation analogized converted merchant cruisers to militias on land, claiming the right to commission them anywhere.[77] The Russian, Italian, and French delegations quickly agreed with the German stance.[78] Similar to their stance when advocating restrictions on naval mines, the British framed their arguments from the standpoint of neutrals and humanity, claiming that neutral shippers would be unable to deter-mine legitimate warships.[79] Italy proposed a compromise solution, allow-ing conversions on the high seas, but only for merchant vessels outside national waters on the outbreak of war.[80] This would have allowed a one-

---

[74] Scott, ed., *1907 Proceedings*, Vol. III, 747.
[75] Behr, Aug. 3, 1907, *Id.*, 920–21.
[76] *See* Satow memoranda of Aug. 22, 1907, Ernest Satow MSS, PRO 30/33/10/16.
[77] Siegel, July 12, 1907, Scott, ed., *1907 Proceedings*, Vol. III, 811.
[78] *Id.*, 811–14.
[79] Lord Reay, July 12, 1907, *Id.*, 813. Belligerent warships possessed certain rights to stop and inspect neutral cargoes on the high seas, creating a risk if a neutral merchant ship failed to recognize and halt for a converted merchant cruiser.
[80] Fusinato, Aug. 30, 1907, *Id.*, 991.

time opportunity for merchant ships to convert into warships, limiting the long-term risk from converted merchant cruisers. Unwisely, the British, as well as the Japanese, rejected the compromise, and scuttled the possibility of any limitation upon conversion.[81]

A subsidiary issue related to the reconversion of merchant cruisers back into non-combatant merchant ships. In the absence of regulation, a ship could transform itself into a warship on the high seas in order to attack commerce, then reconfigure itself as a merchant ship so as to gain access to neutral ports at the end of a successful raid. Austro-Hungarian legal expert Lammasch proposed a ban on this type of vessel, which he colorfully labeled a "naval hermaphrodite."[82] The British delegation seized upon this possibility to argue in favor of neutral rights, but ultimately lost this point when rejecting the Italian compromise.[83]

The final treaty attempted to protect neutral rights by requiring that conversion of merchant ships take place in conformity with the Declaration of Paris of 1856, which included placing the crew under military discipline, and placing the vessel under the direct supervision of the commissioning state.[84] The belligerent commissioning the converted merchant cruiser had a duty to inform neutrals of the conversion "as soon as possible" – a vague standard in an age prior to the general adoption of wireless telegraphy.[85] Like the Submarine Mine Convention, the Convention Relative to the Conversion of Merchant Ships into Warships mentioned the failure of the parties to reach a general agreement on the core issues in its preamble, but unlike the other agreement did not specify that the issue would be reviewed at a future gathering.[86]

Conversion of merchant ships also touched upon other legal issues at the Hague Conference, including the definition of warships, and days of grace. The latter referred to a period often allowed to merchant vessels to leave port at the onset of a conflict. The British delegation noted that the issuance of days of grace had been a matter of convenience, not of customary obligation, and that it would not be extended to vessels the British government deemed capable of conversion into merchant cruisers.

[81] *Id.*, 992.
[82] Lammasch, July 12, 1907, *Id.*, 810.
[83] Lord Reay, Aug. 3, 1907, *Id.*, 921.
[84] "Convention Relative to the Conversion of Merchant Ships into War Ships, Oct. 18, 1907," *American Journal of International Law* 2, no. 1/2 Supplement (1908): Arts. 1 & 4.
[85] *Id.*: Art. 6.
[86] *Id.*

The British delegation did not achieve as many of its goals in this topic as it had in other areas. The unwillingness to compromise on a key issue prevented any legal standard from being framed, leaving future belligerents in an uncertain position.[87] The British government, for its part, intended to enforce its view of international law in future conflicts. Additionally, the British and German positions on the conversion of merchant ships reflected their relative strengths on land and sea. Germany had previously sought stringent restrictions on improvised forces on land, for instance at the 1874 Brussels Conference, subjecting such combatants to the severest terms, at sea the Germans anticipated being the weaker force, and sought rules of conduct favorable to its position. Likewise, Britain, the predominant sea power, abandoned its defense of small state prerogatives where these conflicted with national interest.

CONCLUSION

From the point of view of the British delegation, the results of the Second Hague Peace Conference were mixed. The British delegation introduced significant innovations into the laws of war at sea, gaining acceptance of its concept of distant blockade in return for limitations on the right of capture of neutral vessels. The conference regulated submarine mines about as well as the Admiralty had hoped possible. The prohibition on aerial bombardment was renewed, although ominously far fewer states had signed the document at the close of the conference. Regulations on conversion of merchant ships into warships attempted to allay neutral concern while failing to address core British concerns about commerce raiders.

Britain successfully exploited the rules of war to advance arms control goals. The Admiralty recognized advantages in regulating naval mines and auxiliary cruisers, as a means of maintaining naval superiority. On the larger question of a halt in the arms race, no concrete advance emerged. However, even before the opening of the conference, none was anticipated. The British placed a realistic proposal to exchange

---

[87] There were two arguments currently advanced at the time of the conference regarding state freedom of action in areas where the law remained silent. The older view held that in the absence of clear regulation, a state remained free to take any action desired. See, generally, George B. Davis, "The Launching of Projectiles from Balloons," *American Journal of International Law* 2, no. 3 (1908). The newer view, as contained in the Martens' clause, held that the unwritten law of nations still forbade some conduct.

information before the international community, and gained recognition for the principle of arms limitation. The government had achieved the basic goals it had set for itself. By pragmatically viewing what could be accomplished, and by carefully assessing what value these legal accomplishments would have, the British government displayed a realistic perception of international law.

CHAPTER 8

International Law and Armaments, 1900–1914

INTRODUCTION

Lawyers' and statesmen's perceptions of international law and arms limitation had evolved during the preparations for the Second Hague Peace Conference. The conference witnessed a move away from a utopian role for law in regulating the international community, as discussed in international legal circles and in Parliament before the conference, toward pragmatic steps moderating the arms race. The government encouraged this shift by advocating limited international agreements, which it in turn put into practice in instructions issued to its delegates.[1] Not until the First World War would the public dialogue return to the imperative of an "international federation" or a "league of peace" in halting the arms race.

---

[1] "It has seemed to me, looking back over the history of this very attractive question, that the cause of disarmament has suffered at different times from certain difficulties which, till comparatively recently, seemed to make progress almost hopeless. There was at first a tendency on the part of those who urged schemes of disarmament to evolve their plans in such forms as to bring upon themselves the reproach of being unpractical men, and in consequence the cause of disarmament and of arbitration fell into evil repute .... Your Lordships will see that all these ideal plans have run aground upon the rocks of practical difficulties. The generation in which we live has, therefore, wisely, I think, rather furled its sails and attempted to aim less high, but I am inclined to think that it has obtained more." Lord Fitzmaurice, Under-Secretary of State for Foreign Affairs, *Hansard*, 4th ser., CLVII, 1531–1532, 1535, May 25, 1906.

© The Editor(s) (if applicable) and The Author(s) 2016
S.A. Keefer, *The Law of Nations and Britain's Quest for Naval Security*, DOI 10.1007/978-3-319-39645-3_8

The shift in emphasis from disarmament to arms control paralleled a growing British interest in arms limitation as a means of preserving the United Kingdom's naval position. The rise of numerous great power naval competitors after 1900, with Germany, Japan, and the United States joining the ranks of traditional rivals France and Russia, gave rise to creative attempts to preserve British predominance. Ententes and alliances provided international means of maintaining British security. Arms limitation provided another extension of a diplomatic strategy. Given the evolving geostrategic environment, the shift from disarmament to arms control reflected as much a shift in British interests as a growth in understanding of international law.

Ultimately, the shift was both – an advance in perceptions of law as well as a calculated wielding of law by the British government. The Foreign Office possessed a wealth of precedents for arms limitation by 1904, when American President Theodore Roosevelt called the Second Hague Conference. In the years immediately prior to the 1907 gathering, the Foreign Office reviewed a number of these agreements as part of active diplomacy, including the 1817 Rush-Bagot Agreement and the Argentine-Chilean treaties of 1902 and 1903. Bolstered by these precedents, the government's strengthened advocacy of arms control from 1907 onwards reflected a shift in national interests since the 1899 Hague Conference.

Official support for arms limitation spurred public perceptions of law. Prior to 1900, arms limitation discussion had been limited, and scholarly works often highlighted utopian concepts rather than practical solutions. Even proponents of arms control differed over what role law should play. Before the Second Hague Peace Conference, international lawyers believed that law might influence armaments policy in several ways. First, international law could foster the creation of an international police power capable of enforcing disarmament, an unrealistic solution.[2] Alternatively, lawyers believed that arbitration agreements, by peacefully resolving international controversies, would gradually reduce international tensions and

---

[2] Field, *Draft Outlines of an International Code*; see, generally, Wehberg, *Limitation of Armaments*; Scott A. Keefer, "Building the Palace of Peace: The Hague Conference of 1899 and Arms Control in the Progressive Era," *Journal of the History of International Law* 8 (2006).

lessen states' interest in arming themselves.[3] When addressing the issue of arms competition, academic lawyers reflexively advocated utopian world government, and rarely recommended other models, such as arms control agreements or the rules of war. The experience of the Second Hague Peace Conference shaped scholars' perceptions of international law and the potential role it could play in foreign relations.

Despite the impasse at The Hague, the Foreign Office continued to incorporate international law into strategic planning, recognizing law's potential in the management of the burgeoning naval arms race. After 1907, legal discussions on arms limitations increasingly distinguished between arms control and disarmament. In addressing security concerns, British diplomats crafted legal solutions, codifying the rules of naval war and regulating emerging aerial navigation. These developments were all influenced by arms limitations. Proponents optimistically linked rules of naval warfare to arms reductions, reasoning that security of maritime commerce would reduce German need for a navy. Zeppelin scares and the perceived need to shape the rules of aerial warfare before they entered the realm of practical experience heavily influenced the regulation of aerial navigation.

Parliamentary debates led to the crystallization of concepts, refining subsequent debate on arms control, moving the subject away from grand utopian schemes for "leagues of peace," "international police forces," and "general disarmament," concepts which very few responsible statesmen considered practical. Emphasis in official discourse gradually shifted to limited goals of "exchanges of information," "limitation of expenditure," and eventually toward "arms control." While the public debate often lagged behind the development of international law and proponents continued to herald the "general disarmament" of Europe, the British government framed the arms control question in a limited manner which it pursued in direct negotiations with Germany. Before the Second Hague Peace Conference, Unionist statesmen wishing to discredit the limitation of expenditure on armaments could refer to the folly of "general disarmament," but afterwards they could no longer easily refute arms control by

---

[3] Holls, *The Peace Conference at the Hague and Its Bearing on International Law and Policy*, 92. "Thither point too, though indeed from afar, those propositions for DISARMAMENT which now and then crop up, but which, quite naturally, fade away as quickly as they come, so long as the principle of arbitration does not prevail in Europe." Arnoldson, *Pax Mundi*, 84.

simply associating it with utopian dreams. The arguments of arms control opponents also developed, by turning to concepts later systematized by game theory: Skeptics no longer bemoaned *disarmament* and the impossibility of creating an "international police force," but responded to *arms control* theories.[4]

INTERNATIONAL LAW AND POPULAR PERCEPTION OF ARMS LIMITATION UP TO 1907

Statesmen possessed a broad range of forms in which international law could limit armaments, and associated numerous types of treaties with reductions in expenditures upon armaments. Alliances, ententes, and arbitration agreements reduced the need for weapons, while rules of war, the 1899 Hague arms declarations, and bilateral arms control treaties had provided direct limitations. The British government contemplated all these models as potential means of bringing arms expenses under control. Additionally, the government wrestled with the challenges of enforcing international law, shifting discussion away from broad international governmental institutions to robust state monitoring based on self-interest.

The British government possessed a wide range of legal concepts and models for pursuing arms control at the Hague Conference in 1907. International law could influence the level of armaments in different ways, for instance, by reducing the risk of conflict, which in itself might aid in reducing defense outlays. Former Foreign Secretary Lord Lansdowne noted that the European system of alliances reduced armaments by distributing the burden of defense among several states.[5] Membership in an alli-

---

[4] For instance, some noted that Germany responded to British battleship construction cuts by increasing its own program Moll, "Britain's 1909 Dreadnought 'Gap'," 137. Minutes of Eyre Crowe, *in* Lascelles to Grey, Feb. 12, 1908, *in* Gooch and Temperley, eds., *British Documents*, Vol. VI.

[5] Marquis of Lansdowne, *Hansard*, 4th ser., CLVII, 1543–1544, May 25, 1906. Many international lawyers viewed the system of alliances and ententes as a step in the progressive codification of international law by gradually increasing ties between nations. "There are already in existence certain symptoms which may be considered a partial beginning of disarmament. Such are the *military* alliances which Great States make with one another." Alfred H. Fried, *Friedenswarte*, 1902 at 145, as quoted in Wehberg, *Limitation of Armaments*, 9. Scholars in the early 1900s generally recognized the system of alliances as a form of international law, building on the older ideas of Lawrence, as they were "treaties of union between two or more States for the purpose of defending each other against an attack in war, or of jointly attacking third States, or for both purposes." Oppenheim, *International Law: A Treatise*, Vol. I, 595.

ance also served a deterrent function by increasing the costs of aggression against a state. Lansdowne also posited that the Anglo-French Entente was another means in which law could assist in limiting arms.[6] By eliminating the sources of conflict between nations, ententes allowed states to reduce competitive armament. Thus, by reducing the international tensions that contributed to armaments acquisitions, alliances and ententes could help reduce arms costs as effectively as an arms control treaty.

The rules of war had also limited armaments in the past. The 1899 Hague Conference resulted in a convention regulating actions in warfare, including the use of "needlessly cruel" or poisonous weapons.[7] While the vague terms of this convention did not provide much guidance for states, they did signal a clear intention that the use of weapons would be subjected to limits, influencing further regulations on armament in the twentieth century. Although earlier rules of war had not diminished the costs of armaments, current rules of war issues appeared more likely to do so, such as the regulation of auxiliary cruisers.

The earlier arms agreements in 1899 also developed partially out of the rules of war. By outlawing the *use* of shells designed to diffuse poisonous gas, dum-dum bullets, and exploding bullets, international law provided for a partial ban upon these weapons. Unlike later treaties which forbid the *possession* of weaponry, these early treaties allowed the states to manufacture the proscribed ammunition while banning their use against other parties. Nonetheless, states recognized the difficulties in providing two complete sets of ammunition for their armies.[8] Thus, a partial ban on use resulted in a de facto limitation on possession.

---

[6] Marquis of Lansdowne, *Hansard*, 4th ser., CLVII, 1543, May 25, 1906. French diplomat Paul-Henri-Benjamin d'Estournelles de Constant hoped an arms limitation would follow from the entente, which could be extended to include Germany. Knollys to Selborne, July 11, 1904, Selborne Papers, Adds 13, ff. 117–119.

[7] Art. 22 of the 1899 Convention with Respect to the Laws and Customs of War on Land, stated that "[t]he right of belligerents to adopt means of injuring the enemy is not unlimited," and Art. 23 held that "it is especially prohibited: a. To employ poison or poisoned arms.... e. To employ arms, projectiles, or material of a nature to cause superfluous injury."

[8] As discussed above, this question arose specifically in the 1868 negotiations leading to the Declaration of St. Petersburg. During the negotiations, Russia wanted to maintain the right to use exploding bullets against enemy artillery limbers and ammunition boxes, while banning its use against men, which the delegations deemed to be impossible to regulate. St. George to Secretary for War, Oct. 21, 1868, *in* FO 83/316.

Many parliamentarians and governmental leaders advocated the development of arbitration treaties as a means of limiting armaments. Leaders often believed that arbitration agreements, by providing a peaceful means of resolving disputes, could lead to the gradual decline of war, and hence to the diminution of armaments.[9] A substantial public debate grew out of this faith in arbitration, as many questioned whether disarmament should precede obligatory arbitration agreements, or whether it would naturally occur as a result.[10] Arbitration advocates from the Anglo-American legal tradition viewed the question not only as a matter of prioritizing their energies, but also as a question of security: If the most developed, and most pacific, nations disarmed in the face of "less civilized states," they would merely place the future of civilization at the mercy of the heavily armed barbarians.[11] This debate found its counterpart within British parliamentary discussions on the propriety and timing of arms limitations. The government had to assure peace and security before reducing armaments.[12] In fact, the premature discussion of arms limitation might only worsen tensions between the nations, while the development of arbitration might naturally improve relations.[13]

Finally, both the Foreign Office and Parliament discussed two of the most successful arms control agreements in existence in the early 1900s, the 1817 Rush-Bagot Agreement and the 1902 Argentine-Chilean naval arms agreement. As set out previously, the Foreign Office developed arms control strategies through its participation in these bilateral treaties, exploiting exchanges of information, attaché visits, and the nature

---

[9] Speech of the Bishop of Ripon, House of Lords, *Parl. Deb.* 4th ser., 1906, CLVII, 1523–1528, May 25, 1906; holding that arbitration was preferable as it allowed the peaceful settlement of controversies, while allowing a nation to use force when necessary. "I submit to you that as the principle of peaceful arbitration gains ground it becomes one of the highest duties of Government to adjust those armaments to the newer and happier condition of things." Sir Henry Campbell-Bannerman, as quoted in Speech of E. Robertson, Secretary to the Admiralty, *Hansard*, 4th ser., CLXII, 75, July 27, 1906. Arnoldson, *Pax Mundi*, 84. But see Hobson, "Disarmament," 747–50, claiming that arbitration had not yet evolved sufficiently to foster disarmament, and that even greater international organization was needed prior to disarmament.

[10] "Compulsory Arbitration," *The (London) Times*, July 24, 1907, at 4.

[11] Hobson, "Disarmament," 747.

[12] Lord Sanderson, *Hansard*, 4th ser., 1906, CLVII, 1529–1530, May 25, 1906.

[13] Hague Conference, Extracts from the Times, (Part 5), at 14–15, *in* Second Hague Peace Conference, Inter-Departmental Committee Papers, FO 881/9328*, (1906).

of naval arms construction, as well as assessing the ultimate value and limits of legalized arms limits. Parliament acknowledged these agreements as models of arms limitation, providing tools for any future treaty. However, in the 1906 debates on arms limitation, Parliament still focused upon a multilateral model for arms control, presuming that a large international organization would be required. The unlikelihood of such a scheme succeeding fueled much of the legal criticism of the enterprise. Such an unprecedented cession of sovereignty would incur a strong reaction in Great Britain, and undoubtedly in all the continental powers. International law and international organization in the 1900s rarely exhibited such broad centralizing trends. States had negotiated broad multilateral treaties and formed international organizations for numerous purposes, but had not ceded legislative and executive power as directly as disarmament required.

* * *

In the early 1900s, there were few precedents for powerful international organizations, which might provide a model for an "international police force," boding ill for traditional ideas of disarmament through world government. A sugar convention negotiated in 1902 provided the only recent precedent for a strong international organization, albeit for a decidedly non-security-related purpose. The Convention Relative to the Regime of Sugar created an international body empowered to strike down national sugar tariffs that exceeded allowable levels, thereby limiting the power of the contracting parties to levy export bounties upon sugar.[14] A Permanent Commission had authority to decide questions of national tariff policy by majority vote, and its decisions bound the parties.[15] This constituted a significant precedent in international law, as the Permanent Commission was

---

[14] Convention Relative to the Regime of Sugar, Mar. 5, 1902, Art. VII, *in* Despatch from the British Delegates, No. 4, (March 1902) at 6, Miscellaneous Papers presented to both Houses of Parliament. Great Britain and other states granted bounties to encourage the production and export of sugar, often offsetting the cost through the imposition of tariffs upon imports. George Martineau, "The Brussels Sugar Convention," *Economic Journal* 14, no. 53 (1904) 34–39.

[15] Convention Relative to the Regime of Sugar, Art. VII. Moreover, the parties could not renounce the treaty until five years following ratification, and then had to give 12 months' notice. *Id.* at Art. X. The treaty did provide for a process of appeal, but the same body that reached the initial decision would decide the appeal. *Id.* at Art. VII.

the only international organ possessing the power to alter national law.[16] Sugar policy had been contentious in many states, and the responses to trade wars in sugar led to the development of many concepts of modern trade law.[17] Following ratification, the convention remained highly controversial in Great Britain, a large importer of sugar.[18] This treaty, negotiated by the preceding Unionist government, created significant acrimony in Britain, leading Lansdowne to reason that the public would never accept similar levels of international regulation over arms construction.[19]

Similarly, the Foreign Office expressed significant misgivings about the 1906 Berlin Wireless Telegraphy Conference. This 1906 gathering, held to regulate the brand-new technology, utilized a German draft convention, leading to suspicions of German motives and general wariness of the traps of international regulation. British delegates had refused to sign the final protocol at an earlier conference in 1903, leading Germany to call the 1906 conference and prepare a draft convention as a basis for further negotiations.[20] Britain possessed unique strategic advantages in its submarine telegraphic network and a growing Marconi wireless system and feared these advantages would be sacrificed through international

[16] Paul S. Reinsch, "International Unions and Their Administration," *American Journal of International Law* 1, no. 3 (1907): 604.

[17] E. Castelot, "The Brussels Sugar Conference," Economic Journal 12, no. 46 (1902) 217–220. Concepts such as dumping and anti-dumping duties, subsidies and countervailing duties, entered common discourse with the international sugar disputes. *See* Martineau, "The Brussels Sugar Convention."

[18] The new Liberal government came to power with a goal of renouncing the Sugar Convention, although its opinion changed upon entering office. Early in the new administration, Sir Edward Grey expressed misgivings in the House of Commons, that an international body had the power to dictate policy to Great Britain. M. Geoffray, Memorandum, Apr. 6, 1907, at 2, CAB 37/87/41 (1907), at 2. However, the experience of the new government with this international body convinced it that the organization recognized political realities and would act with moderation. *Id.* This experience possibly contributed to a greater degree of comfort with international law, as many have often found that despite the wording of a convention, political realities often limit the conduct of international organizations. Had the Permanent Commission of the Sugar Convention acted strongly, it would have been with the realization that Great Britain would merely renounce the treaty.

[19] Marquis of Lansdowne, *Hansard*, 4th ser., CLVII, 1545, May 25, 1906. Lansdowne's advocacy of other forms of international law resulted in the major precedents made by his foreign ministry in the preceding Unionist government, including the Anglo-Japanese Alliance, the French Entente, and the Sugar Convention. As the Sugar Convention had come under attack by the new government, he defended the forms of international organization championed by his ministry.

[20] George S. Clarke, Memorandum: The Wireless Telegraphy Conference of 1906, CAB 38/13/14 (Mar. 26, 1907), at 1.

regulation.[21] Echoing British arguments at previous conferences, skeptics feared an international agreement might hinder a nation's ability to develop new technology, diminishing British advantages in wartime.[22] The government would not sacrifice a hegemonic position without commensurate benefits for British interests, refusing to enter into an engagement for the sake of furthering international law.[23]

Britain not only suspected the German hosts of the conference of preparing a legal trap, but also generally disliked the idea of international regulation of wireless telegraphy.[24] The Committee of Imperial Defense expressed concern that an "international bureau" would limit the vital traffic of messages during wartime.[25] The draft treaty called for an interna-

[21] The Wireless Telegraphy Conference of 1906, CAB 38/13/14, at 3. Great Britain needed a secure telegraphic system in time of war, and "[i]f there is the smallest doubt, we must be saved from international entanglements at any cost." George S. Clarke, Wireless Telegraphy, CAB 38/12/51, at 5.

[22] Wireless Telegraphy and the Berlin Conference, CAB 38/12/47, (July 28, 1906), at 2. A further memorandum by the CID suggested that the nations should postpone regulation until the technology had advanced further and its implications were better understood. The Wireless Telegraphy Conference of 1906, CAB 38/13/14, at 7. British diplomats utilized a similar rationale to stall armaments regulation at St. Petersburg in 1868, noting that a general limit on technological innovations would benefit the less developed countries at the expense of nations like Great Britain with highly advanced industry. Sir Arthur Buchanan to Foreign Office, July 25, 1868, *in* FO 83/316. At The Hague in 1899, limits on aerial bombardment only extended five years, to allow the development of new technology, which might ultimately make war more humane. "If such should prove to be the case they were unwilling to renounce this picturesque and efficient means of extermination." Scott, *The Hague Peace Conferences of 1899 and 1907*, Vol. 1, 650.

[23] On the strategic value of communications, *see* Lambert, "Transformation and Technology in the Fisher Era," 272–297. *See also* Paul M. Kennedy, "Imperial Cable Communications and Strategy, 1870–1914," *English Historical Review* 86, no. 341 (1971) 728–752, and Boyce, "Imperial Dreams and National Realities," 39–70, for competing views on British assessment of telegraphy and its impact upon national defenses.

[24] The Committee of Imperial Defence assumed that the Germans must have studied the impact of international regulations upon naval warfare, and accordingly drafted the convention in a manner to best suit German needs. In particular, the use of wireless telegraphy could compensate for the lack of ships possessed by a smaller navy, allowing them to counter a larger adversary. CAB 38/12/47, at 5; CAB 38/12/51, at 5.

[25] CAB 38/12/51, at 2. The Convention as adopted provided only information gathering duties to the international bureau. Art. 13, International Radiotelegraphic Convention, Nov. 3, 1906, *American Journal of International Law* 3, no. 4, 330–377 (Supp. Oct. 1909). Art. 38 did allow the international bureau the minor authority to coordinate the call-signals of different wireless stations, to prevent two stations from using the same name. The arbitration clause contained in the treaty, Art. 18, required the submission of all questions regarding the interpretation or application of the treaty to arbitration, regardless of the interests effected, creating a far greater restriction upon sovereignty.

tional bureau to regulate wireless traffic through majority voting, a "monstrous provision" that would allow Britain to be outvoted by small states or those with little stake in wireless telegraphy like Monaco or Persia.[26] While the Foreign Office preferred direct bilateral negotiations with the great powers on this topic, ultimately Britain participated in a broad multilateral conference in the belief that exclusion from negotiations would be more harmful to British interests.[27] Britain could only influence international policy effectively by engaging with the world.

Notably, neither party emerged as a sole champion of international law. The prior Unionist administration negotiated the Anglo-Japanese Alliance, the Anglo-French Entente, as well as the Berlin Convention on Wireless Telegraphy and the 1902 Sugar Convention, while Liberals led opposition to the Sugar Convention. Both parties recognized the advantages of international agreements in advancing British national interests, and neither uncritically championed international law. Underlying much of the public discussion on international law were lingering concerns regarding the force of law in a security context. Critics of international law noted the fate of treaties in wartime, and rightly observed that a state could not depend solely upon international law for security planning.[28] As treaty enforcement often relied upon reciprocity, and at the most extreme, through the threat of war, the ability of a state to coerce an enemy belligerent appeared meager. Critical speeches in Parliament regularly alluded to the lack of a police force to carry out judgments, rendering any international tribunal powerless to enforce its decisions.[29] The other means of wartime enforcement, through international public opinion and appeals to national honor, also seemed to possess limited value.[30]

---

[26] CAB 38/13/14, at 4.

[27] *Id*, at 6; Extract from Report of British Delegates to the Conference on Wireless Telegraphy at Berlin, CAB 37/84/76, (Oct. 23, 1906) at 2.

[28] John Walton, et. al., Right of Capture of Private Property at Sea, CAB 37/86/14, (8 Feb. 1907), at 40–41.

[29] *See, for example, id.*, at 2; C. Bellairs, *Hansard*, 4th ser., 1906, CLVI, 1397–1398, May 9, 1906; The Next Peace Conference: "The Limitation of Armaments," *The (London) Times*, July 20, 1906, at 4, col. A; Marquess of Lansdowne, former Foreign Secretary, *Hansard*, 4th ser., CLVII, 1544–1545, May 25, 1906; Arthur Lee, former Lord of the Admiralty, *Hansard*, 4th ser., CLXII, 77–78, July 27, 1906.

[30] On the role of public opinion in compliance with international law, *see* Root, "The Sanction of International Law."

The government recognized the limitations of law, but held a more sophisticated view of what it could accomplish. International law, by expressing commonly shared expectations of future behavior, could raise the political costs for a nation which later sought to breach an existing rule.[31] Moreover, public opinion became relevant when a powerful neutral demonstrated a willingness to intervene on behalf of the law, as occurred over the issue of neutral commercial rights in the War of 1812.[32] When preparing for the Second Hague Conference, the Committee of Imperial Defence expressly recognized that law influenced state behavior, while it could never guarantee compliance.[33]

The government further attempted to defuse criticism by disclaiming any intention of disarming at The Hague. As Prime Minister Henry Campbell-Bannerman stated, "[w]ho imagines that the Powers going to The Hague Conference to deal with disarmament are to disarm themselves entirely and present themselves without defence among their neighbours? It is not so. We desire to stop this rivalry, and to set an example in stopping it ..."[34] The government, by assuring Parliament that it sought only limited gains at the conference, responded to criticism by placing international law in the proper context of defense planning. The government then confirmed these broader views of law by formulating and pursuing a pragmatic agenda at The Hague.

SCHOLARS AND THE INTERNATIONAL LAW OF ARMS LIMITATION, 1900–1914

Between the First Hague Conference and the outbreak of the First World War, the pace of change within the international legal system accelerated. This in turn inspired a richer discussion of arms limitation law, leading to

---

[31] At the very least, as argued Lord Loreburn, the Lord Chancellor, when advocating new limits on the right of maritime capture, even if law did could not guarantee that a breach would not occur in war, "[w]e should in that case merely suffer what the existing law allows us to suffer. If no better off, we should at least be no worse off." Immunity of Private Property at Sea in Time of War, CAB 37/88/58, at 5.

[32] Coogan, *End of Neutrality*, 18.

[33] The Hague Conference: Notes on Subjects which might be raised by Great Britain or by other Powers, Oct. 26, 1906, CAB 38/10/76, at 9.

[34] Sir Henry Campbell-Bannerman, *Hansard*, 4th ser., CLXII, 118, July 27, 1906. *See also* Lord Fitzmaurice, Under-Secretary of State for Foreign Affairs, *Hansard*, 4th ser., CLVII, 1531–1532, 1535, May 25, 1906.

a fuller debate on the issues at stake. Increased communication between academic and governmental lawyers, typified by the mixed delegations of military, diplomatic, and academic figures at The Hague, fostered a cross-fertilization of ideas. The Foreign Office followed proceedings at interparliamentary conferences and scholarly gatherings, using their draft agreements in framing British policy at The Hague and elsewhere. In 1898, textbook discussions of arms limitation were spotty and incomplete. By 1914, an emerging awareness of precedents and concepts was taking shape.

Underlying this trend was a shift toward international regulation of a range of issues. The movement for progressive codification of international law, working through multilateral treaties applicable to the majority of the world community, set the core method. The focus upon multilateral instruments was striking.[35] Bilateral agreements had been far more prevalent before the mid-nineteenth century, but afterward states moved increasingly toward multilateral agreements. These new instruments were forward-looking, setting rules for future conduct rather than resolving past disputes, and often open, capable of being adhered to by any state.[36] The 1856 Declaration of Paris set an early example, followed most importantly by the Hague Peace Conferences, the first of which included 26 states, and the second 44. Notably, the regulation of warfare and armaments featured prominently in this development, including the 1864 Geneva Convention and the 1868 St. Petersburg Declaration on Exploding Bullets.

Furthermore, the era saw the emergence of international institutions and dispute resolution mechanisms. The 1899 Hague Peace Conference resulted in the formation of the Permanent Court of Arbitration, an entity still in existence and an ancestor of modern international institutions. Moreover, the growing network of arbitration treaties provided a formalized method of dispute resolution. Such a network suited Britain's national interests, and maintained its position as a global power when facing disputes with smaller countries.[37]

---

[35] Grewe, *The Epochs of International Law*, 513.

[36] Nussbaum, *A Concise History of the Law of Nations*, 192–93.

[37] While the arbitration treaties posed no insurmountable obstacle for a great power to avoid, they effectively bound smaller nations which could not afford to refuse arbitration with a great power. Grewe, *The Epochs of International Law*, 523.

At the same time, scholars increasingly acknowledged "commons problems"[38] and sought international solutions. International legal scholarship increasingly reflected upon problems of interdependence and sovereignty.[39] After the turn of the century, the question of armaments increasingly presented itself as a commons problem, to which lawyers' attention was drawn. In his inaugural lecture at the London School of Economics, Professor A. Pearce Higgins noted the prominence of the question of armaments, along with the rise of arbitration, as the two striking features of the era.[40] According to this view, no single state could safely disarm in the midst of armed neighbors, yet all had a common interest in limiting the arms competition.[41]

As lawyers turned their attention towards solving the problem of armaments, debate sharpened. While nineteenth-century discourse reflexively categorized all limits as disarmament, newer legal works increasingly recognized a distinction between arms control and disarmament.[42] As the legal advisor to the Quai d'Orsay pointed out, "[w]e may say, moreover, that the term 'limitation of armaments' is not synonymous with 'disarmament,' and in no way excludes the possibility of war."[43] Newer works also

[38] Commons problems, such as the overgrazing of common land by sheep, are problems caused by the cumulative actions of many individual actors, which are incapable of solution by any single actor alone.

[39] Thomas Baty, *International Law* (New York: Longmans, Green and Co., 1909), vii. "Since the Hague Conference of 1907 it has become increasingly evident that the nineteenth-century conceptions of International Law must be revised. *Independence is rivaled by Interdependence.*" [Emphasis added.] See also Koskenniemi, *The Gentle Civilizer of Nations*, 181 et. seq.

[40] Higgins, *The Binding Force of International Law*, 29–30. See also Sir Thomas Barclay, *Problems of International Practice and Diplomacy: With Special Reference to the Hague Conferences and Conventions and Other General International Agreements* (London: Sweet and Maxwell, 1907), 125.

[41] "Every individual in every civilized community has been obliged to give up some degree of liberty in order that he may have his compensation in a greater degree of security." Walter S. Logan, "The Mountains Were in Labor and Brought Forth a Mouse," *Lend a Hand* 17, no. 3 (1896): 188.

[42] *See* Barclay, *Problems of International Practice and Diplomacy*, 123 et. seq.; Wehberg, *Limitation of Armaments.* The trend was reflected in international conferences as well. The 1906 meeting of the Interparliamentary Union held discussions on "limitation of armaments." Interparliamentary Union: Official Report of the Fourteenth Conference held in the Royal Gallery of the House of Lords, (1906) at 127.

[43] Jarousse de Sillac, "Periodic Peace Conferences," *American Journal of International Law* 5, no. 4 (1911): 978.

acknowledged more of the arms limitation precedents set in the nineteenth century.[44] Academics advocated specific realistic solutions, while noting the obstacles to limitation. These academic discussions influenced policy-making as the Foreign Office and Admiralty utilized foreign law journals and books in formulating positions on international law.[45]

Many of the precedents and projects for arms limitation were recorded in the works of Hans Wehberg. Wehberg, who as a young pacifist wrote on maritime war and arms limitation before 1914, gained prominence as an international lawyer after the war, participating as a member of the German delegation at Versailles and then as a judge at the Permanent Court of Arbitration.[46] His 1914 *Limitation of Armaments* captured the evolving legal tradition, recognizing distinctions between older concepts of disarmament, and newer ideas of arms control. By the eve of the First World War, precedents such as the 1787 Anglo-French naval agreement, the 1817 Rush-Bagot Agreement, and the 1902–1903 Argentine-Chilean treaties were all becoming part of the lexicon of arms limitation. Additionally, newer agreements such as the 1905 Swedish–Norwegian treaty, and the growing literature on arms limitations projects, were circulated.

The wide range of precedents and possibilities reflected both old and new thinking on the topic. Some authors clung to older utopian models of disarmament, seeking an international police force to uphold arms limits, while arbitration advocates argued for the creation of a world court before turning to the armaments question.[47] The central question of enforcement was addressed through a number of different means. Scholars noted the provision within the Argentine-Chilean treaties for arbitration to resolve disputes.[48] The 1905 Swedish–Norwegian agreement, which called for the

[44] The Czar's program for the First Hague Peace Conference was an early compilation, although focused on academic projects. This program was circulated among the twenty-six attendees of the gathering and followed the assumptions of progressive codification through a systematic review of existing works on armaments. *See Documents Relating to the Program of the First Hague Peace Conference.* Among British works, Barclay, *Problems of International Practice and Diplomacy.* is representative.

[45] *See* Admiralty to Foreign Office, July 3, 1914, *in* Correspondence respecting the Third Peace Conference, FO 881/10528.

[46] Koskenniemi, *The Gentle Civilizer of Nations*, 215–16.

[47] Proposal of Duplessix *in* The Official Report of the Seventeenth Universal Congress of Peace, (1909) 410 *et. seq.*; which recognized disarmament as distinct from arms limitation. *See also* Hobson, "Disarmament," 746–47. Hobson went so far as to link world peace and arms limits to robust naval power. *See also* Proposal of Richet at the 1910 Universal Peace Congress, *in* Wehberg, *Limitation of Armaments*, 46–47.

[48] Wehberg, *Limitation of Armaments*, 24; Wehberg, *Die Internationale Beschränkung Der Rüstungen*, 334–35.

dismantling of fortresses and creation of a neutral zone, also contained notable precedents for international verification and enforcement. Article 5 of this agreement set up a system of verification through a three-party commission, while Article 8 required the submission of disputes relating to the agreement to an improvised arbitral tribunal.[49] This treaty utilized existing systems of arbitration and attaché inspection, allowing individual states to police the agreement rather than depend upon the creation of an international police force. Similarly, a 1913 project by Ludwig Quidde[50] moved the topic decisively away from utopian institutions, incorporating numerous avenues for states to self-enforce. This draft featured safeguard provisions, including a termination clause allowing parties to opt out of rules in case of a violation, and an overall focus on state enforcement of obligations.[51] While self-enforcement was allowed in general international law, it was noteworthy that the draft eschewed more utopian measures.

Many authors opined that budget limitation were more politically expedient than qualitative or quantitative restrictions on weapons.[52] The linkage between naval and land armaments, which had led France before the 1907 Hague Conference to prefer German naval investment as a means of limiting the German army, was acknowledged. One anonymous author sought to measure armaments through a "unit of war," allowing either 50 tons of warships or 10 soldiers for every 700 inhabitants of a country, with the state free to invest these units as it thought best.[53] These concepts presaged later French positions in interwar arms discussions, with their quest for fleet tonnage allotments and land–sea linkage.

Naval arms control concepts became more detailed, and increasingly recognized the ways in which warships could be effectively regulated. Tonnage and numerical limitations, as well as limits on gun caliber, featured promi-

---

[49] Convention Relative to the Establishment of a Neutral Zone and to the Dismantling of Fortifications, Arts. 5 & 8, Parry, ed., *Consolidated Treaty Series*, Vol. 199, at 285.

[50] Quidde was a Reichstag member and a leading figure in the pre-war German peace movement. Roger Chickering, *Imperial Germany and a World without War: The Peace Movement and German Society, 1892–1914* (Princeton, NJ: Princeton University Press, 1975), 85–88.

[51] Speech of Quidde, 1913 Universal Peace Congress, *in* Wehberg, *Limitation of Armaments*, 91–94.

[52] Barclay, *Problems of International Practice and Diplomacy*, 130, 82.

[53] Proposal of Anonymous Author, *Völkerfriede* (1909) at 53, *as quoted in* Wehberg, *Limitation of Armaments*, 74–75.

nently.[54] Additionally, authors further investigated the dynamics of the arms race, and noted means for arms limits to be circumvented. Limitation in one area could lead to increased expenditures in other areas – a concept later known as the "blowback effect." A numerical limit on battleships could lead to an increase in size of smaller vessels, perhaps provoking a race in the next ranked category of warships.[55] This accurately predicted the naval arms race in "treaty cruisers" following the 1922 capital ship limitation at the Washington Conference. Another German author suggested that only an unrealistic total cession of construction would resolve this problem.[56]

Quidde's draft agreement provided responses to many of these questions, and suggested a number of forms of regulation ultimately adopted at the Washington Conference in 1921–1922. At the 1913 Interparliamentary Conference held at The Hague, he called for size and numerical limitations on battleships, with a minimal age before replacement was allowed. Additionally, his draft anticipated the situation of the Turkish dreadnoughts, nearing completion in Britain on the eve of the First World War, by extending treaty regulation to private companies. Finally, his draft dealt with "donated weapons" such as the Canadian dreadnoughts, preventing circumvention of the agreement through third-party gifts and purchases.[57]

Legal scholars also took up the role of non-parties in designing treaty regimes. Legal works increasingly debated the optimal negotiating format for arms control, noting the failure of the multi-state Hague Peace Conferences to achieve results. The Argentine-Chilean agreements were advocated as a model for Anglo-German talks, but many recognized that third parties undermined a bilateral solution.[58] In the aftermath of

[54] Barclay, *Problems of International Practice and Diplomacy*, 130.

[55] Von Ahlefeld, "A Basis for an Anglo-German Agreement," *Deutsche Revue*, May 1912, at 142, *as quoted in* Wehberg, *Limitation of Armaments*, 63–64. As mentioned previously, Ahlefeld even suggested that arms limitation was more popular in Britain due to the development of the battlecruiser, as an intermediate type that would continue to be built after a limit on battleships was in place.

[56] L. Persius, *Berliner Tageblatt*, Mar. 27, 1913, as quoted in *Id.*, 64–65. The German delegate to the Hague in 1899, Baron von Stengel, stated such a limitation would be not only unrealistic, but suicidal. "Wenn jetzt die friedensfreunde verlangen, daß das Deutsche Reich auf diesen Ausbau und eine weitere Verstärkung seiner Seemacht verzichte, so muten sie ihm wahrlich ein geradezu selbstmörderisches Vorgehen zu." Stengel, *Der Ewige Friede*, 31–32; Stengel, *Weltstaat Und Friedensproblem*, 137.

[57] Quidde, Draft of an International Treaty for the Limitation of Armaments Submitted to the Twentieth Universal Peace Congress at the Hague in 1913, Arts. 5, 8, & 9, as quoted in Wehberg, *Limitation of Armaments*, 79 et. seq. Churchill intended on excluding donated Canadian dreadnoughts from the Anglo-German fleet ratio he proposed in 1912.

[58] Schücking, Die Organisation der Welt, (1909) at 78 *et. seq.*, as quoted in *Id.*, 56.

the Second Hague Peace Conference, with another Hague gathering not scheduled until 1915, the 1908 London Universal Peace Congress proposed a limited multilateral negotiation between the great powers.[59] Ultimately, this limited multilateral gathering was never held, although the Foreign Office had come to the same conclusion about negotiating formats. When important maritime warfare issues remained unresolved at The Hague, Grey invited the great powers to discuss the rules at a conference to be held in London.

THE LONDON CONFERENCE OF 1908–1909

The Foreign Office called the London Conference in order to settle maritime law issues left unresolved at the Hague Conference. The British delegation at The Hague viewed the large multilateral gathering as an impediment to progress, particularly where smaller states sought an equal role in rulemaking.[60] The Hague Conference had negotiated an agreement for an International Prize Court, which would hear appeals from national prize courts.[61] In order for Britain to accept this international authority, the law the court would apply needed to be clarified. The London Conference was intended to codify customary rules relating to blockade, contraband, auxiliary merchant cruisers, and the destruction of prizes, thereby providing guidelines for the International Prize Court.

The conference resulted in a grand compromise codifying a list of contraband items and authorizing distant blockade, two British goals, while ending the application of the doctrine of continuous voyage to conditional contraband, a German goal.[62] This latter conditional contraband agreement would allow shipment of goods to Germany through a neutral

---

[59] Proposal of G. H. Perris, *in* Official Report of the Seventeenth Universal Congress of Peace, at 116–117.

[60] Fry to Grey, Oct. 16, 1907, *in* FO 412/90. Legal theorists echoed the judgment, Walter Schücking dismissing the "fetish of unanimity." Schücking, *The International Union of the Hague Conferences*, 216.

[61] Prize courts determined the legitimacy of captures of merchant ships.

[62] The vaguely worded declaration allowed captures within the area of operations of a blockading force, without specifying how far out that area could be, leading to the interpretation. British Delegates to Grey, Mar. 1, 1909, 7, *in* ADM 116/1087 Correspondence and Documents respecting the International Naval Conference Held in London (1908–1909). The Germans interpreted the freedom of neutral ports from blockade as a prohibition of a distant blockade of the North Sea and English Channel. Hull, *A Scrap of Paper*, 144.

Netherlands in wartime. The Admiralty also hoped to regulate the conversion of auxiliary merchant cruisers, another failed goal at The Hague. At the very least, the Admiralty sought a list of vessels which might be possibly converted into warships in wartime.[63] Interdepartmental confusion over the compromise caused a sharp division between the Admiralty and Foreign Office, requiring the matter to be placed before the Cabinet, and nearly causing the collapse of the bargain.[64] The Admiralty raised its proposal for a list of vessels again during exchange of information discussions with Germany, indicating the continued importance the Admiralty attached to these auxiliary warships.

Historians have noted that the Declaration of London, had it been ratified, would have prevented Britain from interdicting trade to Germany through the Netherlands, which would prove to be a significant means of cutting off German trade during the First World War. Several explanations have been advanced to explain British advocacy of an apparently inopportune agreement in light of future conduct. Some have focused on neutral rights, believing that American opposition would have prevented a vigorous application of commerce warfare. Only unexpected American acquiescence allowed the British campaign in 1914.[65] Another theory holds that the Admiralty never intended to honor the agreement in wartime. This builds upon an exchange between the CID Assistant Secretary Maurice Hankey and First Lord McKenna. McKenna reassured Hankey that Britain would exploit the first pretext to tear up the treaty in wartime.[66] Recent scholarship by Christopher Martin questions this second interpretation, and provides a convincing variation on the first explanation.[67] Martin holds that small neutral maritime powers could exert sufficient pressure to

[63] Memorandum by the Director of Naval Intelligence, Sep. 29, 1908, at 20, *in* ADM 116/1079, Part 1. On the importance of conversion of merchant ships into auxiliary cruisers, *see* Seligmann, *The Royal Navy and the German Threat*, 97–102. Seligmann's account provided a full explication of the options and challenges a state had in enforcing obligations in wartime.

[64] *See* correspondence around Dec. 15, 1908 Grey Memo Dec. 14, 1908; Greene to Crowe, Dec. 23, 1908; Greene to Crowe, Dec. 30, 1908, *in* ADM 116/1079, Part 2. *See also,* Lambert, *Planning Armageddon*, 97–98.

[65] Coogan, *End of Neutrality*, 240 *et. seq.*

[66] *Id.*, 137–39; Bernard Semmel, *Liberalism and Naval Strategy: Ideology, Interest, and Sea Power During the Pax Britannica* (Boston: Allen & Unwin, 1986), 112–14; Offer, "Morality and Admiralty," 106–09.

[67] Martin, "The Declaration of London," 749–54.

prevent a broad British interpretation of belligerent rights.[68] This explanation reaffirms the expected role of neutrals in upholding the system of international law, even in wartime.

New scholarship continues to enliven the debate: Nicholas Lambert recently reiterated the second view, arguing that the Admiralty intended to disregard inconvenient treaties or seek pretexts for violating them.[69] Isabel Hull built upon the notion of neutral pressure, noting that Britain had to balance the benefits which would accrue to Britain as a neutral against the costs when Britain was a belligerent.[70] The larger context for the decision-making of the Foreign Office, if not the Admiralty, consisted of the need to consider Britain's interests both as a neutral and as a belligerent when planning for future circumstances.[71] In planning for war, the Foreign Office also had an institutional preoccupation with diplomatic relations with powerful neutrals lacking at the Admiralty, and had to contend with a lengthy history of maritime practices leading to neutral anger.

Beyond this issue, the London Conference provided broader insights into British expectations of international law, including Foreign Office views on the formation of law and the role of neutral states in enforcement. The Foreign Office sought to use a gathering of the great powers to legislate for the world. Significantly, Britain attempted to legitimize its own interpretations of maritime law within the international community to reduce the risk of third-power intervention in future British wars. Moreover, both the Admiralty and the Foreign Office relied on scholarly writing on maritime law, indicating the great extent to which these works reflected existing legal practice.[72]

---

[68] *Id.*, 742–44.

[69] He made the case that Admiralty opinion regarding continuous voyage shifted in 1908, leaving Admiralty delegates with an outdated brief when preparing for the conference, while the Foreign Office failed to grasp the true nature of the Navy's revolutionary new strategy against German finance. Lambert, *Planning Armageddon*, 94–98. Given the significance of the issue and the lengths the Admiralty had gone to convince politicians of the importance of capture when preparing for the Second Hague Peace Conference, it is surprising that such a significant failure in planning could occur, but Lambert provided convincing arguments.

[70] Hull, *A Scrap of Paper*, 144–145. Moreover, she held that the Admiralty and Foreign Office built a consensus around the value of blockade over capture, in contrast to Lambert's account.

[71] *See, for example*, Edmund Slade, Memorandum of Dec. 14, 1908, at 3, *in* ADM 116/1079, Part 2.

[72] *See* Memorandum by the Director of Naval Intelligence, Sep. 29, 1908, *in* ADM 116/1079 citing the 1882 Institute of International Law meeting in Turin.

Grey invited the great powers Austria-Hungary, France, Germany, Italy, Japan, Russia, and the United States to the gathering, also extending invitations to Spain and the Netherlands for diplomatic reasons.[73] Notably, the ten parties probably alone possessed the industrial capacity to build their own dreadnoughts. All but the Netherlands built dreadnoughts within a few years of the conference, with the Dutch plans for construction being only curtailed by the outbreak of the First World War.[74] Thus, the conference reflected a dividing line in naval power excluding weaker states, as all other smaller dreadnought-operating navies purchased their weapons abroad, and generally lacked the ability to maintain them.[75]

Grey's Foreign Office sought to impose great power-made law upon the world, legitimizing a trend in international law towards great power primacy. Generally, treaties only bound the parties ratifying the document. On the other hand, custom bound the entire international community: A state could only opt out if it persistently objected to the customary rule. By crafting a treaty with the most interested powers, the Foreign Office sought to provide a formidable statement of international customary law binding all states, one which the planned International Prize Court would be likely to uphold.

> Is it likely that a court having a majority of judges whose countries negotiated, and subscribed to, the Declaration of London would come to any other conclusion than that the rule upon which the States most directly concerned had, in spite of wide divergence in geographical position, in historical traditions, and in national interests, unanimously agreed, truly represented the justice and equity of the cases.[76]

British instructions held that the government "… would find it difficult to be satisfied with any merely conventional stipulations of limited application, that would leave it uncertain whether the International Court might

---

[73] Grey to Herbert, July 15, 1908; Grey to Howard, July 1, 1908, both in London Conference on International Maritime Law, ADM 116/1080, (1908–1909). The Netherlands had hosted the Hague Conference and Spain had recently been a larger naval power before 1898.

[74] Gardiner, ed., *Conway's 1906–1921*, 366.

[75] Grant, *Rulers, Guns, and Money*, 157, 76, 83.

[76] British Delegates at the Naval Conference to Grey, Mar. 1, 1909, No. 21, 40, *in* ADM 116/1087; *see also* Draft Letter from Grey to Lord Desart, Dec. 1, 1908, 5, *in* ADM 116/1079, Part 2.

not by its decisions introduce rules and principles of naval warfare which would unduly fetter the operations of His Majesty's ships."[77] Britain hoped to avoid "conventional stipulations" of "limited application," by providing an international customary standard applicable to the entire world community.[78] This would eliminate the risk that the International Prize Court would reach surprise decisions upsetting British expectations about rules of maritime conduct.

By setting universally accepted rules of naval warfare, Grey hoped to reduce the risk of third-party intervention in Britain's wars. Britain recognized it could no longer afford to anger powerful neutrals and sought compromises which Britain could enforce.[79] As a Foreign Office memoranda disclosed to the Cabinet, Britain's bargaining position had to reflect the changed strategic circumstances over the past century:

> It is, however, impossible to reproduce the conditions of the Napoleonic wars, or for this country to enforce as against neutrals the belligerent rights which Great Britain enforced a century ago. What enabled her to enforce such rights at that time was the fact that no neutral Power was in a position to compel the observance of neutral rights; even confederations of neutral Powers failed to do so. To-day such conditions no longer exist, there are foreign nations sufficiently powerful at sea to render it impossible for Great Britain in any given war to treat neutral ships and neutral goods in a way that is obviously contrary to the established practice of nations.[80]

A clear code of maritime law would set international expectations and prevent expansion of wars. "It would tend to draw a ring fence round the belligerents, and eliminate the risk of a simultaneous contest with a second Power."[81]

Ultimately, the House of Lords refused its assent to the agreement, fearing that Britain had sacrificed too much of its belligerent rights in return

---

[77] *Id.*, 6.

[78] Similarly, the majority of provisions in the 1982 United Nations Convention on the Law of the Sea restated customary international law, which the United States acknowledged as internationally binding after failing to ratify the treaty.

[79] *See* Memoranda on Meeting in Sir E. Grey's Office, Dec. 15, 1908, *in* ADM 116/1079, Part 2.

[80] The Declaration of London from the Point of View of the Belligerent Rights of Great Britain, Feb. 1, 1911, *in* CAB 37/105/6 (1911).

[81] The Declaration of London from the Point of View of its effects on Neutral Shipping and Commerce, Feb. 1, 1911, *in* CAB 37/105/6 (1911).

for uncertain guarantees. First, Conservatives feared that other states would refuse to honor their obligations in wartime, while Britain would be bound to uphold obligations due to neutral pressure. Additionally, opponents to the treaty believed that without the unfettered ability to block trade into Germany in wartime, Britain could not continue to act as a great sea power. The Declaration of London was the most contentious issue of international law facing the Foreign Office in the years immediately prior to the First World War. It raised direct questions of the utility of international law in regulating state behavior. The Foreign Office still perceived law as a means of shoring up its strategic position in the world, yet had to convince a reluctant public about the wisdom of restricting naval warfare, Britain's unique advantage as a great power.

AERIAL WARFARE AND PREPARATIONS FOR THE THIRD HAGUE PEACE CONFERENCE

British attitudes toward international law can also be gleaned from the Paris Aerial Navigation Conference of 1910. While initially disinterested in the topic of aerial navigation, the Foreign Office belatedly recognized that the proposed treaty would affect British security. Germany proposed a right of over-flight of foreign territory, which would allow German reconnaissance by privately-owned aircraft based in smaller states such as the Netherlands, Belgium, and Denmark.[82] At this point, private aviators operated most aircraft, allowing their access to neutral territory while possibly skirting neutral obligations to prevent belligerent operations from their territory.[83]

Additionally, the Foreign Office position shifted from opposing what was viewed as a bad treaty to seeking a multilateral convention in order to preempt Germany.[84] Without a general convention, Grey feared Germany would bully its smaller neighbors into bilateral agreements providing broad rights of over-flight.[85] Britain organized neutral states against the

[82] The International Conference on Aerial Navigation, July 11, 1910, CAB 38/16/11, (1910) at 2.

[83] In an Anglo-German war where the Low Countries remained neutral, these small states would still be bound to allow Germany to use their territory.

[84] July 29, 1910 Meeting of the Standing-Sub-Committee of the Committee of Imperial Defence, *in* Proceedings of the Committee of Imperial Defence with reference to the International Conference on Aerial Navigation 1910, CAB 38/19/60, (1910), at 14.

[85] Grey to Bertie, Nov. 12, 1910, and Bertie to Grey Nov. 16, 1910, both *in* Correspondence respecting the International Conference on Aerial Navigation, FO 412/95 (1910).

threat to their liberty, similar to British action at the Brussels Conference of 1874.[86] No treaty resulted from the conference, but the negotiations indicated a British desire to exploit law to augment national security. Following the failed 1910 Aerial Navigation Conference, Britain quickly formulated national laws regulating, and hence claiming, its own airspace. Aerial warfare increasingly became part of the international agenda as military applications became viable. Between 1911 and 1914, states gained experience with aerial warfare, [87] necessitating the improvement of military technology, while the topic became more prominent on the international agenda.

The 1899 Hague declaration banning aerial bombardment had a five-year limit, to allow regulation to evolve as experience with the technology increased. In contrast, the 1907 gathering renewed the agreement until the close of a Third Hague Peace Conference, tentatively scheduled for 1915. In the meantime, experience with aerial warfare brought concrete precedents. In the Italo-Turkish War of 1911–1912, Italy employed dirigible airships against villages in Tripolitania.[88] The Balkan Wars witnessed all belligerents operating airplanes flown by foreign mercenaries. The first instance of air–sea warfare arguably occurred in a Mexican insurrection in 1913. This inconclusive episode involved an aircraft operated by a "Constitutionalist" faction dropping bombs on the federal gunboat *Tampico*, while sailors on the gunboat fired rifles at the airplane, everyone missing their target.[89]

The first conflict to raise legal questions about the use of aircraft was the Italo-Turkish War. While Italy had ratified the 1907 Hague Declaration forbidding aerial bombardment, Turkey was not a party.[90] The agreement, applied on a basis of reciprocity, allowed aerial bombardment in conflicts involving non-parties. However, both states had adhered to the Hague rules of land warfare.[91] These rules contained a prohibition on the bombardment of undefended places "by whatever means" which at Italian instigation had included aerial bombardment.[92]

[86] Grey to Bertie, July 29, 1910, *in* FO 412/95.
[87] One summary held that all wars following 1907 involved aircraft. Ellis, "Aerial-Land and Aerial-Maritime Warfare," 261.
[88] "The Use of Balloons in the War between Italy and Turkey."
[89] Ellis, "Aerial-Land and Aerial-Maritime Warfare," 261–62.
[90] Scott, ed., *Hague Conventions*, 222–24.
[91] While neither Turkey nor Italy had ratified the convention, both had signed, and had obligations to refrain from acts which would undermine the purpose of the agreement. *Id.*, 130–31.
[92] "The Use of Balloons in the War between Italy and Turkey," 486–87.

In the years after the Second Hague Peace Conference, military planners increasingly anticipated aerial warfare would play a significant role
in any major European war. As noted presciently in the pages of the
American Journal of International Law, while a Third Hague Peace
Conference scheduled for 1915 might consolidate regulations, "wars do
not wait on conferences ..."[93] Britain, like its continental neighbors, continued researching aerial warfare, including aerial bombardment at sea and
over land.[94] The Royal Flying Corps experimented with torpedoes, and by
1914 included 100-pound bombs in its arsenal.[95] The Corps also began
testing incendiary bullets, capable of igniting the hydrogen in airships,
as a defensive weapon.[96] While these weapons were intended to provide
defense against airships, these experiments raised questions about violations not only of the 1907 ban on aerial bombardment, but also the 1868
prohibition on explosive bullets.

When questions were raised regarding treaty obligations, Grey decided
that although the drafters had not contemplated such use in 1868, and
probably would not have opposed it, the plain terms of the agreement
bound Britain.[97] The 1868 ban on exploding bullets posed a greater
obstacle as it had been ratified by most European countries. In contrast,
Great Britain and the United States were the only parties to ratify the
1907 aerial bombardment prohibition. While all the great powers had
ratified the 1907 convention on rules of war outlawing the bombardment
of undefended places, the aerial bombardment of defended locations such
as enemy troop concentrations and warships was still allowed. Moreover,
many of the Balkan powers had yet to ratify this convention, which would
have justified its non-application in any war involving these states. The
Hague regulations did not forbid the acquisition and testing of military

[93] Ellis, "Aerial-Land and Aerial-Maritime Warfare," 256.
[94] The Royal Flying Corps, First Annual Report by the Air Committee, Committee of
Imperial Defence, June 7, 1913, CAB 38/24/21, (1913).
[95] The Royal Flying Corps, Second Annual Report by the Air Committee, Committee of
Imperial Defence, May 9, 1914, CAB 38/27/22, (1914), at 31.
[96] *Id.*, at 32.
[97] Minutes attached to War Office to Foreign Office, Sep. 17, 1913, *in* Correspondence
regarding Employment of Shells to whose Bursting Charges Substances Generating Noxious
Gases have been added, FO 881/10342, (1913). It should be remembered that Russia initially invented the ammunition to ignite artillery cases, and only questioned its legitimacy
when possible use against soldiers was contemplated.

aircraft, as did other arms control regimes in the twentieth century, but only restricted the use of such weapons.

Aerial warfare remained largely unregulated, and, as its threat increased, Britain viewed international law as a possible solution. In 1910, the Foreign Office specifically stated that the topic should be avoided at the upcoming Hague Peace Conference. However, by 1914 the Foreign Office included the topic as one Britain hoped to see discussed at the gathering.[98] This paralleled Britain's shifting views about investment in aerial technology: Initially, the government opposed innovations which might weaken its insular position, as it had opposed submarines, but once the technology had been adopted by the other powers, British policy had to evolve.[99]

At roughly the same time, the Foreign Office also called on legal advisors to provide an opinion about the legality of exploding shells filled with poisonous gas. The War Office had procured a new gas shell, and posited that as the "sole purpose" of the ammunition was not the diffusion of asphyxiating gas, it was not prohibited.[100] In the discussions which ensued, the Foreign Office provided varied legal positions on such conduct, and approvingly cited academic Pearce Higgins as a leading authority on the topic.[101] After noting that this would virtually make the declaration a dead letter, as all explosive shells arguably lacked the *sole* purpose of diffusing gas, the plain language of the agreement was noted. Lawyers could only look beyond the language of a text if the wording itself was vague, and the present agreement was clearly drafted, thus the new shell would be permissible under the declaration as it had a purpose beyond diffusion of asphyxiating gas.[102] The 1899 negotiations witnessed a debate over the advantages of highly specific regulations as opposed to agreements expressing a larger spirit. Yet even technically correct legalistic arguments

[98] July 29, 1910 Meeting of the Standing-Sub-Committee of the Committee of Imperial Defence, *in* CAB 38/19/60, at 14; Third Peace Conference, Mar. 24, 1914, CAB 37/119/48, (1914).

[99] Report of the Technical Sub-Committee of the Committee of Imperial Defence on Aerial Navigation, Airships, July 30, 1912, CAB 38/19/32, (1912).

[100] War Office to Foreign Office, Sep. 17, 1913, *in* FO 881/10342.

[101] Memorandum of Davidson, Sep. 26, 1913, enclosure in War Office to Foreign Office, Sep. 17, 1913, *in* FO 881/10342. Higgins was a professor of international law at the London School of Economics and government international legal advisor during the First World War.

[102] *Id.*

had to account for likely objections. The Foreign Office had to chart national strategy around an uncertain set of circumstances.

Britain began preparations for the Third Hague Peace Conference in early 1914. The Foreign Office noted that a number of "legacy" topics from the Second Hague Peace Conference would be raised at the next gathering. The 1907 mine convention called on parties to renew negotiations, and the aerial bombardment declaration only remained in effect until the close of the upcoming conference. Additionally, the 1907 armaments resolution called for continued study of the question. The Foreign Office anticipated further discussions of maritime issues, which would include naval mines, but had no intention of raising the larger armament issue at the new gathering. Notably, statesmen recognized that scholarly international legal conferences would influence the agenda.[103] In preparing for the upcoming conference, the Foreign Office sought to prepare draft agreements in advance, rectifying what was seen as a shortcoming in preparations for the last conference. Given the turmoil of the 18 months prior to May 1914, Grey saw little prospect of a gathering taking place in 1915.[104] Ultimately, this was correct, but for very different reasons.

CONCLUSION

By 1914, international legal thought on arms control had matured. Academic writing had moved away from utopian projects and increasingly recognized a discrete and pragmatic role for law in reducing arms competition. Knowledge of arms control precedents increased significantly, providing a broader range of models for treaty terms. These developments were not confined to academia, but also influenced British thinking on arms control. Politicians and the public were exposed to a broader range of roles for international law through the Second Hague Peace Conference, shaping the

[103] Third Peace Conference, Mar. 24, 1914, at 1, *in* CAB 37/119/48 (1914).

[104] *Id.* "[The Foreign Office has] been unable to give as much attention as they would have wished to the questions connected with the general organisation of peace, which constitutes the real province of The Hague Conference, owing to the fact that their efforts have necessarily been largely directed to the solution of the acute problems arising from the actual prevalence and threatened spread of war." Grey to Mensdorff, June 16, 1913, *in* Correspondence respecting the Third Peace Conference, FO 881/10528, (1912–1914). The date was moved back to 1916, and ultimately to 1917. Grey to Barclay, July 9, 1914, *in Id.*

post-conference dialogue on armaments. Thus, when facing an arms race with Germany, the Foreign Office possessed a wide range of legal precedents which could be applied to naval arms limitation. This shift was essential to real progress, as early multilateral projects for arms limitation often featured utopian goals of world disarmament or an international police force. By fostering greater understanding of pragmatic applications of law, including the bilateral and limited multilateral arms agreements, scholars shifted debate away from unrealistic plans to regulations which were feasible.

Negotiations on a range of security issues overlapped with arms limitation and provided further treaty models. The rapid development of aircraft made The Hague rules on aerial bombardment relevant rather than merely of theoretical interest. Moreover, one British response to the threat of dirigible aircraft, namely incendiary bullets, revived the older issue of exploding bullets. In the London Conference in 1908–1909, the most important security-related diplomatic gathering between the Second Hague Peace Conference and 1914, the Foreign Office discussed ways of legitimizing rules set by the great powers within the broader international community. The creative use of legal custom in the resulting London Declaration provided a means to enforce great power hegemony, while sidelining the trend toward equality of states at the Second Hague Peace Conference. As international competition in dreadnoughts increased after 1907, and as smaller states purchased these weapons, these trends provided new means to contain a growing arms race through international law.

CHAPTER 9

The *Dreadnought* Competition and Arms Control up to 1914

INTRODUCTION

Unsurprisingly, the Hague Conference failed to resolve the central challenge of the naval arms race. Pre-conference diplomacy, which laid bare German objections, had presented the best prospect for an agreement. However, the gathering did result in a number of arms-related advances, through the regulation of naval mines and the conversion of merchant ships into auxiliary cruisers. More importantly, British negotiating strategy altered from the First to the Second Hague Conference. Britain realized the need to engage with the international community. While Britain stood out in 1899 as the only state to refuse ratification of any arms limitations, in contrast by 1907 Britain championed all arms limits. Moreover, the armaments resolution at the 1907 gathering provided Britain with the opening to continue bilateral discussions directly with Germany. After 1907, British proposals for exchanging information provided the model for progress.

The naval arms race between Britain and Germany influenced the development of arms control concepts. The Liberal government exhibited ambivalence about negotiations with Germany: German reluctance to negotiate and refusal to separate armaments from political questions made Grey's Foreign Office wary of a diplomatic trap. British politicians expressed concerns that willingness to negotiate would show weakness, spurring Germany's naval ambitions. The concomitant suggestion was

© The Editor(s) (if applicable) and The Author(s) 2016
S.A. Keefer, *The Law of Nations and Britain's Quest for Naval Security*, DOI 10.1007/978-3-319-39645-3_9

that Britain should increase its naval construction to signal a determination to win the race. Additionally, the Admiralty wavered between the advantages of openness and that of secretiveness in construction policy. Ultimately, German demands for concessions outweighed the potential benefits of arms limitation, preventing a deal from being reached.

Coming to power pledged to reduce naval expenditure, the Liberal government would have faced considerable discontent from its radical backbenchers if arms control efforts were abandoned. While statesmen debated whether or not arms control was a good idea or if Germany would consent to agreement, they accepted that such an agreement *could* be reached through a treaty. Statesmen believed that international law could limit tensions within the confines of the existing international system, without the creation of powerful international institutions. The British response to the 1909 Dreadnought Scare highlighted this point. The scare fully exposed the German naval challenge, while undermining the premises on which British construction policy rested. Suddenly the public feared that Germany could, undetected, build as many ships, and as rapidly as Britain, allowing no time for a response. Here, law could play a concrete role in security, by formalizing attaché visits and exchanges of information. Significantly, the only Anglo-German arms treaty to reach the drafting stage before the war was an exchange of information agreement.

Britain took a central role in the development of arms control in the decade prior to the First World War. While Anglo-Germman negotiations were ultimately fruitless, the efforts indicated that contemporary statesmen possessed a more sophisticated assessment of international law than is often acknowledged. Moreover, the efforts provide evidence of how the Foreign Office viewed the contemporary environment, and how they thought the future might unfold. Arms control was perceived as possible within the existing international system, and without the need to create utopian international institutions. The failure to realize these goals should not obscure this fact.

Anglo-German Naval Arms Control and International Law 1908–1914

Between 1908 and 1914, Anglo-German naval arms limitation negotiations reflected pragmatic views of international law. International law provided an asset that allowed parties to communicate vital interests to both domestic and foreign audiences, strengthened mutual interests, and increased predictability in international affairs. While other arms treaties, such as the Argentine-Chilean and Rush-Bagot agreements, strengthened mutual interests between the parties, there appeared little prospect of an Anglo-German accord warming relations, given the incompatible British and German goals for negotiations. Yet international law could still play a key role by increasing predictability, thereby fostering greater transparency in naval construction. Given the growing perception of a German naval challenge, the Foreign Office sought an agreement for this reason. Moreover, British expectations of international law influenced the Foreign Office's negotiating stance. Law mattered and had an independent effect, and could contribute to an agreement by depoliticizing arms construction and by increasing predictability.

The following sections will assess the legal underpinnings of the British negotiating stance in the arms discussions. Previously unutilized Admiralty and Foreign Office materials will be incorporated, providing new evidence of British arms control strategies. These materials support the argument that law played a significant role in arms control strategy. The Foreign Office intended a legally binding agreement to reduce the risk of a German breach, by setting terms clearly in writing. In turn, the British government sought terms which could be easily monitored through existing diplomatic practices, especially attaché inspections. Efforts to reach an exchange of information agreement confirm this expectation of law, with the Foreign Office attempting to depoliticize attaché visits, removing them from the whims of the admiralties. Much of the larger concern about arms control centered on the difficulty in using a bilateral agreement to halt a more general arms race. Finally, the possibility of a non-binding understanding to halt the arms race provided further evidence of what statesmen expected law to contribute to an agreement.

The Admiralty had consistently followed a naval construction policy that maximized the strengths of British industry. Britain relied upon its ability to build ships faster than any competitor, and in larger numbers. Such a policy could be utilized to either hasten or hinder the adoption of new technology: In the mid-century rivalry with France, Britain awaited French construction of both steam-driven ships-of-the-line and ironclad battleships, answering the *Gloire* with the superior *Warrior*. Fisher utilized this policy in advocating new technology, incorporating more advanced weapons upon confirmation that German construction was tied to an inferior type:

THE GREAT SECRET IS TO PUT OFF TO THE VERY LAST HOUR THE SHIP (big or little) that you mean to build (or PERHAPS NOT BUILD HER AT ALL!). You see all your rivals' plans fully developed, their vessels started beyond recall, and then in each individual answer to each such rival vessel you plunge with a design 50 per cent better! knowing that your rapid shipbuilding and command of money will enable you to have your vessel fit to fight as soon if not sooner than the rival vessel.[1]

The construction of the *Invincible* exemplified this process, as well as a newer pattern of exploitation of secret construction and disinformation. The German navy, convinced that Britain's new armored cruiser would be armed with 9.2-inch guns, responded with their equivalent 8.2-inch-gunned *Blücher*.[2] However, the British battlecruiser was instead armed with a 12-inch gun main armament, solidly outclassing its German rival, and rendering it obsolete before completion. The introduction of the *Dreadnought*, then the 13.5-inch-gunned super-dreadnoughts, and the fast 15-inch gun *Queen Elizabeth* similarly utilized superior industrial resources to quickly trump capital ships built by competitors.

This policy not only depended on rapid construction methods, but also presumed that foreign construction would be detected with sufficient time to respond. Notably, White asserted that the Admiralty could always uncover construction plans of its foreign rivals.[3] Existing practices of naval attaché visits, together with public sources of information on warship construction and the lengthy period it took to complete a battleship all combined to make this "wait-and-see" approach viable.

The premises that underlay this construction policy collapsed in 1909. Suddenly, fears arose that Germany could build as rapidly as Britain, in as large numbers, and in a new environment of secrecy. These fears crystallized at the same time as the *Dreadnought* erased the comfortable margin of superiority in older battleships, raising concerns that Germany could out-build Britain. The standard international practices involving attaché visits to foreign naval yards complemented British construction policy, allowing timely receipt of information.[4] In 1907, the year of the Hague

---

[1] Fisher to Churchill, Feb. 13, 1912, *in* Marder, ed., *Fear God Dread Nought*, No. 351, at 431.

[2] Sumida, *In Defense of Naval Supremacy*, 158–159.

[3] White, "Modern Warships," 868.

[4] *See* Seligmann, *Spies in Uniform*, 108.

Conference, a reduced naval program of one battleship was justified, partly on information gathered by the British naval attaché in Germany. The attaché personally viewed five of the six German battleships under construction, including three of the four dreadnoughts being built.[5] Britain had initiated the policy of secrecy in capital ship construction with the *Dreadnought*, which, coupled with the rapid construction time of the warship, increased the political impact of its completion. As mentioned above, the Admiralty utilized secret construction with the *Invincible*. Germany, in turn, began restricting attaché access – weapons manufacturer Krupps forbade attaché access to heavy gun, armor, and projectile manufacturing facilities in 1907 and shipyards reduced visits in 1909 before ending them completely in 1910.[6]

British inability to confirm German construction fueled suspicions precisely when German capabilities were being reassessed. Revelations of German construction practices and capacity brought Britain's previous policy into question. Evidence suggested that German shipbuilders were stockpiling nickel steel, guns, and other time-sensitive capital ship components.[7] In capital ship construction, turrets and heavy guns needed the greatest lead-time, requiring ordnance contracts to be placed prior to laying down the hull.[8] The record-breaking construction time for the *Dreadnought* had only been accomplished by borrowing four turrets destined for two other battleships.[9] The shift to dreadnought-type battleships with their "all-big-gun armament" increased the importance of turret and gun manufacturing as a determinant of construction capacity, as it greatly increased the number of heavy guns and turrets carried by battleships.[10]

Simultaneously, the Admiralty questioned earlier assumptions about longer German construction times, reaching the sobering conclusion that

---

[5] Lord Tweedmouth, Future Battleship Building, Nov. 21, 1907, CAB 37/90/101, (1907), at 4.

[6] Seligmann, *Spies in Uniform*, 107–08.

[7] Grey to Goschen, 4 January 1909, Correspondence Respecting the Limitation of Armaments, FO 412/96 (1909–1910); Marder, *Dreadnought*, 153–54.

[8] Sir William White, "British and Foreign Warship Building Capacity," *The Times*, Nov. 15, 1906, at 17. Winston Churchill estimated that turret orders needed to be placed three months prior to laying down the hull. Churchill, Battleship Programme, 1914–15, Enclosure I, *in* German Navy Law and Comparisons with Strength of the Royal Navy [an incomplete paper], Jan. 10, 1914, CAB 37/118/6 (1914).

[9] Gardiner, ed., *Conway's 1906–1921*, 21–22.

[10] Sir William White, Feb. 15, 1909, *in* Churchill, Naval Expenditure, July 15, 1910, CAB 37/103/32, at 6 (1910).

Germany could build capital ships at the same rate as Britain.[11] In January 1909, the Admiralty avowed that the German Navy would possess 17 capital ships by early 1912, and estimated that Germany might have as many as 21 if full capacity was realized. Against those numbers, Britain would possess a slim margin of superiority under then-current construction programs, with eighteen dreadnoughts.[12] While Britain possessed a preponderance in pre-dreadnought battleships, both the public and politicians increasingly believed only dreadnoughts mattered.[13]

The immediate solution, encapsulated in the slogan "we want eight, and we won't wait," called for a dramatic increase in British naval construction. Historians have questioned whether the scare was manufactured to secure warship orders, although recent scholarship confirms that the perception of threat by the navy was genuine.[14] Regardless, Grey and the Foreign Office responded to the German naval expansion as a genuine threat, and guided the Cabinet in countering this challenge. Four capital ships were authorized for immediate construction, and another four contingent ships, technically part of the following year's naval budget, could be started if deemed necessary. Ultimately all eight were commenced in 1909, along with two battlecruisers commissioned by Australia and New Zealand, bringing the total of capital ships begun to a staggering total of ten.[15]

Britain followed established international legal protocol and requested clarification about the apparent arms build-up and German intentions.[16] German Ambassador Metternich claimed that private companies stockpiled materials prior to receiving contracts and commenced several ships before their allotted dates under the Navy Law at the shipbuilders' discretion.[17] Nonetheless, inability to determine German ship construction,

---

[11] Edmund Slade, Note Drawn up at the Request of the First Lord of the Admiralty by the Director of Naval Intelligence, Jan. 8, 1908, CAB 37/91/2 (1908); Battleship Building Programmes of Great Britain, Germany, France, United States, Italy, and Austria (June 1909), July 14, 1909, CAB 37/100/97 (1909), at 2–3.

[12] Marder, *Dreadnought*, 154–55.

[13] Goschen to Grey, May 20, 1909, Gooch and Temperley, eds., *British Documents*, Vol. VI, at 272, 73.

[14] *See* Matthew S. Seligmann, "Intelligence Information and the 1909 Naval Scare: The Secret Foundations of a Public Panic," *War in History* 17, no. 1 (2010).

[15] Data compiled from Marder, *Dreadnought*, 439, 41.

[16] Grey to Goschen, Jan. 4, 1909, FO 412/96.

[17] Grey to Goschen, Feb. 3, 1909, Gooch and Temperley, eds., *British Documents*, Vol. VI, 239.

coupled with misstatements about the extent of the German naval program, left significant suspicions. Planning British shipbuilding by worst-case scenario seemed the best reply. The long term solution pursued by the Foreign Office included an agreed arms limit as well as an exchange of information to clarify German intentions.

Under the Liberal government, Britain had reduced its naval program from the four armored vessels called for annually in the Cawdor Memorandum. Yet British unilateral moderation had only been met by an escalation of German efforts in 1906–1907.[18] King Edward VII raised the issue of armaments while visiting Germany in the summer of 1908, but the monarch lacked interest in his role as emissary, and nothing came of the endeavor.

Anglo-German naval arms negotiations began in earnest with the summer 1909 accession of Theobald von Bethmann Hollweg to the Chancellorship in Germany. In October, Germany began negotiations with Britain for both a political treaty, guaranteeing British neutrality in the event of a continental war, and a naval agreement, focusing on capital ship numbers and fleet ratios. The negotiations stalled over two elements. First, the timing of the political and naval treaties hampered negotiations, with Germany seeking a political treaty first, while the British Foreign Office viewed a political treaty as worthless unless naval spending was limited. Eventually, the parties agreed to negotiate both treaties simultaneously, but British suspicions about the political treaty never receded and ultimately came to overshadow interest in a naval treaty. Second, Germany refused to reduce its overall naval construction program. Germany offered to reduce its construction tempo for the next few years, with the understanding that later annual programs would have to be increased in order to complete the fleet by 1920. This offer would have reduced annual construction programs through 1911 from four ships to three, while requiring an increase over the two ships planned annually from 1912 to 1918 to make up the difference. Faced with an offer which ultimately would not reduce naval expenditures, the Foreign Office stalled. However, by August 1910 the Foreign Office reconsidered, and agreed to negotiate on the basis of no increase in construction to prevent further inflation of costs.[19]

---

[18] Moll, "Politics, Power, and Panic: Britain's 1909 Dreadnought 'Gap'," 137.

[19] Memorandum respecting Agreement with Germany, *in* Minute by Grey, May 24, 1911, Gooch and Temperley, eds., *British Documents*, Vol. VI, 631–36.

Negotiations continued sporadically from autumn 1909 to the summer of 1911, Britain seeking a pause in the winter of 1909–1910 and again in the winter of 1910–1911, as the Foreign Office contemplated replies to unsatisfactory German offers. German Admiral Tirpitz's original plans held that a large German fleet, even if smaller than the British Navy, would pose such a threat in war that Britain would become more amenable to German diplomatic goals. Tirpitz wrongly assumed that Britain's rivalry with France and Russia was incapable of solution, so that if faced with a German threat, Britain would be forced to back down in order to focus upon its permanent enemies. In order for the German threat to materialize, Germany had to pass through a "risk zone" after Britain recognized the threat but before the German Navy was too big for a preemptive strike. But as Britain gradually recognized the German threat and increased its navy in response, the risk zone lengthened indefinitely, posing an insoluble problem to the Tirpitz Plan. In response, figures in both the German Army and Foreign Ministry sought to exploit the naval race in a bargain with Britain that would end an apparently futile build-up. Tirpitz held out before 1909, buttressed by the fixed long-term construction set in Germany's Naval Law, but increasingly he recognized the need to bargain with Britain.[20] The British eight ship construction program of that year rendered a rude shock, and the increasingly irresistible demands of the army for a larger share of military funding necessitated an agreement to prevent Germany from losing ground.

In May 1911, Germany withdrew its offer to slow the construction tempo, claiming that it could no longer do so while still completing the fleet on schedule. The Agadir Crisis in July 1911 halted negotiations until the end of the year. By 1912, increases in French and Russian military programs required an increase in funding to the German Army, with the British Admiralty recognizing this would divert funds from the German Navy. With this background, in February 1912, nongovernmental contacts by German industrialists brought about an abortive discussion in Berlin led by the British Secretary of State for War, Viscount Richard Haldane. While Grey had been willing to negotiate a colonial concession, Germany overplayed its hand. Prior to the meetings in Berlin, Bethmann Hollweg announced a new naval *Novelle*, predicating negotiations on the

---

[20] Michael Epkenhans, "Was a Peaceful Outcome Thinkable? The Naval Race before 1914," in *An Improbable War*, 120–22.

rate of increase of the German fleet.[21] Haldane could only warn Germany that any increase would be met by a two to one response. Following the unsuccessful conference, Germany offered to cut a battleship from the planned expansion, harkening back to Britain's tepid offer in 1906, derided by Arthur Lee in Parliament as a "piece of toasted cheese to catch unwary mice."[22] Unsurprisingly, Britain refused to budge. Both sides had misinterpreted the other's intentions, and the negotiations confirmed the gap between their positions. Subsequently, the Foreign Office sought no direct negotiations on the question, fearing the discussion would only worsen relations. Following the failure of negotiations, Churchill made his naval holiday offer in the spring of 1912, coupling it with a threat to respond at 2:1 for any German construction above the stated program.

German insistence on a political treaty guaranteeing British neutrality undermined arms negotiations. Throughout the period 1909–1912, leading figures echoed Sir Eyre Crowe's fears that a political agreement, guaranteeing Germany against unprovoked British attack, would undermine Britain's ententes with France and Russia.[23] The diplomatic cost greatly outweighed the advantages to be gained from meager German arms offers, diminishing the desirability of a treaty.

While interest in an agreement wavered, statesmen had firm expectations about what benefits an arms control treaty would bring. Numerous legal negotiations indicated that policy-makers recognized that treaties would be enforced through self-help. The legal concept of self-enforcement in turn harmonized with Admiralty construction policy. If Britain discovered that extra warships were being built in breach of an agreement, the Admiralty would need to quickly discover the violation, and then utilize superior industrial facilities to rapidly respond. In a prospective agreement, Britain enjoyed unique advantages both from its predominant fleet, which would provide a buffer against violations, and from its industrial might, which allowed a rapid, overwhelming response.

These conditions applied throughout most of the preceding century, except during the period around 1908–1911, before the numerical lead in dreadnoughts reaffirmed Britain's position. During this transition period, the Admiralty altered its naval calculations to take into account the slim

---

[21] Stevenson, *Armaments and the Coming of War*, 206.

[22] Tate, *The Disarmament Illusion*, 335–36.

[23] *See* notes *attached to* Goschen to Grey, May 10, 1911, *in* Further Correspondence respecting the Limitation of Armaments, FO 412/103 (1911–1912).

margin of superiority and the ability of Germany to rapidly close the gap. Cabinet notes from 1909 indicate these calculations were being made, as government leaders estimated the length of time for Germany and Britain to build a battleship, while querying "when we get the evidence is it too late? You are not sure till the ship is a year old. Only safe policy is to keep ahead."[24] Similarly, when Germany offered to convert an exchange of information agreement into what would essentially be an annual arms limit, Kiderlen chided his British colleague that the exchange would only relate to one year, too short a period to alter the balance.[25] The key point is that both sides understood the dynamic of naval construction and how this dynamic affected treaty enforcement.

A purely bilateral arms control agreement could be enforced by state action. However, the multilateral dimension of the naval arms race complicated matters. When discussing the possibility of converting an exchange of information agreement into an annual naval arms treaty, Crowe noted the matter touched:

> ... upon one of the most fundamental difficulties which as I have repeatedly pointed out, stand in the way of HMG making an agreement respecting limitation of armaments with one Power only, whilst third Powers, some of them allied, and others perhaps in secret understanding with Germany (Turkey, Brazil, Sweden?) remained free to build what they liked as rapidly as they liked .... If the limitation of armaments is to have any practical value for this country, it must be based on a far more comprehensive foundation than the present German proposal ...[26]

A naval arms treaty needed to address third-party construction as much as potential German violations.

GLOBAL NAVAL ARMS COMPETITION AND INTERNATIONAL LAW

The advent of the *Dreadnought* brought a radical change in naval arms competition as the new type of battleship became universally adopted. In calculating naval balances, the Admiralty had to consider not only the

---

[24] Notes *attached to* CAB 37/100/97.
[25] Goschen to Grey, Mar. 30, 1911, *in* FO 412/103.
[26] Notes *attached to* Goschen to Grey, Mar. 30, 1911, *in* FO 412/103.

balance in the Mediterranean, but also Latin American, Far Eastern, and Greco-Turkish rivalries when calculating the potential naval strengths in the North Sea. While regional considerations were not new, the extent to which peripheral navies influenced the balance of power was novel (Table 1.4). The Foreign Office advocated a number of legal responses, including escape clauses in any Anglo-German agreement and innovative declarations which would bind the entire international community. Conversely, Foreign Office diplomats also discouraged regional arms agreements which threatened British strategic interests. While Britain completed no naval arms agreements, the intensity of these deliberations indicates that the Foreign Office possessed a greater appreciation of the strengths of law than had previously been acknowledged.

Before the dreadnought, a greater diversity of battleship types coexisted. Small powers generally built coastal-defense battleships which could be ignored in great power calculations because of their limited suitability for fleet actions. After 1906, the dreadnought became a universal currency of naval strength, with small powers building or purchasing their own, significantly altering naval calculations. In calculations publicized in 1896, the great powers possessed 96 first-class battleships built or building, to two built among the smaller states.[27] In 1912, the ratio was 101 great power dreadnoughts, to 11 small power vessels, either built or under construction.[28] These 11 ships constituted a larger potential force than that possessed by any great power besides Britain, Germany, or the United States, and nearly equaled the 12 dreadnoughts built or building by the latter. The range of small state dreadnoughts comprised a naval force in its own right.

The rise of small power capital ship fleets was new and upset systematic calculations of naval strength. A Cabinet paper in 1912 noted that:

[British naval power] will be diminished with the growth not only of the German Navy, but by the simultaneous building by many Powers of great ships of war .... The existence of a number of Navies all comprising ships of high quality creates possibilities of adverse combinations being suddenly formed against which no reasonable standard of British naval strength can fully guard.[29]

[27] With an additional third under construction in Turkey but unlikely to ever be finished. J. Scott Keltie, *The Statesman's Year-Book: Statistical and Historical Annual of the States of the World for the Year 1896* (London: Macmillan Co., 1896), xxix.
[28] *Figures compiled from* Gardiner, ed., *Conway's 1906–1921.*
[29] Memorandum on the General Naval Situation, Aug. 26, 1912, CAB 37/112/100, at 8 (1912).

Moreover, smaller powers lacking stable finances or government were often the purchasers of dreadnoughts, with little evident capacity to maintain these expensive warships for long. This raised the specter that dreadnoughts would return to the open market. As Churchill stated a year later:

> The simultaneous building by so many powers great and small of capital ships, and their general naval expansion, are causes of deep anxiety to us. Germany may fall behind in the race she has herself provoked, and we may yet be left to face a great preponderance of loose Dreadnoughts wh[ich] at v[er] y short notice, a diplomatic grouping or regrouping may range against us.[30]

Since 1909, the Foreign Office had known that Italy and Austro-Hungary planned to build dreadnoughts. While these two German allies competitively armed against one another, Britain needed to calculate these fleets when assessing naval requirements. This became a matter of increasing urgency by 1912, with the completion of the first Austro-Hungarian dreadnought. One solution involved a division of responsibilities with France, with that nation protecting mutual interests in the Mediterranean while Britain protected the French northern coast against German attack. While the Foreign Office avoided legal obligations to France in the 1912 Mediterranean agreement, this type of arrangement paralleled British thinking prior to the Second Hague Peace Conference, when Parliament explored different models for limiting arms through law.

Additionally, the Foreign Office contemplated arms control with Austria-Hungary. At the height of the Agadir crisis, Charles Hardinge, the Permanent Under-Secretary at the Foreign Office, hinted to the Habsburg Foreign Minister that Austria could act "as a drag on any ambitious naval policy which the German government might be tempted to pursue," causing a minor scandal in the Austro-Hungarian press.[31] A year later, a newspaper report, believed to be officially inspired by the Austrian government, suggested that its naval program might be dropped in return for security guarantees. Churchill sought to exploit this opening, advocating that Britain provide the Mediterranean powers with a treaty guaranteeing their possessions, and an unlimited arbitration agreement with Austria-Hungary as a means of abating the naval

---

[30] Churchill to Grey, Oct. 24, 1913, Gooch and Temperley, eds., *British Documents*, Vol. IX, 721.

[31] Nicolson to Grey, Aug. 1, 1911, Grey Manuscripts – Foreign Office Memoranda, FO 800/93, (1909–1911).

rivalry in the region.[32] This updated version of the 1887 Mediterranean Agreement borrowed much from contemporary international law, and from the Argentine-Chilean model in particular, with its package of arbitration, guarantee, and armaments treaties. Despite Churchill's eagerness, Grey ended the project, reasoning it lacked official support in Austria.[33]

* * *

Beyond Mediterranean calculations, the resurgence of Latin American naval rivalries further complicated the European balance. Brazil ordered a pair of dreadnoughts in Britain, to be commenced in 1908, and contemplated a third, thereby drawing a reluctant Argentina into an arms race. Argentina sought British assistance, referring directly to Britain's role in concluding the successful 1902 agreement with Chile.[34] While acknowledging the earlier precedent, the Foreign Office held unequivocally that an arms deal would not be in Britain's interest:

> We are not asked to recommend this proposal to the Brazilian gov[ernmen]t and, even if we were, it would scarcely be to our interest to do so. The three battleships will do us no harm as long as they are retained by the Brazilians (in whose hands they will probably deteriorate rapidly), whereas the addition of even one of them to the navy of "another Power" might necessitate an increase in our own naval estimates.[35]

If "another Power," meaning Germany, purchased the ships, Britain would be forced to add to its own program. The two Brazilian ships then completing could have provided Germany with parity or even an advantage. Given German capacity to build ships at the same rate as Britain, this addition would greatly spur the Anglo-German arms race by evening

[32] Churchill to Grey, July 31, 1912, FO 800/87.

[33] *See* notes *attached to* Churchill's Secretary to Grey, Aug. 1, 1912, FO 800/87.

[34] Henderson to Grey, Aug. 12, 1908, *in* Brazil, FO 371/403 (1908).

[35] Notes *attached to* S. American Armaments, Aug. 11, 1908, *in* FO 371/403. Grey minuted these notes "[w]e certainly cannot recommend Brazil to sell." The Foreign Office steadfastly maintained this attitude towards British intervention, although when fears were expressed in the autumn of a potential South American war, Hardinge provided a counterpoint, claiming "[i]t is to be hoped that prudent counsels may prevail and that S. America may give a lead to Europe by a scheme of proportionate disarmament." Notes *attached to* South American Naval Armaments, Sep. 19, 1908, FO 371/403.

the odds.[36] Further documents reiterated the point that dreadnoughts in Argentine or Brazilian hands would rapidly deteriorate,[37] removing the risk of their influencing the European balance. Accordingly, the Foreign Office refused Argentine requests for intervention.

The Argentine government hoped Brazil would cancel its program, or, at the very least, transfer one ship to Buenos Aires, keep one, and sell the third on the world market, saving Argentina the expense of purchasing its own dreadnought squadron.[38] Ultimately, Brazil recognized that Argentine construction would spur Chilean building, and that Chile would assist in maintaining a balance against its eastern neighbor.[39] Chilean support for Brazil doomed the Argentine arms control project.

The possibility of a regional arms agreement reemerged in early 1911. By that time, Brazil possessed two dreadnoughts and was building a third, Argentina had started two battleships of its own in reply, and Chile was following suit. In 1910, Brazil suffered a naval mutiny, cooling its desire for dreadnoughts. Brazil's third dreadnought, then under construction at Armstrong's yard, was up for sale and Brazil appeared poised to sell its other two. Brazil could not divest itself of these vessels if its neighbors were building their own, but Argentina was also willing to dispose of its dreadnoughts.[40] Upon realizing that the Latin American states were reaching an arms agreement on their own accord, the Foreign Office nearly panicked. "There seems to be a risk of five 1st class battleships – 3 Brazilian & 2 Argentine – being put on the market more or less simultaneously."[41]

The Foreign Office revised earlier views that the dreadnoughts would rapidly become worthless, expressing a fear that if Germany purchased the warships, it could quickly refurbish them and add them as potent units of the fleet.

---

[36] By the end of 1908, Britain had one dreadnought and two battlecruisers completed, and seven more under construction, compared to nine German capital ships under construction, although more of the British ships were nearing completion. Gardiner, ed., *Conway's 1906–1921*, 1 et. seq. and 134 et. seq.

[37] Notes *attached to* Sale of Brazilian Battleships, Aug. 21, 1908; Townley to Grey, Aug. 28, 1908, *both in* FO 371/403.

[38] Townley to Grey, Aug. 10, 1908, *in* FO 371/403.

[39] Cheetham to Grey, Aug. 18, 1908, *in* FO 371/403.

[40] Haggard to Grey, Feb. 3, 1911, *in* Brazil, FO 371/1051 (1911).

[41] Notes *attached to* Brazilian Dreadnoughts, Feb. 27, 1911, *in* FO 371/1051. In 1911, Britain had 27 capital ships of dreadnought-type built or building to 20 German vessels, thus five ships if purchased by Germany, would nearly balance the odds at 27 to 25. Gardiner, ed., *Conway's 1906–1921*, 1 et. seq. and 134 et. seq.

As German policy seems to be to reduce the present naval inequality between herself & Great Britain at about any cost it would conceivably be worth her while to give a fancy price for these ships – which after a short period of docking would be as good ships as any at present afloat – & with our present very narrow margin of superiority the sudden acquisition by Germany of two first class fighting ships would be a serious factor in the political situation.[42]

Since 1908, the possibility of instability caused by a regional arms limit had only grown as the number of dreadnoughts in question expanded. In 1903, the Admiralty purchased the two Chilean battleships at the center of the Argentine-Chilean arms race, but these warships proved difficult to incorporate in the British fleet because of technical differences.[43] Similar challenges in incorporating the Brazilian ships may have reduced Admiralty interest in the vessels.[44] Thus, Britain may have had little interest in purchasing the expensive warships, yet may have found it necessary in order to stave off a German acquisition.

Britain could have played a significant role in resolving the regional arms race, possessing the same assets enabling enforcement as in 1902. Similarly to the Argentine-Chilean negotiations, in 1908 the warships in question were building in British yards and British financiers could exercise a check on excessive naval programs. While the Brazilians opposed a limit in 1908, all parties expressed a degree of interest in limiting armaments by 1911. British inaction prevented further instability in the European naval balance, at the expense of heightened South American rivalry.[45]

*　*　*

These proceedings, which occurred at the same time as the Anglo-German negotiations, undoubtedly influenced Crowe's wariness when Germany

---

[42] Notes *attached to* Sale of Dreadnoughts, Feb. 13, 1911, No. 5136, *in* FO 371/1051. The Admiralty noted that the 12-inch guns on the Brazilian dreadnoughts used different ammunition from German guns and questioned whether Germany would want them. Admiralty to Foreign Office, Feb. 14, 1911, *in* FO 371/1051.

[43] Gardiner, ed., *Conway's 1906–1921*, 39.

[44] However, the Brazilian dreadnought purchased by Turkey ultimately found its way into the British Navy on the eve of the First World War.

[45] Ultimately, Argentina and Brazil kept two dreadnoughts apiece, Brazil selling its third battleship to the Ottoman Empire before completion. Chile ordered two super-dreadnoughts from Armstrong, which were seized before completion at the start of the Great War.

sought to modify the exchange of information into an annual naval arms limit. The Foreign Office founded its attitudes toward arms control agreements on calculations of British interest, opposing limitation when it appeared to introduce greater uncertainty in the European balance of power. In this case, rather than fearing law was impractical the Foreign Office worried that it would prove effective.

Given the uncertainty created by the global dreadnought rivalry, the Foreign Office sought an escape clause in any Anglo-German agreement, hampering negotiations. Similar challenges had hampered earlier British negotiations. When contemplating an arms limitation offer to Russia in 1838, Lord John Russell noted:

> It will be necessary not to bind ourselves with respect to our own force, the Navy being our principal arm, and we having to consider other Powers, and their strength at sea, as well as Russia. Still, a friendly representation may do good, though it may not altogether preclude the necessity for strengthening our Navy.[46]

Germany's initial offer in November 1909 called for a three-to-four-year limit on the number of capital ships, "which neither of the two countries shall yearly be able to exceed."[47] Crowe expressed a fear that Britain would be bound "not only as against Germany, but as against the rest of the world …. She may leave her allies to build fleets, or she may conclude fresh alliances with the owners of fleets, or buy their ships for a future contingency."[48] The Foreign Office stalled, eventually replying to the proposal in 1910 that Britain would "seize the opportunity of knowing exactly what Germany proposed to build, to reduce our Naval construction as far as we safely could having due regard to our position as a Power to whom strength at sea meant everything."[49] When pressed again for a firmer commitment, Goschen equivocated, claiming His Majesty's Government "would on their side restrict their shipbuilding programme to what was necessary to preserve a safe proportion to the existing German programme as long as the latter continued to be, as it necessarily was at present, the chief factor in determining British naval construction."[50] Crowe ultimately

[46] As quoted in Bartlett; *Britain and Sea Power*, 121.
[47] Notes attached to Goschen to Grey, Nov. 4, 1909, FO 412/96.
[48] *Id.*
[49] Goschen to Grey, Aug. 19, 1910, FO 412/96.
[50] Goschen to Grey, Oct. 12, 1910, FO 412/96.

sought draft clauses of an agreement that would preserve British freedom to build against third parties, so as to maintain the two-power standard.[51] Another legal response lay in the creation of a doctrine binding the entire legal community to an arms limit. The evidence suggests that in 1909 Britain contemplated a novel strategy to bind the international community through a bilateral Anglo-German declaration. Hardinge provided an intriguing reference in August 1909. When preparing a memorandum on a possible limit, he told Grey that "'Declarations' are in vogue and I think it is the form most suitable for any agreement to which we *and other Powers* can subscribe."[52] The treaty would not only be open to third parties, but then-current British legal doctrine implied a special significance for declarations. Standard international law did not differentiate between forms of agreement,[53] but the Foreign Office had been seeking support for a distinction at the London Conference of 1908–1909. At that gathering, the Foreign Office argued that while conventions bound only the parties to the agreement, a declaration could frame a general rule of international law binding upon the whole community.[54] While it is unclear if the Under-Secretary to the Foreign Office knew that such a distinction had been advocated by his government at a major conference held in his capital in the previous year, knowledge of this distinction might imply that he intended to create a rule binding the entire international community.

A tension had evolved within international law between concepts of sovereign equality and formal recognition of a special role for the great powers.[55] This special role had been justified as necessary for the maintenance of a balance of power. While the great powers possessed a de facto ability to shape the diplomatic environment, efforts to legitimize this distinction

---

[51] Notes attached to Goschen to Grey, Oct. 12, 1910, FO 412/96.

[52] Emphasis added. Hardinge to Grey, Aug. 25, 1909, FO 412/96.

[53] Oppenheim, *International Law: A Treatise*, Vol. I, Peace 551–52.

[54] "A la différence d'une 'convention,' créant de règles particulières aux États Contractants, la 'déclaration' projetée doit être, dans l'opinion du Gouvernement de Sa Majesté, la reconnaissance par les Puissances les mieux qualifiées et les plus intéressées, délibérant en commun, que, dans l'état actuel des relations mondiales, il existe véritablement un droit commun des nations, dont elle entend dégager les principes dans l'intérêt de tous." Proceedings of the International Naval Conference held in London, December 1908 – February 1909, Parliamentary Papers, Miscellaneous, No. 5 (1909) Cd. 4555. Lemnitzer recently described a similar strategy contemplated by the Foreign Office when drafting the Declaration of Paris in 1856. *See* Lemnitzer, *Power, Law and the End of Privateering*, 67.

[55] *See* Simpson, *Great Powers and Outlaw States*.

conflicted with principles of universality. At the Hague Conferences, the small powers had espoused the preeminence of sovereign equality, but at a practical cost of impeding negotiations. After the interminable discussions at The Hague, the London Conference represented a swing back toward the special role of the great powers, as well as an attempt to crystallize that distinction. British arms control efforts took place in this evolving legal environment, reflecting tensions in the international system.

EXCHANGE OF INFORMATION NEGOTIATIONS

In the midst of the Dreadnought Scare, Grey suggested an arms agreement to Metternich. Metternich ruled out the possibility of a reduction and reaffirmed Germany's adherence to its Navy Law. Grey countered by offering to regularize an exchange of information.[56] Reiterating the point a week later, Grey suggested the only solution

> was for the two Admiralties to put all their cards on the table, and to let the Naval Attachés see all the yards in which ships were being built, in order to learn all the facts, not of course as to the designs, but as to the actual progress of shipbuilding.[57]

Subsequently, the exchange of information negotiations ran parallel to the broader quest for a naval arms limit. Given the immediate role an exchange of information agreement would have on arms procurement, these negotiations were much more focused than the arms limitation talks, and came close to yielding a practical solution to the arms race dynamic. Significantly, an exchange of information agreement was viewed as an alternative that would allow Britain to maintain its construction policy.

The exchange of information negotiations between 1909 and 1911 offered an alternative form of arms control. An exchange of information agreement would have provided Britain with the essential information to frame its shipbuilding policy, offsetting the apparent ability of Germany to construct capital ships as rapidly as Britain. In mid-1910, Anglo-German naval arms limitation discussions had reached an impasse, focusing on either cutting the German Navy Law or retarding the construction tempo of German ships. Attempting to rekindle discussions, Grey suggested a

---

[56] Grey to Goschen, Mar. 10, 1909, British Documents, Vol. VI, 241–242.
[57] Grey to Goschen, Mar. 17, 1909, British Documents, Vol. VI, 242–243.

third possibility – an agreement not to increase naval construction coupled with an exchange of information.[58] Despite concern expressed in German quarters that an exchange of information would only exacerbate tensions, Admiral Tirpitz agreed to discussions. By early 1911, the framework of the exchange had been negotiated and the form of the agreement was under discussion. Negotiations hit obstacles in the spring and summer of 1911, but by May of that year discussions had proceeded sufficiently for the Foreign Office to place the issue before the Cabinet. By August, the Agadir Crisis halted talks until Germany revived the topic in November. Internal British correspondence intensified in December 1911–January 1912, with the Admiralty significantly reducing the information sought from such an agreement. A final agreement was nearly reached in early 1912, only to be eclipsed by the naval arms discussions of the Haldane mission, before the topic faded from the agenda.

The Admiralty and Foreign Office had experience with information exchanges from other negotiations. While negotiating with Germany in the summer of 1911, the Foreign Office brokered a similar exchange with Japan. Article VII of the Anglo-Japanese Alliance mandated regular consultations by naval and military authorities, which the Admiralty interpreted as requiring the parties to "exchange full information as to their intended building programme each year in advance."[59] Marder noted that the exchange included intended building programs, technical data, as well as force dispositions and other elements of intelligence. He claimed the Admiralty exploited the exchange of information as defense against Japan, in case the alliance was not renewed.[60] The government recognized the strategic potential of such an arrangement, reinforcing the point that the Anglo-German negotiations were not novel.

The exchange of information discussions contained two major elements – an exchange of written details of upcoming construction programs, and procedures for attaché visits to confirm these details. The Admiralty initially sought information on dimensions of vessels, protection, armament, speed, horsepower, as well as when ships would be laid down

---

[58] Memo *attached to* Grey to Goschen, July 29, 1910, No. 28, *in* FO 412/96.
[59] Anglo-Japanese Alliance, Aug. 12, 1905, *in* Hurst, ed., *Key Treaties*, Vol. II, at 771. On the Admiralty interpretation, *see* Anglo-Japanese Agreement of August 12, 1905: Proposals for Concerted Action – Memorandum by the Admiralty, Dec. 7, 1905, CAB 38/10/88 (1905).
[60] Marder, *Dreadnought*, 235.

and completed.[61] The Admiralty communicated its terms to the Foreign Office in December 1910, which forwarded them to the German Imperial Chancellor Bethmann Hollweg in February 1911.[62] The Germans agreed to these terms in March, but requested simultaneous exchanges of information between October 1 and November 15 while leaving the details of inspection visits for naval authorities to arrange.[63] Moreover, the German government sought to make the information provided by each party binding, preventing either party from adding ships or altering their qualities upon learning the construction program of the other.[64]

Before the agreement had been completed, the Admiralty was rethinking the wisdom of the proposal. Internal Admiralty correspondence indicated intense debates over the exchange of information. After receiving Kiderlen's memorandum, Grey requested the Admiralty's opinion. First Sea Lord Arthur Wilson averred "[t]he action of the Foreign Office in making these proposals at all is extremely unfortunate."[65] Graham Greene, then Assistant Secretary to the Board of Admiralty, drafted two letters in reply to the Foreign Office.

One version highlighted Admiralty reservations about and opposition to the exchange of information. Objections arose from the impossibility of binding the government not to alter its naval program after details had been exchanged, as required in the German draft. Britain also had an advantage as Germany set its numbers in advance with its Navy Law. "This has been hitherto a great advantage to us and it is advisable to call attention to it as little as possible."[66] Additionally, details would have been exchanged prior to presenting them to Parliament, and the country would have been bound even before the government had assented

[61] Notes *attached to* Report No. 41 by Naval Attaché, Berlin, Oct. 24, 1910, *in* Exchange of Naval Information between British and German Governments, ADM 1/8195 (1910–1912).

[62] Goschen to Grey, Feb. 8, 1911, FO 412/103.

[63] Goschen to Grey, Mar. 25, 1911, *in* FO 412/103.

[64] Goschen to Grey, Mar. 30, 1911, *in* FO 412/103.

[65] Memo *attached to* Periodical Exchange of Naval Information, Apr. 5, 1911, *in* ADM 1/8195. The memorandum expressed the expectation that a prior communication in November 1910 would have ended the project. However, this earlier document made no mention of ending negotiations, affirmatively listed the information the Admiralty sought from an agreement, and merely expressed pessimism about the chances of success. Memo *attached to* Report No. 41 by Naval Attaché, Berlin, Oct. 24, 1910, *in* ADM 1/8195.

[66] Draft Letter, April 1911, *attached to* Periodical Exchange of Naval Information, Apr. 5, 1911, *in* ADM 1/8195.

to the new building program. Alternatively, if the Admiralty had been allowed to present the program to Parliament before exchanging details with Germany, the information would already have been public. Finally, as Germany was not Britain's only naval rival, it would have been impossible to base its program solely on German construction. The Admiralty segregated ship numbers from construction details in this draft, noting that details were often modified before the ship was laid down, and sought to retain flexibility in this area. Ultimately, the letter expressed a hope "that if circumstances admit of the whole matter being quietly dropped without ostentation or giving offence it would be very desirable to do so."[67]

The Admiralty never sent this letter to the Foreign Office, instead concealing its internal deliberations, while accepting and altering the exchange of information. Two exchanges of information were now envisaged – the first, stating only a "bare number of ships of each type," would be exchanged at a predetermined annual point, and the second, including technical details of tonnage, speed, and armament, would be submitted at the laying of the keel.[68] Subsequent historians have focused on the timing issues raised by these two submissions of information.[69] Depending upon the submission date, one party might have been advantaged over another if the exchange occurred before programs were determined. Moreover if exchanges of information were simultaneous, when the parties would forward technical details remained unclear as these usually evolved after the annual program was set.[70]

The real issue laid not in the timing of the exchange but in British desires to hide details. The Admiralty's desire for secrecy became more salient in 1911. In July, a similar internal debate occurred, with two letters drafted for the Foreign Office – one favoring a less-revealing exchange, and the other upholding a wide exchange.[71] In spite of shifting priorities, the advantages of openness continued to outweigh the advantages of secrecy.

---

[67] *Id.*

[68] Graham Greene to Foreign Office, May 16, 1911, *in* FO 412/103.

[69] *See* Thomas Otte, "'What we desire is confidence': The Search for an Anglo-German Agreement, 1909–1912," in *Arms and Disarmament in Diplomacy*, Keith Hamilton & Edward Johnson, eds., (London: Valentine Mitchell, 2008), 45; Woodward, *Great Britain and the German Navy*, 292 et. seq.

[70] This difficulty was resolved by the Admiralty plan to include technical details with the *next* year's submission of ship numbers. Thomas to Foreign Office, Aug. 21, 1911, *in* FO 412/103.

[71] Memorandum, July 27, 1911, attached to Exchange of Naval Information, July 13, 1911, *in* ADM 1/8195; Thomas to Foreign Office, Aug. 21, 1911, *in* FO 412/103.

Following the Agadir crisis, negotiations lapsed until Germany reopened the matter in November 1911. The Foreign Office provided the Admiralty with another opportunity to revise its goals. The Admiralty considered forwarding the Germans the August 21 letter, but ultimately drafted a new statement of policy, changing the handling of technical details. The initial draft noted "that it would be preferable to let drop altogether the proposal for the interchange of technical information except data of a most general character."[72] Yet the Admiralty ultimately was unwilling to abandon the project, and again submitted terms for exchanging technical information.

The Admiralty noted that the more detailed the information to be exchanged, the greater the difficulty in verifying it, creating risks of mutual suspicion and recrimination. Moreover, the Admiralty disowned any intent to pry into special features of warships, claiming they "are quite content to assume that every ship in each class will represent the last word of the naval science of the constructing Power upon the subject."[73] Now the Admiralty only sought verification of the numbers of ships of each class, and dates of launching and completion. While not explicitly excluding verification of technical details such as displacement, horsepower, and armament, these categories were not discussed in conjunction with verification.[74] Instead, a monetary account of the contract price allotted to hulls, armament, and engines was proposed "… without trenching at all upon the peculiarities of construction, [which] would probably be found in practice to provide a much truer measure of the scale of naval preparation than any other which could be adopted."[75]

This shift was further confirmed by other alterations. An early draft listed "displacement, horse-power, and armament" as details to be exchanged, armament being scratched out and subtly altered with "the number of guns constituting the main armament …"[76] In this fashion, gun caliber was deftly excluded by the Admiralty through focusing on the number of cannons. Additionally, the initial draft specified attaché verification by allowing a "walk through all the yards capable of constructing war vessels"

---

[72] Draft December 1911, *in* Anglo-German Relations – Exchange of Naval Information Between British and German Governments, ADM 116/940B (1902–1914).

[73] Greene to Foreign Office, Dec. 12, 1911, *in* FO 412/103.

[74] An early version even suggested submitting a statement of costs of each ship in lieu of exchanging technical details. Draft December 1911, ADM 116/940B.

[75] Greene to Foreign Office, Dec. 12, 1911, *in* FO 412/103.

[76] Draft of Dec. 8, 1911, attached to Exchange of Naval Information, July 13, 1911, *in* ADM 1/8195.

while a later version modified this to the narrower "inspect the building slips …" This possibly excluded a thorough inspection of the entire navy yard, including the attendant armor, turret, and gun-assembly works.[77] Given the Admiralty's initial desire to regain access to this information and conviction that these subsidiary industries formed a more precise index of warship construction, this exclusion is striking.[78]

The process of naval revolution described by Nicholas Lambert provides a background to this shift.[79] The navy sought continuous improvements in fighting ships to outclass foreign counterparts. What probably ended the Admiralty equivocation about exchanging technical details between August and December was the appointment of the new First Sea Lord Winston Churchill, who immediately determined upon an untried 15-inch gun for the next year's naval program. The *Queen Elizabeth* class, destined to carry these weapons, was designed before the naval ordnance had even been built.[80] So intense was the secrecy surrounding the gun design, that it was even referred to as "the 14-inch experimental" in official documents to hide its true characteristics.[81] As the navy became more comfortable in its lead over Germany, the advantages of subterfuge outweighed openness.

In spite of the Admiralty's declining interest in exchanging technical ship data, its final list of terms in December 1911 included – for the first time – a request for information on merchant ships capable of transformation into auxiliary merchant cruisers.[82] The inclusion of new terms sug-

---

[77] *Compare* Draft of Dec. 8, 1911, *id.*, with Draft of Dec. 5, 1911, *in* ADM 116/940B.

[78] In discussing British requirements from the exchange of information, the naval attaché in Berlin, Captain Watson, specifically mentioned the need to visit both "ship-building and armament yards." Watson to Goschen, Mar. 30, 1911, enclosure in Goschen to Grey, Mar. 30, 1911, *in* FO 412/103. Although it is possible later documents used the more general term shipbuilding yards to include attendant factories, the lack of their explicit inclusion would belie stated Admiralty goals of having all details set in writing.

[79] See, generally, Lambert, *Sir John Fisher's Naval Revolution*.

[80] Moreover, these new super-dreadnoughts were designed with a significant speed advantage over all existing battleships to form a fast tactical wing to the fleet, another element the Admiralty would have been loathe to divulge.

[81] Winston S Churchill, *The World Crisis, 1911–1914* (London: Thornton Butterworth Limited, 1923), 123–24.

[82] Greene to Foreign Office, Dec. 12, 1911, *in* FO 412/103. The Admiralty wanted a list of all merchant steamers of 14 knots speed or greater that Germany intended to arm, with facilities for attaché inspections. *Id.*

gests that the Admiralty still found ways in which an agreement could be useful, and thus did not abandon the project.[83] The Foreign Office communicated these terms to Germany in January 1912, but the matter receded after the Haldane mission.

*   *   *

Grey and the Foreign Office attached great value to an exchange of information agreement, not just as a prelude to an arms treaty. An agreement could have dampened a qualitative arms race by reducing the imperative of "going one better in the dark."[84] Even after it became apparent that continued negotiations for a naval limit would only exacerbate relations with Germany, the Foreign Office continued to pursue an exchange of information.[85] Moreover, during the early months of negotiations, the Admiralty conceded that Britain had more to gain from an agreement as British information was more publicly available than German data.[86] The negotiations were also undertaken in the aftermath of the Dreadnought hoax, which humiliatingly demonstrated the Navy's inability to maintain secrecy.[87]

International law influenced expectations of what an exchange of information could achieve. Law could have depoliticized the issue, regularizing the exchange without increasing ill-feelings that would have accompanied information requests made during crises.[88] Statesmen believed a binding international agreement was necessary to remove the scheduling of attaché visits from the purview of naval authorities, as well as to prevent evasion.[89]

---

[83] *See* Seligmann, *The Royal Navy and the German Threat*, 133–134.

[84] Watson to Goschen, Mar. 30, 1911, *enclosure in* Goschen to Grey, Mar. 30, 1911, *in* FO 412/103.

[85] Grey to Churchill, Apr. 12, 1912, *in* FO 800/87.

[86] Admiralty to Foreign Office, December 3, 1910, *in* ADM 1/8195.

[87] The Dreadnought hoax was an incident in which Virginia Woolf and several friends, masquerading as an Abyssinian delegation in black face and fake beards, received an inspection of the new *Dreadnought* with full honors. Greene to Grey, Feb. 10, 1910, *in* FO 800/87.

[88] Notes *attached to* Diary of Lord Haldane's visit to Berlin, Feb. 10, 1912, Gooch and Temperley, eds., *British Documents*, Vol. VI, 684–85. The 1871 revision of the Black Sea Treaty provided experience, when British diplomats only allowed passage of the Turkish Straits by warships where necessary to enforce the Treaty of Paris. The alternative in 1871 was to allow Turkey to decide when to allow warships to pass, a power of dubious value as it might prove diplomatically impossible to refuse Russian requests during a crisis without worsening relations. *See* Chap. 3. Diplomats made conscious use of legal instruments to remove political implications of decision-making, regularizing a course of conduct.

[89] Notes attached to Goschen to Grey, Mar. 25, 1911, *Id.*, Vol. VI, 610–11.

Responding to a German desire to allow attachés to settle the details, Sir Eyre Crowe noted the German practice of "jockeying" Britain out of negotiated advantages, averring "[t]he only prudent and safe course is to have everything settled and agreed to before anything is signed."[90] The Admiralty echoed these concerns. When negotiating the exchange of technical details, the Admiralty advocated an annual submission of technical details with the following year's program.[91] An international legal agreement would crystallize the terms of an information exchange, reducing the risk of jockeying or noncompliance.

Along with firm obligations, the Foreign Office and Admiralty pursued unambiguous terms to facilitate compliance. The Admiralty stressed the need for "simple *and easily verifiable* facts ..." and warned against the risk of confusion and recrimination if minute details needed to be conveyed and confirmed.[92] To avoid the ambiguity surrounding the completion date of warships, the Admiralty suggested that the date of the public ceremony attendant with launching could be used as an easily confirmed benchmark.[93]

Correspondence between the Foreign Office and the Admiralty indicated that they anticipated a legally binding agreement. Internal January 1911 discussions showed Admiralty concerns that the document be "sufficiently elastic to permit the inclusion of other items which ... might hereafter acquire importance and special significance."[94] Further negotiations confirmed expectations that the parties contemplated a binding engagement. The German reply in the spring of 1911 suggested that once information had been exchanged, no alteration would be allowed. While this would have prevented either party from exploiting the infor-

---

[90] Notes attached to de Salis to Grey, July 1, 1911, *Id.*, Vol. VI, 640–41. Crowe noted "[w]e have had repeated and unhappy experience of the practice of concluding agreements and leaving some essential part to be arranged subsequently. It is to my mind an absolutely unsound method ..." *Id.*

[91] Notes, July 27, 1911, attached to Exchange of Naval Information, July 13, 1911, ADM 1/8195.

[92] [Italics added.] Greene to Foreign Office, Dec. 12, 1911, *in* FO 412/103.

[93] Draft Letter to Foreign Office, April 1911, attached to Periodical Exchange of Naval Information, Apr. 5, 1911, *in* ADM 1/8195. After launching, ships underwent significant further construction, trials, and fitting out, which often ran over a year, making a firm date for when the ship was actually fit for naval service difficult to determine.

[94] Grey to Goschen, Jan. 27, 1911, FO 412/103. *See also* Greene to Crowe, Jan. 11, 1911, *and* Crowe to Greene, Jan. 12, 1911, *both in* ADM 116/940B.

mation by altering its shipbuilding program, it would also convert the agreement into an annual naval arms control limit. The Admiralty and the Foreign Office recognized the implications of such an arrangement and refused to convert the exchange of information into a naval arms agreement.[95] British hesitation about converting an exchange of information into a naval arms treaty reflected fears about the repercussions of limiting Britain to a bilateral agreement while third parties continued to build.[96] Consistent with an exchange of information, the British wished to allow alterations to the information, but only after disclosing the changes to the other party.[97] Secretary of State Kiderlen had previously held that if either party needed to modify the details, these modifications would form the basis of "a friendly discussion" between the parties, and incorporated these provisions into the terms of the agreement.[98] Ultimately, the parties contemplated a binding agreement, but the legal obligations only extended to exchanging information.

While both German and British negotiators sought a simple document, favoring an exchange of notes over a more formal agreement,[99] a binding treaty could have been created through an exchange of notes. By reducing the formality, the parties could have reduced the public glare that would accompany an armaments agreement, reaching an arrangement that might otherwise have been politically impossible. Similarly, the agreement was easier to complete than an arms limitation treaty, as it intruded less conspicuously into naval construction.

* * *

Before the agreement was completed, the strategic context had shifted. While Germany remained willing to complete the agreement, by late 1911, the Admiralty was no longer interested. Stevenson has argued that the Anglo-German naval arms race peaked after 1909, and by 1912 the new relationship was being solidified, alleviating German fears of a Copenhagen-style pre-emptive strike.[100] After the destabilizing

[95] Admiralty to Foreign Office, May 16, 1911, *in* FO 412/103.
[96] Notes attached to Goschen to Grey, Mar. 30, 1911, *in* FO 412/103.
[97] Grey to Goschen, June 1, 1911, *in* FO 412/103.
[98] Goschen to Grey, Mar. 30, 1911; De Salis to Grey, July 1, 1911, *both in* FO 412/103.
[99] Goschen to Grey, Feb. 7, 1911, *in* FO 412/103.
[100] Stevenson, *Armaments and the Coming of War*, 174–75.

introduction of the *Dreadnought*, Britain also gained confidence when the naval ratio stabilized.

The exchange of information was most relevant in the 1909–1912 transition period. While both states had fewer than ten dreadnoughts, the margin of superiority was a matter of one year's construction program, and Britain feared that Germany might secretly close the gap in naval construction. Once no single year's program could undermine the British margin of superiority, Britain gained confidence, and the Admiralty lost interest in the exchange and again saw the advantages in the secretive introduction of new technology, like the 15-inch gun. Yet during that transition period, an exchange of information was sought in order to remove such issues as attaché visits from the hands of naval officials and setting them as a matter of course. International law brought regularity to the equation. When attempting to maintain open, if not cordial, relations in the face of a series of international crises, the de-politicization of armaments policy provided a means of removing one area of contention.

THE NAVAL HOLIDAY AND INFORMAL ARMS CONTROL

In addition to treaty negotiations, Britain also sought an informal, non-binding arrangement with Germany to limit naval armaments. Advocacy of an informal agreement provides insight into the role of law, indicating where law was perceived as unnecessary or disadvantageous. Conversely, the ambiguities of informal agreements highlight the contributions of law to arms control. Throughout the years of Anglo-German negotiations, various statesmen questioned the utility of formal negotiations, believing that the quest for a treaty only worsened relations and added impetus to the arms race.[101] During the visit of King Edward VII to Cronberg in 1908, Hardinge suggested an informal arrangement as an alternative to a binding treaty. "Reverting to the general question of naval expenditure, I expressed the hope that moderate counsels would still prevail, and

---

[101] *See, e.g.* Lascelles to Grey, August 14, 1908; Goschen to Nicolson, October 28, 1910, *both in* Gooch and Temperley, eds., *British Documents*, Vol. VI, 181–82, 539; Minutes of Eyre Crowe, February 18, 1913, in Goschen to Grey, February 10, 1913, Gooch and Temperley, eds., *British Documents*, Vol. IX, 669, 71. The less Britain protested German naval construction, the less political fuel would be fed to the German naval party. Report by Captain Watson, enclosure no. 2 in Goschen to Grey, October 15, 1913, Gooch and Temperley, eds., *British Documents*, Vol. IX, 710, 14.

that although friendly discussion between the two Governments might as the Emperor insisted, be barred, still I was convinced that His Majesty's Government *would require no written formula nor verbal statement* from the German Government but only a visible proof that the programme of naval construction had been modified or slackened, in order to make a similar modification or slackening in their own."[102] By making the offer, the Foreign Office hoped to circumvent the domestic disapproval in Germany that would be engendered by a formal renunciation of the Navy Law.

A non-binding agreement remained a possibility throughout subsequent negotiations, and was most squarely raised by Churchill's naval holiday proposals in 1912–1913. He presented his first naval estimates as First Lord in March 1912, shortly after the unsuccessful Haldane mission indicated that formal arms control had reached an impasse. When justifying the large naval claims, he linked expenditure squarely to Germany, openly admitting the 60 percent standard which had been in place since 1909, and seeking an informal solution. He suggested a "naval holiday," whereby neither party would commence construction of new warships, though without any formal obligation. "Here, then, is a perfectly plain and simple plan of arrangement whereby without diplomatic negotiation, without any bargaining, *without the slightest restriction upon the sovereign freedom of either Power*, this keen and costly naval rivalry can be at any time abated."[103] Churchill coupled the offer with a threat to match any German capital ship construction beyond the current Navy Law at a rate of two to one. As Germany was then debating expansion of the Navy Law, this would create a disincentive for further increases. Finally, Churchill incorporated the standard caveat for third-party construction, pledging Britain only "in the absence of any unexpected development in other countries."[104]

One major difference between formal and informal agreements lay in the vagueness of informal terms, which could be both an advantage and a disadvantage. Misunderstanding or intentional misrepresentation could be exploited to build beyond the tacitly agreed levels. During the Dreadnought Scare in 1909, vagueness increased mistrust, such as when Metternich assured Britain about the number of dreadnoughts Germany was building, but excluded battlecruisers from the figure.[105] Churchill's

---

[102] Emphasis Added. Memorandum by Hardinge, Aug. 16, 1908, Gooch and Temperley, eds., *British Documents*, Vol. VI, 187.

[103] Emphasis added. Churchill, *Hansard*, 5th ser., XXXV, 1558, Mar. 18, 1912.

[104] *Id.* 1556.

[105] Grey to Goschen, Mar. 17, 1909, Gooch and Temperley, eds., *British Documents*, Vol. VI, 242–44.

offer of a ratio in 1912 not only contained the by-then standard caveat for third-party construction, but also excluded dreadnoughts building for British colonies and dominions. Australia and New Zealand had purchased battlecruisers in 1909, New Zealand presenting its vessel to the British Navy, while Malaya donated a super-dreadnought of the *Queen Elizabeth* class and the Admiralty courted the Canadian government for an order of three battleships.[106] Grey exploited informal arms discussions in 1913 to avoid explaining the status of these colonial vessels under the 1.6–1 ratio.[107] Britain could also exploit private industrial resources by purchasing dreadnoughts built for other nations in British yards. Moreover, as Germany shifted funding from its navy to its army, Britain had less interest in tying itself to a formal ratio, while conversely Tirpitz's interest increased.[108]

Both sides sought to circumvent the tacit naval balance through third-party construction, Germany through Austria-Hungary and Italy, Britain through construction by dominions and colonies, and both utilized naval agreements with alliance and entente partners to alter the naval balance.[109] Furthermore, when the Canadian Parliament refused plans to build dreadnoughts in the summer of 1913, the Admiralty sought British replacements, drawing complaints from Germany.[110] The balance broke down even before the war, although diminishing German efforts in the naval arms race masked this breakdown.

The Foreign Office had long-standing objections to informal arrangements, Crowe complaining in 1909 of "false and non-binding assurances,"[111] and again opposing an informal understanding arising from the Haldane mission.

---

[106] Gardiner, ed., *Conway's 1906–1921*. On the British desire for Canadian dreadnoughts, *see for example* Draft Memorandum for Publication, Sep. 20, 1912, CAB 37/112/105 (1912).

[107] Grey to Goschen, Mar. 5, 1913, Gooch and Temperley, eds., *British Documents*, Vol. IX, 687–88.

[108] John H. Maurer, "The Anglo-German Naval Rivalry and Informal Arms Control, 1912–1914," *Journal of Conflict Resolution* 36, no. 2 (1992): 300.

[109] *Id.* at 296. Maurer also noted that the agreement did not halt the qualitative aspects of the arms race either. *Id.* at 298–99.

[110] Goschen to Nicholson, June 5, 1913, Gooch and Temperley, eds., *British Documents*, Vol. IX, 704–05.

[111] Notes *attached to* Goschen to Grey, Mar. 23, 1909, *Id.*, Vol. VI, 247–49.

Such a form of "understanding" has of course no binding effect. If a political incident intervened, or if merely the German gov[ernmen]t were to renew the press campaign against this country which they allowed to flourish during the last 6 months, they would be fully justified in saying that, in view of the state of public feeling, they could not, with the best intention, avoid going beyond their assurances. Therefore an assurance, having no conventional force, is useless for the only purpose for which we should require it.[112]

British opinion changed as it became apparent that formal arms control initiatives only worsened relations with Germany, and as the necessity for a limit was receding.

Agreements codified in treaties provided a stronger statement than an informal arrangement. Law provided clearer statements to the international community, thereby increasing predictability.[113] Foreign Office notes continuously indicated a belief that Germany would be less likely to breach a binding commitment. A non-binding agreement provided a less certain alternative, which could function if an unequivocal exchange of information agreement were in place.

CONCLUSION

By 1914, British arms control policy reflected a richer understanding of the opportunities and limits of international law. In Anglo-German negotiations, statesmen recognized that treaties could restrain Germany more effectively than non- binding understandings, reducing the risk of the Wilhelmine government "jockeying" Britain out of agreed concessions. Legal strategies could be integrated seamlessly with naval construction policy, allowing simple practices like attaché visits to increase predictability in international affairs. Statesmen perceived that law could assist in depoliticizing the volatile topic of warship construction, providing space for the German government to rein in armaments while removing exchanges of information from the whims of admiralties.

Yet if law provided opportunities, statesmen acknowledged its limitations. The Foreign Office feared Germany might breach treaty obligations,

---

[112] Notes *attached to* Diary of Lord Haldane's Visit to Berlin, Feb. 10, 1912, *Id.*, Vol. VI, 684–85.

[113] Alternatively, a secret treaty, as contemplated by Crowe, might also halt the arms race without causing a political uproar in Germany, although Britain would be reluctant to enter such an agreement. *Id.*

but responded by seeking firm, clear terms. For instance, when negotiating the exchange of information, the Admiralty repeatedly pursued simple and easily verifiable facts to prevent violations. The inability of bilateral Anglo-German negotiations to respond to a multilateral strategic situation impeded a deal. In addressing a multilateral arms competition, diplomats refused to bind Britain to a bilateral agreement with Germany unless these third party concerns were addressed. The Foreign Office explored creative legal strategies such as issuing a wide-ranging declaration or including an escape clause in a treaty. Yet the inability to regulate a global environment through a bilateral treaty hindered Anglo-German negotiations. While law had its limits, British official opinion generally recognized its utility.

Unfamiliarity with international law did not prevent statesmen from resolving the naval arms race by agreement prior to the First World War. The British record indicates that the opportunities of law were clearly understood and incorporated into diplomacy. In fact, Britain's opposition to Latin American arms control indicated a clear belief that such a treaty was likely to succeed, rather than skepticism. The Foreign Office recognized how law could contribute to national security and exploited the possibilities offered by treaties. Negotiations foundered on other rocks, in particular, German insistence on a political treaty, and the resultant mistrust it engendered in Britain. Had political will been present, international law would have provided a way.

CHAPTER 10

Conclusion

By 1914, Britain had significant experience employing international law as part of security planning. Britain had been central in the framing of numerous precedents for arms limitation, indicating an understanding of the potential of law in this area. The Anglo-French Declarations of 1787, the Rush-Bagot Agreement of 1817, the Black Sea Treaty of 1856, and the 1902 Chilean-Argentine Naval Arms Treaty had all been negotiated by British statesmen. The 1868 St. Petersburg Declaration and the Hague Conventions and Declarations of 1899 and 1907 all reflected British influence, while the 1897 Greco-Turkish negotiations and 1909–1912 Anglo-German talks both exemplified a high degree of comfort working with legal arms limits. Statesmen possessed and recognized the range of legal precedents for limiting armaments, and drew on these precedents when they advanced British interests.

Likewise, when statesmen disavowed the possibility of legal limits, they often did so for reasons of policy, rather than a lack of belief in the potential of law. In 1899, the legal impossibility of disarmament had been used to foil inconvenient arms limitation proposals that no great power wanted yet could not openly denounce. Salisbury's true opinion can be gleaned from his secret naval arms limit proposal to Russia that year, as well as his representatives' offer to accept a submarine ban at The Hague. Legal qualms had a way of disappearing when the limit advanced British interests. Similarly, Grey's opposition to Latin American arms control after 1908 reflected a cold calculation of Britain's interests, not legal impossibility.

© The Editor(s) (if applicable) and The Author(s) 2016   285
S.A. Keefer, *The Law of Nations and Britain's Quest for Naval Security*, DOI 10.1007/978-3-319-39645-3_10

While the Foreign Office debated the usefulness and wisdom of treaties, and while not every politician grasped the nuances of international law, overall the government comprehended the opportunities offered by law.

By the decade prior to 1914, the terms of post-war naval arms control had already taken shape. Before 1899, imprecise terminology conflated arms control with disarmament, but by 1914 the distinction between the two concepts had been established. Legal terminology evolved as greater experience was gained, and as scholars increasingly circulated that knowledge after 1899. Britain had incorporated or evaluated numerous methods for limiting armaments. Ship numbers, particularly capital ships numbers, had long served as the preferred criteria, figuring in the 1817, 1856, and 1902 agreements. Numbers were easily verifiable and allowed simple calculations of relative power, and at The Hague in 1907 and in the subsequent Anglo-German negotiations the Admiralty continued to prefer this form of regulation. Technical details including ship weight, vessel dimensions, protection, speed, horsepower, and armament – both gun caliber and numbers – had all been proposed as limitation terms. The Admiralty consistently sought terms that could be easily verified through existing diplomatic means, and steadfastly opposed forms of limitation that sacrificed British advantages, such as battleship size limits in 1907. Concepts such as naval construction holidays, expenditure limitations, exchanges of information, the role of naval bases in calculating relative naval strength, and linkage of naval and land armaments had all been debated. These concepts all found their way into naval arms negotiations in the 1920s and 1930s, providing a framework for future discussions. Pre-war naval arms control left an extensive legacy.[1] Arms limitation was not a novelty in the pre-war Foreign Office.

Several other larger themes also emerge from the pre-war experience. First, to be properly understood, arms limitation negotiations from 1899 to 1914 need to be viewed in their nineteenth-century context, rather than as the first steps in twentieth-century developments. The nineteenth-century precedents mentioned above served as the starting point for British arms control policy at The Hague and in Anglo-German negotiations.

---

[1] *See*, for example, J. W. Headlam-Morley, Historical Summary of Proposals for the Reduction of Armaments, Oct. 27, 1921, Annex P *in* Washington Conference Memoranda 1921, FO 412/118 (1921) listing naval arms control agreements and negotiations including the 1817, 1899, 1902, and 1907 precedents.

Moreover, in 1909 when Britain asserted the customary legal right of a state to demand assurances from a neighbor engaged in an arms buildup, it drew upon traditional diplomatic practice. Britain had similarly sought assurances from Russia in 1833, and France in 1793 and 1840, and had also attempted to manage competition with France in the 1860s through diplomatic discussions. The past provided a model for peacefully managing competition, with traditional international law serving as a framework for negotiations.

When Britain prepared for the 1899 Hague Peace Conference, its representatives studied the 1868 St. Petersburg Declaration and the 1874 Brussels Conference as models for the probable political dynamic at the gathering and the most likely form of a final agreement. The Czar's circular in 1898 was little different from earlier proposals by French Emperor Napoleon III or Czar Alexander I, and diplomats approached the conference with these inauspicious examples in mind. In later negotiations, like the Paris Aerial Navigation Conference of 1910, the Foreign Office also drew upon the political model of the 1874 Brussels Conference, attempting to unite the smaller states against the large continental military powers. Expectations at turn-of-the-century conferences were greatly influenced by the results of similar initiatives in the past.

One of the core assumptions of the international legal system, regarding state enforcement of obligations and war, revealed beliefs about future conflict. War was the ultimate form of state enforcement, and statesmen predicated the international system on a belief in limited wars. Britain expected rules of war to be enforced by neutral great powers. Moreover, statesmen designed these rules of war to foster a rapid return to peaceful relations, hoping to minimize enmity by setting clear standards of expected behavior. The expectations encapsulated in rules of war can only be explained in terms of the world before 1914, not what came afterwards.

The tendency in historiography has been to obscure the nineteenth-century roots of pre-war arms control. Works have either consigned the Hague Conferences to a wistful footnote about a doomed counter-current before the deluge in 1914, or placed arms limitation in the context of the post-1919 evolution of international legal institutions. The former view focuses on the peace movement, itself an ephemeral manifestation, while ignoring state interest. The latter view tends to define law in terms of ever more-powerful international institutions, seeking precursors before 1914. This in turn overlooks how law functioned at the turn of the century, and tends to underestimate the influence of these earlier treaties.

Second, British statesmen's pragmatic approach to law remained constant over the nineteenth century. In spite of terminological ambiguity surrounding disarmament before 1899, statesmen recognized how arms limitation would function. Diplomats recognized that treaties could not determine the behavior of competing states, but could influence actions as an "obstacle, rather than a barrier." In spite of technical violations, Britain maintained the 1817 Rush-Bagot Agreement after repeated internal debates from the 1890s to 1912. These deliberations acknowledged small-scale American breaches, but held that the treaty prevented worse abuses, affirming that it was better "to let sleeping dogs lie." Similarly, Palmerston expected Russia to eventually abrogate the 1856 Black Sea Treaty. His administration had to design an agreement that could best meet British interests in the roughly ten years it expected the treaty to last. In the event, the treaty proved a significant obstacle: Despite strenuous efforts by the Czar, Russia took 14 years to overturn the treaty. This outlook towards law colored the overall British negotiating position at The Hague in 1907. When discussing a renewal of the 1899 ban on aerial bombardment at the Second Hague Peace Conference, the Foreign Office recognized that law could never guarantee compliance. However, the creation of a general norm would raise the political costs of violations, reducing the likelihood of this form of attack. On repeated occasions, British diplomats crafted agreements that could advance national interests while recognizing the limitations of law.

Nor were there major divides between Conservatives and Liberals in their approach toward legalized arms control. While at times the parties differed on the necessity of arms limitation, they agreed on how treaty limits would function. The great Liberal drive for economy after 1905 exaggerated the differences between the parties on arms limitation. However, Conservatives also championed arms control when they viewed it as being in the national interest. Balfour's administration had led the push for a ban on naval mines, and had even contemplated calling a conference to ban these mines before the Second Hague Peace Conference was organized. Even Salisbury, an apparent critic of arms limitation before the Hague Conference of 1899, secretly parlayed for a naval arms agreement with Russia in March of that year, after spending the previous year renegotiating an arms limit with the United States, and he publicly sought a ban on submarines at The Hague. Despite outward differences, both parties perceived advantages in law and employed it in arms control strategies.

Statesmen from both parties sought agreements that would be workable in the existing legal system. Britain ruled out complex verification systems with France in 1787 as impractical, whittled down the terms of the Black Sea neutralization in 1856 to easily ascertainable warship characteristics, and rejected grandiose Austrian arms limitation projects for the Black Sea in 1871 as unworkable. The exchange of information discussions featured a quest for "simple and easily verifiable facts" while exploiting traditional diplomatic procedures such as attaché visits. Statesmen were untroubled by the lack of international organizations before 1914. Rather than seeking impractical institutions to manage their security, they moved nimbly within the existing system.

Third, international law and arms rivalry developed their own dynamic, in turn influencing popular perceptions of international law. Up to the 1890s, Britain had been able to focus on two potential European rivals, usually France and Russia. The rise of multiple naval competitors in the 1890s complicated this calculation. This problem was then compounded by the wide acceptance of the *Dreadnought* as the standard in battleship construction, bringing smaller states more directly into reckonings of power. Bilateral treaty models had evolved to respond to limited naval competition, as with the Great Lakes or Argentine-Chilean rivalries and buttressed the more often-used customary legal right to demand assurances in response to naval build-ups, as they had been employed with France and Russia. As competition became widespread, it became increasingly likely that multilateral negotiations would be needed, yet early legal thought on multilateral arms limitation had featured the cession of significant amounts of state power to international institutions, in effect the "international police force." In order for any progress to be made, these unrealistic proposals had to be discarded in favor of workable multilateral solutions. Thus, the increasingly multinational arms race influenced the development of international law, by pushing negotiations from the utopian into the pragmatic.

While pragmatism underlay these negotiations, the evolving arms race provided an opportunity for learning, by applying concepts of law in new contexts. Scholars in the nineteenth century predicated disarmament schemes around ideals of progressive codification of international law and the goal of gradually building a system of world government that would make disarmament possible. Twentieth-century scholarly works shifted to more limited roles for international institutions in managing arms competition. Lord Salisbury's apparently inconsistent views, denouncing arms limitation at The Hague as unenforceable while negotiating arms control with the United States and Russia, may reflect more than disingenuousness. There may have been an implicit assumption that what was at stake at The Hague could only be viewed as world government, fundamentally differing from the practical bilateral agreements of the past. Yet limited agreements could be adapted to the new forum. By the Second Hague Peace Conference, the Foreign Office showed far greater interest in building a network of legal agreements strengthening British interests, arriving with a clear agenda.

A workable system of arms control, as with a workable system of international law, involved a larger "give-and-take" of numerous limited agreements often designed to solve immediate problems rather than to set permanent relationships. Statesmen employed agreements in an attempt to channel the rapid development of military technology in the industrial age into acceptable, and less strategically destabilizing, weapons. Limitations of mines, auxiliary cruisers, aerial bombardment, expanding and exploding bullets, and poison gas reflected attempts to regulate discrete armaments in order to advance national interest. Rather than resulting in the creation of international government, arms control initiatives reinforced the role of states in the international system.

The interlocking naval arms races required further adjustments as it became clear that the Hague Conference proved too unwieldy for real negotiations. When a question solely concerned two or three great powers, this could be resolved by direct negotiation, but when all the great powers, as well as many small countries, were acquiring dreadnoughts, a multilateral solution was required. The Foreign Office considered several strategies. The naval holiday with Germany could have provided an opportunity, by effectively creating an annual, if informal, arms control agreement that could be exited if either state was threatened by third-party construction. Building on the model of the 1908–1909 London Conference, a declaration might be used in an attempt to bind the entire community, without the necessity of conducting multilateral negotiations. The terms could be enforced through great power domination of finance and construction facilities, a lesson Britain fully understood from ongoing Latin American arms discussions between 1900 and 1914. Ultimately, the Washington Treaty combined these approaches in 1922, with the great powers setting qualitative terms for warship exports, creating a de facto global treaty regime.[2]

[2] Scott Keefer, "'Big Ships Cause Big Wars, Little Ships Cause Little Wars, and No Ships Cause No Wars:' International Law and Arms Control Policy in the Interwar Era," in *War, Society, and the Ingenious Arts: Essays in Honor of Thomas H. Buckley*, Kelly K. Chaves and William A. Crafton, eds., (Tulsa: University of Tulsa Press, 2009), 45.

A fourth theme relates to the nature of that extant international system and the role of great powers within it. In the nineteenth century, the central role played by the great powers in shaping international law became more overt. This role had long been justified as necessary in order to uphold a balance of power, and thus to maintain peace. However, in the past, this precedence had been tacit, and diplomats still acknowledged the theoretical sovereign equality of states. By the late nineteenth century, international lawyers sought to legitimize the de facto preeminence of the great powers, formally legitimizing their special capacity to make law.

The small states' desire for a legal system based on sovereign equality and great powers quest for an unfettered ability to resolve world questions led to tensions. Small states sought greater representation at the Hague Conferences, while the great powers sought the ability to resolve questions among themselves unimpeded by unwieldy negotiations with dozens of states. In response to this development, the British Foreign Office sought to limit invitations to the 1908–1909 London Conference to the great powers. The Foreign Office also anticipated that the resulting 1909 Declaration of London would be enforced by the International Prize Court against the small powers. The Foreign Office expected rules crafted by the states most interested in naval warfare, the great powers, would bind the entire legal community without its consent.

Similarly, the Foreign Office often sought only great power consensus in setting arms control norms. In 1899, Goschen directed his naval reduction offer in Parliament to the other great powers. At the 1899 Hague Conference, when Russia requested a unanimous ban on submarines, the British delegation replied that only great power adherence was necessary to make the rule effective. In planning for the Second Hague Peace Conference, the key Foreign Office memoranda by Hurst contemplated an arms control system monitored by the great powers. In 1909, in recommending an armament declaration to halt the dreadnought race, Hardinge probably advocated this type of instrument to allow enforcement of the new regulations against the smaller states. The Foreign Office generally sought consensus among the great powers as a prerequisite, rather than universality, which was significantly more difficult to achieve. While near-universal adherence to arms control norms placed added pressure on recalcitrant states to comply, security could more often be advanced through the participation of the largest naval powers.

The great powers exploited their predominance in imposing arms limits. When the concert of the powers settled the 1897 Greco-Turkish War, they contemplated stripping the Greek Navy of its battleships. Moreover, the great powers had stripped Montenegro of the right to maintain warships in the Treaty of Berlin of 1878,[3] theoretical though that right may have been. The British role in the 1902 Chilean-Argentine Naval Arms Treaty followed this pattern. British financiers threatened to withhold funding for further warships, while British shipyards agreed not to deliver battleships destined for Chile, allowing the Foreign Office to monitor the terms of the agreement. The 1856 Black Sea Treaty imposed by Britain, Austria, and France also falls into this category, as defeated Russia had little real choice about the terms of this agreement. While the disparity in power between Russia and its adversaries was temporary, it nonetheless was real and decisively influenced the 1856 negotiations.

The role of the great powers relates, in turn, to a fifth theme. Law was most effective when it took into account national interest and power. The British government acknowledged this reality when discussing the fate of the Black Sea Treaty in 1871. When confronted with the collapse of that treaty, Parliament debated two solutions – either create powerful international legal institutions or craft agreements that states could enforce. The government accepted the latter solution, advocating the pragmatic enforcement of treaties through great power participation rather than world government.

The creation of world government was unrealistic in 1871, but by 1918 popular opinion supported the creation of powerful international institutions. The breakdown of international order in the Great War led to the belief that inadequate legal institutions contributed to conflict, and that world government could prevent a recurrence of hostilities. Historians interpreted pre-war arms limitation as being merely the first steps in progressive codification of international law, while overlooking the achievements of the old system.

Pre-war lawyers often recognized that world government was a chimera. The decision to work within the existing system of international law reflected as much a belief in the impracticality of world government as a recognition that states lacked support for powerful institutions. Advocacy of world government came at a cost in the effectiveness of extant international law.

---

[3] Treaty of Berlin, Art. XXIX.

Is it quite certain that if International Law is discredited now, we shall not need its help, before the Powers will be ready to replace the *bâtons* of their marshals by those of the Universal Constabulary? Surely, to diminish the authority of an existing law by slighting allusions to it, made through admiration of an alternative system which is entirely speculative and unpractical, is a course leading directly to anarchy.[4]

The quest for world government after 1919 obscured the accomplishments in the pre-war era and failed to address a key element of the international legal system – state power. Strong international institutions merely channeled state interest, and a system based on these institutions was still no stronger than the mutual interests of the great powers anchoring it. Populations and politicians placed too great a faith in strong international institutions, and when these institutions also failed to prevent war, the failure undermined support for an older and more practical form of international law. Only through understanding how international law functions as an element of diplomacy, can publics, politicians, and historians properly assess what law can and cannot achieve. In order for law to play a role in world affairs, such a pragmatic evaluation is essential.

[4] Baty, "The Basis of International Law," 280–81.

BIBLIOGRAPHY

UNPUBLISHED PRIMARY SOURCES

Cabinet, Foreign Office, War Office, Committee of Imperial Defence, and Colonial Office papers; The National Archives, Kew.
Ardagh MSS, Public Record Office, Kew.
Asquith MSS, Bodleian Library, Oxford.
Campbell-Bannerman MSS, British Library.
Clarendon MSS, Bodleian Library, Oxford.
Crowe MSS, Bodleian Library, Oxford.
Grey MSS, Public Record Office, Kew.
Salisbury MSS, Hatfield House.
Satow MSS, Public Record Office, Kew.
Selborne MSS, Bodleian Library, Oxford.

ADMIRALTY ARCHIVES, THE NATIONAL ARCHIVES, KEW

ADM 1/7340b, American Lakes: Naval Force to be Maintained by United States and Great Britain, (1897-1898).
ADM 1/7474, Canada: American Warships on the Great Lakes, (1892-1905).
ADM 1/8195, Exchange of Naval Information between British and German Governments, (1910-1912).
ADM 3/262, Admiralty Special Minutes, (1816-1824).
ADM 116/98, Peace Conference, (1899-1900).

© The Editor(s) (if applicable) and The Author(s) 2016
S.A. Keefer, *The Law of Nations and Britain's Quest for Naval Security*, DOI 10.1007/978-3-319-39645-3

ADM 116/1079, London Conference on International Maritime Law, (1908-1909).

ADM 116/1080, London Conference on International Maritime Law, (1908-1909).

ADM 116/940B, Anglo-German Relations – Exchange of Naval Information Between British and German Governments, (1902-1914).

CABINET ARCHIVES, THE NATIONAL ARCHIVES, KEW

CAB 37/59/142, Draft Dispatch from Lansdowne to MacDonald, Dec. 24, 1901, (1901).

CAB 37/72/137, Correspondence Relating to the Dogger Bank Incident, (Nov. 3, 1904).

CAB 37/73/134, Law Officers of the Crown to the Marquis of Lansdowne. (Oct. 29, 1904).

CAB 37/84/76, Extract from Report of British Delegates to the Conference on Wireless Telegraphy at Berlin. (Oct. 23, 1906).

CAB 37/86/14, Walton, John , et. al. Right of Capture of Private Property at Sea. (8 Feb. 1907).

CAB 37/87/41,Geoffray, M. Memorandum. (Apr. 6, 1907).

CAB 37/87/42, Walton Committee. Report of the Inter-Departmental Committee appointed to consider the Subjects which may arise for Discussion at the Second Peace Conference. (Apr. 11, 1907).

CAB 37/88/58, Lord Loreburn. Immunity of Private Property at Sea in Time of War. (n.d., c. Apr. 1907).

CAB 37/89/63, Foreign Office. Memorandum. (May 31, 1907).

CAB 37/90/101, Lord Tweedmouth, Future Battleship Building, Nov. 21, 1907, (1907).

CAB 37/91/2, Edmund Slade, Note Drawn up at the Request of the First Lord of the Admiralty by the Director of Naval Intelligence, Jan. 8, 1908, (1908).

CAB 37/100/97, Battleship Building Programmes of Great Britain, Germany, France, United States, Italy, and Austria (June 1909), July 14, 1909, (1909).

CAB 37/103/32, Churchill, Naval Expenditure, July 15, 1910, (1910).

CAB 37/105/6, The Declaration of London from the Point of View of the Belligerent Rights of Great Britain, Feb. 1, 1911, (1911).

CAB 37/112/100, Memorandum on the General Naval Situation, Aug. 26, 1912, (1912).

CAB 37/112/105, Draft Memorandum for Publication, Sep. 20, 1912, (1912).

CAB 37/118/6, German Navy Law and Comparisons with Strength of the Royal Navy [an incomplete paper], Jan. 10, 1914, (1914).

CAB 37/119/48, Third Peace Conference, Mar. 24, 1914, (1914).

CAB 41/30/69, [Campbell-Bannerman] Cabinet Letters, (1906).CAB 41/31/21, [Campbell-Bannerman] Cabinet Letters, (1907).

Committee of Imperial Defence, Cabinet Archives, The National Archives, Kew

CAB 4/1/42B, Chamberlain, Austen. Submarine Mine Defences. (Nov. 13, 1904).

CAB 4/1/52 B, Committee of Imperial Defence. Submarine Automatic Mines. (Mar. 13, 1905).

CAB 38/8/13, Defence of Canada: Memorandum by the Admiralty. (Feb. 24, 1905).

CAB 38/10/76, The Hague Conference: Notes on Subjects which might be raised by Great Britain or by other Powers. (Oct. 26, 1905).

CAB 38/10/88, Anglo-Japanese Agreement of August 12, 1905: Proposals for Concerted Action – Memorandum by the Admiralty, Dec. 7, 1905, (1905).

CAB 38/11/17, Clarke, George S. The Hague Conference: Arbitration and Reduction of Armaments. (Apr. 20, 1906).

CAB 38/11/20, The Hague Conference. (May 15, 1906).

CAB 38/12/47, Wireless Telegraphy and the Berlin Conference. (July 28, 1906).

CAB 38/12/51, Wireless Telegraphy. (Sep. 14, 1906).

CAB 38/13/14, Memorandum: The Wireless Telegraphy Conference of 1906. (Mar. 26, 1907).

CAB 38/16/11, The International Conference on Aerial Navigation, July 11, 1910, (1910).

CAB 38/19/32, Report of the Technical Sub-Committee of the Committee of Imperial Defence on Aerial Navigation, Airships, July 30, 1912, (1912).

CAB 38/19/60, Proceedings of the Committee of Imperial Defence with reference to the International Conference on Aerial Navigation 1910, (1910).

CAB 38/24/21, The Royal Flying Corps, First Annual Report by the Air Committee, Committee of Imperial Defence, June 7, 1913, (1913).

CAB 38/27/22, The Royal Flying Corps, Second Annual Report by the Air Committee, Committee of Imperial Defence, May 9, 1914, (1914).

Colonial Office Archives, The National Archives, Kew

CO 537/496, War Vessels on the Great Lakes, (Mar. 7, 1912).

Foreign Office Archives, The National Archives, Kew

FO 5/113, Castlereagh to Bagot, Drafts, (1816).

FO 5/114, Bagot to Castlereagh, (1816).

FO 5/115, Bagot to Castlereagh, (1816).

FO 5/2598, Armed Ships on the Great Lakes, (1892-1905).

FO 16/316, Chile – Diplomatic, (1898).

FO 16/317, Chile – Diplomatic, (1898).

FO 16/324, Chile – Diplomatic, (1899).

FO 16/331, Chile – Diplomatic, (1901).

FO 16/336, Chile – Diplomatic, (1902).

FO 16/356, Argentina-Chile Boundary Arbitration, Parts I to III, (1896-1902).

FO 16/357, Chile-Argentine Arbitration, Nov. 7, 1902, *in* Argentine-Chile Boundary Arbitration, (1902).

FO 16/358, Argentine-Chile Boundary Arbitration, Parts I-III, (1903-1905).

FO 27/25, Eden Correspondence, (May-Sep. 1787).

FO 27/26, Eden & Grenville Correspondence, (Sep.-Dec. 1787).

FO 27/1163, Lord Clarendon Paris Conference Drafts, (Feb.-Apr. 1856).

FO 27/1168, Paris Conference, Archives, Lord Clarendon to Lord Palmerston, Drafts, (Feb. 17-Mar. 12, 1856).

FO 27/1169, Paris Conference, Archives, Lord Clarendon to Lord Palmerston, Drafts, (Mar. 13-Apr. 20, 1856).

FO 83/316, Use of Explosive Projectiles in Time of War, (1868 and 1869).

FO 83/485, Brussels Conference Volume V, Rules of War and Miscellaneous, (Sep. 28, 1874-Aug. 31, 1875).

FO 83/1652, Papers respecting the Bombardment of Unfortified Towns, Requisitions, etc., (1834-1898).

FO 881/5716, Edward Herstlet, Memorandum Respecting the Number of British and Foreign Ships of War in the Mediterranean, (January 28, 1889).

FO 881/7356, Reports by the Law Officers of the Crown, (1899).

FO 371/13, Brazil, (1906).

FO 371/403, Brazil, (1908).

FO 371/1051, Brazil, (1911).

FO 412/15, Conference at Brussels on the Rules of Military Warfare Correspondence, Part I, (Apr.-July 1874).

FO 412/16, Conference at Brussels on the Rules of Military Warfare Correspondence, Part II, (June-July 1874).

FO 412/18, Conference at Brussels on the Rules of Military Warfare Correspondence with Major-General Sir A. Horsford, (July-Sep. 1874).

FO 412/22, Correspondence Respecting the Protection of Submarine Cables in Time of War, (1886-1887).

FO 412/65, Correspondence Respecting the Peace Conference Held at the Hague in 1899, (1898-1900).

FO 412/79, Correspondence Respecting the Convocation of a Second Peace Conference at the Hague, (1907).

FO 412/86, Further Correspondence respecting the Second Peace Conference at the Hague, (Jan. 1906-June 1907).

FO 412/87, Further Correspondence respecting the Second Peace Conference at the Hague, (July 1907).

FO 412/88, Further Correspondence respecting the Second Peace Conference at the Hague, (Aug. 1907).

FO 412/89, Further Correspondence respecting the Second Peace Conference at the Hague, (Sep. 1907).

FO 412/90, Further Correspondence respecting the Second Peace Conference at the Hague, (Oct.-Dec. 1907).

FO 412/95, Correspondence respecting the International Conference on Aerial Navigation, (1910).

FO 412/96, Correspondence Respecting the Limitation of Armaments, (1909-1910).

FO 412/103, Further Correspondence respecting the Limitation of Armaments, (1911-1912).

FO 800/61, Grey Correspondence: Germany, (1906-1909).

FO 800/87, Admiralty – Grey Correspondence: Admiralty 1905-1913, (1905-1913).

FO 800/93, Grey Manuscripts – Foreign Office Memoranda, (1909-1911).

FO 881/1816, E. Hammond, Memorandum – Russia and Turkey and the Treaties of 1856, Nov. 1, 1870, (1870).

FO 881/1825, E. Hertslet, Memorandum Respecting the Passage of Foreign Ships of War through the Straits of the Dardanelles and Bosphorus, Nov. 18, 1870, (1870).

FO 881/1901, Correspondence respecting the Treaty of March 30, 1856, (Nov. 1870-Feb. 1871).

FO 881/6907, Ardagh, Memorandum on Hostilities between Turkey and Greece, Mar. 23, 1897, (1897).

FO 881/6994, Further Correspondence Respecting the Affairs of South-Eastern Europe, (May 1897)

FO 881/9328x, (Part 2), Note on General Points Which Might be Raised at the Hague Conference.

FO 881/9328x (Part 5), Hague Conference, Extracts from the Times, (1906).

FO 881/9328x, (Part 12), Hurst, Cecil. Memorandum on Disarmament, Dec. 1906.

FO 881/10342, Correspondence regarding Employment of Shells to whose Bursting Charges Substances Generating Noxious Gases have been added, (1913).

FO 881/10528, Correspondence respecting the Third Peace Conference, (1912-1914).

WAR OFFICE, PUBLIC RECORDS OFFICE, KEW

WO 106/40/B1/5, Sir John Ardagh & Percy Lake, Naval Action in Defence of the Question of the Great Lakes, Mar. 28, 1896, (1896).
WO 106/40/B1/10, G.S., Admiralty Memo on the Defence of Canada, (Mar. 24, 1905)
WO 106/40/B1/15, Grant-Duff, Armed Vessels on the Great Lakes, Defence and Operational Plans, (Nov. 1907).

PARLIAMENTARY PAPERS

Proceedings of the International Naval Conference held in London, December 1908 – February 1909, Parliamentary Papers, Miscellaneous, No. 5 (1909) Cd. 4555.

UNITED STATES DOCUMENTS

Message from the President of the United States, Naval Forces on the Lakes, July 1, 1840, H.R. Exec. Doc. No. 26-246, (1840).
Message from the President of the United States, in Response to Senate Resolution of April 11, 1892, Relative to the Agreement between the United States and Great Britain Concerning the Naval Forces to Be Maintained on the Great Lakes, Dec. 7, 1892, S. Exec. Doc. No. 9, (1892).
Message of the President of the United States, War Vessels on the Great Lakes, Feb. 27, 1900, H.R. Doc. No. 56-471, (1900).

PUBLISHED PRIMARY SOURCES

Hansard: *Parliamentary Debates.*
The Times (London).
The New York Times.
Documents Relating to the Program of the First Hague Peace Conference: Laid before the Conference by the Netherland Government. Oxford: Clarendon Press, 1921.
Gooch, G P, and H Temperley, eds. *British Documents on the Origins of the War.* London: H M Stationery Office, 1926-1938.
Interparliamentary Union. *Official Report of the Fourteenth Conference held in the Royal Gallery of the House of Lords,* (1906).
Lepsius, Johannes, Albrecht Mendelssohn Bartholdy, and Friedrich Thimme, eds. *Die Grosse Politik Der Europäischen Kabinette, 1871-914: Sammlung Der Diplomatischen Akten Des Auswärtigen Amtes.* 40 vols. Berlin: Deutsche Verlagsgesellschaft für Politik und Geschichte, 1922-1927.

Metternich, Klemens von. *Memoirs of Prince Metternich.* Translated by Gerard W. Smith. Edited by Prince Richard Metternich. Vol. V: 1830-1835. London: Richard Bentley & Son, 1882.

Newton, Lord. *Lord Lyons: A Record of British Diplomacy.* Volume I. London: Edward Arnold, 1913.

Scott, James Brown, ed. *The Proceedings of the Hague Peace Conferences: Translation of the Original Texts.* Edited by James Brown Scott. Conference of 1907, Vol. I-III. New York: Oxford University Press, 1921.

————, ed. *The Proceedings of the Hague Peace Conferences: Translation of the Original Texts.* Edited by James Brown Scott. Conference of 1899. New York: Oxford University Press, 1920.

State, U.S. Department of. *Papers Relating to the Foreign Relations of the United States with the Annual Message of the President 1899.* Washington: Government Printing Office, 1901.

————. *Papers Relating to the Foreign Relations of the United States with the Annual Message of the President 1907,* Part II. Washington: Government Printing Office, 1910.

Universal Congress of Peace. *The Official Report of the Seventeenth Universal Congress of Peace,* (1909).

TREATIES AND INTERNATIONAL AGREEMENTS

1713 Treaty of Peace and Friendship between France and Great Britain, signed at Utrecht, Apr. 11, 1713. Clive Parry, ed., *Consolidated Treaty Series* Vol. 27, 482: Dobbs Ferry, New York: Oceana Publications, 1969.

1739 Definitive Treaty of Peace between the Emperor and Turkey, signed at Belgrade, Sep. 18, 1739, Parry, ed., *Consolidated Treaty Series* Vol. 35, 431.

1787 Reciprocal Declaration between France and Great Britain, signed at Versailles, Aug. 30, 1787, *in* Parry, ed., *Consolidated Treaty Series,* Vol. 50, 211.

1787 Reciprocal Declarations between France and Great Britain, signed at Versailles, Oct. 27, 1787, *in* Parry, ed., *Consolidated Treaty Series,* Vol. 50: 245.

1807 Armistices between France and Russia, signed at Tilsit, June 25, 1807, Parry, ed., *Consolidated Treaty Series* Vol. 59, 203.

1815 (Second) Treaty of Paris, signed at Paris, Nov. 20, 1815, *in* Michael Hurst, ed., *Key Treaties for the Great Powers 1814-1914* (Newton Abbot: David & Charles, 1972), Vol. 1, 128.

1817 Exchange of Notes between Great Britain and the United States Relative to Naval Forces on the American Lakes, signed at Washington, Apr. 28, 29, 1817, *in* Parry, ed., *Consolidated Treaty Series,* Vol. 67, 154.

1828 Peace Treaty between Russia and Persia, signed at Turkmanchai, Feb. 22, 1828, *in* Georg F. Martens, ed., *Nouveau recueil de traités,* (1829) Vol. VII, 564.

1830 Treaty of Navigation and Commerce between France and Tripoli, signed at Tripoli, Aug. 11, 1830, *in* Parry, ed., *Consolidated Treaty Series*, Vol. 81, 105.

1831 Preliminary Treaty of Peace between Bolivia and Peru, signed at Tiquina, Aug. 25, 1831, Parry, ed., *Consolidated Treaty Series*, Vol. 82, 150.

1840 Preliminary Convention of Peace and Commerce between Bolivia - and Peru, signed at Lima, Apr. 19, 1840, Parry, ed., *Consolidated Treaty Series*, Vol. 90, 104.

1841 Convention Respecting the Straits of the Dardenelles and of the Bosphorus, signed in London, July 13, 1841, *in* Hurst, ed., *Key Treaties*, Vol. I, 259.

1854 Treaty of Constantinople, Mar. 12, 1854, *in* Hurst, ed., *Key Treaties* Vol. I, 299.

1855 Treaty of Stockholm, Nov. 21, 1855, *in* Hurst, ed., *Key Treaties* Vol. I, 315.

1856 Convention between Russia and Turkey, limiting their Naval Force in the Black Sea, *in* Hurst, ed., *Key Treaties* Vol. I, 331.

1856 Treaty of Paris, signed Mar. 30, 1856, Art. XIV, *in* Hurst, ed., *Key Treaties*, Vol. I, 321.

1856 Convention Respecting the Aland Islands, signed at Paris, Apr. 27, 1856, *in* Hurst, ed., *Key Treaties*, Vol. I, 333.

1856 Declaration of Paris, Apr. 16, 1856. *American Journal of International Law* 1, no. 2 Supplement (1907): 89–90.

1864 Geneva Convention for the Amelioration of the Condition of the Sick and Wounded of Armies in the Field, Aug. 22, 1864. *American Journal of International Law* 1, no. 2 Supplement (1907): 90–92.

1867 Treaty Relative to the Grand Duchy of Luxemburg and the Duchy of Limburg, signed at London, May 31, 1867, *in* Hurst, ed., *Key Treaties*, Vol. I, 447.

1868 Declaration of St. Petersburg, of 1868 to the Effect of Prohibiting the Use of Certain Projectiles in Wartime, Nov. 29, (Dec. 11) 1868. *American Journal of International Law* 1, no. 2 Supplement (1907): 95–96.

1871 Declaration of London, Jan. 17, 1871, *in* Hurst, ed., *Key Treaties*, Vol. II, 439.

1871 Treaty of London for the Revision of Certain Stipulations of the Treaties of 30th March, 1856, Relative to the Black Sea and Danube, Mar. 13, 1871, *in* Hurst, ed., *Key Treaties*, Vol. II, 467.

1874 Project of an International Declaration Concerning the Laws and Customs of War, Adopted by the Conference of Brussels, Aug. 27, 1874. *American Journal of International Law* 1, no. 2 Supplement (1907): 96–103.

1878 Treaty [of Berlin] for the Settlement of the Affairs of the East, July 13, 1878, *in* Hurst, ed., *Key Treaties*, Vol. II, 551.

1882 First Treaty of Triple Alliance between Austria-Hungary, Germany and Italy, May 20, 1882, Hurst, ed., *Key Treaties*, Vol. 2, 611.

1887 British Note to the Italian Government in Regard to a Mediterranean Agreement, Feb. 12, 1887, Hurst, ed., *Key Treaties*, Vol. 2, 635.

1892 Draft of Military Convention between France and Russia, 1892, Hurst, ed., *Key Treaties*, Vol. 2, 668.

1899 Convention with Respect to the Laws and Customs of War on Land, signed at The Hague, July 29, 1899. *American Journal of International Law* 1, no. 2 Supplement (1907): 129–59.

1899 Declaration Concerning Aerial Bombardment, signed at The Hague, July 29, 1899. *American Journal of International Law* 1, no. 2 Supplement (1907): 153–55.

1899 Declaration Concerning Asphyxiating Gas, signed at The Hague, July 29, 1899. *American Journal of International Law* 1, no. 2 Supplement (1907): 157–59.

1899 Declaration Concerning Exploding Bullets, signed at The Hague, July 29, 1899. *American Journal of International Law* 1, no. 2 Supplement (1907): 155–57.

1899 Final Act of the Peace Conference, signed at The Hague, July 29, 1899. *American Journal of International Law* 1, no. 2 Supplement (1907): 103–07.

1902 Convention Relative to the Regime of Sugar. Mar. 5, 1902, *in* Despatch from the British Delegates, No. 4, (March 1902), Miscellaneous Papers presented to both Houses of Parliament.

1902 Convention between Chile and the Argentine Republic Respecting the Limitation of Naval Armaments, May 28 1902. *American Journal of International Law* 1, no. 3 Supplement (1907): 294–97.

1902 General Arbitration Treaty between the Argentine Republic and Chile, May 28, 1902. *American Journal of International Law* 6, no. 2 Supplement (1912): 79–82.

1903 Agreement Concluded and Signed between the Argentine Republic and Chile, Giving Effect to the Terms of the Convention of May 28, 1902, for the Limitation of Naval Armaments, January 9, 1903. *American Journal of International Law* 1, no. 3 Supplement (1907): 297–99.

1904 Declaration Between the United Kingdom and France respecting Egypt and Morocco, Apr. 8, 1904; Hurst, ed., *Key Treaties*, Vol. II, 760.

1905 [Anglo-Japanese Alliance] Agreement Respecting the Integrity of China, the General Peace of Eastern Asia and India, and the Territorial Rights and Special Interests of the Parties in those Regions, signed in London, Aug. 12, 1905, Hurst, ed., *Key Treaties*, Vol. II, 770.

1905 Convention Relative to the Establishment of a Neutral Zone and to the Dismantling of Fortifications, Oct. 26, 1905, Parry, ed., *Consolidated Treaty Series*, Vol. 199, 285.

1906 International Radiotelegraphic Convention, signed Nov. 3, 1906, *American Journal of International Law* 3, no. 4, Supplement (Oct. 1909): 330–377.

1907 Declaration Prohibiting the Discharge of Projectiles and Explosives from Balloons, signed at The Hague, Oct. 18, 1907. *American Journal of International Law* 2, no. 1/2 Supplement (1908): 216–18.

1907 Convention Regarding the Laws and Customs of Land Warfare, signed at The Hague, Oct. 18, 1907. *American Journal of International Law* 2, no. 1/2 Supplement (1908): 90–117.

1907 Convention Relative to the Conversion of Merchant Ships into War Ships, signed at The Hague, Oct. 18, 1907. *American Journal of International Law* 2, no. 1/2 Supplement (1908): 133–38.

1907 Convention Relative to the Laying of Submarine Mines, signed at The Hague, Oct. 18, 1907. *American Journal of International Law* 2, no. 1/2 Supplement (1908): 138–45.

1907 Convention Respecting the Rights and Duties of Neutral Powers in Naval War, signed at The Hague, Oct. 18, 1907. *American Journal of International Law* 2, no. 1/2 Supplement (1908): 202–16.

1907 Final Act, signed at The Hague, Oct. 18, 1907. *American Journal of International Law* 2, no. 1/2 Supplement (1908): 1–43.

1909 Declaration of London, Feb. 26, 1909. *American Journal of International Law* 3, no. 3 Supplement (1909): 179–220.

1922 Washington Treaty Limiting Naval Armament, Feb. 6, 1922. *American Journal of International Law* 16, Supplement (Apr. 1922): 41–56.

1925 Geneva Protocol for the Prohibition of the Use in War of Asphyxiating, Poisonous or Other Gases, and of Bacteriological Methods of Warfare, June 17, 1925, United States Treaties Vol. 26, 571.

PRIMARY SOURCES ON LAW AND ARMAMENTS

Arnoldson, K. P. *Pax Mundi: A Concise Account of the Progress of the Movement for Peace by Means of Arbitration, Neutralization, International Law and Disarmament*. London: Swan Sonnenschein and Co., 1892.

Austin, John. *The Province of Jurisprudence Determined*. London: John Murray, 1832.

Barclay, Sir Thomas. *Problems of International Practice and Diplomacy: With Special Reference to the Hague Conferences and Conventions and Other General International Agreements*. London: Sweet and Maxwell, 1907.

Baty, Thomas. "The Basis of International Law." *Macmillan's Magazine* 78, no. 466 (1898): 279–83.

———. *International Law*. New York: Longmans, Green and Co., 1909.

Boutell, Henry Sherman. "Is the Rush-Bagot Convention Immortal?" *North American Review* 173, no. 3 (1901): 331–48.

Campbell-Bannerman, Henry. "The Hague Conference and the Limitation of Armaments." 1 *The Nation*, Mar. 2, 1907.

Castelot, E. "The Brussels Sugar Conference." *Economic Journal* 12, no. 46 (1902): 217–220.

Choate, Joseph. *The Two Hague Conferences.* Princeton, NJ: Princeton University Press, 1969.

Cobden, Richard. *The Political Writings of Richard Cobden.* Vol. II. London: William Ridgway, 1867.

Crandall, Samuel B. *Treaties, Their Making and Enforcement.* New York: Columbia University Press, 1904.

Crosby, Ernest. "A Precedent for Disarmament: A Suggestion to the Peace Conference." *North American Review* 183, no. 6 (1906): 776–79.

Davis, Cushman K. *A Treatise on International Law Including American Diplomacy.* St. Paul, Minnesota: Keefe-Davidson Law Book Co., 1901.

Davis, George B. "The Launching of Projectiles from Balloons." *American Journal of International Law* 2, no. 3 (1908): 528–29.

———. *Outlines of International Law: With an Account of Its Origin and Sources of Its Historical Development.* New York: Harper and Brothers, 1887.

de la Grasserie, Raoul. *Des Moyens Pratiques Pour Parvenir a La Suppression De La Paix Armée Et De La Guerre.* Paris: Ancienne Librairie Germer Baillière, 1894.

de Sillac, Jarousse. "Periodic Peace Conferences." *American Journal of International Law* 5, no. 4 (1911): 968–86.

Diplomaticus. "The Vanishing of Universal Peace." *Fortnightly Review* 65, no. 389 (1899): 871–80.

Ellis, Wilmot E. "Aerial-Land and Aerial-Maritime Warfare." *American Journal of International Law* 8, no. 2 (1914): 256–73.

Eversley, Lord George. "Naval Scares." *Contemporary Review* 90 (1906): 624–38.

Field, David Dudley. *Draft Outlines of an International Code.* New York: Baker, Voorhis and Co., 1872.

Fried, Alfred H. *Die Zweite Haager Konferenz: Ihre Arbeiten, Ihre Ergebnisse, Und Ihre Bedeutung.* Leipzig: B. Elischer Nachfolger, 1908.

Hall, William Edward. *A Treatise on International Law.* 3rd ed. London: Henry Frowde, 1890.

Halleck, H. W. *Elements of International Law and Laws of War.* Philadelphia: J. B. Lippincott & Co., 1866.

Hershey, Amos S. *The International Law and Diplomacy of the Russo-Japanese War.* London: Macmillan and Co., 1906.

Higgins, A. Pearce. *The Binding Force of International Law.* Cambridge: Cambridge University Press, 1910.

———. *The Hague Peace Conferences and Other International Conferences Concerning the Laws and Usages of War: Texts of Conventions with Commentaries.* Cambridge: Cambridge University Press, 1909.

Hobson, Richmond Pearson. "Disarmament." *American Journal of International Law* 2, no. 4 (1908): 743–57.

Holls, Frederick W. *The Peace Conference at the Hague and Its Bearing on International Law and Policy.* London: Macmillan and Co., 1900.

Kamarowski, Count. "Quelques Réflexions Sur Les Armements Croissants de l'Europe." *Revue de Droit International et de Législation Comparée* 19 (1887): 479–86.

Lawrence, Thomas Joseph. *Essays on Some Disputed Questions in Modern International Law.* 2nd ed. Cambridge: Deighton, Bell & Co., 1885.

———. *A Handbook of Public International Law.* Cambridge: Deighton, Bell & Co., 1885.

———. *The Principles of International Law.* 4th ed. Boston: Heath and Co., 1910.

Lieber, Francis. *Instructions for the Government of Armies of the United States in the Field.* New York: D. Van Nostrand, 1863.

Logan, Walter S. "The Mountains Were in Labor and Brought Forth a Mouse." *Lend a Hand* 17, no. 3 (1896): 185–89.

Lorimer, James. "La Question du désarmement et les difficultés qu'elle soulève au point de vue du droit international." *Revue de droit international et de législation comparée* 19 (1887): 472–78.

Mahan, Alfred Thayer. *Armaments and Arbitration: Or, The Place of Force in the International Relations of States.* New York: Harper and Brothers, 1912.

Maine, Henry Sumner. *International Law, a Series of Lectures Delivered before the University of Cambridge, 1887.* New York: Henry Holt & Co., 1888.

Maitland, F. W. "A Prologue to a History of English Law." *Law Quarterly Review* 14, no. 53 (1898): 13–33.

Martineau, George. "The Brussels Sugar Convention," *Economic Journal* 14, no. 53 (1904): 34–39.

Mérignhac, Alexandre. *Traité théoretique et pratique de l'arbitrage international.* Paris: Librairie du recueil général des lois et des arrêts, 1895.

Moltke, Helmuth von, and Johann Kaspar Bluntschli. "Les lois de la guerre sur terre." *Revue de droit international et de législation comparée* 13 (1881): 79–84.

Moore, John Bassett. *A Digest of International Law.* Washington: Government Printing Office, 1906.

Oppenheim, Lassa. *International Law: A Treatise.* 2nd ed. II vols. Vol. I. London: Longmans, Green and Co., 1912.

Phillimore, Sir Robert. *Commentaries Upon International Law,* Vol. I. Philadelphia: T & J.W. Johnson Law Booksellers, 1854.

———. *Commentaries Upon International Law,* Vol. II. Philadelphia: T & J.W. Johnson Law Booksellers, 1855.

———. *Commentaries Upon International Law,* Vol. III. Philadelphia: T. & J.W. Johnson & Co., 1857.

———. *Commentaries Upon International Law.* Vol. I. 3rd ed. London: Butterworths, 1879.

Porter, J. B. *International Law, Having Particular Reference to the Laws of War on Land.* Fort Leavenworth, Kansas: Press of the Army Service Schools, 1914.

Reinsch, Paul S. "International Unions and Their Administration." *American Journal of International Law* 1, no. 3 (1907): 579–623.

Ridges, Edward Wavell. *Constitutional Law of England.* London: Stevens & Sons, 1905.

Rolin-Jaequemyns, M. Gustave. "Limitation conventionelle des dépenses et des effectifs militaires." *Revue de droit International et de législation comparée* 19 (1887): 398–407.

Root, Elihu. "The Sanction of International Law." *American Journal of International Law* 2, no. 3 (1908): 451–57.

Schücking, Walther. *The International Union of the Hague Conferences.* Translated by Charles G. Fenwick. Oxford: Clarendon Press, 1918.

Scott, James Brown. *The Hague Peace Conferences of 1899 and 1907: A Series of Lectures Delivered before the Johns Hopkins University in the Year 1908.* 2 vols. Baltimore, MD: Johns Hopkins Press, 1909.

———, ed. *The Hague Conventions and Declarations of 1899 and 1907.* New York: Oxford University Press, 1915.

Smith, Frederick Erwin. *International Law.* 2nd Edition ed. London: Dent and Co., 1903.

Souchon, A. "La question du désarmement." *Revue générale de droit international public* 1 (1894): 513–22.

Stengel, Karl von. *Der Ewige Friede.* Munich: Carl Haushalter, 1899.

———. *Weltstaat Und Friedensproblem.* Berlin: Verlag Reichl, 1909.

Stockton, Charles H. *Outlines of International Law.* New York: Charles Scribner's Sons, 1914.

Taylor, Hannis. *A Treatise on International Public Law.* Chicago: Callaghan and Co., 1901.

Twiss, Travers. *The Law of Nations Considered as Independent Political Communities.* Vol. I On the Right and Duties of Nations in Time of Peace. Oxford: Oxford University Press, 1861.

———. *The Law of Nations Considered as Independent Political Communities.* Vol. II On the Rights and Duties of Nations in Time of War. Oxford: Oxford University Press, 1863.

"The Use of Balloons in the War between Italy and Turkey." *American Journal of International Law* 6, no. 2 (1912): 485–87.

Von Martens, G. F. *A Compendium of the Law of Nations.* Translated by William Cobbett. London: Corbett & Morgan, 1802.

Wehberg, Hans. *Die Internationale Beschränkung der Rüstungen.* Stuttgart: Deutsche Verlags-Anstalt, 1919.

———. *The Limitation of Armaments: A Collection of the Projects Proposed for the Solution of the Problem, Preceded by an Historical Introduction.* Translated by Edwin H. Zeydel. Washington: Carnegie Endowment for International Peace, 1921.

Westlake, John. *Chapters on the Principles of International Law.* Cambridge: Cambridge University Press, 1894.

Wheaton, Henry. *Elements of International Law, with a Sketch of the History of the Science.* Philadelphia: Carey, Lea & Blanchard, 1836.

White, Andrew Dickson. *The First Hague Conference.* Boston: World Peace Foundation, 1912.

White, Sir William. "Modern Warships." *Journal of the Society of the Arts* 54 (1906): 866–71.

Secondary Sources

Bartlett, C. J. *Great Britain and Sea Power, 1815-1853.* Oxford: Clarendon Press, 1963.

Baumgart, Winfried. *The Peace of Paris 1856: Studies in War, Diplomacy, and Peacemaking.* Translated by Ann Pottinger Saab. Santa Barbara: ABC Clio, 1981.

Beckett, Eric. "Sir Cecil Hurst's Services to International Law." *British Yearbook of International Law* 26 (1949): 1.

Bederman, David J. "The 1871 London Declaration, Rebus Sic Stantibus and a Primitivist View of the Law of Nations." *American Journal of International Law* 82, no. 1 (1988): 1–40.

Beeler, John F. *British Naval Policy in the Gladstone-Disraeli Era, 1866-1880.* Stanford: Stanford University Press, 1997.

Bell, Christopher M. "Sir John Fisher's Naval Revolution Reconsidered: Winston Churchill at the Admiralty, 1911-14." *War in History* 18, no. 3 (2011): 333–356.

Bolton, G C, and B E Kennedy. "William Eden and the Treaty of Mauritius, 1786-7." *Historical Journal* 16, no. 4 (1973): 681–96.

Bourne, Kenneth. *Britain and the Balance of Power in North America, 1815-1908.* London: Longmans, Green & Co., 1967.

Boyce, Robert W. D. "Imperial Dreams and National Realities: Britain, Canada and the Struggle for a Pacific Telegraph Cable, 1879-1902." *English Historical Review* 115, no. 460 (2000): 39–70.

Buckley, Thomas H. *The United States and the Washington Conference, 1921-1922.* Knoxville, Tennessee: University of Tennessee Press, 1970.

Burr, Robert N. "The Balance of Power in Nineteenth-Century South America: An Exploratory Essay." *Hispanic American Historical Review* 35, no. 1 (1955): 37–60.

———. "By Reason or Force: Chile and the Balancing of Power in South America, 1830-1905." *University of California Publications in History* 77 (1965): 1–322.

Callahan, James Morton. *The Neutrality of the American Lakes and Anglo-American Relations*, Baltimore, MD: Johns Hopkins Press, 1898.

Chayes, Abram. "An Inquiry into the Working of Arms Control Agreements." *Harvard Law Review* 85, no. 5 (1972): 905–69.

Chickering, Roger. *Imperial Germany and a World without War: The Peace Movement and German Society, 1892-1914.* Princeton, NJ: Princeton University Press, 1975.

Churchill, Winston S. *The World Crisis, 1911-1914.* London: Thornton Butterworth Limited, 1923.

Coogan, John W. *The End of Neutrality: The United States, Britain, and Maritime Rights 1899-1915.* Ithaca: Cornell University Press, 1981.

Davis, Calvin DeArmond. *The United States and the First Hague Peace Conference.* Ithaca, New York: Cornell University Press, 1962.

———. *The United States and the Second Hague Peace Conference: American Diplomacy and International Organization 1899-1914.* Durham, North Carolina: Duke University Press, 1975.

Delbrück, Jost, ed. *Friedensdokumente aus Fünf Jahrhunderten: Abrüstung, Kriegsverhütung, Rüstungskontrolle.* Strasbourg: N.P. Engel, 1984.

Dülffer, Jost. "Chances and Limits of Arms Control 1898-1914." In *An Improbable War: The Outbreak of World War I and European Political Culture before 1914,* edited by Holger Afflerbach and David Stevenson, 95–112. New York: Berghan Books, 2004.

———. *Regeln Gegen den Krieg? Die Haager Friedenskonferenzen von 1899 und 1907 in der Internationalen Politik.* Berlin: Ullstein, 1981.

Dunne, Finley Peter. *Dissertations by Mr. Dooley.* New York: Harper & Bros., 1906.

Dupuy, R Ernest, and Trevor N Dupuy. *The Encyclopedia of Military History: From 3500 B.C. To the Present.* 2nd edition ed. New York: Harper and Row, 1986.

Epkenhans, Michael. "Was a Peaceful Outcome Thinkable? The Naval Race before 1914." In *An Improbable War: The Outbreak of World War I and European Political Culture before 1914,* edited by Holger Afflerbach and David Stevenson. New York: Berghan Books, 2007.

Ferrari, Gustavo. *Conflicto Y Paz Con Chile (1898-1903).* Buenos Aires: Editorial Universitaria de Buenos Aires, 1968.

Ferreiro, Larrie D. "Mahan and the "English Club" of Lima, Peru: The Genesis of the *Influence of Sea Power Upon History.*" *Journal of Military History* 72 (2008): 901–06.

Fisher, John Arbuthnot. *Records by Admiral of the Fleet Lord Fisher.* London: Hodder and Stoughton, 1919.

Fotakis, Zsis. *Greek Naval Strategy and Policy, 1910-1919.* London: Routledge, 2005.

France, Anatole. *The Red Lily.* New York: Boni & Liveright.

Gardiner, Robert, ed. *Conway's All the World's Fighting Ships, 1906-1921.* 3rd ed. London: Conway Maritime Press, 1985.

Gardiner, Robert, ed. *Conway's All the World's Fighting Ships, 1860-1905.* London: Conway Maritime Press Ltd., 1979.

Glete, Jan. *Navies and Nations: Warships, Navies and State Building in Europe and America, 1500-1860*. Stockholm: Historiska Institutionen, 1993.

Gluek, Alvin C. "The Invisible Revision of the Rush-Bagot Agreement, 1898-1914," *Canadian Historical Review* 60, no. 4 (Dec. 1979): 466–484.

Gollin, Alfred. *The Impact of Air Power on the British People and Their Government, 1909-1914*. London: Macmillan, 1989.

Grant, Jonathan A. *Rulers, Guns, and Money: The Global Arms Trade in the Age of Imperialism*. Cambridge: Harvard University Press, 2007.

Grewe, Wilhelm G., ed. *Fontes Historiae Iuris Gentium: Sources Relating to the History of the Law of Nations*. 3 vols. Vol. 3. Berlin: Walter de Gruyter, 1992.

Grewe, Wilhelm G. *The Epochs of International Law*. Translated by Michael Byers. Berlin: Walter de Gruyter, 2000.

Hamilton, C. I. *Anglo-French Naval Rivalry 1840-1870*. Oxford: Clarendon Press, 1993.

Haydon, F. Stansbury. "A Proposed Gas Shell, 1862." *Journal of the American Military History Foundation* 2, no. 1 (1938): 52–54.

Herkless, J. L. "Lord Clarendon's Attempt at Franco-Prussian Disarmament, January to March 1870." *Historical Journal* 15, no. 3 (1972): 455–70.

Herrmann, David G. *The Arming of Europe and the Making of the First World War*. Princeton, NJ: Princeton University Press, 1996.

Herwig, Holger H. "Strategic Uncertainties of a Nation-State: Prussia-Germany, 1871-1918." In *The Making of Strategy: Rulers, States and War*, edited by Williamson Murray, 242, 1996.

Howard, Christopher H. D. *Britain and the Casus Belli, 1822-1902: A Study of Britain's International Position from Canning to Salisbury*. London: Athlone Press, 1974.

Howard, Michael. *War in European History*. Oxford: Oxford University Press, 1976.

Hull, Isabel. *Absolute Destruction: Military Culture and the Practices of War in Imperial Germany*. Ithaca: Cornell University Press, 2005.

———. *A Scrap of Paper: Breaking and Making International Law during the Great War*. Ithaca: Cornell University Press, 2014.

Hurst, Michael, ed. *Key Treaties for the Great Powers 1814-1914*. Newton Abbot: David & Charles, 1972.

Keefer, Scott A. "International Control of Biological Weapons." *Nova Journal of International and Comparative Law* 6 (1999): 107–41.

———. "Building the Palace of Peace: The Hague Conference of 1899 and Arms Control in the Progressive Era." *Journal of the History of International Law* 8 (2006): 1–17.

———. "Building the Palace of Peace: The Hague Conference of 1907 and Arms Control before the World War." *Journal of the History of International Law* 9 (2007): 35–82.

———. "'Big Ships Cause Big Wars, Little Ships Cause Little Wars, and No Ships Cause No Wars:' International Law and Arms Control Policy in the Interwar Era." In *War, Society, and the Ingenious Arts: Essays in Honor of Thomas H. Buckley*, edited by Kelly K. Chaves and William A. Crafton, 35–61. Tulsa: University of Tulsa Press, 2009.

———. "'An Obstacle, though not a Barrier': The Role of International Law in Security Planning during the Pax Britannica." *International History Review* 35, no. 5 (2013): 1–21.

———. "'Explosive Missals': International Law, Technology, and Security in Nineteenth-Century Disarmament Conferences." *War in History* 21, no. 4 (2014): 445–464.

Kennedy, Paul M. "Imperial Cable Communications and Strategy, 1870-1914." *English Historical Review* 86, no. 341 (1971): 728–752.

Keltie, J. Scott. *The Statesman's Year-Book: Statistical and Historical Annual of the States of the World for the Year 1896*. London: Macmillan Co., 1896.

Knaplund, Paul. "Documents: The Armaments on the Great Lakes, 1844," *American Historical Review*, 40, no. 3 (Apr. 1935): 473–474.

Koskenniemi, Martti. *The Gentle Civilizer of Nations: The Rise and Fall of International Law 1870-1960*. Cambridge: Cambridge University Press, 2001.

Lambert, Andrew. *The Crimean War: British Grand Strategy, 1853-56*. Manchester: Manchester University Press, 1990.

Lambert, Nicholas A. "Transformation and Technology in the Fisher Era: The Impact of the Communications Revolution." *Journal of Strategic Studies* 27, no. 2 (2004): 272–97.

———. *Sir John Fisher's Naval Revolution*. Columbia, SC: University of South Carolina Press, 1999.

———. *Planning Armageddon: British Economic Warfare and the First World War*. Cambridge, MA: Harvard University Press, 2012.

———. "On Standards: A Reply to Christopher Bell." *War in History* 19, no. 2 (2012): 217–240.

Leiner, Frederick C. "The Unknown Effort: Theodore Roosevelt's Battleship Plan and International Arms Limitation Talks, 1906-1907." *Military Affairs* 48, no. 4 (1984): 174–79.

Lemnitzer, Jan Martin. *Power, Law and the End of Privateering*. Houndsmills, Basingstoke: Palgrave Macmillan, 2014.

Lhéritier, Michel. *Histoire diplomatique de la Grèce de 1821 a nos jours*. Vol. IV. Paris: Les Presses universitaires de France, 1926.

Marder, Arthur J. *The Anatomy of British Sea Power: A History of British Naval Policy in the Pre-Dreadnought Era, 1880-1905*. 3rd Edition 1972 ed. London: Frank Cass, 1940.

———. *From the Dreadnought to Scapa Flow*. 3rd Edition ed. Vol. I. London: Oxford University Press, 1972.

———, ed. *Fear God and Dread Nought: The Correspondence of Admiral of the Fleet Lord Fisher of Kilverstone*. Vol. II Years of Power, 1904-1914. Oxford: Alden Press, 1956.

Martin, Christopher. "The 1907 Naval War Plans and the Second Hague Peace Conference: A Case of Propaganda." *Journal of Strategic Studies* 28, no. 5 (2005): 833–56.

———. "The Declaration of London: A Matter of Operational Capability." *Historical Research* 82, no. 218 (2009): 731–55.

Maurer, John H. "The Anglo-German Naval Rivalry and Informal Arms Control, 1912-1914." *Journal of Conflict Resolution* 36, no. 2 (1992): 284–308.

McKercher, B. J. C., ed. *Arms Limitation and Disarmament: Restraints on War 1899-1939*. Westport, Conn: Praeger, 1992.

McNeill, William H. *The Pursuit of Power: Technology, Armed Force, and Society since A.D. 1000*. Chicago: University of Chicago Press, 1982.

Medlicott, W. N. *Bismarck, Gladstone, and the Concert of Europe*. London: Athlone Press, 1956.

Modelski, George and William R. Thompson. *Seapower in Global Politics, 1494-1993*. London: Macmillan, 1988.

Moll, Kenneth J. "Politics, Power, and Panic: Britain's 1909 Dreadnought 'Gap'." *Military Affairs* 29, no. 3 (1965): 133–44.

Morrill, Dan L. "Nicholas II and the Call for the First Hague Conference." *Journal of Modern History* 46, no. 2 (1974): 296–313.

Morris, A J A. "The English Radicals' Campaign for Disarmament and the Hague Conference of 1907." *Journal of Modern History* 43, no. 3 (1971): 367–93.

Mosse, W. E. *The Rise and Fall of the Crimean System 1855-1871: The Story of a Peace Settlement*. London: Macmillan & Co., 1963.

———. "Russia and the Levant, 1856-1862: Grand Duke Constantine Nicolaevich and the Russian Steam Navigation Company." *Journal of Modern History* 26, no. 1 (1954): 39–48.

Neff, Stephen C. *War and the Law of Nations: A General History*. Cambridge: Cambridge University Press, 2005.

Neilson, Keith. "*The British Empire Floats on the British Navy': British Naval Policy, Belligerent Rights, and Disarmament, 1902-1909*." In *Arms Limitation and Disarmament: Restraints on War 1899-1939*, edited by B. J. C. McKercher, 21–41. Westport, Conn: Praeger, 1992.

Nicholls, David. "Richard Cobden and the International Peace Congress Movement, 1848-1853." *Journal of British Studies* 30, no. 4 (1991): 351–76.

Nish, Ian H. *The Anglo-Japanese Alliance: The Diplomacy of Two Island Empires 1894-1907*. London: Athlone Press, 1966.

Nussbaum, Arthur. *A Concise History of the Law of Nations*. New York: Macmillan Co., 1947.

Offer, Avner. *The First World War: An Agrarian Interpretation.* Oxford: Clarendon Press, 1989.

———. "Morality and Admiralty: 'Jacky' Fisher, Economic Warfare and the Laws of War." *Journal of Contemporary History* 23, no. 1 (1988): 99–118.

———. "The Working Classes, British Naval Plans and the Coming of the Great War." *Past and Present* 107 (1985): 204–26.

Otte, Thomas G. "Grey Ambassador: The *Dreadnought* and British Foreign Policy." In *The Dreadnought and the Edwardian Age,* edited by Robert J. Blyth, Andrew Lambert, & Jan Ruger, 51–78. Farnham, Surrey: Ashgate Publishing, 2011.

———. "'What we desire is confidence': The Search for an Anglo-German Agreement, 1909-1912." In *Arms and Disarmament in Diplomacy,* edited by Keith Hamilton & Edward Johnson, 33–52. London: Valentine Mitchell, 2008.

Otway, Arthur, ed. *Autobiography and Journals of Admiral Lord Clarence E. Paget.* London: Chapman & Hall, 1896.

Parkes, Oscar. *British Battleships: "Warrior" 1860 to "Vanguard" 1950, a History of Design, Construction and Armament.* London: Seeley Service & Co., 1957.

Parkinson, Roger. *The Late Victorian Navy: The Pre-Dreadnought Era and the Origins of the First World War.* Chippenham, United Kingdom: Boydell Press, 2008.

Parry, Clive. "Foreign Policy and International Law." In *Foreign Policy under Sir Edward Grey,* edited by F. H. Hinsley, 89–110. Cambridge: Cambridge University Press, 1977.

———, ed. *A British Digest of International Law, Part VII Organs of States.* London: Stevens & Sons, 1965.

———, ed. *Consolidated Treaty Series.* Dobbs Ferry, New York: Oceana Publications, 1969.

Podsoblyaev, Evgenii F., Francis King, and John Biggart. "The Russian Naval General Staff and the Evolution of Naval Policy, 1905-1914." *Journal of Military History* 66, no. 1 (2002): 37–69.

Price, Munro. "The Dutch Affair and the Fall of the Ancien Regime, 1784-1787." *Historical Journal* 38, no. 4 (1995): 875–905.

Punch, or the London Charivari, July 10, 1907, Vol. CXXXIII, (1907).

Rich, Norman. *Friedrich Von Holstein: Politics and Diplomacy in the Era of Bismarck and Wilhelm II.* Cambridge: Cambridge University Press, 1965.

Ropp, Theodore. *The Development of a Modern Navy: French Naval Policy, 1871-1904.* Annapolis, Maryland: Naval Institute Press, 1987.

Rose, J H, W Pitt, W W Grenville, and Wm Eden. "The Missions of William Grenville to the Hague and Versailles in 1787." *English Historical Review* 24, no. 94 (1909): 278–95.

Salisbury, Robert Arthur Talbot Gascoyne-Cecil, 3rd Marquis. "The Land Question of Ireland: Issued by the Irish Land Committee," *Quarterly Review*, 151, no. 302, (Apr. 1881): 535–567.

Sandler, Stanley. "The Day of the Ram." *Military Affairs* 40, no. 4 (1976): 175–78.

Schell, Jonathan. "The Folly of Arms Control." *Foreign Affairs* 79, no. 5 (Sep.-Oct. 2000): 22–46.

Seligmann, Matthew S. "Intelligence Information and the 1909 Naval Scare: The Secret Foundations of a Public Panic." *War in History* 17, no. 1 (2010): 37–59.

———. "New Weapons for New Targets: Sir John Fisher, the Threat from Germany, and the Building of HMS *Dreadnought* and HMS *Invincible*, 1902-1907." *International History Review* 30, no. 2 (2008): 303–31.

———. *Spies in Uniform: British Military and Naval Intelligence on the Eve of the First World War*. Oxford: Oxford University Press, 2006.

———. "Britain's Security Mirage: The Royal Navy and the Franco-Russian Naval Threat, 1898-1906." *Journal of Strategic Studies* 35, no. 6 (2012): 861–886.

———. *The Royal Navy and the German Threat, 1901-1914: Admiralty Plans to Protect British Trade in a War Against Germany*. Oxford: Oxford University Press, 2012.

———. "The Renaissance of Pre-First World War Naval History." *Journal of Strategic Studies* 36, no. 3 (2013): 454–479.

Semmel, Bernard. *Liberalism and Naval Strategy: Ideology, Interest, and Sea Power During the Pax Britannica*. Boston: Allen & Unwin, 1986.

Sidorowicz, Andre T. "The British Government, the Hague Peace Conference of 1907, and the Armaments Question." In *Arms Limitation and Disarmament: Restraints on War 1899-1939*, edited by B. J. C. McKercher, 1–19. Westport, Conn: Praeger, 1992.

Simpson, Gerry. *Great Powers and Outlaw States: Unequal Sovereigns in the International Legal Order*. Cambridge: Cambridge University Press, 2004.

Stacey, C. P. "The Myth of the Unguarded Frontier 1815-1871." *American Historical Review* 56, no. 1 (1950): 1–18.

Steinberg, Jonathan. "The Copenhagen Complex." *Journal of Contemporary History* 1, no. 3 (1966): 23–46.

Steiner, Zara. *Britain and the Origins of the First World War*. London: Macmillan, 1977.

Stevenson, David. *Armaments and the Coming of War: Europe 1904-1914*. Oxford: Oxford University Press, 1996.

Sumida, Jon Tetsura. *In Defence of Naval Supremacy: Finance, Technology and British Naval Policy, 1889-1914*. London: Routledge, 1989.

Sumner, B. H. "The Secret Franco-Russian Treaty of 3 March 1859." *English Historical Review* 48, no. 189 (1933): 65–83.

Tate, Merze. *The Disarmament Illusion: The Movement for a Limitation of Armaments to 1907*. 2nd ed. 1971 ed. New York: Russell and Russell, 1942.

Tyrrell, Alexander. "Making the Millenium: The Mid-Nineteenth Century Peace Movement." *Historical Journal* 21, no. 1 (1978): 75–95.

Updyke, Frank A. *The Diplomacy of the War of 1812.* Baltimore: Johns Hopkins Press, 1915.

Vagts, Alfred, and Detlev Vagts. "The Balance of Power in International Law: A History of an Idea." *American Journal of International Law* 73, no. 4 (1979): 555–80.

Vagts, Detlev. "The Hague Conventions and Arms Control." *American Journal of International Law* 94, no. 1 (2000): 31–41.

Volwiler, A. T. "Harrison, Blaine, and American Foreign Policy, 1889-1893." *Proceedings of the American Philosophical Society* 79, no. 4 (1938): 637–48.

von Bismarck, Otto. *Otto Von Bismarck, The Man and the Statesman.* Translated by A. J. Butler. New York: Harper & Brothers, 1899.

von Rauch, George. *Conflict in the Southern Cone: The Argentine Military and the Boundary Dispute with Chile, 1870-1902.* London: Praeger, 1999.

Wetzel, David. *The Crimean War: A Diplomatic History.* Boulder: Columbia University Press, 1985.

Wilgus, A. Curtis. "The Second International American Conference at Mexico City." *Hispanic American Historical Review* 11, no. 1 (1931): 27–68.

Woodward, E. L. *Great Britain and the German Navy.* 2nd ed. London: Frank Cass and Co., 1964.

Worcester, Donald E. "Naval Strategy in the War of the Pacific." *Journal of Interamerican Studies* 5, no. 1 (1963): 31–37.

Wright, Carroll D. *The Statesman's Yearbook: Statistical and Historical Annual of the States of the World for the Year 1899.* New York: Macmillan Co., 1899.

INDEX

© The Editor(s) (if applicable) and The Author(s) 2016   317
S.A. Keefer, *The Law of Nations and Britain's Quest for Naval
Security*, DOI 10.1007/978-3-319-39645-3

217, 223, 212n36, 214n44,
247, 248, 241n62
rules of war, 48, 49, 96, 106, 111,
115, 178, 193, 194, 204, 223,
204n5, 227–35, 251, 287
scholars and, 235–41
status quo, 100, 121, 207
verification of, 101, 139
violation of, 110, 111, 129, 166,
167
arms limitation-naval
forms of naval limitation, 169, 200
limitation on submarines, 108, 113,
124–7, 171n128, 249, 288,
291
warship armament limitation,
32n69, 113–15
warship numerical limitation, 239,
240
warship size limitation, 167, 185,
197–200
arms race
Anglo-American, 11, 139, 160, 166
Anglo-French, 18, 98, 166, 178,
238, 285
Anglo-German, 4, 8, 9, 14, 142,
150, 157, 175, 209n17, 240,
254–63, 266–9, 282, 285, 286,
290, 291
Argentine-Chilean, 3, 8, 138,
140–8, 155–8, 166, 175, 226,
230, 238, 255, 265, 267, 289
expenses of, 147, 148, 196
generally, 9, 101, 103, 122, 127,
134, 191, 220, 223, 283
naval, 9, 137, 140, 157, 172, 183,
199, 209n17, 227, 240, 253,
274, 278, 281, 283, 290
preemptive strike, 113, 140, 142,
204, 260
attaché, 4, 8, 173, 239, 254–7, 271,
274–9, 282, 272n61, 272n65,
275n78, 275n82, 289

Austria-Hungary
and 1816–1830s arms control
initiatives, 282, 288, 291
and 1870 proposals to modify the
Black Sea Neutralization Treaty,
48n145
and diplomacy prior to the 1907
Hague Peace Conference, 99,
191
and dreadnought rivalry, 268

B
Bethmann Hollweg, Theobald von,
259
Bismarck, Otto von, 81n89
Black Sea Neutralization Treaty of
1856
and renegotiation in 1870, 48n145
and verification, 36, 38, 166, 170,
175, 288
generally, 48n145
Russian antipathy of, 33n76,
48n145
strategic value of Black Sea, 37, 59,
73, 167, 174, 175, 224,
276n88
Bolivia
and South American diplomacy,
140
and War of the Pacific, 140
bombardment. *See* aerial
bombardment
Brazil
and Latin American arms race, 142
and Latin American balance of
power, 157
Brussels Conference, 48, 49, 49n150,
50n152, 83, 86, 87, 96, 104,
116, 223, 205n6, 247, 287
Brussels Declaration on the Laws and
Customs of War of 1874,
50n154, 86, 106, 112

CPSIA information can be obtained
at www.ICGtesting.com
Printed in the USA
BVOW06*1054100917

494478BV00009B/62/P